Urban Redevelopment and Modernity in Liverpool and Manchester, 1918–39

Urban Redevelopment and Modernity in Liverpool and Manchester, 1918–39

Charlotte Wildman

Bloomsbury Academic
An imprint of Bloomsbury Publishing Plc

B L O O M S B U R Y
LONDON · OXFORD · NEW YORK · NEW DELHI · SYDNEY

Bloomsbury Academic
An imprint of Bloomsbury Publishing Plc

50 Bedford Square
London
WC1B 3DP
UK

1385 Broadway
New York
NY 10018
USA

www.bloomsbury.com

BLOOMSBURY and the Diana logo are trademarks of Bloomsbury Publishing Plc

First published 2016

British Library Cataloguing-in-Publication Data
A catalogue record for this book is available from the British Library.

ISBN: HB: 978-1-4742-5736-7
ePDF: 978-1-4742-5738-1
ePub: 978-1-4742-5737-4

Library of Congress Cataloging-in-Publication Data
Names: Wildman, Charlotte, author. Title: Urban redevelopment and modernity in Liverpool and Manchester, 1918–1939 / Charlotte Wildman. Description: London; New York: Bloomsbury Academic, an imprint of Bloomsbury Publishing Plc, 2016. | Includes bibliographical references and index. | Description based on print version record and CIP data provided by publisher; resource not viewed. Identifiers: LCCN 2016021077 (print) | LCCN 2016010855 (ebook) | ISBN 9781474257374 (epub) | ISBN 9781474257381 (epdf) | ISBN 9781474257367 (hardback) | ISBN 9781474257381 (PDF) | ISBN 9781474257374 (ePub) Subjects: LCSH: Urban renewal–England–Liverpool–History–20th century. | Urban renewal–England–Manchester–History–20th century. | City and town life–England–Liverpool–History–20th century. | City and town life–England–Liverpool–History–20th century. | Social change–England–Liverpool–History–20th century. | Social change–England–Liverpool–History–20th century. | Liverpool (England)–Social conditions–20th century. | Manchester (England)–Social conditions–20th century. | Liverpool (England)–Economic conditions–20th century. | Manchester (England)–Economic conditions–20th century. | BISAC: HISTORY / General. | HISTORY / Europe / Great Britain. | HISTORY / Modern / 20th Century. Classification: LCC HT178.G72 (print) | LCC HT178.G72 L538 2016 (ebook) | DDC 307.3/4160942–dc23 LC record available at https://lccn.loc.gov/2016021077

Cover design: Catherine Wood
Cover image © Manchester City Council

Typeset by Deanta Global Publishing Services, Chennai, India
Printed and bound in Great Britain

To Daniel and Daphne - for standing close by.

Contents

List of Illustrations and Tables   viii

List of Abbreviations   xi

Acknowledgements   xii

Introduction: Urban Redevelopment and Modernity in Liverpool
and Manchester, 1918–39   1

Part One   Civic Culture

1   'Soaring Skyward': Urban Regeneration   21

2   Civic Week Celebrations   49

Part Two   Consumer Culture

3   'For Profit or Pleasure': New Cultures of Retail, Shopping and
Consumer Culture   83

4   Performing Fashionable Selfhoods in the Transformed City   112

Part Three   Catholic Urban Culture

5   Gender and Religious Selfhoods in Manchester   143

6   The Cathedral That Never Was?   167

    Conclusion: The Second World War and the Challenge to Interwar
Urban Culture   190

Appendix   203

Notes   208

Bibliography   260

Index   285

List of Illustrations and Tables

Figure 1.1 'Houses – Old and New'   32
Source: Manchester Corporation, *Centenary Celebration of Manchester's Incorporation: Official Handbook to the Exhibition of Civic Services May 2–7 1938* (Manchester: Percy Brothers, 1938), 84.

Figure 1.2 'A Vision of the Future of Kingsway'   35
Source: *Liverpolitan*, January 1935, 15.

Figure 1.3 'Modern Manchester'   41
Source: Manchester Corporation, *How Manchester Is Managed* (1938), inside cover.

Figure 2.1 A mannequin parade held aboard the Cunard liner *Franconia* during Liverpool's Civic Week in 1925   63
Source: Getty Editorial Image 2668798.

Table 3.1 Clothing shops, Liverpool 1922–38   87
Source: Kelly's Trade Directories, Liverpool 1922, 1932, 1938.

Figure 3.1 Proportion of shops in Liverpool expressed as percentages, 1922–38   87
Source: Kelly's Trade Directories, Liverpool 1922, 1932, 1938.

Table 3.2 Clothing shops, Manchester 1922–38   89
Source: Kelly's Trade Directories, Manchester 1922, 1932, 1938.

Figure 3.2 Numbers of advertisements placed by department stores, 1920–38   99
Source: *Liverpool Echo* and *Manchester Evening News*, 1920, 1932, 1938.

Figure 3.3 Number of department store advertisements in the *Manchester Guardian*, 1920–38   100
Source: *Manchester Guardian*, 1920–38.

Figure 3.4   Department store advertisements in the
             Liverpool Echo, 1920–38   102
             Source: *Liverpool Echo*, 1920–38.

Table 4.1   G. H. Lee's sales and customers, 1925–36   121
             Source: John Lewis Archive Box 180/3/a.

Figure 4.1   Graph depicting gap between customers and sales at
             G. H. Lee's, 1925–36   121
             Source: John Lewis Archive Box 180/3/a.

Figure 4.2   Window shoppers outside Messrs Kendal, Milne & Co in
             Deansgate, Manchester, 27 August 1931   126
             Source: Getty Editorial Image 99174504.

Table 4.2   G. H. Lee's number of customers in relation to
             department, 1933   137
             Source: John Lewis Archive Box 180/3/a.

Figure 5.1   Number of participants in the Catholic processions,
             1903–34   151
             Source: Salford Catholic Diocese. *The Authorised Official
             Programme of the Catholic Whit-Friday Procession*
             (Manchester), 1895–1934.

Figure 5.2   St Michael's Roman Catholic parish, Ancoats, c. 1910s   153
             Source: MCL LIC Ref m69150.

Figure 5.3   Roman Catholic walk, c. 1918   153
             Source: MCL LIC Ref 1313026.

Figure 5.4   St William's procession, Angel Meadow, Salford, 1926   158
             Source: MCL LIC Ref N4101.

Figure 5.5   Children of Mary, Catholic Whit procession, 1927   159
             Source: MCL LIC Ref 905039.

Figure 6.1   Image of scale model of Liverpool Catholic Cathedral,
             designed by Edwin Lutyens, at Museum of Liverpool.
             Copyright, Mike Peel   173

Figure 6.2   Temporary altar during the ceremonial laying of the
             foundation stone, 1933   181
             Source: Stuart Bale Archive, National Museums and
             Galleries on Merseyside, 1613–114.

Copyright

List of Abbreviations

DC	*Daily Courier*
LCR	*The Cathedral Record: the Official Organ of the Archdiocese of Liverpool*, or *Liverpool Cathedral Record*
LAA	Liverpool Archdiocesan Archive
LHC	Liverpool Housing Committee
LCL LSC	Liverpool Local Studies Collection
LPM	*Liverpool Post and Mercury*
MCL LSC	Manchester Central Library Local Studies Collection
MCL LIC	Manchester Central Library Local Image Collection
TH CM	Manchester Town Hall Committee Council Minutes
MEN	*Manchester Evening News*
MG	*Manchester Guardian*
NYT	*New York Times*
PRO	National Archives
NW SA OTC	North West Sound Archive Oral Testimony Collection
SDA	Salford Diocesan Archives

Acknowledgements

This book has been a long time in the making and I have relied on the support, assistance and cajoling from many over this period. First, I am indebted to the Arts and Humanities Research Council, who funded my doctoral thesis, which provided the foundations of this monograph. I have received much support from my intellectual home, the Department of History at the University of Manchester. In particular, I thank Bertrand Taithe and Max Jones who were supportive and kind PhD supervisors. I thank my thesis examiners Frank Mort and Simon Gunn, whose feedback helped to shape the book into its revised form. I have found the History department to be a great place to work and I thank my all my colleagues and students, past and present. Outside of Manchester, Matt Houlbrook and Chris Otter have been kind enough to read and offer invaluable feedback on various forms of my work. Thanks also to the anonymous readers whose suggestions helped to sharpen the aims and scope of this monograph. At Bloomsbury, I thank Frances Arnold, Emily Drewe and Emma Goode for their help and assistance in bringing this book to publication.

I benefited from the rich expertise from many archivists and librarians throughout the country. I spent a great deal of my time researching this book at Manchester Central Library and Liverpool Central Library, and my gratitude goes to all their archivists and librarians. Major programmes of refurbishment have transformed both of these libraries in recent years and they are certainly wonderful places to work now, although I do not quite have the same 'colourful' stories from my early days of research. Elsewhere, I am grateful to Judy Faraday at the John Lewis Archive, Father David Lannon at the Salford Diocesan Archive and Meg Whittle at the Liverpool Archdiocesan Archive, along with staff at the University of Manchester Library, British Library, University of Liverpool Library, the National Archives, University of Sussex Special collections, Getty Images and the Bodleian Library at the University of Oxford.

Thanks to all my friends who have kept me entertained and distracted, particularly Justine Gordon for her kindness and her British Library hospitality, and Katharine Melvill whose friendship continues from afar. Katherine Davies, Lucinda Matthews-Jones, James Mansell and Jo Laycock have understood the privileges and pressures of academic life and remain great sources of advice. My family, Margaret, Jim, Tommy and John, first fuelled my interest in history through frequent trips to Birkenhead Library (along with an illicitly acquired copy of a Kellogg's history book...) and have remained supportive of my academic career, many thanks to them and also to my extended family. The memories of my grandmothers, Veronica Cruikshank and Irene Wildman, two fashionably dressed young women in 1930s Liverpool, undoubtedly sowed the seeds of this project. Finally, I dedicate this book to Daniel and Daphne, Mario and Metta, who have kept me company, reminded me that there is more to life than academia, and continue to cheerlead me through the tough times with tea and cake, the NBA and the occasional mug of wine – thank you for standing close by.

Introduction: Urban Redevelopment and Modernity in Liverpool and Manchester, 1918–39

In 1924, architectural expert Sir Charles Reilly proclaimed that 'Liverpool, like New York, is soaring skyward. In all parts of the city splendid new buildings, such as the Adelphi Hotel, reflect the influence of the best modern American architecture. The face of some leading shipping streets is thus being gradually transformed, and the city's business houses bear witness in stone to the stability of their trade.'[1] Reilly referred to the new commercial architecture, which included the Adelphi Hotel (completed 1914) and the shipping and business buildings under completion, such as the India Buildings (1924–32), built by Liverpool architect Herbert Rowse, who had studied under Reilly. In Manchester, civic leaders made similar declarations that emphasized the city's vibrancy and in 1926 the Lord Mayor, Sir Miles Ewart Mitchell, argued that Manchester was 'more than the "cotton metropolis," as some like to call it'. Instead, he claimed, 'it is a city into whose being are knit threads as diverse and coloured as go to make up the like of any city. In it are practised almost all the trades and industries ... it draws the material of its staple industry from the Far West and sends its finished goods to the Far East, and deals indifferently with all that lies between.'[2]

By drawing attention to the vitality of the cities' architecture and commercial stability and diversity, these depictions are at odds with the generally negative images of both Liverpool and Manchester between the two world wars. More familiar images of interwar Liverpool, for instance, stress the city's 'dampness, the dilapidation, the darkness'.[3] The city's experience of poverty and unemployment as a result of severe challenges to its port trade marked it out as one of the worst suffering between the two world wars. By 1929, 597 per 10,000 people in Liverpool received poor relief, 'a higher percentage than in any other city'.[4] By implication, living standards were notoriously poor in parts of the city. In 1931, a survey on poverty and housing by Liverpool University Settlement Society found dwellings with 'defective roofs ... decayed windows were common features. The ceilings of the windows were stuffed with rags. The furniture was often completely unsuitable for the rooms, and .... (the) mattress served as a general ground by day and a ... resting-place by night.[5] Liverpool was not the only city to suffer from problems of deprivation and *The Times* highlighted the 'grave position' of both Liverpool and Manchester in 1921, where unemployment 'grows steadily worse' as a consequence of the decline of the cotton industry.[6] In Manchester, the inability to revive its ailing cotton industry ensured the city's unemployment problem remained 'extremely grave' throughout the 1920s.[7] There, the unemployment rate of insured workers hit 18.7 per cent by 1931.[8] Again, living conditions were significantly low in parts of the city and in 1923 even the city's Town Clerk admitted 'it would be difficult to find worse houses in England'.[9]

Such images of urban decay and poverty remain associated with Liverpool and Manchester's interwar experience and overshadow the level of innovation and redevelopment that occurred in these cities between the two world wars. Although poverty, unemployment and social divisions persisted in both cities, a focus on these problems neglects the level of dynamism and civic ambition displayed by local politicians, planners, businessmen and religious leaders. Rather, the statements by Reilly and Manchester's Lord Mayor reflect a wider culture of boosterism and investment in urban redevelopment. Local politicians responded to economic, political and social turbulence by investing in ambitious programmes of urban redevelopment. Urban transformation reinvigorated civic, consumer and religious local cultures and this book stresses the overall ambition, modernity and vitality of interwar Liverpool and Manchester. Liverpool and Manchester witnessed pioneering developments in civic design and architecture; in retail and shopping; and in cultures of religion and popular worship. Their analysis draws out the complexities of local and regional modernity more generally in interwar Britain.

Historicising Liverpool and Manchester's twentieth-century experience

A reassessment of interwar urban culture challenges historical accounts of Liverpool and Manchester's twentieth-century experience, which emphasize these entrenched narratives of urban decay and deprivation. Writing in 1982, economic historian Sheila Marriner suggested that Liverpool was 'synonymous with vandalism, with high crime rates, with social deprivation in the form of bad housing, with obsolete schools, polluted air and a polluted river, with chronic unemployment, run-down dock systems and large areas of industrial dereliction'.[10] Similarly, Manchester's image 'is invariably gloomy' as 'twentieth-century changes have created a sense that the city and its people have been deserted and abandoned'.[11] In particular, Liverpool and Manchester's interwar experience remains central to this image of their twentieth-century demise. This period of British history remains indelibly associated in both popular memory and scholarship as being as an era of contradictions, contrasts and disunity, placing these cities firmly on the negative side of a prosperity versus poverty debate. In his classic *English History*, for example, A. J. P. Taylor wrote, 'The nineteen-thirties have been called the black years, the devil's decade. ... Yet, at the same time, most English people were enjoying a richer life than any previously known in the history of the world ... the two sides of life did not join up'.[12]

These historical accounts reflect contemporary representations of the period, which contrast unemployment marches and dole queues, especially in northern industrial towns and in South Wales, with flappers and glamorous mill girls in 'cheap artificial stockings, cheap short-skirted frocks, cheap coats, cheap shoes, crimped hair, powder and rouge'.[13] In contrast, the writings of J. B. Priestley were key in shaping perceptions of the affluent South and famously depicted 'the England of arterial and by-pass roads, filling stations and factories that look like exhibition buildings, of giant cinemas and dance-halls and cafes, bungalows with tiny garages, cocktail bars, Woolworth's, motor coaches, wireless, hiking, factory girls looking like actresses, greyhound racing and dirt tracks, swimming pools, and everything given away for cigarette coupons'.[14] By implication, northern industrial towns and cities, including Liverpool and Manchester, remain overly clichéd as sites of urban decay.

Central to these stereotypical images of interwar Britain is the emphasis on an economic north–south divide. Seminal accounts by economic historians such as Derek Aldcroft, John Stevenson and Chris Cook, and Tim Hatton stress the higher levels of unemployment in northern towns and cities in comparison to the prosperous South and the North's relative inability to recover from the economic depression of 1929–31.[15] Perhaps more long-lasting in influence, however, is the notable work of contemporary left-wing intellectuals who used Lancashire, in particular, as a canvas with which to engage readers with important contemporary issues relating to class and poverty. Most famous is George Orwell and his depictions of working-class life in Wigan remain indelibly linked with Northern England's interwar experience. Orwell's descriptions of Wigan stressed a place of filth and poverty, hunger and deprivation, such as, 'As you walk through the industrial towns you lose yourself in labyrinths of little brick houses blackened by smoke, festering in planless chaos round miry alleys and little cindered yards where there are stinking dustbins and lines of granny washing and half ruinous W. C.s.'[16] Yet Orwell was not the only left-wing intellectual to use Lancashire as a way to communicate wider social problems to their audiences. The research movement Mass Observation, like Orwell, charted working-class life in Lancashire by undertaking an in-depth study of Bolton and attempted, with mixed success, to infiltrate daily life and with the aim of using their findings to bring about political reform.[17] As we shall see, Mass Observation often misinterpreted or misunderstood working-class culture. In doing so these commentators helped to manifest the perceived 'otherness' of the northern working classes, which shapes wider historical discourse about a north–south divide between the two world wars.

In a similar vein to the writings of Orwell and Mass Observation on Lancashire more generally, contemporary autobiographies and popular literature set in interwar Liverpool and Manchester also stressed narratives of deprivation and urban decay. Helen Forrester's autobiographical novel, *Tuppence to Cross the Mersey*, recalled the horror she felt arriving in Liverpool in 1930 after her middle-class family fell on hard times. 'How terrified I had been!' she wrote, 'How menacingly grotesque the people had looked ... grim and twisted, foul-mouthed and coarse ... I had to make what I could of this grimy city and its bitterly humorous inhabitants and share with them their suffering during the Depression years.'[18] Forrester's account presented the impact of unemployment on Liverpool's already precarious port and shipping trades, exacerbated by wider economic problems and the Wall Street Crash. In 1932, 44 per cent of Liverpool's insured labour force in shipping was unemployed and, along with underemployment and low wages, unemployment caused widespread problems throughout the city.[19] 'Irish Slummy', Pat O'Mara's account of life in the Scotland Road area of Liverpool, a section of poor housing between the city centre and docks associated with the city's Irish migrants, described the poverty and deprived living conditions inhabitants faced because of these problems. Homes were 'like cells in a penitentiary', he wrote, where 'the customary domestic procedure ... was to drink and fight.'[20]

Depictions of Manchester also stressed its social problems. The city's reputation as the 'shock city' of the industrial revolution ensured many commentators and writers charted its poor living standards from the early nineteenth century, perhaps most famously in Friedrich Engels' *The Condition of the Working Class* (1845) and the novels of Elizabeth Gaskell, including *North and South* (1854) and *Mary Barton* (1848). Such depictions of Manchester and the surrounding area continued after 1918 but became especially impactful following the decline of the cotton industry, which had 'made' Manchester. In 1835, for instance, 90 per cent of the British cotton industry was concentrated in Lancashire and Cheshire and the Manchester's weekly trade rose from £1 million in the 1850s to £10 million by the 1880s.[21] Yet the collapse of Lancashire's cotton industry after the First World War was sudden, catastrophic and irreversible and by 1939, cloth exports amounted to only one-fifth of their 1913 levels.[22] After 1918, foreign competitors were able to provide cotton at far cheaper prices and Lancashire not only lost its monopoly but struggled to compete in the global cotton market. Whereas Manchester exported 1,500 million pounds of cotton in 1912, by 1930 this fell to just 450 million and continued to decline until 1950.[23]

The decline of Manchester's cotton industry provided an important background to literature set in the city. In his 1932 novel *Love on the Dole*, Walter Greenwood's influential tale of poverty and frustrated ambitions, highlighted the problems of unemployment faced in neighbouring Salford. Greenwood describes streets 'where blue-grey smoke swirls down like companies of ghosts ... jungles of tiny houses cramped and huddled together ... where men and women are born, live, love and die and pay preposterous rents for the privilege of calling grimy houses "home"'.[24] Similarly, Howard Spring's 1934 novel *Shabby Tiger* depicted Manchester as a lifeless, dark and lacklustre city. It described 'the black facades of Portland Street warehouses, grim and strong as prisons, silent, at that hour, as the grave ... the University's inky mass piled against the last of the sunlight like education's redoubtable Bastille ... a street of mean houses and mean shops'.[25] These contemporary writings are important because they helped to nurture a powerful image of a north–south divide and contributed to an overly stereotypical image of poverty and urban decay in Liverpool and Manchester. They drew attention to the problems they faced without addressing the steps taken by the local government to address them, leaving a strong influence on historical debates.

Key historical debates

This book offers an alternative interpretation of Manchester and Liverpool's interwar experience than the narrative usually presented by contemporary novels and autobiographies and most historical scholarship. The re-examination of Liverpool and Manchester's interwar experience offered here contributes to a number of key scholarly debates relating to twentieth-century British history. First, although class is not utilized as the main organizing category, its centrality to twentieth-century British history ensures its relevance here, and, indeed, many existing studies of interwar Britain are organized around class experiences.[26] Secondly, although issues relating to class and living standards in interwar Britain have particularly attracted significant scholarly attention, historians' interpretations remain divided. For instance, a number of studies emerged in the late 1970s that stressed the interwar period as one of a rise in living standards and general prosperity for the working classes.[27] This scholarship sought to locate the roots of the post-war age of affluence in the 1930s and, in doing so, stressed the rise of mass consumer culture and a general increase in living standards during the period 1918–39.

By contrast, in the 1980s, accounts of poverty and class experience in interwar Britain emerged in response to the 1979 Conservative victory and the advent of the Thatcher era. For instance, historian Margaret Mitchell made an explicit link between histories of class and poverty in interwar Britain and a broader protest against Thatcher's policy of state retrenchment. Mitchell suggested the political context of the 1980s ensured the study of the interwar period had 'assumed a new urgency'. Mitchell cited the similarities between Britain's economy in the 1930s and the 1980s, and the emerging evidence that linked unemployment with poor health.[28] Like Orwell and Mass Observation before them, we can see that accounts of poverty and unemployment in interwar Britain by left-wing scholars remained important as ways to challenge the prevailing political situation.

In the early 1990s, influential scholarship by Andrew Davies and Steven Fielding responded to studies that stressed interwar affluence by highlighting the continued centrality of poverty in working-class life after 1918. Both in their individual research and in their jointly edited collection, *Workers' Worlds*, they offer rich analyses and understandings of working-class culture in Manchester and Salford during the early twentieth century.[29] In his monograph *Leisure, Gender and Poverty*, for instance, Davies stresses that although retrospective narratives suggest poverty was less severe after 1918, 'accounts of working-class life during the inter-war decades are still laced with references to poverty, and the visual symbols of poverty, so familiar in accounts of the Edwardian years, such as jam-jars used as cups and raggedy dressed children, still appear frequently in descriptions of the 1930s'.[30] Davies shows that an examination of poverty and gender roles needs to be central to an assessment of working-class culture and although this monograph is interested in how urban cultures fostered forms of shared identity other than class, Davies' findings and approach illuminate this study's interest in urban redevelopment in interwar Liverpool and Manchester. Building on Fielding's *Class and Ethnicity*, which examines working-class Irish migrants in Manchester and Salford, for instance, this research is interested in how the transformed urban environment provided opportunities for individuals to express other forms of community identities, including Catholicism, in order to offer a more nuanced and detailed assessment of how other social identities shaped and interacted with class.[31]

This monograph also contributes to more recent histories of class, including Selina Todd's *The People*, which demonstrates the stress unemployment and poverty placed on working-class communities interwar, but also draws attention to the problems caused by government policy that reflected their mistrust of the poor. Todd highlights the continued importance of class as a conceptual framework throughout twentieth-century Britain and emphasizes its importance as an analytical category for British historians.[32] Similarly, Ross McKibbin's *Classes and Cultures* draws attention towards the continuing divisions and differences between Britain's class groups in the early twentieth century. McKibbin suggests that the middle classes dominated culture and politics between the two world wars, whereas the working classes remained divided and fractured.[33] Yet Jon Lawrence's recent research re-examines debates about working-class affluence and, in doing so, points to the gap between official and vernacular understandings of social class in twentieth-century Britain. For Lawrence, the period was one of change for class identities but he emphasizes the agency of working-class people in shaping and changing their worlds: 'Working people, in their great diversity, remade their lives consciously from the bottom up across the middle decades of the twentieth century. In the process, they dissolved many of the intellectual and political constructions imposed upon them about what it meant to be "working class".'[34] Examining the way in which civic, consumer and religious urban cultures in interwar Liverpool and Manchester helped to offer individuals different forms of shared identity, my research contributes to wider understandings of how class might intersect with other forms of collective identities in regionally specific ways. An analysis of urban redevelopment and modernity in these cities illuminates the ways in which individuals contributed to a refashioning of their own selfhoods through their participation with a range of urban cultures.

As this rich scholarship attests, class rightly remains the key organizing category in academic scholarship on Britain's twentieth-century experience. Nevertheless, looking at other forms of identity alongside class divisions offers a different perspective of Liverpool and Manchester's interwar experience. In particular, the interwar period has received increased scholarly attention over the past decade and there has been a shift towards thinking about connections, rather than differences, between individuals, classes and communities.[35] Historians of gender, such as Liz Conor in *The Spectacular Modern Woman*, for example, argue that the rise of mass media, film and consumer culture across Western industrial societies led to a reshaping of feminine identity, closely linked to the emerging visual culture.[36] Conor also contributed to the Modern Girl Around the World Research Group, which claims that the Modern Girl, defined by her apparent disregard of traditional female roles, emerged as a global phenomenon between the two world wars.[37] This scholarship suggests that the characterization of the interwar period as a divided and fractured one might need further investigation, particularly by thinking about the connections between individuals and communities, and perhaps between women more specifically.

An interest in the relational connections between individuals, alongside a focus on urban redevelopment, urban culture and experience as a way to understand identities reflects a broader shift in urban history. Traditionally, urban historians concentrated on understanding the mechanics of the city, like transport, public health and governance.[38] However, the 'spatial turn' asks historians to think of space not as a passive background but as an active actor.[39] Key texts by Edward Soja, David Harvey and Denis Cosgrove highlighted the importance of landscape and environment in understanding the relationships with social identities, but also contributed to rich debates about the use of 'space' over 'place', which continues among urban historians.[40] The influence of Michel Foucault, in particular, significantly reshaped approaches to urban scholarship and encouraged historians to think about the city as a site of power, leading to a number of accounts that considered the use of light, architecture and mapping as tools of governmentality in the mid-Victorian city.[41] Similarly, the work of Henri Lefebvre remains influential, especially as his 1974 work, *The Production of Space*, distinguished between spatial practice, representations of space and representational spaces.[42] These texts ask historians not only to consider the relationship between identities and urban space but also to think carefully about the conceptualization of urban space itself.

The book develops ongoing debates about spatial analysis and applies a cultural urban history lens to the case studies of Liverpool and Manchester as two of Britain's most important provincial cities. It provides a counterpoint to recent influential cultural histories of London, particularly those by Frank Mort, Lynda Nead, Judith Walkowitz and Matt Houlbrook. Influenced by these theoretical approaches, their scholarship has woven together material relating to images and representations of the city with sources concerned with urban experience as a way to consider broader social and cultural change and the dialectal relationship between individuals and the city.[43] In *Queer London*, for example, Houlbrook writes: 'Male sexual practices and identities do not just take place *in* the city; they are shaped and sustained *by* the physical and cultural forms of modern urban life just as they in turn shape that life.'[44] This book offers a much-needed shift away from a focus on the metropolis and applies the cultural–historical framework utilized by Houlbrook et al. to assess the experience of two of Britain's key cities. It shows that Manchester's and Liverpool's redevelopment changed the way people used the cities, which, in turn, reshaped the urban environment. Investment in comprehensive public transport systems, for example, physically altered the urban fabric and changed the parts of the cities people visited, drawing in increasing numbers of people into the city centres for leisure and pleasure, as well as for work. In doing so, it suggests that Liverpool and Manchester's transformed urban environments became important for individuals, especially women, to perform a range of shared identities that obscured class divisions. Like the men who frequented Houlbrook's *Queer London*, there was a reciprocal relationship between identity and urban space in Liverpool and Manchester.

Linked to its contribution to urban history more generally is the book's interest in planning and regeneration. It builds on recent literature that highlights Britain's vibrant cultures of urban planning, particularly during and after the Second World War.[45] However, by drawing attention to the innovative approaches to planning and civic design in interwar Manchester and Liverpool, it demonstrates continuities between post-war trends, which undermines the narrative of the 'New Jerusalem' and of post-war 'reconstruction'.[46] At the same time, the ambitious programmes of urban redevelopment that emerged in interwar Liverpool and Manchester drew on international approaches to design and cutting-edge trends in urban planning that reflected a wider international culture of planning that emerged in the early twentieth century.[47] Urban planning and civic design were, from its formative years, international and collaborative. For example, the Town Planning Conference in London in 1910, credited as a seminal moment in the development and professionalization of planning, was 'a self-consciously international' meeting.[48] The conference brought together 1,400 planners and architects and papers delivered in French, Dutch, German, Italian,

Danish, Norwegian and Swedish, to audiences from most European countries, Australia, the United States and Canada. At the conference banquet, Daniel Burnham, famous for building one of the first American skyscrapers and as the designer of the World's Columbian Exposition in Chicago (1893) and the City of Chicago Plan (1909), heralded the international spirit of the town planning movement. Burnham declared: 'Men have come all over to realise a universal thought. This town planning has spread all over the world. In America there are hundreds of city planning commissions, in Germany there are hundreds of them. … We hear of them in Japan, in Australia. The idea has become universal.'[49] Yet historian William Whyte stresses the 'international indifference' towards the conference, arguing that architects were driven by national concerns rather than transnational issues and suggests that 'the 1910 Conference was big news – and of immediate importance – almost nowhere outside Britain.'[50] Nevertheless, its significance lies in the openness of planners in Britain to ideas and trends pioneered abroad and the international conversations that took place between civic designers during the early twentieth century. British and American planners made frequent visits across the Atlantic throughout the period, which contributed to a dynamic culture of international exchange.[51] As we shall see, planners and architects in Liverpool were especially enthusiastic about engaging with wider trends and approaches, which shaped the nature and style of the city's redevelopment. Nor were international trends limited to the redesign and regeneration of the urban fabric, and urban transformation produced new forms of consumer and religious cultures that were similarly outward-facing and drew on wider trends, particularly from across the Atlantic.

Although the book stresses the vitality of internationalism on Liverpool and Manchester's interwar urban culture, it reflects a new interest in the local and in regional experiences among scholars of twentieth-century Britain. Historians of interwar Britain tend to focus on showing the national shared identity that emerged in response to the chaos and disruption of the First World War, particularly around Stanley Baldwin's unifying rhetoric of 'Englishness', to the detriment of civic and local identities.[52] By implication, narratives of the decay of Northern England's industrial cities are usually associated with accounts of the decline of localism. Historians, such as Simon Gunn, typically view 1914 as a turning point in the dramatic demise of civic power.[53] Robert Morris, for instance, suggests that the powerful municipal culture of the late nineteenth and early twentieth centuries relied on the influence and reach of local elites. By the 1920s and 1930s, however, 'key institutional structures which had supported all this began to be diminished, undermined and replaced. … The towns were abandoned by their elite.'[54] Yet, recent scholarship on civic engagement in the early-twentieth-century challenges the narrative of elite disengagement, suggesting the re-examination of interwar cultures of civic pride offered here is timely.[55]

The book's interest in post-1918 urban cultures and local modernities reflects emerging scholarly concern with regional identities and cultures in early-twentieth-century Britain, especially in the North.[56] It demonstrates the importance of civic pride and localism in interwar Liverpool and Manchester as the local elite drove the cities' redevelopment. Post-1918 cultures of civic pride reflected the specific context of the period and were part of an effort to engage with the electorate that reflected a wider culture of 'civics', which stressed a mutual relationship between the individual and the local, and particularly the city.[57] This strategy of using civics to communicate with the electorate and to promote a local shared identity aimed to engage citizens through cross-class rhetoric at a time of political and economic turmoil. I go further here, however, and suggest that civics also shaped the revitalized consumer and religious cultures in Liverpool and Manchester's redeveloped cityscapes as businessmen and Catholic leaders adopted this populist rhetoric to communicate with shoppers and worshippers, which reflected trends seen in wider political culture more generally. We should not view local identities as being parochial or backward-looking and the material presented here stresses the importance of localism to wider processes of modernity.

This book's interest in local modernity coincides with a wider attempt by academics and journalists to reassess Liverpool and Manchester's past more generally, perhaps as part of a renewed interest in localism and regionalism, but also to reflect a change in the cities' fortunes since the mid-1990s.[58] Liverpool celebrated the 800th anniversary of its charter in 2007 and became European Capital of Culture in 2008. John Belchem, an expert in Liverpool history, wrote that he hoped that Liverpool's 800th anniversary would lead to the production of a comprehensive history, as 'the need is imminent'.[59] Belchem published his edited tome on eight hundred years of Liverpool's history, covering the city's economic, cultural and social development in 2006, triggering greater historical interest in the city's past.[60] In Manchester, the 1996 IRA bomb contributed to a wider programme of financial investment and regeneration, fuelling an economic boom around a number of prestige projects around leisure, hospitality and retail.[61] Recent scholarships including an architectural history of Manchester, on local government, and on post-war planning, are examples of recent attempts to expand historical understandings of the city's twentieth-century experience.[62]

This book goes further than these recent studies of Liverpool and Manchester, however, and analyses the implications of regeneration and economic diversification by assessing a range of forms of urban culture, including civic, consumer and religious. There is a flourishing body of work that debates Britain's experiences of secularization, but twentieth-century urban historians have largely neglected to incorporate it into research.[63] For instance, the *Cambridge Urban History of Britain, Volume III 1840–1950*, published in 2000 and a landmark in the urban history of modern Britain, contains no chapters on religion.[64] Moving away from a focus on 'formal' expressions of religiosity, such as church attendance, an analysis of Liverpool and Manchester's redevelopment instead highlights the importance of religion to urban cultures, but shows religious identities could be episodic and not fixed. By examining Catholic leaders' responses to wider urban redevelopment and by assessing their ambitions and building plans in Liverpool and Manchester, interwar urban redevelopment is shown to have been far reaching in its scope and impact. Catholic leaders were no means passive or reluctant in these processes and instead utilized the opportunities to strengthen their own influence and power in the redeveloped cityscapes.

Finally, the monograph's interest in a range of forms of urban culture permits this study to contribute to wider debates about the relationship between gender and the modern city. Since the publication of Leonore Davidoff and Catherine Hall's seminal *Family Fortunes* in 1987, historical research focuses on a spatial analysis of gender that aligns femininity with the private sphere of home and family, and masculinity with the public sphere of work and the outside world.[65] By implication, the experience of women in cities tends to emphasize the modern city as a dangerous and threatening space for women, or stresses anxieties about women's vulnerability and their subjection to forms of surveillance and control.[66] However, other approaches aim to offer new insights into the relationship between femininity and the urban environment and, for example, current scholarship by historians of planning draws attention towards women's roles as town planners and architects.[67] Such perspectives are important in raising innovative ways of thinking about the relationship between urban space and social identities. For instance, Elizabeth Darling and Lesley Whitworth's edited collection *Women and the Making of Built Space in England* not only draws attention to the range of actors and organizations that shaped the built environment but also demonstrates that urban historians must move away from focusing on architects and engineers towards a consideration of those who use and experience the urban environment, particularly women as housewives, activists and philanthropists.[68] As Helen Meller's chapter in the collection illustrates, women made important contributions towards addressing problems with the urban environment and developed new ways of urban living on a local level.[69] This book supports the findings of the collection by highlighting women's role in shaping the redeveloped cityscapes of Liverpool and Manchester and stresses that the important influence of women lay in their roles as visitors to civic celebrations, as shoppers and as Catholic worshippers. It offers an assessment of the multifarious ways in which women shaped the transformed urban environment, and draws attention to the agency and variety of roles for women in Liverpool and Manchester's transformed cityscapes. In doing so, this monograph contributes to a wider and more nuanced analysis of how such women experienced modernity, which tends to remain limited to a focus on bourgeois women's participation in relatively elite spaces.[70]

Regional modernity

An interest in women's experiences of the city, alongside a new emphasis on the overall ambition and modernity and vitality of interwar Liverpool and Manchester, contributes to a re-reading of regional modernity. British modernity tends to be associated with the decline of the role of the church from the late nineteenth century, alongside the rise in mass consumerism, changes in women's roles and rights, a new imperialism, new innovations in technologies, and accompanied by a sense of crisis as contemporaries attempted to make sense of these changes. This definition can be criticized for assuming religion and modernity are incompatible and for focusing on metropolitan sites of modernity, such as London's West End.[71] By implication, Liverpool and Manchester tend to be characterized in scholarship as separate from wider social and cultural change and as 'out of step' from the wider processes of modernity. Liverpool, in particular, is depicted by historians as an 'exceptional' city in ways that evoke parochialism: 'Liverpool's apartness, indeed, is crucial to its identity,' Belchem claims.[72] The image of Manchester's 'exceptional' history also persists through its image as the original 'shock city' of the industrial revolution but that stresses its reputation as the 'first modern city', built on cotton and world famous: 'All roads led to Manchester.'[73]

Their reputation as exceptional cities contributes to Liverpool and Manchester's marginalization in twentieth-century cultural history, which remains dominated by a focus on London. Yet James Vernon's recent re-examination of British modernity claims it emerged as a product of rapid population growth and urbanization and created a society of strangers. Vernon suggests ways that society adapted to these new conditions, which included new forms of localism.[74] Vernon's approach signals a new way of thinking about modernity that places localism at the heart, rather than the periphery, of analysis. This monograph develops Vernon's analysis and follows Martin Daunton and Bernhard Rieger's assertion that British modernity should be studied through close readings within specific sites and localities.[75] Such an approach permits an examination and evaluation of modernity in regional-specific ways and a consideration of the similarities and differences with the metropolitan model. In doing so, this book challenges Liverpool and Manchester's image as exceptional cities and places them into wider discourse about modernity in Britain. Although their modernity possessed important local characteristics, it had more in common with mainstream and metropolitan cultures of modernity than historians tend to suggest. Rather than claiming that modernity in Liverpool and Manchester was unique to the interwar period, or indeed suggesting that my claims that Liverpool and Manchester were 'modern' is new, the book is interested in broadening the scholarly enquiry to think about regional modernities more broadly conceived.

Urban modernity tends to be associated with fantasy and spectacular urban images, which perpetuated imagined visions of the modern city.[76] For instance, plans for London after the First World War represented 'an exercise in the contemporary urban imagination'.[77] Frank Mort's article on planning in London during the 1940s draws on John Harley's notion of 'subliminal geography' and uses urban fantasy 'to denote the conscious construction of an imagined urban scene that was in excess of the socially possible or politically acceptable'.[78] Mort focuses on the power of visual depictions of the 1943 County of London plan and accompanying exhibition to argue that plans for London's reconstruction in the 1940s 'possessed a rich fantasy life, in that they dramatized elaborate and highly inventive images of the city, as much as actual policies for the rebuilding of London'.[79] As we shall see, a proliferation of images accompanied urban transformation in Liverpool and Manchester and there was a fantasy element to some of the discourse that emerged alongside the new civic, consumer and religious cultures. Nevertheless, the monograph engages critically with these urban images and is interested in the incompleteness of redevelopment alongside the role of citizens shaping the transformed environment and accepting or rejecting the images disseminated by the council, businessmen and Catholic leaders. In doing so, it aims to offer a multifaceted analysis of how cities develop and contributes to a more complicated examination of urban modernity.

Methods and approach

This examination of urban transformation in interwar Liverpool and Manchester takes a detailed approach to understanding urban modernity. We shall see that local politicians' investment in housing, transport, civic architecture and civic celebrations shared similarities with shop owners' new approach to marketing and shopping culture, and that Catholic leaders also attempted to create new images of urban modernity. Examining Liverpool and Manchester, two of Britain's most important provincial cities, not only challenges the generally negative image of these cities in historical scholarship, but contributes to a more detailed analysis of the experience of Britain's cities more generally between the two world wars. London remained Britain's metropolis throughout the twentieth century and with a population of around 8.6 million, being the second largest city in the world, dwarfed all other British cities. Nevertheless, cities like Manchester and Liverpool remained important to the country's economy and infrastructure. Greater Manchester encompassed a total population of 2,700,000 in the 1930s, including around 300,000 Catholics. In common with London, Greater Manchester encompassed smaller satellite towns and districts, such as Stockport and Trafford to the south, and Bolton, Bury and Rochdale to the north. Yet Manchester Corporation actually governed around 775,000 people and covered a relatively small circular area around the city centre, including Ardwick, Cheetham, Didsbury and Crumpsall. Lying 35 miles west of Manchester, Liverpool encompassed a radius area of around five miles from the city's port, including Bootle, Speke and Crosby. Liverpool's population stood at around 750,000 between a third and half of which was Roman Catholic. These social, cultural and geographical factors shaped urban transformation and the forms of urban modernity that emerged in Liverpool and Manchester and explain why it is important to offer a detailed examination of the interwar urban culture that looks beyond the metropolitan experience.

Focusing on the implications of Liverpool and Manchester's interwar redevelopment and the manifestation of regional forms of modernity uncovers the rich and wide-ranging forms of urban cultures that emerged in interwar Liverpool and Manchester. The book is organized into three parts. Part One charts the ambitious programmes of urban development implemented by local politicians and urban planners in response to economic turbulence and political instability. Whereas historians tend to associate the post-1918 urban landscape with decay and with the decline of the power of civic culture, Chapter 1 shows how local politicians, planners and architects invested in dramatic programmes of urban transformation, accompanied by extensive publicity campaigns. It argues that not only did urban redevelopment take place within international cultures of planning, but it was publicized in ways that fostered distinct urban images around the transformed cities. This publicity and communication were essential in the age of mass suffrage and the investment local politicians made in civic design and transformation aimed to engage with the newly enfranchised classless citizen. Their work reflected a more demotic and populist civic culture that represented a departure from Victorian approaches to civic pride and urban governance. Building on the material on urban transformation, Chapter 2 explores how civic celebrations promoted and publicized the transformed cityscapes to citizens. It shows that waves of Civic Week exhibitions marked the 1920s, the first of which was held in the Wembley Exhibition Hall (location of the Great Empire Exhibition) and others in the cities themselves. The celebrations guided the gaze of their citizens away from the persisting slums and unemployment problems and towards the new architecture and grandiose schemes of public works. Both chapters stress, however, that the process of transformation remained incomplete and the proliferation of urban images was an attempt to mask ongoing social problems and tensions.

Part Two illustrates the ways in which the redevelopment of Liverpool and Manchester revitalized shopping practices and permitted the emergence of a vibrant and demotic retail culture. Chapter 3 demonstrates that urban redevelopment reinvigorated urban consumer culture. It shows that shop managers, led by those of department stores, responded to economic depression by making use of the transformed cityscapes and borrowed trends and innovations from American retailing to transform local shopping culture. Department stores pioneered the emergence of this new vibrant and populist shopping culture as they increasingly sought to encourage a broad range of shoppers, rather than solely targeting middle- and upper-class customers. Their tactics were copied by other retailers, which transformed the visual appearance of shops, shopping streets and the city centres overall. Chapter 4 demonstrates that this vibrant culture of shopping brought fashionably dressed women, of varying ages, into the urban environment, to see and be seen. The chapter shows how working-class women could participate in this culture of shopping, especially through window-shopping, and demonstrates the imaginative means they employed in order to achieve the fashionable feminine identities they saw in these shops and to imitate Hollywood movie stars, in particular. As the chapter emphasizes, these fashionably dressed women shoppers obscured class divisions and women were able to have a significant amount of agency within the transformed urban environment.

Part Three demonstrates the rich and exotic cultures of religion that emerged in the transformed cities. Although religion tends to be viewed as incompatible with modernity, the material presented here shows cultures of Catholicism contributed to and shaped Liverpool and Manchester's modernity. Chapter 5 examines women's involvement in Manchester's Whit processions to understand the ways in which the transformed urban environment could act as a stage for the performance of episodic religious identities and highlights women's access to both religious and consumer cultures in interwar Britain. Chapter 6 continues these themes by focusing on the attempt to build the largest cathedral outside of Rome in 1930s Liverpool. The chapter argues that Catholic leaders created a powerful Catholic urban fantasy around the cathedral through their fundraising campaign and, although the cathedral remained unbuilt, it helped to transform perceptions of English Catholicism and marketed Liverpool as a centre of Catholicism. In doing so, the book highlights Catholic leaders' enthusiasm towards modernity and in creating a specific form of Catholic modernity that embraced modern trends.

This analysis of urban regeneration and modernity in interwar Liverpool and Manchester employs a variety of sources, including municipal publications, photographs, films, dress and fashion, advertisements, historical material from Mass Observation, statistical information from trade directories, personal testimony and material from Catholic archives. The diverse application of sources provides a vivid and detailed understanding of interwar urban culture and each relevant chapter discusses its specific use of source material in detail. Common to all chapters is the use of the press, both national and local. Research by Adrian Bingham has encouraged historians to make greater use of newspapers and has reminded scholars of how crucial the press was to social, cultural and political life in early-twentieth-century Britain.[80] Although early modern scholars make effective use of the provincial press, however, historians of the twentieth century tend to focus on the national dailies.[81] Here, the local press is shown to have been a lively and energetic force in Britain's industrial cities. In the increasingly competitive market for audiences, the local press mirrored the tactics of the nationals including a lively and sensationalist approach to news, the introduction of women's pages, a greater use of images and larger, more eye-catching advertisements. Reflecting a burgeoning scholarly interest in the civic role of the local press, an assessment of Liverpool and Manchester's newspapers shows they maintained a significant civic voice and actively promoted urban redevelopment and their reportage helped to foster the vibrant civic, consumer and religious cultures that emerged in interwar Britain.[82] The local press was neither parochial nor inward-looking, however, and regularly reported important national and international events. By implication, the methodological approach employed here shows that the press did much to foster the new urban images of Liverpool and Manchester and possessed an important role in interwar cultures of civic pride and boosterism. As Chapter 1 will show, it was through the local and national press that municipal leaders, architects and urban planners promoted new images of Liverpool and Manchester as they publicized their ambitious programmes of redevelopment, which were important responses to a range of social, political and economic problems. As we shall see, redevelopment had profound implications for civic, consumer and religious urban cultures and manifest local forms of modernity that reflected similarities and differences with British modernity more generally.

Part One

Civic Culture

'Soaring Skyward': Urban Regeneration

The redevelopment of Liverpool and Manchester was a product of the unique post-1918 period and the challenges they faced. In particular, both cities confronted a number of problems in the immediate aftermath of war. Although the First World War finally ended in 1918 and was strongly welcomed by the millions who marched across Britain on the Peace Day of July 1919, the transition to peace did not always remain smooth.[1] For example, waves of racially motivated riots occurred in several port cities in 1919, including Cardiff and London. Provoked by concerns about unemployment and miscegenation, violence targeted black seamen and dock workers.[2] Liverpool saw the worst of the violence with murderous results: a young black sailor named Charles Whootton died following a chase through the city by a lynch mob; pursued by a baying crowd which shouted 'let him drown!' he was either pushed or jumped into the docks.[3] In the same year, Liverpool also experienced the highest proportion of strike action in the Police Strike of 1919, in comparison with London, with five times as many policemen striking.[4] The strikes led to considerable unrest throughout the city and 'resulted in wholesale destruction of property, much looting and the eventual repayment via the public taxes'.[5] Although Manchester did not witness this kind of violence, it did also experience significant social tensions. For instance, in 1926, the General Strike brought the city to a standstill and the city suffered from numerous attacks by the Irish Republican Army (IRA) throughout the 1920s.[6]

These post-war social tensions emerged alongside persistent economic instability in both Liverpool and Manchester. The problem of unemployment plagued Britain's northern industrial cities more generally throughout the post-First World War period as they were particularly ill-affected by economic depression: whereas London's official unemployment rate stood at 12 per cent in 1932, the peak of the economic depression, it reached nearly 27 per cent in North West England and approached 30 per cent in the North East.[7] As the old staple industries such as coal, steel, cotton and shipbuilding collapsed dramatically in England's industrial heartlands, the new light industries, such as the factories manufacturing consumer durables like radios and washing machines, emerged in the South East and the Midlands.[8] Northern England's landscape became strongly associated with poverty and decay: 'You could see the scarred mess that greedy men have made of this handsome country', the documentary film-maker Paul Rotha wrote when he visited Lancashire during the 1930s.[9] As we shall see, both Liverpool and Manchester experienced severe challenges to their economies, which, in conjunction with wider social tensions, brought new concerns about instability.

At the same time as social and economic turmoil, the advent of mass democracy prompted considerable debates about the nature of the electorate.[10] Britain had a cross-class electorate for the first time after the First World War and, as the rest of Europe and Russia witnessed political turbulence and the rise of political extremism, both national and local politicians took important steps to engage and communicate with the new electorate. Although the impact of mass suffrage on national politics has attracted notable scholarly attention, especially regarding the implications for political marketing, the impact on local politics remains notably under-researched.[11] Rather, historians tend to assume that a fall in the influence of local government heralded the decline of England's provincial cities. In particular, scholars tend to view 1914 as a turning point in the dramatic demise of civic power.[12] Yet, Richard Trainor has drawn attention to J. B. Priestley's assertion in 1934 that England was 'the country of local government'.[13] By highlighting the involvement of the middle classes, rather than the industrial elite, more generally, Trainor suggests that the idea of decline in the 1920s and 1930s remains exaggerated.[14] This chapter goes further and suggests that civic pride thrived in Liverpool and Manchester between the two world wars in response to post-First World War turbulence, but it was a civic culture that was different from the one that had flourished during the nineteenth century. Then, the great men of the industrial revolution invested in their cities to boost trade and to dwarf their competitors but also, and perhaps more importantly, as a way to wield power over the urban working class.[15] After 1918, the building of public and grandiose monuments remained no less important, but the civic culture that emerged was more demotic and populist and reflected the new mass democratic age.

Local politicians in Liverpool and Manchester responded to the unique problems they faced after 1918 by investing in ambitious programmes of urban transformation that fostered a rich culture of civic pride. By focusing on housing reform, public transport and new forms of civic and commercial architecture, this chapter highlights the innovative and imaginative strategies employed by Liverpool's and Manchester's local politicians and urban planners in the face of potentially crippling economic and social problems. Although formal, published plans did not emerge in Britain until the Second World War, interwar urban transformation was heavily publicized in the press and through municipal publicity material with a proliferation of images of the transformed urban environment, both real and imagined.[16] Urban transformation and the accompanying publicity material helped to create new urban images that reinvigorated local cultures and boosted the local economies. The symbolic impact of these grandiose schemes – including those that remained incomplete by 1939, such as housing reform – was profound. Urban transformation and the accompanying urban images had important implications for urban culture more generally. As subsequent chapters explore, the ambitious programmes of redevelopment uncovered here revitalized local culture and produced new forms of civic, consumer and religious urban cultures that reflected an important localized manifestation of modernity.

Innovation and civic design in the age of political and economic turbulence

The image of Liverpool and Manchester as dynamic and innovative cities does not match the typically bleak image associated with northern towns and cities more generally between the two world wars. The 'old' staple industries such as coal mining, shipbuilding and cotton suffered from increased competition from abroad and decreased domestic demand, which caused high levels of unemployment in Northern England, Scotland and parts of Wales.[17] Liverpool experienced severe challenges to its port trade and its share of national imports fell significantly across the period, from 33 per cent in 1915–20 to just 20 per cent for 1924–38.[18] Just as damaging were the losses in passenger trade. The more lucrative north Atlantic trade shifted towards the newer ports, especially Southampton. Several shipping companies, most notably Cunard, moved their headquarters out of Liverpool and caused significant white-collar unemployment in the city.[19] Unemployment rates hit 33 per cent in 1932 and it is no surprise that Liverpool suffered from particularly high levels of poverty as a result of the city's economic problems.[20] By 1932, 700 people per 10,000 claimed poor relief, in comparison with just 297 per 10,000 nationally.[21] Yet Liverpool was never officially designated a depressed area because it suffered less than other struggling towns and cities.[22] Instability, rather than simple decline, characterized its interwar economy. The economic landscape shaped the marketing of interwar urban redevelopment, which fuelled an image that stressed commercial stability and faith in the city's future.

Lancashire did not escape post-First World War economic turbulence and its famous cotton industry collapsed irrecoverably during the 1920s. By 1939, cloth exports amounted to only one-fifth of their 1913 levels.[23] The collapse severely affected mill towns throughout the region, such as Blackburn, where the cotton industry had accounted for 60 per cent of employment; however, it had an unemployment rate of 46.8 per cent in 1931.[24] By contrast, the city of Manchester was better equipped to cope with the cotton industry's collapse. Certain parts of the city experienced crippling levels of unemployment and poverty. In 1934, for example, a study by Manchester University found that a quarter of all households had no member in employment and the overall unemployment level never fell below 42.5 per cent while the survey was undertaken. Nevertheless, other parts of the city saw greater prosperity and overall levels of unemployment never reached the national rate.[25] It was also a period of striking innovation and commercial diversification for the city. Manchester's Ship Canal (completed in 1894) became particularly important in developing and diversifying trade between the wars. Trafford Park, an industrial zone to the south of the city, attracted significant investment and, by 1933, was home to over two hundred American firms and also to a municipal airport, which was opened in 1929.[26] The economic context explains why presentations and depictions of Manchester's urban transformation highlighted its diverse economy and portrayed a shift away from the city's Victorian image of 'Cottonopolis'.

Alongside economic turmoil, political change characterized the decades following the First World War with the advent of mass suffrage. The national Conservative Party proved to be the most effective party in communicating across class divisions. In particular, the leadership of Stanley Baldwin fostered an inclusive rhetoric of 'Englishness' and a cosy approach to political broadcasting that enabled the party to engage effectively with voters across class lines.[27] Yet historians often characterize Liverpool, in particular, as being outside of the national political culture and marginalized from Baldwin's unifying rhetoric.[28] The apparent exceptionalism of cities such as Liverpool does seem to have been overstated, however, since the Conservative Party remained the majority party in municipal elections in both Liverpool and Manchester throughout the interwar period but lost some seats following a rise in support for Labour, largely mirroring national trends.[29] We can see urban transformation and the accompanying images promoted to inhabitants as part of a broader scheme by the local Conservative Party to engage with the new mass electorate. The approach made by local politicians to engage with the newly enfranchised citizen, therefore, reveals similarities to marketing tactics adopted by the national Conservative Party in response to anxieties about mass suffrage in the early 1920s.[30]

The more demotic local political culture adopted in Liverpool and Manchester between the wars emerged within a wider internationalist and innovative culture of urban planning. From the 1900s, for example, the work of American planner Daniel Burnham and his peers responded to criticisms that planners had spent far too much time expanding the infrastructure of cities such as Chicago to the detriment of the quality of civic culture and urban life.[31] The link between planning and a demotic and inclusive approach to citizenship was also clear in Liverpool and Manchester: in 1925, Manchester's Town Planning Special Committee was instructed to prepare a general survey of the city's needs because 'the publication of a survey as suggested should do much to assist the municipal government and the Citizens in general to visualise living and other conditions within the city and to create a greater sense of citizenship'.[32] Planners and politicians in Liverpool and Manchester, thus, adopted wider ideas about planning as a means to communicate with the classless urban citizen. Their strategy promoted a new kind of civic culture that represented a shift away from cultures that reinforced the middle-class power and dominance in the Victorian city.[33]

Local politics, urban planning, architectural innovation and civic pride were interlinked and often overlapped in Liverpool and Manchester between the two world wars. The energetic ambitions of a few local and influential individuals helped to drive the vibrancy of urban redevelopment. Manchester's key figure was Lord Ernest Simon, who donated land to the south of the city for the council's ambitious project to build the Wythenshawe housing estate, the largest municipal estate in Europe.[34] An ardent socialist, Simon was politically active at both national and local levels and was particularly interested in improving housing for the working classes. Simon also campaigned for a more comprehensive approach to town planning with greater state involvement and advocated the municipalization of urban land.[35] Manchester established a number of civic societies with links to the council and Alderman Sir Percy Woodhouse was central in convening a civic committee in 1930 to 'take advantage of any and every opportunity arising to retain existing industries in Manchester and to seek the introduction of new industries'.[36] Manchester was notable for appointing a city architect, Henry Price, in 1902, who retired in 1932 and was replaced by George Noel Hill, who was charged with overseeing all municipal building projects and advising on planning and civic design.

Sir Charles Reilly, architectural expert and emeritus professor at the University of Liverpool, was instrumental in driving redevelopment in Liverpool and, to a certain degree, also in Manchester and beyond.[37] Reilly's legacy lay less in his own architectural work and more in importing American ideas and trends in planning and civic design to Britain. Impressed with what he witnessed while travelling through America just before the First World War, Reilly became devoted to promoting the role of architecture in British society. He became a prolific journalist, a role in which he championed American innovations in architecture and planning, called for British cities to take on these trends and celebrated those that did.[38] Reilly visited America on numerous occasions, often returning with large stacks of planning material and periodicals, and during one trip, he made a dash to Chicago to take up an opportunity to meet with Burnham, whom he much admired.[39] Reilly's architectural critiques of Liverpool and Manchester, published in the early 1920s, are landmarks in the emergence of a greater interest in planning and urban redevelopment in both cities, which owed much to his experiences of America.[40] Reilly was highly effective in developing the professionalization of town planning through the University of Liverpool's School of Architecture. The school established the *Town Planning Review*, and he convinced Lord Lever to finance the first-ever professorship in planning in 1912. Reilly's friend Patrick Abercrombie, holder of the chair from 1915 to 1935, was also important in developing the discipline and together they pursued a holistic approach to regional planning.[41] Reilly's colleague John Brodie, city engineer from 1898, provided a direct link between Liverpool Corporation (the city's government) and the university, following the creation of a special lectureship for him in engineering. Brodie's achievements were striking: he was one of the first to suggest an electric tram system for Liverpool, designed the Mersey Tunnel (inspired by New York's Holland Tunnel) and pioneered a circumferential boulevard around the city. Brodie also led experimental use of prefabricated housing, assisted in the planning of New Delhi and, as his proudest achievement, invented the nets used in football matches.[42]

In politics, the role of Sir Archibald Salvidge (chairman from 1892 to 1928) was fundamental in shaping the Conservative Party's approach to local politics. Nicknamed the 'King of Liverpool', Salvidge fashioned a deliberate 'Tory democrat' image for the Conservatives in reaction to Labour's first parliamentary seat in Liverpool in 1923.[43] Salvidge remained concerned about the rise of Labour and the implications of universal suffrage on local politics. Following the municipal elections in May 1926, Salvidge lamented the loss of three key districts and 'urged councillors, in their own interests, to give more time and attention to the affairs of the respective Wards to meet the ceaseless propaganda of their opponents'.[44] Yet such concerns were not limited to the Conservative Party. In the preface to Simon's 1926 publication, A City Council from Within, for example, the political psychologist and educationalist Graham Wallas explained that the book was aimed at younger members of the Labour Party. Wallas warned that the 'inevitable transference of power from the middle to the working classes in our English cities might be so directed as to be disastrous in some cases to administrative efficiency'.[45] Salvidge and Wallas thus exposed the tensions and anxieties both between and within the Labour and Conservative parties on a local level over the issue of mass suffrage.

One of the most influential individuals who helped to promote Liverpool's and Manchester's economies abroad was Sir Harry Gloster Armstrong, consul general in New York from 1920 to 1931. Armstrong and his wife were extremely popular in New York society and contributed much to the social, civic and religious culture of the city.[46] They left New York in 1931, to many farewell dinners and celebrations, after Armstrong obtained an unprecedented two extensions to his term and served until he reluctantly retired at the age of seventy.[47] On retirement, Armstrong moved to Manchester to become chairman of the Manchester Ship Canal and established its first American office in New York. Armstrong did much to forge close relationships between British and American cities and, as we shall see, he organized highly publicized visits from Liverpool's and Manchester's mayors in 1931. Armstrong's success was notable and on his death in 1938, the British ambassador Sir Ronald Lindsay paid tribute: 'His duty has been in New York to look after British interests and British subjects and British commerce, and I think he has done it with energy and with success.'[48] Armstrong was, therefore, symbolic of an attempt to publicize and promote British cities abroad, despite a broader strategy of economic protectionism pursued by the national government.[49]

Local politicians, planners and architects were able to finance their ambitious programmes of urban transformation and accompanying propaganda campaigns because their rateable incomes and loans from the central government increased (above inflation) between the two world wars. They also received increased profits from public transport and amenities such as electricity and gas. Liverpool Corporation had a total income of £5,366,155 in 1924 (£2,753,508 from rates), rising to £9,400,589 by 1935 (£4,367,220 from rates).[50] Manchester Corporation's income also rose substantially, from £4,947,920 in 1924 (£2,872,912 from rates) to £8,621,477 in 1935 (£4,623,801 from rates).[51] This increase occurred partly because rates nearly doubled between 1915 and 1922.[52] Both the corporations invested heavily in their respective cities. For example, Manchester Corporation consistently invested far more money in libraries and art galleries (£126,864 in 1935) than on maternity and child welfare (£83,732 in 1935). There were also revealing distinctions in how each corporation spent its income. Manchester Corporation spent significantly more money on streets: £450,528 in 1926, compared to Liverpool's expenditure of £229,027. By contrast, Liverpool's civic leaders invested more in policing, perhaps by way of response to the 1919 Police Strike, and in 1927, Liverpool Corporation spent £799,562 on policing, in comparison with Manchester's £484,745.[53] The choice to invest in transforming the urban environment, rather than in health and welfare, was key to local politicians and planners' ambitions to revitalize their urban landscapes. Both Liverpool and Manchester Corporations began these programmes of redevelopment and regeneration by starting with housing reform.

Housing reform

Housing was a priority in Britain after the First World War ended and the national government took significant steps to assist councils and private builders in demolishing inadequate dwellings and to construct state-subsidized replacements.[54] As they were home to some of the poorest housing in the country in 1918, it is unsurprising that both Liverpool and Manchester Corporations embraced housing reform.[55] In Liverpool, Sir Lancelot Keay, city architect and director of Housing, undertook much of the work from 1925 until 1948. The corporation rehoused 140,000 people (15 per cent of its population) in 33,355 purpose-built suburban houses between the wars.[56] Like much of the rest of the country, the council embraced suburbanization, and in 1934, the Social Survey of Merseyside reported that 96 per cent of corporation houses built after 1919 were located in the suburbs.[57]

Progress made in housing reform was striking, yet incomplete. In July 1928, Liverpool's housing committee abandoned a plan to clear congested areas near the city centre in favour of supplying cheap houses nearby to relieve the acute shortage of affordable accommodation.[58] Scotland Road, the area between the port district and the city centre, was home to a large Irish Catholic population and epitomized 'squalid Liverpool' to late Victorian health reformers. It remained a site of great poverty and unemployment in the interwar period and was not subject to major clearance until the 1950s.[59] Those rehoused to the suburbs often experienced feelings of alienation and isolation due to the lack of community and social amenities. Nevertheless, many inhabitants were enthused about suburban life, although the negative sentiments towards the new suburbs by residents are well documented.[60] Liverpool Corporation did include the provision of shops in the new estates, but such businesses struggled financially, and the council often denied permission for the newly emerging chain stores, such as Woolworths, to open in the new estates as they wished to control the types of trades undertaken.[61]

Although Liverpool's process of housing reform remained varied in its scope and success, municipal leaders publicized their progress to encourage confidence in the city's economy. 'Nowhere has the appalling post-war problem of house shortage been more bravely and successfully tackled,' announced Lord Mayor Thomas Dowd in 1924. Dowd continued,

> It would have been impossible for the city to undertake works of such magnitude as this if its financial stability were not impregnable. But happily, Liverpool's financial credit is high – so high, indeed, that on more than one occasion it has been able to borrow money in the open market more cheaply than the Imperial Government itself.[62]

Lord Mayor Edwin Thompson repeated these sentiments in 1931, when he also turned to the changing urban environment to express optimism in the city's commercial future. 'Evidence of this faith in the future meets us at every hand on both sides of the river,' he declared, 'it is to be read in ... the vast development of our suburbs; in the contemplated attacks on our slum areas; in our new arterial roads and town and regional planning schemes.'[63] Municipal leaders acknowledged that Liverpool's programme of housing reform was incomplete, but claimed it was 'progressing step by step, thanks to enlightened civic management and courageous private enterprise. ... Liverpool, believing in its own future, is equipping itself for the good times ahead, and at the same time lengthening her lead over all rivals, both as a city and as a port.'[64] There was, thus, a clear attempt to promote the city's progress within a broader narrative of optimism concerning the city's economy.

The 'booster' narrative around Liverpool's investment in housing was strikingly effective and became associated with the city's international reputation. The *New York Times* made several reports on Liverpool's housing schemes between the wars and in 1933 the newspaper suggested that the city was home to 'one of the greatest slum clearance schemes produced in England'.[65] As early as 1925, the *New York Times* celebrated Liverpool's success in housing following the visit of Helen Hanning, chairman of the City Parliament of Community Councils, to examine the use of state credit in the provision of working-class housing in Britain. Hanning visited several of Britain's industrial cities but chose to highlight Liverpool's specific success in housing reform at a meeting of the City Parliament. 'This city was supposed to have the worst slums in England,' she reported:

> The development there is wonderful – both in the densely populated districts and in the suburbs. … They had also worked out a scheme and were about to erect 1000 electrically equipped and heated houses, the plan being a joint project of the Housing and Electrical Commission, the latter being city-owned. This plan contemplated selling electricity at a very low rate … great thought has been given to recreation and playgrounds provided for even the most densely populated centres. … I was much impressed by the many moderate-sized parks with their tennis courts, ball grounds, bowling greens and children's playgrounds, always crowded in the evenings, even dancing facilities having been provided in most of them.[66]

Such a glowing report in the *New York Times* was the kind of positive publicity for Liverpool that money could just not buy. Although it was promoting housing, the reportage gave an image of an entrepreneurial and innovative city and undermined Liverpool's association with urban decay and economic deprivation.

Manchester was also ambitious in tackling housing reform and built 21,859 new suburban council houses by 1933.[67] Manchester's famous Wythenshawe estate, established on a large stretch of land to the south of the city centre, provided suburban homes specifically for the working classes:[68] a total of 40,000 inhabitants occupied 8,145 homes in Wythenshawe by 1939, which was nearly half way towards the corporation's goal of 100,000 people.[69] The corporation's investment in housing led to rather grand claims about the success of housing reform and Lord Simon claimed that no cellar dwellings were remaining in

Manchester by 1938, and whereas there had been 10,000 back-to-back houses prior to 1918, there were less than forty by 1938: 'Really bad slums, which are still common in other cities, do not exist in Manchester.'[70]

The Wythenshawe estate was the corporation's showpiece in its ambitious programme of urban redevelopment. It was 'a bold experiment' and the first to combine important planning principles such as parkways, neighbourhood unit planning and agricultural belts: 'In no other example have all these elements been correlated and combined to form one self-contained entity,' explained the *Town Planning Review* in 1935.[71] Wythenshawe incorporated the use of neighbourhood units, where 'the land is divided into large sectors for housing purposes, each sector being bounded by traffic routes, and having the school near the centre of it'.[72] Historical scholarship on Manchester Corporation's interwar investment in housing tends to present it as an extension, or 'last gesture' of Victorian civic pride.[73] Yet municipal publicity material presented the new suburbs as symbols of a clear break with the city's Victorian past. A brochure, published in 1938 to celebrate the corporation's centenary anniversary, encouraged citizens to recognize the improvement in the city's housing stock. During the Victorian years,

> slums were crowded, and street after street of cheap little houses was rushed up, often without foundations, and with walls half a brick in thickness, crowded together to make the builder's profit out of a piece of land as high as possible. … We are now in the city of today, as clean and as healthy as the town we have just described was dirty and horrifying.[74]

Figure 1.1 shows the corporation directly contrasted housing from the mid-nineteenth century and the 1930s. Indeed, publicity material consistently presented a negative image of Victorian Manchester, particularly following the collapse of the cotton industry.[75] A local newspaper, the *Manchester City News*, also compared the Victorian slums with the new suburbs in an article entitled 'Hulme Vs Wilbraham Estate'. 'Instead of dreary, depressing long rows of houses opening onto the street front … and backing onto narrow, dirty passages', the article claimed, 'we have … houses into which the sunlight can penetrate … with good gardens and plenty of space.'[76] Manchester's inhabitants were encouraged to see the new suburbs as a symbol of change, presented as a tangible example of the city's broader development.

Celebratory representations of housing reform in Manchester masked a darker reality, however. In 1930, the pressure on housing was acute and Manchester Corporation decided to delay the clearance of Hulme, an area

HOUSES—OLD AND NEW.
UPPER : HULME.   LOWER : WYTHENSHAWE.

Figure 1.1 'Houses – Old and New'

Source: Manchester Corporation, *Centenary Celebration of Manchester's Incorporation: Official Handbook to the Exhibition of Civic Services May 2–7 1938* (Manchester: Percy Brothers, 1938), 84.

close to the city centre, until rehousing was available to its inhabitants.[77] The need for more housing was urgent and there were 10,000 people waiting for corporation housing in 1931.[78] A report by Manchester Corporation in 1932 found that 30,000 houses in Manchester needed clearing but, since that was impossible because of the acute demand for homes, the report recommended that a target of 15,000 by 1938 was more realistic.[79] Under pressure, Manchester Corporation modified its plans for housing reform. In 1932, a report for the corporation on the Hulme Clearance Area was undertaken by the Manchester Salford and Counties Property Owners' Association, which claimed that there were no back-to-back houses in Hulme, that each had a private yard, all but nine had water carrier systems and at 4.43 persons per house 'cannot be taken as serious overcrowding'.[80] The report suggested that the Wythenshawe estate was an impractical alternative location for Hulme residents because of travelling expenses and that 75 per cent had already refused to move to the Platt Lane Estate, which was much closer. Clearing the area, recommended the report, would merely increase overcrowding in the surrounding areas.[81] In response, the architect's report suggested that a better alternative was the destruction of half the houses in Hulme near the city centre. The plans show that the aim was to create as many open spaces as possible and suggested reducing density to twenty-five houses an acre with a focus on reconditioning surviving houses.[82] Corporation propaganda was careful to ensure that the grandiosity of the Wythenshawe estate overshadowed older types of housing that did survive, such as that in Hulme. Although a striking and ambitious project, Wythenshawe did not represent the reality of all housing in Manchester by the mid-1930s. Nevertheless, the ambition in Manchester was strong and planners went further to transform Manchester in a way that revitalized local culture.

'Transport is vital to a modern city:' Replanning the city and defining the 'civic centre'

Ambitious plans for urban transformation were not limited to housing reform in Liverpool and Manchester. The interwar period was the golden age of mass public transport in both cities as impressive transport networks were established in these cities during this era. By as early as 1924, trams in Liverpool covered Allerton, Woolton and Walton on the city outskirts and, during the morning and evening peak hours, three hundred cars entered and left the Pierhead.[83] By 1939, Liverpool Corporation claimed that its public transport system carried 282,045,776 passengers and covered 24,620,064 miles every year.[84] Public transport expansion ensured that large numbers of people congregated in two key areas of the city, notably the Pierhead and St George's Hall. The Pierhead became 'the transport hub of the city' and 'a bustling interchange between ships and trains, ferries and trams'.[85] From there, the 'majority of routes radiate in fanlike formation' and an estimated four thousand trams visited the Pierhead every day.[86]

Investment in public transport reshaped the urban environment and, in particular, led to more clearly defined civic centres. In Liverpool, rather than build new civic architecture, the extended mass transport system was organized around St George's Hall, which cemented its position as the city's civic centre. This shift was a response to anxieties from around the time of the First World War that although St George's Hall was the 'finest example of trabeated stone architecture in Europe ... very few people seemed to have seen it. It is curious how great works of art can, as it were, disappear into a cloud.'[87] As Figure 1.2 shows, the expansion of Liverpool's public transport accentuated the role of St George's Hall, which had become the main terminus by 1935. The picture depicts how planners understood the impact of the Mersey Tunnel (completed in 1934) as they envisioned St George's Hall to be the centre of all forms of transport. By presenting an image of a coherent and ordered transport system around Liverpool's grandest and most impressive building, the image evokes a sense of grandeur. The image features Liverpool's other impressive Victorian buildings alongside St George's Hall, including the Walker Art Gallery and Lime Street Station. Planners in Liverpool appropriated these grand symbols of Victorian civic pride, when Liverpool thrived commercially, to nurture a sense of continuity with the present. For instance, the laying of the foundation stone of St George's Hall commemorated Queen Victoria's coronation, although the building was not actually completed until 1854.[88] Situated above the city and adjoining Lime Street Station (built in 1836 and rebuilt in 1850 and 1871), planners specifically chose the site of St George's Hall because it expressed 'the pride and confidence of the thriving town'.[89] By placing St George's Hall at the centre of the city's interwar public transport network, therefore, planners drew attention to Liverpool's strong history of commercial success in order to inspire confidence in its future.

The image featured in Figure 1.2 is notably similar to the system of traffic circulation proposed for public places by Eugène Hénard. Hénard, the French architect, urban planner and expert in traffic studies, designed to reduce conflict in currents of traffic.[90] Hénard presented his work at the 1910 Town Planning Conference in London, where Brodie was also in attendance.[91] Brodie, like Hénard, was especially interested in the role of boulevards in urban planning and was responsible for Queen's Drive, a circumferential boulevard around Liverpool that was a minimum of 84 feet in width, going up to 108 feet in places.[92]

A VISION OF THE FUTURE OF KINGSWAY

Figure 1.2 'A Vision of the Future of Kingsway'
Source: Liverpolitan, January 1935, 15.

Brodie described the road as the 'lungs' of the city and credited Burnham's *Plan of Chicago* with shaping his designs.[93] 'By using this road it will be possible for traffic coming in by any of the main approaches to the town to skirt the busy business centre and to reach any part of the city without passing through the congested area,' Brodie wrote.[94] The links and influences between Hénard, Burnham and Brodie are important because they illuminate the international cultures of planning and the global influences on urban transformation in Liverpool between the two world wars. These connections and shared influences on urban design demonstrate that local cultures of modernity were outward-looking and in no way parochial.

Brodie was especially influential in designing and implementing Liverpool's interwar transformation. Brodie's greatest triumph was the Mersey Tunnel (although he personally claimed it was the invention of the nets for football goal posts), which connected Liverpool and Birkenhead and became the world's longest and largest subaqueous road tunnel. The Holland Tunnel, connecting New Jersey and Manhattan under the Hudson River, which was begun in 1920 and was completed seven years later, inspired the Mersey Tunnel. It was championed by Sir Archibald Salvidge, chairman of the Conservative Party in Liverpool from 1892 until his death in 1928, who, claimed Reilly, 'ruled Liverpool almost like an American boss'.[95] He displayed a passionate civic loyalty and an energetic commitment to civic pride. Known as the 'King of Liverpool', Salvidge embraced a more inclusive approach towards local politics in response to Labour's first parliamentary seat in Liverpool in 1923.[96] For Salvidge, the only way for the local Conservative Party to face the threat from Labour was to take a more active role in civic culture and to focus on economic regeneration. Salvidge's populist approach was to prove fundamental in Liverpool's interwar urban redevelopment, and he realized that a prestige project like the tunnel would encourage investment and boost the local economy by improving traffic to the city's port trade. Salvidge received the Freedom of Liverpool for his success in obtaining 50 per cent funding from the central government for the tunnel with the passing of the Mersey Tunnel Act in 1925.[97] The tunnel project was not without problems, however, and cost 26 per cent more than original estimates allowed and the project borrowed a further £1,369,04 from the Ministry of Health.[98] Sadly, Salvidge never lived to see the tunnel, dying in 1928, and Brodie only just lived to see its completion, dying just four months later in November 1934. Nevertheless, the tunnel proved to be one of the most symbolically important innovations in Liverpool's interwar programme of redevelopment.

The importance of the tunnel lay not only in its potential benefits to the city's economy but also in its 'booster power' that such a grandiose project would make about Liverpool to the rest of the country. For example, the tunnel was described proudly by its chairman as 'a mighty piece of engineering, the tunnel will rank as one of the wonders of the world, as well as a monument to the civic enterprise of the city of Liverpool and the borough of Birkenhead'.[99] King George V formally opened the tunnel on 18 July 1934, amid great pomp and ceremony during a 'Royal Tunnel Week'. The Lord Mayor accompanied the King, alongside other municipal councillors, and the Anglican Bishop, who formally offered God's blessing to the tunnel.[100] Liverpool used the tunnel's opening celebrations to promote its history in order to encourage confidence in its future. The celebrations included a pageant of women dressed as the 'Spirit of Liverpool' in medieval clothes and bearing beacons of virtues such as charity, progress, vision and commerce.[101] Crucially, accompanying publicity material and rhetoric presented the tunnel as a symbol of confidence in the city's economy: 'What, indeed, is the great new Merseyside Road Tunnel but an act of faith unmatched probably in all of Europe?' asked the Lord Mayor in a 1931 speech to the city.[102]

As in Liverpool, investment in public transport was also important to Manchester's redevelopment. Manchester's buses carried 6.9 million passengers in 1925, increasing to 20.2 million in 1929 and by 1938, at least one tram passed through the main shopping street in the city centre, Market Street, every 24 seconds.[103] Again, there was a link between improving transport and alleviating unemployment in the area: in 1929, a Report of Works for the Unemployed Special Committee proposed a comprehensive programme of road works in Manchester over a period of five years, with 60 per cent of the cost expected from the central government.[104] Municipal publicity material consistently presented developments in Manchester's public transport as a symbol of the city's progress. Manchester's *Commercial Year Book* of 1925 declared, 'Transport is vital to a modern city,' and it offered statistics to 'enable every citizen to study our great municipal enterprise'.[105]

In the 1930s, municipal publicity material continued to stress the progress made in the city's public transport in comparison with the Victorian years. In 1935, the corporation asked its citizens to contrast the 'early motor buses', which 'were a somewhat doubtful proposition from the point of view of reliability and were anything but quiet and smooth', with Manchester's newer system of operating 'motor buses parallel with and supplementary to the tramway services, each type of vehicle functioning to the best of its ability'.[106] The article further claimed that 'Manchester has always been a pioneer in transport'.[107] Public transport was also an important aspect of the centenary celebrations of Manchester's incorporation in 1938. The *Manchester Guardian*'s article, 'From Horse Bus to Motor Bus', encapsulated the way public transport was used to portray municipal progress. It contrasted Manchester's first omnibus of 1824, 'a relatively exclusive conveyance' which was 'narrow and cramped', with the sophisticated and comfortable public transport available in 1938.[108]

The impact of mass transport had a profound impact on shaping a clearly defined civic centre in Manchester. Again, evidence suggests Manchester's transformation emerged within an international culture of knowledge exchange. First was the influence of Robert Pilcher, who trained as an electrical engineer at the Montreal Street Railway before becoming the general manager for the Manchester Corporation Transport Department in 1929 until 1946. Pilcher advocated the promotion of public transport among local citizens and actively encouraged the link between civic pride and mass transit.[109] Secondly, the role of Town Clerk was also instrumental in fostering international influences on urban planning in Manchester. In 1925, Percy Heath held the post and he represented

Manchester in the International Town, City and Regional Planning Conference in New York. On his return, Heath reported that Philadelphia was a city that afforded comparisons with Manchester:

> With many other cities, Philadelphia, population 1,894,500, affords a good example of what is being done in a built-up area by the construction, at a cost of 30,000,000 dollars, of a new artery in the form of a magnificent parkway from the City Hall in the centre of the city to an existing park on the outskirts of the city. Private citizens take considerable interest in all matters relating to the well-being of the towns and cities, and considerable co-operation exists between the municipalities and commercial bodies or individuals in all matters relating to town planning and development.[110]

These international influences ensured that the expansion of public transport in Manchester possessed a prominent role in civic culture and contributed to the emergence of a clearly defined civic centre in the heart of the city. Following expansion, the tram system terminated in Piccadilly and many ran past the rear of the Victorian Town Hall (completed 1877). 'The routes extend from the districts beyond the City on all sides and pass through the centre of the City, thus affording the opportunity of transferring from one route to another,' described one public transport handbook in 1928.[111] The area behind the Victorian Town Hall (St Peter's Square) became the focus of civic culture with the building of Manchester Central Library (1934) and the Town Hall extension (1938). The impact of public transport expansion was fundamental to this shift and municipal investment in the library and public transport went hand in hand.[112]

The interest in reshaping civic space in Manchester followed numerous criticisms of the city's civic design and architectural form that emerged in the early 1920s and led by Reilly, but his calls for reform gained momentum quickly. In 1921, for instance, the *Manchester Guardian Yearbook* complained that

> Manchester does not rank highly among the world's beauty spots. ... Manchester is a conglomeration of architectural accidents that sprang up as commercial interests of the moment dictated. A finely conceived city should have its great public and administrating buildings grouped for combined effect in a stately civic centre. ... The root of the trouble is a lack of organic planning and corporate imagination.[113]

These kinds of criticisms helped to provoke a new interest in planning and development from the early 1920s. Concerns focused particularly on the area where the corporation eventually built the new library and Town Hall extension. In 1924, the area, then known as 'Jackson's Row' and covering 1,618 square yards, was considered the 'heart of the city' and described as 'an exceptional site'. A report commissioned by the corporation warned against piecemeal allocation, but suggested that the area should not be left vacant. It recommended that a representative 'should be appointed and charged with the duty of immediately preparing comprehensive schemes for the utilisation *en bloc* of these extensive and important sites'.[114] The new approach to the 'heart of the city' appears to have emerged directly from the Town Clerk's trip to the regional planning conference held in New York City in 1925. His report states that the redevelopment of Manchester was to 'be properly regulated in conformity with a pre-determined plan of development', in response to the trends and innovations he witnessed at the conference.[115]

In 1925, and perhaps again in response to the Town Clerk's experience in New York, the Town Hall committee – originally set up to oversee the care of all monuments and statues owned by the corporation – decided that a new library was in 'urgent need', alongside an extension to the Town Hall.[116] By 1931, however, the committee (renamed the Town Hall extension committee) reported that the Unemployed Grants Committee, which the committee hoped to claim from, no longer considered grants towards Town Hall schemes and the plans for Jackson Row were postponed for two years.[117] Despite these delays, the corporation finally completed the Manchester Central Library which was opened amid great pomp and ceremony by King George V on 17 July 1934. Costing almost £600,000, the library accommodated one million volumes and seated over three hundred readers in the Great Hall, which made it, in size, second only to the British Museum's reading room.[118] Manchester Corporation presented the library within a rhetoric of populist civic culture: in 1938, municipal publicity material claimed the building was 'used by all classes in the community'.[119] Again, the corporation presented the library as a sign of the city's progression and suggested a 'story of pioneer experimental work'.[120] The library was adjacent to the Town Hall and Town Hall extension, creating a cluster of civic buildings. Manchester also hoped to build a new art gallery, but financial restrictions hampered the project.[121] Nevertheless, great admiration greeted the new building and Reilly envisioned its impact in characteristically dramatic terms:

Whatever forms of architectural expression Manchester today maybe choosing, she is undergoing one great change. A single building, it seems to me, is altering her whole aspect … the new Reference Library will, I think, change Manchester. Already its magnificent outline can be seen complete from St Peter's Square. It is like the Colosseum, a great isolated building planted down in the centre of the town and having no truck with its surroundings.[122]

The library thus represented an important shift in architectural design in Manchester and became a new kind of civic monument that was unprecedented in the city.

Adjacent to the library, the Town Hall extension, designed by English architect Vincent Harris, opened in 1938 as part of the centenary celebrations of Manchester's incorporation. Costing £750,000, the building represented a notable departure from Victorian town halls: the new extension included a new council chamber, Gas and Electricity Departments with their own showrooms, cinemas and demonstration rooms. Gas showrooms represented 'a public gathering place', particularly for women.[123] The showroom in the Town Hall extension reflected a specifically female form of citizenship and articulated a wider attempt by the corporation to define the female citizen through her consumption of corporation goods and services, especially gas and electricity.[124] However, despite their important public role and link to women's citizenship, the new building marginalized such showrooms. In 1924, for example, the Town Hall committee decided that they would locate the showrooms in the basement of the extension as 'anything in the nature of shop windows would detract from the general appearance of the building, and would not be a desirable feature'.[125] This decision hints at tensions within the decision-making process as the committee attempted to design a civic area that appealed to the new franchise, both in terms of class and gender.

Crucially, Manchester Corporation fostered a populist rhetoric around the Town Hall extension and claimed it was 'the absolute property of the Citizens'.[126] It claimed the building was 'designed with a view to the convenience of the public' and provided 'the seat from which the city's municipal affairs are directed, and is the centre of much of the social life of the community'.[127] Victorian town halls, such as Manchester's, were associated with the imposing power of the industrial elite, seeking to impose their power over the new cities.[128] In contrast, in the 1930s, Manchester Corporation aimed to foster a more inclusive and demotic culture around its civic architecture and as Figure 1.3 shows, these new buildings were not just the civic centre of the city, but also represented 'Modern Manchester', from which the Victorian Town Hall appeared marginalized.

MODERN MANCHESTER.

Figure 1.3 'Modern Manchester'
Source: Manchester Corporation, *How Manchester Is Managed* (1938), inside cover.

New commercial architecture

Municipal leaders' investment in civic architecture reflected a period of increased scrutiny about the Liverpool's and Manchester's older architecture, led by Reilly. Reilly championed New York's architectural style and canvassed planners and architects to rebuild Manchester using American methods: 'New York is developing a new kind of architecture – perhaps even a world style – before our eyes. ... The skyline then of the new New York which is forming now will be unlike that of any other city in the world. It will be more romantic than that of any other city', he wrote in the *Manchester Guardian*.[129] Redesigning the city centres, thus, became a greater priority by the 1930s, following key developments in housing reform and public transport. In 1929, for instance, Manchester's city architect,

Henry Price, claimed that demolition in the centre had already begun and the 'general appearance is fast changing.'[130] In Manchester, planners and architects developed new forms of architecture that moved away from the city's Gothic heritage.[131] Whereas Manchester's Victorian architecture was associated with the cotton trade, the most notable buildings of the interwar period reinforced the portrayal of a commercially diverse and cosmopolitan city.

Manchester's planners and architects took up Reilly's challenge and the first in the new architectural style was the Ship Canal building (1926), which was far taller than any other buildings in the city and required an act of Parliament to overrule pre-existing regulations on building height and intended to be 'the focal point of a comprehensive development of the area.'[132] Reilly claimed it was the 'tallest office building in the country' and hoped that Manchester would build further tall buildings to imitate the effect such tall buildings had on the New York skyline.[133] Although Manchester never reached the heights and scale of New York's skyscrapers, important buildings did emerge in the 1930s. They included Lee House, Great Bridgewater Street (1931); Sunlight House, Quay Street (1932), then the city's tallest commercial building; Kendal Milne's, Deansgate (1938); and Edwin Lutyens' Midland Bank on King Street (1935). The light Portland stone of Manchester's interwar commercial architecture represented a clear visual break from darker Victorian architecture of sandstone and terracotta.

The new architecture was celebrated in municipal publicity material and the local press. The Ship Canal building was 'a sign the city was progressing' and, as we shall see in Chapter 2, a central attraction of Manchester's Civic Week 1926 when it was decorated with lights to provide an important aspect of evening entertainment.[134] This celebration of the Ship Canal building reflected a new and more positive approach to Manchester's architecture. Between 1926 and 1937, the *Manchester Guardian's* semi-regular feature titled 'A New Building for Manchester' celebrated the city's new architecture, including those that were not built, such as proposals for a seventeen-storey 'skyscraper', which the newspaper claimed 'Manchester was promised.'[135] In 1927, the mayor praised Manchester's 'recent improvement in its buildings', suggesting 'it was good architects now studied not only the framework of a building but the work that was to be carried in it. ... Newspapers and especially the "Manchester Guardian" were doing great service by showing that there was something in architecture than mere building.'[136] The new buildings were consistently marketed in the press to emphasize the diversity and strength of Manchester's economy. Rylands

Building, for example, was described as 'another symbol of Manchester's enterprise' in 1930.[137] Similarly, the new Kendal Milne department store was considered a 'modern building ... one of the largest in the country'.[138] There was a far more celebratory attitude to architecture in Manchester's press from the late 1920s onwards and this boosterism was used to emphasize a new era for a city that drew attention to the vitality of the city's economy.

In Liverpool, Reilly's energy and his role at the Liverpool School of Architecture ensured that the city was at the forefront in innovations of design and urban architecture. The wealthy industrialist William Lever had become interested in American architecture at the end of the nineteenth century. Lever opened offices in New York City and Philadelphia in 1895 and was responsible for Reilly's first visit to the East Coast in 1909. Reilly was very impressed: 'Ordinary American citizens ... even knew the names of the architects of their chief buildings. It was very different to the outlook of the ordinary Manchester or Liverpool citizen about his town to which I was not accustomed.'[139] The experience inspired Reilly to import American trends in civic design and architecture into Britain. As the *Manchester Guardian* reported in 1923, Reilly's contribution ensured that 'the Liverpool School is the one English School of Architecture which has persistently followed American methods and has established connections in America'.[140] The School of Architecture emerged to become a world leader under Reilly's energetic leadership and during Reilly's thirty-year tenure his students received the Prix de Rome scholarship on more occasions than any other architectural school in Britain.[141] One of Reilly's most successful innovations was to send a handful of fourth-year students to gain experience of American architectural offices and Reilly expected these students to return and share their experiences with their fellow students during their fifth year of study. Two of these students even worked on the Empire State Building.[142] Reilly's most famous student was Herbert Rowse, who visited America at the same time as Reilly, but stayed longer.[143] Rowse's experience of America heavily shaped the style of buildings that emerged in Liverpool during the 1930s, which are in the New York modernist style.[144]

New York's influence on architecture in Liverpool is clear from 1930, when a flurry of neo-classical and, later, modernist buildings were completed. They included India Buildings (1930), Martins Bank (1927–32), Philharmonic Hall (1939) and George's Dock Ventilation and Control Station (1932), which were all designed by Rowse. Architect and writer Harry Stuart Goodhart-Rendel described the fashion for American commercial architecture, which, he claimed, most English architects in 1930s Britain were unable to imitate. Rowse's work was the exception, he wrote:

> That an Englishman should have produced single-handed a specimen equal to America's best is undoubtedly gratifying, although the flawless magnificence of Martins Bank at Liverpool may evoke in us admiration unmingled with affection. This building is a remarkable one, displaying great technical accomplishment on the part of its designer.[145]

Again, depictions of changes to Liverpool's urban environment aimed to encourage citizens' optimism and faith in the city's economy. As we saw in the opening paragraph to this book, in as early as 1924, Reilly claimed that 'Liverpool, like New York, is soaring skyward. In all parts of the city splendid new buildings, such as the Adelphi Hotel, reflect the influence of the best modern American architecture.'[146] By suggesting favourable comparisons with American architecture, and New York particularly, Reilly hoped to present an optimistic and positive image of Liverpool more generally.

Liverpool's planners and politicians went further to forge links with New York City and in 1931 the Lord Mayor, Edwin Thompson, made a much-publicized civic visit to New York and was the first Liverpool mayor to cross the Atlantic during office.[147] Invited by New York's Mayor Walker, the visit was part of a broader attempt to improve trade between Britain and America, but Thompson, unsurprisingly, ensured that Liverpool would benefit most.[148] Huge crowds gathered to see the mayor's ship leave Liverpool for New York in the company of a large British commercial delegation heading to Washington for the congress of the International Chamber of Commerce. Organizers lit the ship, the *Britanic*, brightly for the occasion and the Lord Mayor broadcast a message to the city. He explained 'he was going out to cement still closer the close relationship between the two cities. Liverpool was the natural gateway to Lancashire and the industrial North and he wanted to emphasise this point by personal contact with the municipal and commercial life of New York.'[149]

On his arrival, the City Hall officially received Thompson to great celebrations, including performances by Martha Atwood, formerly of Metropolitan Opera Company, singing the 'Star-spangled Banner', and from the Municipal Band, broadcast locally and nationally.[150] In his arrival speech, Thompson stressed the well-established links between Liverpool and New York. 'Ever since the first regular steamship service between Liverpool and New York started in 1847', he said, 'the commercial interests of the two ports had been identical.'[151] Thompson described Liverpool to his New York counterpart as the 'most American of English cities', and claimed Liverpool would also build skyscrapers.[152] In doing so, the Lord Mayor hoped to evoke confidence in Liverpool's economy and Thompson also used the trip as an opportunity to encourage a positive image for Liverpool's commercial position. 'Commenting briefly on current business conditions, Lord Mayor Thompson said he believed there was too much pessimism about them, and that a definite feeling of optimism was well justified now', reported the *New York Times*.[153] Also aiming to boost international trade, businessmen in Liverpool sought to establish links with Chicago through publicity stunts.[154] The ceremony at the opening of Chicago's new Board of Trade in 1930, for example, saw a message of greeting from the Liverpool Corn Association appear on the trading floor. A wireless phone conversation between John Bunnell, president of the Chicago Board of Trade, and Charles Sydney Jones, deputy mayor of Liverpool, also took place. In their conversation, Bunnell 'expressed hope that the occasion would help to cement the relations between the two cities'.[155] What emerges from these exchanges is an image of Liverpool as an innovative and outward-looking city whose leaders sought to extend existing links with Chicago and New York, the cities that the world was watching, in order to boost its own profile.

Not to be outdone, Manchester's Lord Mayor, George Frank Titt, also made a civic visit to New York City in October 1932. Assisted by Harry Armstrong, Titt ensured that his trip had greater pomp and fanfare than his Liverpool counterpart had. To drum up support prior to his departure, for instance, Titt delivered a radio broadcast in New York, in which he emphasized the interdependence of all nations. Titt spoke of his enthusiasm to 'tell the United States about Manchester. Manchester was looking forward to better times. ... Manchester was confident in its ability to consolidate its position in the world, and to attract new enterprises.'[156] Not just designed to sell Manchester to New York, the trip also aimed to sell Manchester to its own inhabitants. Prior to his departure, the Lord Mayor assured the Town Hall committee that he

> would leave no stone unturned to draw particular attention in America to the importance of Manchester, not only as a city, but as a great port, and, in his opinion, the greatest distributing and consuming centre in the whole of the United Kingdom. That had never been stressed as much as it ought to be, because in the past, he feared Manchester people had not 'boomed' themselves quite as much as they might have done.[157]

The *New York Times* also reported that the visit was aimed to cement friendship and cooperation of trade between Manchester and New York. It quoted the Lord Mayor as saying, 'Manchester people have not advertised the city as much as they might have done in the past, and I hope this delegation will place before the American people the great importance of Manchester and draw attention to the fact that Manchester is a far greater city than many might be inclined to imagine.'[158] The Lord Mayor's speeches are important because they illuminate the duality of interwar urban transformation in Manchester, which intended to encourage economic growth but also to engage with citizens at a time of political and social disruption.

Armstrong's contacts and enduring popularity in New York ensured that Manchester's Lord Mayor's visit made a real splash in the city. Titt received a gold medal by the Lord Mayor of New York and a reception of the National Industrial Conference Board and the New York Chamber of Commerce held a luncheon for him.[159] Titt also visited the New York Cotton Exchange, which suspended trading in his honour, where he called on the American market to buy more British goods and claimed that Manchester could produce the best quality goods. 'Manchester found that she must advertise as well as produce articles of good quality, and Manchester was fully alive to the new challenge and prepared to meet it,' Titt declared to a cheering audience.[160] Following on from his visit to New York, the Lord Mayor went on to 'visit Washington to be presented to President Hoover ... attend the celebrations in Boston on Columbus Day at the invitation of Mayor Curley' and, to reinforce the civic aspect of his tour, Titt then travelled to Manchester, New Hampshire and Manchester, Connecticut.[161] On his return, Titt assured a welcome party at the Town Hall that 'the visit had been a great success' and went further:

> He assured them Manchester had been well advertised, and suggested that they would be amazed if they knew how many influential people they had met ... who had not realised how important Manchester was as a banking clearing-house, as a port, and as an industrial centre which covered many important industries in addition to our staple trade.[162]

The visit to America, thus, reflected Manchester's broader attempt to embrace a period of economic diversification, which the city needed to do in order to weather a very challenging economic storm.

Conclusion

Civic visits by British mayors to New York City were an important symbol of attempts made by planners and politicians to boost the image of Liverpool and

Manchester. Local politicians in these two cities responded to economic, political and social turmoil by investing in ambitious and grandiose programmes of urban transformation. Some projects, such as housing reform, remained incomplete, but redevelopment helped to create new images of these cities. These programmes of urban transformation emerged within a culture of international knowledge exchange. As we have seen, Reilly and the Liverpool School of Architecture were fundamental to the importation of East Coast American trends in planning, architecture and civic design. Reilly even claimed to have turned down a chair in architecture in Chicago, managed to get the American immigration laws waived for his visiting architectural students and became an honorary corresponding member of the American Institute of Architecture.[163] Reilly was also integral to fostering a more public role for architecture through his prolific journalism, which advertised and promoted both international developments, including the new forms of architecture that were emerging in Britain.[164] Yet Reilly's protégées and collaborators, most notably Rowse and Brodie, could implement their ideas only due to the vision and ambition of local politicians. Salvidge of Liverpool and Simon and Woodhouse of Manchester were notable for their energetic and imaginative responses to economic and political turbulence. Harry Armstrong's popularity in New York and links to North-West England were also important in helping local politicians to build links with East Coast America. During a celebratory dinner for Armstrong in London in 1931, for example, he regarded this closer relationship as the legacy of his consulship: 'Relations between Great Britain and the United States, he said, are now better than ever before. "American newspapers carry a great deal more news about British affairs than British papers print about America."'[165] As we have seen, the New York Times reported favourably on Liverpool's programme of housing reform, in particular.

The local press heavily promoted urban transformation in Liverpool and Manchester alongside civic handbooks printed by the councils to publicize the new urban landscape to citizens. In doing so, their reportage helped to foster new urban images of the transformed cities. As we have seen, in Manchester, representations of redevelopment portrayed a new period for the city and evoked an image of an ordered, carefully planned city with a diverse economy, whereas Liverpool sought to foster a sense of stability and of confidence in its commercial future. In both cities, urban transformation related closely to citizenship and its representation functioned as a communication that engaged with the classless urban citizen. It is difficult to know how far citizens accepted these images; the work of local politicians to communicate with the citizens lends weight to the suggestion that there was a greater interest in 'the people' between the wars.[166]

Faced with a turbulent economic and political climate, therefore, municipal leaders in Liverpool and Manchester invested in grandiose and ambitious programmes of urban transformation. Yet, it is important to emphasize that the work of planners, architects and local politicians in interwar Liverpool and Manchester reflected a shift away from the civic pride that had dominated these cities during the nineteenth century, which had emphasized the power of the industrial middle classes. Rather, what emerged between the two world wars was a rich civic culture that attempted to foster a more inclusive and demotic urban culture that sought to engage citizens. As we shall move on to see, politicians in both cities could not manage to avoid criticism or silence the threat of instability completely, but the civic celebrations that Liverpool and Manchester invested in encapsulated the link between urban transformation and citizenship. Civic celebrations became crucial strategies to promote positive images of these cities and to engage the classless citizen in local culture more explicitly, but also reflected the intense civic rivalry between Liverpool and Manchester.

Civic Week Celebrations

Between the 18th and 25th of September 1924, thousands of Liverpudlians left their city and made the long journey down to London to visit the Empire Exhibition Hall at Wembley for Liverpool's first Civic Week. Once there, they (along with numerous visitors from throughout Britain and the world) found their city recreated as an exhibition in incredible and minute detail. One newspaper described the scene:

> All day long the Hall is inundated with visitors from every part of the universe who simply marvel as they view the beauty of our art treasures, the magnificence of our shipping display, the delightful exhibits from our noble Cathedral, the weird models from our School of Tropical Medicine, the display from our technical schools, the illustrations of our great civic enterprises, the massive beauty of our shire horses.[1]

Considered such a resounding success by politicians and businessmen in Liverpool, the week at Wembley inspired further civic celebrations to publicize and promote the city. In 1925, for instance, Liverpool took Civic Week back to the city and the celebrations became a regular part of the civic calendar throughout the late 1920s.[2] Liverpool's efforts inspired Manchester Corporation to invest in large-scale celebrations. The city also hosted its own Civic Week Exhibition in 1926 and elaborate celebrations in 1938 to celebrate the centenary of the city's incorporation. This chapter shows the celebrations both reflected and exposed a tense rivalry between the two cities that had a long history but that intensified during the challenging interwar economic climate. Liverpool was somewhat of a pioneer in these kinds of civic celebrations and other cities followed its lead, including Carlisle, which held a Civic Week in 1928; Hull and Bolton in 1929; and Blackpool hosted a Pageant of Progress in 1930. These celebrations reflected a rich culture of civic pride not usually associated with the post-1918 period.

Of course, large-scale exhibitions and civic celebrations were by no means new. The British tradition of grand exhibitions developed in conjunction with Victorian declarations of industrial power. The lasting image of the 1851 Great Exhibition, hosted in the purposefully built grandiose glass display case and triumph of mid-nineteenth-century engineering that was Crystal Palace, 'symbolized Victorianism', especially 'Britain's supremacy in industrial production'.[3] More particularly, exhibition culture and civic celebrations emerged hand in hand with the great industrial cities of Victorian Britain. Simon Gunn's seminal text, *The Public Culture of the Victorian middle class*, highlights the importance of spectacular public pageants in the Victorian city. Described as 'festivals of capitalism', Gunn writes, 'they were theatrical events played out in the monumental stage-set of the Victorian city with its warehouses, exchanges and town halls'.[4] Lavish ceremonies and celebrations were organized for the opening of new buildings and railway stations, the unveiling of statues and art collections, and visits or funerals of notable individuals until the end of the late nineteenth century.[5]

The decline of these civic celebrations remains closely linked with the demise of civic Liberalism and of the reduced influence of the industrial middle class on local politics at the beginning of the twentieth century.[6] Instead, large exhibitions increasingly focused on the promotion of Britishness and nationalism through celebrations of imperialism and Empire, especially after 1918. The British Empire Exhibition of 1924–5 at Wembley aimed to celebrate the contribution made by the Empire to Britain's success in the war and to promote a new form of imperialism for the post-war era.[7] Similarly, the 1938 Empire Exhibition in Glasgow acted as a representation and celebration of the British Empire.[8] Grand exhibitions remained an important feature of displays of British nationalism throughout the twentieth century, despite the demise of the British Empire, including the 1951 Festival of Britain and, more recently, the Millennium Experience at London's Millennium Dome in 2000.[9]

How, then, do we understand the numerous civic celebrations held by the corporations that governed Liverpool and Manchester between the two world wars? Again, we can see the vigour and energy with which Liverpool and Manchester Corporations invested in the celebrations reflected their focus on promoting citizenship and on improving the local economies by advertising trade and infrastructure to local, national and international audiences. In part, the civic celebrations aimed to promote and advertise the ambitious programmes of urban transformation we witnessed in Chapter 1. However, they also reflected a competitive game of one-upmanship between civic politicians and businessmen in Liverpool and Manchester that built on a tradition of economic rivalry and hard-toothed business strategies that emerged during the mid-nineteenth century. These rivalries intensified over Manchester's building of the Ship Canal (a severe and bold challenge to Liverpool's port trade) but that became ever more crucial during the interwar economic decline.[10] Yet the celebrations also had a key function in promoting citizenship and reflected a broader culture of engagement with inhabitants and the new form of local politics fostered by politicians in Liverpool and Manchester in response to economic and political turbulence.

Central to the celebrations was the issue of citizenship. Like exhibition culture more generally, twentieth-century citizenship in Britain remains associated with national identity.[11] However, citizenship was not only under debate at a local level, but there were clear attempts to define who the local citizen was and how they were expected to fulfil their roles and obligations to the local state. The age of mass suffrage triggered a dynamic period for local citizenship and civic celebrations are an example of rich debates that aimed discuss and define citizenship, which shows that central government did not necessarily have ownership over the concept.[12] Interwar civic celebrations reveal that definitions of local citizenship had a shared civic culture at its centre and pointed to a more demotic political culture. Yet, as Chapter 1 noted in its analysis of the women-focused spaces in the new municipal buildings, despite mass suffrage local citizenship remained gendered. Civic celebrations focused on appealing to women through their activities as shoppers and, as Chapters 3 and 4 illustrate, reflected a wider articulation of women's local citizenship through their roles as consumers. Women's roles as shoppers and consumers shaped discourse around citizenship more generally in interwar Liverpool and Manchester. As Chapters 5 and 6 demonstrate, local Catholic leaders also embedded consumer culture within ideas about women's identities as religious citizens. The civic celebrations therefore articulate an important moment wherein important debates about local citizenship occurred within a context of wider social and cultural change and needed to encompass shifting ideas about class and gender. The gendered nature of local citizenship also suggests parallels with wider national trends as women's citizenship more generally became associated with domesticity.[13]

Citizenship was key to the interwar civic celebrations. The analysis of civic celebrations exposes Liverpool and Manchester's rich interwar civic culture, but they reflected the new, democratic age and moved away from Victorian manifestations and declarations of the power and prestige of the industrial elite, towards a more demotic and cross-class celebration of local culture. As a case study, they suggest that historians need to pay greater attention to civic culture in British cities after 1918 but also that the very concept of 'the civic' needs to be reconsidered for the twentieth century. Yet despite the redefinition of civic pride in the new age of mass democracy, the competitive spirit between Liverpool and Manchester was not lessened and, in contrast, intensified and became even more aggressive during the challenging economic circumstances both cities faced after 1918.

Which 'Second City'?

Civic Week celebrations emerged during a period of intense competition between Liverpool and Manchester and became a vehicle for civic patriots to reignite older rivalries. Indeed, the very decision to host the celebrations reflected the desire of local politicians in both cities to appear innovative and not to fall behind in promoting and supporting their local economies. The determination and vision of the Lord Mayor, Sir Arnold Rushton, drove Liverpool's week at Wembley after he visited the Civic Hall in Wembley. The opportunity to host a week first came from the organizers of the 1924 British Empire Exhibition, for which the Wembley Exhibition Hall was built, and, after his visit, Rushton reported that he 'was deeply impressed with the magnitude of the Scheme'.[14] Crucially, the appeal to Rushton lay in the support offered by the colonies, with Canada reputedly spending £250,000 on goods and services promoted at Wembley during the British Empire Exhibition. Rushton claimed that the support of the colonies convinced him that 'it is not only the bounden duty but the privilege of the large Cities and Municipalities to be associated with the scheme'.[15] For the Lord Mayor, therefore, the exhibition was part of a broader tradition of imperial citizenship. More pressing for Rushton, however, was the anxiety that other cities might take the opportunity sooner and overshadow and outmode Liverpool. With the knowledge (or rumour) that two other large cities had already booked their week at Wembley, the Lord Mayor admitted that 'what I am anxious to do – and there should be no delay – is that the City of Liverpool shall at once give in her name as being associated with the movement'.[16] Liverpool Corporation and associated businessmen, including representatives of Cunard, White Star Line and Liverpool Chamber of Commerce, passed the Lord Mayor's motion unanimously at a special meeting. For them, the idea of missing an opportunity to promote the city to the country and its colonies, which other cities were taking up, was too much to bear. In the spirit of civic competition and rivalry, they were keen to foster an image of Liverpool as a cutting-edge and forward-thinking city.[17]

Manchester Corporation was initially far less enthusiastic than their Liverpool counterparts about the idea of a civic celebration. Although several members of the council visited Wembley Exhibition Hall during its construction in February 1924, when they were considering the idea of a Manchester Civic Week, the corporation was reluctant to commit to the plan.[18] In September 1924, Manchester's Town Hall committee received a letter from the Empire Exhibition Hall Board inviting Manchester to follow other cities, including Liverpool, Hull and Salford, to host a Civic Week in Wembley. The committee was told by the Empire Exhibition committee that 'the value of these periods though never doubted by ourselves was a matter of some controversy in the early part of the year' but for those cities that had participated, 'there is no doubt that Civic periods have been an emphatic success and have accomplished even more than was originally contemplated'.[19] The committee decided to defer a decision to the invitation, particularly due to a forthcoming conference of delegates from other city corporations on the topic of civic celebrations held at the British Empire Exhibition. Perhaps the lack of an impassioned individual to drive the civic celebrations forward meant there was a lack of urgency in keeping pace with other city's initiatives, or it may have been that politicians in Manchester were reluctant to follow the strategies of smaller cities, focusing instead on their own initiatives.

Nevertheless, Manchester Corporation certainly felt a sense of urgency to participate in civic celebrations after learning of the great success of Liverpool's week at Wembley in 1924. In 1925 and following a further invitation from Wembley to host a week at the British Empire Exhibition Hall, Manchester's Town Hall committee sent a representative to speak to Liverpool's Lord Mayor and key members of the council to find out more information about their success at Wembley. The subsequent report found that the

> The experience of Liverpool municipal representatives of their Civic Period had been very encouraging – the Lord Mayor being enthusiastic about its success – over 50,000 persons per diem in the period having visited the Civic Hall and been supplied with information about Liverpool. The Lord Mayor expressed himself as satisfied that Liverpool must benefit by the experience out of all proportion to the expense; and he would strongly support a civic period in 1925 if available.[20]

Rushton reported to the Manchester Corporation that the 'greatest ceremony has been exercised and I am pleased to be in a position to present such a favourable report'.[21] Manchester's Civic Week Sub-committee decided not to host a week at Wembley, however, after receiving a report relating to a conference that had occurred in the previous November. There, councillors from Manchester had attended alongside representatives from Birmingham, Bristol, Huddersfield, Northampton, Salford, Hull and Cardiff. Hull's representative explained that their week at the British Empire Exhibition had been a success and cited the example of one local business who had participated in Hull's Civic Week at Wembley who 'had done more fresh business during their fortnight there than they had done during the previous two years'.[22] There were no representatives from Liverpool Corporation, however, since their Civic Week Committee had decided to host a civic 'At Home' week in the city and refused the opportunity to spend another week at Wembley. The absence of Liverpool's representatives at the conference and the city's decision not to host a second exhibition at Wembley seem to have been an important influencing factor in the Manchester committee's decision to decline the invitation to participate in the British Empire Exhibition.[23] Instead, Manchester's Special Sub-Committee Report on Civic Week concluded 'having regard to the undoubted benefits which will accrue to the trade and commerce of the City, it is unanimously recommended that a "Civic Week" be held in Manchester in 1926'.[24] It seems the corporation were motivated by the promised boost to local businesses and, clearly impressed by the success demonstrated by Liverpool's week at Wembley, a sense of wishing to stay in keeping with current trends and fashions in local government and civic culture. They wanted to avoid being left behind as other corporations displayed notable innovation and ambition in their strategies to improve local economies.

As with interwar urban transformation more generally, politicians and men of commerce in Liverpool were particularly important in shaping the style of these civic celebrations after deliberately moving away from the style and form of the previous exhibitions held by other cities at Wembley. Liverpool was not the first city to host a week at Wembley but the form and content of their exhibition reflected a significant and ambitious departure of previous celebrations hosted by other cities. 'Salford made a trade show of theirs', reported the *Daily Courier*, 'but the Liverpool committee decided that Liverpool was worthy of something better than that.'[25] Liverpool Corporation's definition of 'civic' did, however, incorporate the local economy and the one of the key aims of the first exhibitions was to market Liverpool as the 'Second City of the Empire' and to criticize and undermine Manchester's claims to the title. This rivalry was common to all the civic celebrations hosted by both cities during the 1920s.[26] In 1926, for example, the *Liverpool Post* complained rigorously about what it considered to be Manchester's erroneous claims to the title of 'Second City',

> Manchester now comes out with a title that is commonly used in Liverpool to refer to Liverpool … We shall ignore Manchester's pretensions … but the double claim may be confusing to people in other parts of the country. It would be a good thing, perhaps, to have Liverpool's letters marked 'No connection with any other "second city". Beware of imitations!'[27]

Interestingly, although other northern towns and cities including Salford, Hull and Bolton held Civic Weeks, Manchester and Liverpool were only directly competitive with each other. Neither engaged with the idea of Glasgow being competitor for the title of Second City. Prior to Manchester's Civic Week in 1926, for instance, an article titled 'Manchester Vs Liverpool' in the *Manchester Dispatch* revealed the organizers' determination that the celebrations should outshine Liverpool's. 'Last year Liverpool scored with success the great idea of a Civic Week', stated the newspaper, 'this year Manchester has gone one better with the Civic Week idea and putting on her best party frock, has arranged a gorgeous and unparalleled display of attractions for the visitor.'[28] The display and aims of the festivities reflected the competition between Liverpool and Manchester as their organizers engaged in a game of one-upmanship. The cities competed aggressively for the title of 'Second City of the Empire' as the title possessed real implications for their economies and for civic pride.

'The high peak of civic patriotism was reached today': Liverpool's Civic Weeks

Liverpool Corporation took a significant gamble in hosting a week at Wembley, especially by changing the focus of the exhibition away from its original concern with trade and industry, as followed by cities such as Salford. The nature of Liverpool's risk is clear from the press coverage leading up to its week at Wembley as sceptics feared the exhibition could actually damage the city's reputation and cause further problems for its economy. 'Civic Week, if it fails, will do more harm than good than if Liverpool had wholly ignored Wembley', the *Daily Courier* warned.[29] Part of the problem was the corporation's move away from a narrow focus on promoting the city's trade in favour of a broader celebration of Liverpool's cultural and civic life. In contrast to previous weeks at Wembley,

'Liverpool's week will be principally a "civic" week, the pick of the city's best in commerce, art, science and municipal endeavour will fill the Civic Hall.'[30] The *Manchester Guardian* reported Liverpool's acceptance to host a Civic Week at Wembley with great suspicion and, rather deviously, claimed that Liverpool Corporation paid four times the amount of rent for use of the Civic Hall than had been offered to Manchester Corporation.[31]

Unlike previous Civic Weeks hosted by cities at Wembley, which were more like trade fairs, Liverpool's week recreated the city within the Hall. As the week drew closer, Wembley was 'gradually becoming representative of Liverpool. A model of the docks, models of giant ocean liners, the chairs used by the King and Queen at the Cathedral ceremony, an array of pictures and other works of art, are being placed into position.'[32] The Exhibition Hall presented Liverpool as a city with a strong history of commercial and cultural success. The city's reconstruction at Wembley was selective and focused on portraying the city in such a way that, in the words of the Lord Mayor, 'You can stroll around and visualise Liverpool's greatness.'[33] Civic Week celebrated Liverpool's scientific, cultural and economic achievements and, quite literally, turned the city into an exhibition. Crucially, this involved careful choices about what was and what was not included. One advert epitomized the decisions around what to include and exclude in the celebrations. With the caption 'Packing His Trunk', the illustration shows Liverpool preparing for Civic Week and, although items relating to trade were included (chemicals, tobacco, world's trade route, ship building), so were items relating to civic pride (art, architecture, pottery). The advert indicates Civic Week had dual aims: it promoted the city's trade to the outside world, but advertised Liverpool's cultural and civic endeavours to its own population and asked them to see the cultural gems possessed by the city, albeit on display elsewhere.[34]

In the weeks prior to Liverpool's week at Wembley, the *Courier* proclaimed, 'The principle object of the Civic Week is to advertise Liverpool to the Empire and the World.'[35] The *Liverpool Post and Mercury* reiterated this aim two weeks later:

> Civic Week will be something more than a Liverpool invasion of Wembley – though it will be that on a large scale. It will be a means of letting all-comers to the Exhibition, and particularly the overseas visitors, know more about Liverpool and her achievements – about her far-flung shipping interests, her pre-eminence as a distributing centre for the North and Midlands, her great industrial enterprises; and her contributions to art, science and the higher things in life.[36]

Newspaper reports thus indicate that before Civic Week began, commentators anticipated it primarily intended to promote Liverpool's commercial prowess to overseas visitors. Yet promotional material produced by the corporation suggests Civic Week's organizers were also concerned with directly promoting Liverpool to its own inhabitants. One advert placed in the *Daily Courier* shows the Lord Mayor specifically invited people from Liverpool to the Exhibition and asked them to make the trip down to Wembley. 'Liverpool's Greatness Revealed', promised the advert.[37] The decision by the organizers to stage a civic celebration, rather than merely a trade fair, lay in their desire to encourage visitors from Liverpool itself.

Many people from Liverpool did manage to make the trip to see their city recreated at Wembley. The *Liverpool Echo* provided inexpensive train tickets for Liverpudlians to travel to the exhibition and demand was apparently so high the newspaper had to keep releasing more and more.[38] An estimated 50,000 people visited on the Saturday alone and a total of 250,000 across the whole week.[39] Amid great excitement over the presence of Liverpool's inhabitants at Wembley, the *Post and Mercury* declared, 'The high peak of civic patriotism was reached today.'[40] However, observers noted the lack of recognition people from Liverpool felt when they saw their city recreated at Wembley: 'Citizens from Liverpool failed to recognise their own city. Many of them knew more about Westminster Abbey than they knew of Liverpool Cathedral,' reported the *Evening Express*.[41] Civic Week led to calls for a more permanent promotion of Liverpool. As the *Evening Express* proclaimed, 'Liverpool, for a great city, is singularly tongue-tied about its own virtues. ... The ball set rolling by the Civic Week at Wembley must not be allowed to come to a standstill.'[42] And so, the corporation sought to reinforce the message of Civic Week and display a positive image of Liverpool to its own citizens more permanently.

Sir Henry McMahon, chairman of the management committee for the British Empire Exhibition Board, recognized the success of Liverpool's work at Wembley and immediately invited the city to return to the Exhibition Hall for the following year.[43] Although the idea of a further Civic Week was popular in Liverpool, many of the firms who had contributed to the Wembley exhibition were concerned about the cost, particularly because they had been required to contribute to a £70,000 guarantee fund in 1924. A journalist for *The Times* suggested that the Harbour Board and shipping lines would be 'satisfied if no more is heard of the proposal to reopen the exhibition'. The journalist claimed the Liverpool Cotton Board would refuse to cooperate if the corporation chose to host a further week at Wembley.[44] Concerns about costs and anxieties about the cooperation of such important firms alongside the sentiment that efforts to promote Liverpool needed to be extended and developed, rather than curtailed, encouraged Liverpool Corporation to stage the next Civic Week in Liverpool itself. The experience at Wembley paved the way for new forms of civic celebrations that transformed the city itself into an exhibition.

Liverpool's Civic Week of 1925 therefore focused on promoting the city to its own inhabitants, although attracting external and overseas investment remained important. The continued duality of its role was clear, as the *Manchester Guardian* reported in a slightly warmer article than Liverpool's week at Wembley had garnered,

> The Liverpool citizen is invited to lift his mind from his little struggle for existence and take a look round at his own city, with its museums, its public halls, its biscuit, match, cable, chocolate, piano. And clothing factories, and its ships. ... Everything should tend ... to awaken a livelier civic pride in Liverpool people themselves, and to induce in the visitors a sense of Liverpool's importance and its advantages as a trading centre.[45]

The celebrations placed all the positive aspects of the city on display and tours of the city, or rather, of carefully selected parts of the city, became a regular part of the Civic Week celebrations. 'Motorbuses will leave St George's Hall and proceed to Cathedral (half an hours stay), thence via Princes Park, Aigburth Road etc., to Allerton House (for tea), and then through Calderstones Park to Childwall Abbey, returning via Broadgreen Road, Edge Lane etc., to St George's Plateau.'[46] Organized tours allowed the corporation to control what parts of Liverpool were seen and ensured only parts of the city which could be celebrated were included on the tour, with a particular focus on the shipping trade: large crowds visited the liners *Samaria* and *Laconia* and 10,000 people received tours around the ships by the end of the first afternoon alone.[47] Civic Week reinforced the image of Liverpool as a commercially successful port trade and emphasized international links. One of the most celebrated moments of the 1925 Civic Week was the congratulatory message from the Lord Mayor of New York City, who wrote, 'We felicitate you on your interesting celebration, and wish it every success, and assure you of our hearty reciprocation of our sentiments for the strengthening of the good will already existing between Liverpool and New York.'[48] The Civic Week was therefore part of the broader attempts made by the corporation to invest in publicity material that aimed to present Liverpool and an outward-looking, global and commercially successful city.

Liverpool hosted annual Civic Week celebrations in the city until 1928. Their place in the civic and cultural life of the city relied heavily on the energy and vision of Liverpool Organization, founded in 1926. Frederick James Marquis (later Lord Woolton, most famous for his role as Minister of Food during the Second World War) led Liverpool Organization and was the driving force behind its work and agenda. Born in Salford to ambitious lower middle-class parents, Marquis (1883–1964) became very interested in social issues as a teacher in Burnley, before training as an economist at the University of Manchester. As Warden of the David Lewis Hotel and Club Association in Liverpool, a social experiment established by the Liverpool branch of the retailing firm Lewis's in the city's docklands area that aimed to improve living conditions in the city, and as warden of the Liverpool University Settlement, he came into direct contact with Liverpool's poor. In 1920, Marquis joined Lewis's department store, where he achieved notable successes and responsibility for its rapid expansion and development, becoming director in 1928 and chairman in 1936. At Lewis's, Marquis was able to combine his interest in social issues with business and commerce throughout the 1920s and 1930s and, as we will see in Chapter 3, made important contributions to reviving retail culture in Liverpool. Although he refused to declare any clear political leanings or affiliations, Marquis was a key figure linking business with government at both a local and national level. As well as his chairmanship of Liverpool Organization, Marquis was a member of the advisory council of overseas development committee (1928–31); member of the advisory council of the Board of Trade (1930–4); member of the advisory council to the General Post Office (1933–47); member of the Cadman committee on civil aviation in 1937; and member (1936–9), and then chairman (1939), of the Council for Art and Industry. Marquis received a knighthood in 1935 in recognition of his dedication to business and social issues and as Minister of Food in 1940 became fundamental to the ability of the British Home Front to survive limitations on food during the Second World War.[49]

Marquis epitomized the strength and influence of local men of commerce and business in Liverpool, which, rather than demising after 1918, was revitalized in the context of economic depression and political instability. As chairman of Liverpool Organization, Marquis worked to ensure close collaborative links between business and local government. Liverpool Organization worked 'advancing the interests of Liverpool' and possessed five related aims: encourage Liverpool's port trade; attract industrialists to manufacture their goods on Merseyside; teach the surrounding towns that Liverpool was 'the business and cultural centre round which they revolve'; educate the 'Liverpool people themselves in the needs and the advantages of their own City'; and inculcate a 'higher pride of citizenship' within the city.[50] It pursued a focus on 'community advertising', which aimed to focus on the existing needs of citizens by investing in Liverpool and claimed to be the first city in Britain to do so.[51] The Civic Week celebrations epitomized all these aims and was an ambitious attempt at civic publicity and was also the pinnacle of the efforts of Liverpool Organization, which included campaigning for an airport for the city in order to boost the port trade.[52]

Marquis secured an annual grant of £2,000 in 1926 for Liverpool's Civic Week, guaranteed for the next five years and on the provision that Liverpool Organization found at least £3,000 extra each year and required the admittance of at least three council representatives to the Organization.[53] Civic Week occupied most of the annual budget but, nevertheless, the amount of publicity material and campaign work Liverpool Organization produced was impressive. In 1927, for example, Liverpool Organization produced and disseminated 2,500 special posters advertising Liverpool as an industrial city and displayed on London, Midland and Scottish railways among others, plus advertisements in *The Times*, the *Manchester Guardian*, the *Glasgow Herald*, the *Journal of Commerce* and the Liverpool press.[54] In 1929, Liverpool Organization also reported the publication of over seventy articles promoting Liverpool in the New Zealand and Australian press alone.[55] One of their main strategies was to make closer links between Liverpool and America, which reflected wider efforts to strengthen connections as we saw in Chapter 1. First was the focus on attracting American business investment and in 1929, Liverpool Organization sent out 4,000 personal letters to business owners in America:

> Each manufacturer was given the reason why his particular class of goods could be made with profit in Liverpool, both for the home and export trade. A map illustrating the industrial character of Merseyside accompanied each letter. The campaign aroused considerable interest in America, and many encouraging replies were received.[56]

The organization was confident that this strategy had been a success and claimed it had ensured Liverpool would be a serious contender for any American business considering expanding abroad.[57] Secondly, Liverpool Organization sought to market Liverpool as a holiday destination, focusing on American tourists. The Organization claimed to have arranged itineraries for more than twelve times the number of visitors in June and July 1928 in comparison to the three summer months of 1927 and reported that the June 1929 numbers were double that of June 1928.[58] Liverpool Organization aimed to increase the number of American visitors by offering them Social Study Tour of Liverpool 'with the object of attracting tourist traffic to Liverpool and keeping overseas visitors in the City, for three or four days'.[59]

Despite these other ambitious activities, Civic Week remained Liverpool Organization's priority and held further celebrations throughout the late 1920s, in which 'Liverpool citizens were shown their own city'.[60] The dual aim of promoting trade and industry and presenting a positive image of Liverpool to its citizens persisted and the celebrations remained popular, and the number of spectators was staggering as one million people attended Civic Week in 1926.[61] In 1927, the number of visitors to Civic Week rose to 1.4 million people when Liverpool tramways department estimated the city's trams carried 5.6 million passengers.[62] These visitors came to see Liverpool put on display. In 1928, Civic Week included a marathon that ended at Liverpool football ground, processions, dancing displays, pageant of youth and a firework display. The accompanying guidebook described: 'Miscellaneous attractions include visits to ocean liners in dock, aeroplane flights at £1 GP, view from Royal Liver Tower, University, Abattoir, Cotton, Corn, Fruit and Produces Exchanges Open and free invitations to visit local factories'.[63] Early-twentieth-century guidebooks were important in shaping the modern city and the ways in which it was seen and experienced.[64] Liverpool Civic Week Committee used tours and the accompanying guides to ensure the attractions shaped the way people perceived the city. Organizers did not leave visitors to wander the city alone but carefully guided spectators to see specific parts of the city in order to maintain the representation of Liverpool that they wished to promote.

Civic celebrations also allowed Liverpool Organization to celebrate the city's interwar redevelopment and narratives of progress ensured Liverpool's past helped to celebrate its present and future. Celebrations of public transport were especially important and were popular features of Civic Week that offered excitement and entertainment. Liverpool's Civic Week of 1927, for example, included a race between a former and a contemporary form of public transport in Liverpool. The poster advertised: '"The Old Times" the original Liverpool – Chester and Shrewsbury Flying Stage Coach, on steel springs, with a guard all the way, and "The New Wonder", Municipal Motor Omnibus – latest patent, 1927'.[65] Liverpool's civic celebrations were an opportunity for municipal leaders to promote the city's urban redevelopment within a wider narrative that celebrated progress through commercial stability. Nowhere was this more apparent than the representation of Liverpool's docks, which organizers used deliberately to promote a sense of prosperity in the city, particularly around the Gladstone Docks, designed to take the largest trans-Atlantic steam ships and completed in 1927. For example, a promotional map from 1924 claimed, 'Facilities are systematically kept several years in advance of the demands of commerce so that it is always ready to handle more business and new kinds of business.'[66] The docks were something of a star attraction during Civic Week: processions usually began at the Pierhead, before following on to the docks, and publicity material often advised visitors to Civic Week to visit the docks as part of their tour.[67] The celebrations were a way to promote the new, positive images of Liverpool but they also turned the city into an exhibition more directly.

Liverpool's department stores were also fundamental to the city's Civic Week celebrations: as the *Manchester Guardian* reported in 1925, 'The great stores have joined the movement, showing dress-designing on living models, giving lectures on cookery and architecture, and providing concerts.'[68] The involvement of department stores is a revealing example of the interconnections between businessmen and local government and also shows how these civic celebrations involved gendered spaces, which emphasized women's roles as consumer-citizens. As Figure 2.1 depicts, there was even a mannequin parade (where models displayed the latest fashions, almost a precursor to catwalk shows and a common feature of interwar shopping culture, as we shall see in Chapter 4) on the Cunard liner *Franconia* in 1925. The mannequin parade included the slightly odd feature of a female model wearing a model ship for a hat and a model of the world around her middle, flanked by two (rather bored looking) costumed children. The event on the *Franconia* suggests a rather surreal attempt to combine Liverpool's industry and shopping culture and hints at the almost fantastical nature of the celebrations.[69]

Like the mannequin parade that took place on the *Franconia*, department stores organized special fashion promotions and specifically appealed to women. In 1925, for instance, Bon Marché hosted a special Civic Week Exhibition of 'continental fashions and exposition of draping on the living model.'[70] Shops led the way in decorating their fronts and windows, described in 1925 as being 'at their gayest, with window displays suggestive of a shopping carnival.'[71] Asa Briggs suggested Lewis's department store managers were encouraged to actively 'preserve the good name of the store in his city and support worthy civic causes' during the 1920s and this would be particularly true in Liverpool, with Marquis playing such an important role in both Liverpool Organization

Figure 2.1 A mannequin parade held aboard the Cunard liner *Franconia* during Liverpool's Civic Week in 1925
Source: Getty Editorial Image 2668798.

and in Lewis's, one of Liverpool's largest and popular department stores.[72] Women in Liverpool clearly enjoyed these events, as the 21-year-old diarist Hilda Baines recorded in 1928, 'It is Liverpool Civic Week, mother and I at Lewis's to hear the staff choir singing and the mann. [*sic*] parade.'[73] Sometimes Liverpool's women responded rather dramatically to such events and in 1926 the West End actress Gladys Cooper caused a near-riot when she appeared at one of the department stores as part of the Civic Week celebrations. As the *Manchester Guardian* described,

> Her visit to the establishment was the signal for an invasion on the part of women who thronged the streets, eager to get a glimpse of her, and Miss Cooper was nearly mobbed. In their anxiety to see her women climbed on the counters and mounted the galleries, and for a considerable time the press was so great that it put a complete stoppage to business.[74]

Liverpool Organization and the corporation may have got more than they intended for in this case, but it shows what a popular aspect of Civic Week department stores held. It illustrates that the close connections between government and businessmen, epitomized by Marquis, were vital to the positive image of Liverpool created through the civic celebrations.

Not all of Liverpool's Civic Week events attracted the same hysteria as Gladys Cooper's visit to a department store but they did attract significant audience numbers and received positive reviews and responses from both the press and individuals, with the *Manchester Guardian* estimating that over half a million people from outside Liverpool visited during Civic Week in 1926.[75] Furthermore, it also reported the difficulty of getting tickets for some events because they sold out so quickly and that ticket agencies throughout England and Wales had to make repeat orders.[76] Perhaps by implication, the *Manchester Guardian* seemed won over by the impact of the celebrations and claimed repeatedly that Civic Weeks were an important success from a commercial point of view. In 1925, for example, the newspaper reported that 'record business is being done at the Liverpool shops during Civic Week. The main thoroughfares are as thronged as though it was the height of the Christmas shopping season, and some of the shops are so busy that crowds have been queuing to gain admission.'[77] The newspaper repeated these claims a year later,

> On the commercial side of Civic Week there is exceptional business to be recorded so far as the city shops, restaurants, and places of entertainment are concerned. There have been queues everywhere and the shops crowded to their full capacity. There is a chorus of gratitude from the shop managers, who declare that the visitors are buyers more than sightseers and estimates said to be on a moderate basis show that the business actually done is 50 per cent greater than that of Civic Week last year.[78]

The celebrations were also considered to have brought more trade and industry to the city. Liverpool Organization reported that the during the 1927 Civic Week 'an impressive world advertisement was received by Liverpool, and as a result of that advertisement the new direct shipping services were established by Leyland Line.'[79]

Of course, the civic celebrations were not just about trade and economy, and the organizers of Civic Week were confident that they did manifest a much greater sense of civic pride among Liverpool's inhabitants. As Matthew Anderson, Civic Week manager, declared in 1926, 'Each succeeding year local patriotism grows more fervent; all interests in the community become more accustomed to act together for the common good, and every citizen becomes consciously, or unconsciously, an ambassador for its city wherever he goes.'[80] There were, however, some dissenting voices. In its coverage of Liverpool's Civic Week of 1927, *Manchester Guardian* highlighted the city's American links by describing a concert by a group of mouth-organists, which was part of the celebrations.

It reported the popularity of these concerts in America, remarking that 'it has, of course, always been to Liverpool's advantage to provide home comforts for Americans'. Yet, the article continued, the mouth-organ concert

> Illustrates the tendency of these 'civic weeks' to become amorphous and wide-sprawling. One cannot help feeling that they would gain by a certain tightening-up. ... A lopping off of the extraneous and a concentration on things that really are of civic significance. Merely to have a lot of things going on in the city is not necessarily to make any useful comment in the city's customary civic life.[81]

It is difficult to know how fair the *Manchester Guardian* was in its criticism here, or whether the newspaper was jealous of, or perhaps even snobbish towards, Liverpool's comprehensive approach to civic pride. Nevertheless, the celebrations also involved a marginalization of certain aspects of Liverpool culture and they were as much, if not more, about excluding parts of urban life as celebrating the positive parts. There were hints that the police were instructed to be especially heavy-handed in the run-up to the civic celebrations and in 1927 two habitual criminals, William Humphries (52) and Charles Walsh (52), attracted media attention for complaining about their arrest on a charge of frequenting with intent to commit a felony, just prior to Civic Week. One of the criminals apparently remarked, 'You might have left us until after Civic Week.' While in the dock, Walsh said 'he knew from personal experience the methods adopted by the police'. 'They wanted to get us in for Civic Week', he added.[82]

Those who did attend Liverpool's civic celebrations seemed to have enjoyed them, although it is difficult to trace any clear acceptance of the messages of civic patriotism that Liverpool Organization hoped to impart. Local diarist Hilda Baines wrote of her trip to the Civic Week mannequin parades, 'I had not seen one before. We enjoyed it all immensely.'[83] Nevertheless, local people were encouraged to be actively involved with the celebrations and one of their most popular features was a competition to make a slogan for the city. In 1926 it was 'Liverpool, any ware, anywhere', and in 1928 it was 'show Liverpool, shout Liverpool and sing Liverpool'.[84] In 1928, a competition in the commercial newspaper *Irwin's* asked children to submit written accounts of their experiences of Civic Week. The responses *Irwin's* published give some sense of how local people in Liverpool felt about Civic Week and the kind of impact it had on their experiences of the city. 'I was delighted with our Civic Week celebrations', wrote Mabel Malone aged ten, 'I had such a nice time and all free, it made me feel quite proud of our own city, and the beautiful liners, the grand buildings and nice bright shops.'[85] 'After such an interesting week of sightseeing we must be contented to wait another twelve months before we have the opportunity of seeing such things again', lamented Edna Scragg, aged thirteen.[86] Their responses offer some indication of what it was like for individuals to see and experience Liverpool as an exhibition and the language used is illustrative of the way in which children receive, internalize and repeat discourse they experience.[87]

Manchester joins in: Civic Week, 1926

The sheer success of Liverpool's Civic Week celebrations caused a dilemma for Manchester Corporation. On the one hand, there were strong concerns that the city's trade and industry would suffer from not hosting a Civic Week on a similar scale to Liverpool.[88] At the same time, and perhaps a worse fate, there were concerns that in hosting their own Civic Week, Manchester looked like they were merely following and imitating their great rivals. Once the decision was finally made to host a Civic Week in 1926, anxiety seized the press and councillors about what the city could deliver. In a thinly veiled swipe at Liverpool, the *Manchester Guardian* reported, 'Admirable as it may be to have a band playing continuously in Piccadilly for a week and an extra dose of illumination applied to the tramcars, these things in themselves are hardly likely to extend the prestige of the city in quarters where it would be advantageous to make an impression.'[89] Even on the first day of the celebrations, a nervous article in the *Manchester Guardian* asked, 'Does Manchester Do Justice to Itself?'[90] The city's businessmen and politicians clearly felt the pressure to deliver successful and productive celebrations particularly because of the intense rivalry with Liverpool.

In an attempt to distance Manchester's Civic Week from Liverpool's, the celebrations were marketed as being less-showy and more serious. There was a focus on 'the city's effort to know itself': 'It is not intended that "Civic Week" should be simply a standing in the world's market place in order to bawl our wares with the spot-light on them: it will be seriously an effort to get to know our own city, its story, its present achievements, its possibilities.'[91] Russell Brady, one of the key organizers of Manchester's Civic Week celebrations, was especially determined that it would not be 'a shopping week' and hinted the suggestion that Liverpool's was.[92] Despite the attempt to distance the celebrations from Liverpool, the idea that Manchester had 'copied' their rivals fuelled an even greater competitive spirit between the two. 'The city (Liverpool) adopted this method of community publicity before Manchester saw the merit', the *Manchester Guardian* admitted, 'and is not now a little flattered that Manchester has followed its example. But since it has provoked Manchester to emulation it is just a little nervous lest its best efforts be outshone ... a brilliant Tale of Two Cities is being prepared by the experts in modern publicity methods.'[93]

The intense rivalry with Liverpool may explain why Manchester Corporation found a more generous budget for Civic Week than their competitors had: Manchester Civic Week Executive committee agreed to pay half the costs of decorating the Town Hall, Albert Square and surrounding streets and expenses incurred 'of purely a civic character' only, at a total of £897.10.[94] In total, Manchester Corporation offered £3,050 in expenses plus a £1,000 donation for feeding the poorest children of the city, but refused a request of £400 for refreshments for military officers and naval visits.[95] The corporation appointed a Civic Week Sub-committee, instructed by the corporation 'to confer and cooperate with any body, company, associate, or person who may be interested in the subject, and to take steps as they consider desirable in the matter'.[96] The directors of Manchester's Ship Canal Building were particularly supportive of Manchester's Civic Week and were one of the first commercial groups to pledge their support and cooperation with the corporation.[97] The aim of Manchester's Civic Week was to dwarf their competitors'. Taking another swipe at Liverpool, the *Manchester Guardian* suggested that rather than host a 'decorative "shopping week" combined with the high spirits of a fair', the objective was 'to show Manchester as a place where the whole world may come shopping on the largest conceivable scale'.[98]

The decision to host a Civic Week in 1926 was no accident since it was a key year and a turning point in Manchester's interwar transformation. Also in 1926, Manchester Corporation began to produce a yearbook, *How Manchester Is Managed*, the land at Wythenshawe was purchased for the ambitious municipal housing project and the Manchester Ship Canal Building on King Street (one of the first buildings of the period which used Portland stone and was architecturally distinct from the city's gothic saw tradition) was completed. These landmarks were mooted as the reasons behind the celebrations: Manchester was 'keeping open house', for the week, declared the *Daily Telegraph*, 'so that those who look may learn'.[99] Primarily it was, in the words of the *Manchester Guardian*, 'an education week for citizens of Manchester'.[100] However, 1926 also saw the General Strike, which delayed Manchester's Civic Week, and suggests the celebrations came at a time of particular vulnerability for the local state.[101] The context helps to explain claims by the *Manchester Guardian* that identified Civic Week's main intention as being 'that citizens should become acquainted with their own city. ... There is so much worth seeing.'[102] The link with citizenship was therefore central to the ways in which the press and municipal publications presented (and justified) Manchester's Civic Week to inhabitants. Writing five years after the Civic Week, the organizers claimed the purpose of the celebrations was 'to make Manchester aware of itself'. They explained,

> Few communities have a livelier sense of local patriotism, but the mere size of the city makes it impossible for the citizen, unaided, to take in and realise the scale and variety of the social activities of which it is the scene or centre.[103]

Organizers portrayed the purpose and aims of Manchester's Civic Week as promoting civic pride among Manchester's inhabitants. Their strategy reflected local politicians' wider attempts at engaging and communicating with the new electorate within a volatile climate of upheaval and uncertainty.

Organizers also attempted to place Manchester's citizens at the heart of the celebrations, which helped to make their Civic Week more distinct from Liverpool's. Celebrations focused on citizens in similar ways to their attention towards Manchester's buildings, industry and culture. *Manchester Guardian* reported, 'Manchester is preparing to show the world that, although commerce and industry have quietened down due to external happenings, her citizens have not lost the enterprise and vigilance for which they have so long been noted.'[104] Thus, part of the atmosphere of excitement and celebration created through Manchester's Civic Week aimed to rally the support of the city's inhabitants. Yet, at the same time, the celebrations were also an opportunity for Manchester to show the range of its commerce and industry. As in Liverpool, Manchester's civic celebrations included tours of the city and highlighted the diversity of the city's economy,

> Visitors in their thousands, it is hoped, will attend the exhibitions, one of the chief of which is the Textile Exhibition at Belle Vue ... and see the pageants, one historical and the other related to industry. The University and Whitworth Hall will be open to the public, and the institutions that may be visited include the Shirley Institute, Portico Library, Chamber of Commerce ... Chetham's Hospital and Library, M.R.I., Y.M.C.A., Manchester Royal Exchange, Post Office, Telephones, Ryland's Library and the Manchester Coal Exchange.[105]

Manchester's Civic Week also promoted and advertised the city's redevelopment and emphasized the break with the city's Victorian past. The *Manchester*

Guardian's guide to the festivities advised visitors, 'in its public buildings the city has much to be proud of, the commercial architecture being far in advance of that of Victorian days and the domestic architecture considerably improved.'[106] Manchester's civic celebrations clearly intertwined with the desires of municipal leaders and influential businessmen to reshape perceptions of the city and reinforce the idea that there was a new era for the city. At the same time, the celebrations used the city's past to celebrate its future. Manchester's Civic Week historical pageant, for example, represented an opportunity 'for its citizens to get involved, and to celebrate themselves'.[107]

Municipal leaders also used Manchester's Civic Week to show they had changed their approach to municipal publicity, following their investment in urban redevelopment. 'For one glorious week, Manchester, perhaps the shyest of cities, jumps out of her shell', claimed the Lord Mayor.[108] The celebrations portrayed a new start for Manchester, from which civic leaders would promote the city more assertively. The corporation explained in the *Official Handbook*,

> The rise of lusty young competitors abroad has in the past century made trade a harder mistress to satisfy, but Manchester, with the help of the old and the new blood, is still in the van of commercial progress. ... You are asked to look at Manchester, posed openly before your eyes, and to see how it does the trick of leading the world industrially. Manchester believes that this is a trick worth knowing and a trick worth showing, and that is why Manchester is holding a Civic Week.[109]

Civic Week reinforced the image of a new era in Manchester, which, as we saw in Chapter 1, was a key motif of the city's transformation. Through such publicity material, the organizers asked inhabitants to see the city with a fresh gaze.

Civic Week saw Manchester's dramatic visual transformation to ensure visitors were impressed with the city they saw. One newspaper described Manchester's transformation 'from a cold prosaic city to a place of bright, infectious gaiety. It is almost as if some magical performance of Aladdin's wonderful lamp was taking place, so rapid, complete, and extensive is the transformation.'[110] The main thoroughfares and streets were each assigned a specific colour scheme and decorated with ribbons and banners: St Peter's Square was decorated in naval and military colours; Albert Square in blue and yellow; Mosley Street had nautical flags; Portland Street was covered in autumnal shades; St Ann's Square in green and cerise; Deansgate gold and blue; and Whitworth Street in flags of all nations and 'decorations of a foreign type'.[111] These decorations contributed to the dramatic and celebratory image of Manchester, as Civic Week would be

> A week of wonders, of ever-open doors, of pageantry and pomp and picturesque ceremony. Days of delight and evenings of open entertainment will crowd upon one another, and all the might and majesty of the city will be displayed before the eyes of the citizen and the gaze of the stranger.[112]

Organizers used artificial lighting particularly effectively to guide the eyes of the citizen and gaze and the stranger during Civic Week. Extra lighting around the main streets and buildings allowed the celebrations to carry on into the evening and private firms received free electricity to brighten up the streets.[113] Chapter 3 shows Manchester's shops increasingly used light to decorate their shop fronts, transforming the visual experience of the city centre and Civic Week appropriated similar methods of decoration and allowed the corporation to ensure the gaze of visitors remained focused on the newly built parts of the city.

The use of illuminations was expected to have a magical effect on Manchester by uncovering the jewels in its crown: 'The addition of brilliant lighting during the evening, an addition which will lift from their comparative flatness the sheer cliffs of the warehouse streets, showing them for what they are, the material evidences of strength and energy'.[114] It was commonplace for corporations to illuminate important buildings in Britain's industrial cities, initially during civic celebrations, becoming a matter of course in the late nineteenth century.[115] Similarly, the use of electric light as a 'technology of rule' emerged within the governance of the Victorian liberal city, 'through which a vigorous economy and stable society can be held in place without resorting to armies or terror'.[116] In the 1920s therefore, Victorian technologies were reinvented to re-imagine the city and during Manchester's Civic Week, light drew attention on the city's most important buildings. For example, the organizers lit the Ship Canal building, to 'rise in a white illumination' and the Tower of Refuge, an insurance building (completed 1910), as well as the Town Hall.[117] As the *Daily Dispatch* reported, this seemed to have a dramatic impact: 'By far the most interesting building by the night glares was the latest skyscraper – the new offices of the Manchester Ship Canal Company. The contractors had just removed the scaffolding from the building in time for the celebrations, and the clean bold lines stood out in all their classic boldness'.[118] Civic Week therefore specifically highlighted Manchester Corporation's successful investment in urban infrastructure and also drew attention to the city's public transport system and electricity supplies. The Electricity and Tram Departments collaborated during Civic Week to produce 'a very brilliant spectacle'. They produced a tram covered in electric light, 'it will have 3,000 lamps of 30 watts each, which will require nearly thirteen electrical horsepower to light. The whole car is to flame, not with a steady illumination, but with a ripple which should get the best out of the red, white and green.'[119] One side spelt '1901 Still the Best' and the other, '1926 Stood the Test', in lights. The illuminated tram sought to symbolize Manchester's transition from the nineteenth century to 1938 and the city's claim to be a pioneer in municipal government.

As well as highlighting municipal progress, Civic Week possessed an important commercial role. At the beginning of the celebrations, the *Manchester Evening Chronicle* raised this issue by asking, 'Will Manchester citizens really take to heart the word and lesson of Civic Week and support the local manufacturers wherever possible?'[120] Their question suggests the celebrations were an opportunity for municipal leaders and men of commerce to encourage the city to be economically self-sufficient. Local companies undertook specific advertising campaigns around Civic Week to target those attending the celebrations. An advert for a Manchester cigarette company declared,

> Next week Manchester will tell the world that Manchester-made goods are the best. … For Civic Week smoke the following City produced cigarettes – any of which will prove the claims to superiority of Manchester-made cigarettes.[121]

Further promotional material made grander claims about Manchester's consumer culture. A special supplement, 'Civic Week Shopping', in the *Manchester Guardian*, claimed in Manchester 'the luxury of the present day is unique because it is universal … it would be difficult to say, comparatively speaking, one class is more luxurious than the other.'[122] This idea of an illusion of classlessness in shopping culture was not uncommon in Manchester from the later 1920s and became an important theme to consumer culture within the city, as we shall see in more detail in Chapter 3.

As Chapter 4 will demonstrate, between the two world wars the female shopper became an important figure in Manchester Corporation's attempt to present the economy as being diverse and cosmopolitan. Despite municipal politicians' insistence that the celebrations would not be a 'shopping week', advertisements and publicity material envisioned Manchester as a shopping destination. It provides an example of an early strategy of using consumer culture as a method of promoting urban improvement and economic growth. The *Manchester Guardian* recognized the vital role the city's shops possessed in the celebrations and claimed that 'the Manchester shops are taking Civic Week very seriously'.

The article suggested that their decorations and events were not just frivolous and nor were shopkeepers using the opportunity to draw in the Civic Week crowds to raise profits, rather 'they are fully aware of their responsibility to the city's activities'.[123] In particular, during Civic Week women were told that there was no other place that could satisfy their shopping needs like Manchester's shops could: 'No Manchester woman … need set out to buy a particular article and come home without it. Everything that she can possibly want is provided for her, with a wide margin of variations in case her whim should swerve'.[124] Shops, such as Affleck and Brown department store, one of the city's more traditionally upmarket and exclusive stores, held mannequin parades and promotional events as Civic Week allowed the store to promote its most exotic fashions, in this case 'the latest modes from Paris and London'.[125] Kendal Milne, perhaps Manchester's most famous department store, also hosted a mannequin parade for Civic Week. One journalist described the event as being overwhelming in scale: 'One was left with a feeling of mental indigestion, a feeling that one had partaken of too many good things at once'.[126] The image emphasized here was that Manchester could offer so much, if not too much, to the fashion-conscious shopper.

Although the department store attractions did not appear to have caused riot-like behaviour in Manchester as they had done in Liverpool, Manchester's Civic Week attractions certainly drew in large crowds. An estimated million people attended the Civic Week attractions and news reports emphasized the crowded streets, with 100,000 reportedly in attendance at the historical pageant in Heaton Park.[127] The organizers of Manchester's Civic Week certainly appeared to be pleased about the apparent impact of the celebrations. 'At present day there is no part of the world in which the name of Manchester is unknown', they claimed in 1929 and credited Civic Week with creating such important publicity.[128] Similarly, Manchester's Lord Mayor made confident assertions about the impact of Civic Week, claiming,

> Civic Week has justified itself from every possible point of view, and has realised the highest expectations. There have been more people in the city during the past week than any week in its history, and trade locally has benefited enormously. … No better means of advertising Manchester could have been devised.[129]

Manchester's civic celebrations did not take place without controversy, however. Whereas Liverpool's celebrations seem to have taken place with little apparent conflict, Manchester's military tattoo provoked a great outrage among many local people, who felt it was inappropriate in the aftermath of the Great War. 'If we are to have a tattoo during the Civic Week', wrote one correspondent to the *Manchester Guardian*, 'let it show the reality of war, with all its degradation, its horror, and its untold suffering.'[130] Despite this criticism, many people did turn up to watch the military tattoo and so it seems the criticism featured in the *Manchester Guardian*, although noisy, was not widespread.

Criticism also came from those who objected to the corporation's investment in a lavish exhibition at a time when social problems needed to be tackled. *Northern Voice*, a self-styled working-class periodical, complained 'amongst the junketing and chronicling of Civic Week … I have seen no reference to one little island near the heart of the city.' Referring to the slum area of Ancoats, the article gives some sense of the way in which the celebrations marginalized the less salubrious areas of the city.[131] Civic Week was especially criticized for the cost: 'A large number of citizens are much opposed to such a scheme at the present time', one correspondent to the *MEN* complained, 'what I, along with numbers of other ratepayers want to know is: "Who's footing the bills?" If it is coming out of the public purse the sooner a protest meeting is held the better.'[132] There do not seem to be any records of protest meetings, although these controversies and criticisms perhaps explains why Manchester, unlike Liverpool, did not host civic celebrations again on this scale until 1938.

Criticism did not end once the celebrations were over. When Manchester's Civic Week ended, the Secretary of State for Dominion Affairs called for a more reciprocal relationship between Manchester and the Empire, as it was 'no less essential that Manchester itself should be conscious of its partnership in and interdependence with the rest of our country and of the Empire.'[133] This suggests the national government was concerned about the potential impact of the Civic Week celebrations and feared it nurtured municipal economic self-sufficiency, rather than one the Empire Marketing Board sought to promote.[134] Despite these problems, Manchester Corporation was keen to develop the longer-term implications of Civic Week and the celebrations forged a clear link between citizenship and loyalty to the city and Corporation. As the *Manchester Guardian* urged, 'Do your duty by this great and noble city. Forget pessimism. Forget doleful, dismal Jeremiahs, and remember there is a silver lining to every cloud.'[135] Manchester Corporation's drive to attract greater investment in Manchester and to promote the city's economy throughout the world did not wane following Civic Week. The Town Hall committee invited representatives of the 'Come to Britain' movement (established by the Department of Overseas Trade to boost tourists and to encourage the sale of British goods by attracting holiday-makers) to visit Manchester 'with instructions to request the government to endeavour to get Chinese representatives to visit the city'.[136] There was a significant shift by the 1930s, however, and Manchester's civic celebrations, rather than promoting trade and municipal publicity, focused on teaching inhabitants how to be citizens.

1938 centenary celebrations

Manchester may have been reluctant to host further Civic Week celebrations because they were so closely associated with Liverpool's efforts to nurture civic pride. Or, it may have been because the corporation remained occupied with the ambitious Wythenshawe estate, town hall extension and new public library. Perhaps the ongoing economic problems also made the idea of a showy, spectacular celebrations seem inappropriate, ineffective or even unpalatable. Economic challenges remained acute, especially as the corporation's attempts to revive the cotton industry remained unsuccessful.[137] In 1938, however, and once their ambitious building plans were making good progress, the centenary anniversary of Manchester's incorporation offered the corporation to invest in civic celebrations that would be more unique and specific to the city. Yet again, the 1938 celebrations manifest a positive civic culture that emphasized distinct urban images about Manchester and specifically sought to teach inhabitants about citizenship. As Manchester's Lord Mayor proclaimed, the celebrations of 1938 intended to,

> Stimulate interest in all our citizens and help them to realise even more fully that by a free vote and by inspiring well-informed public opinion that they may enhance the utility of local government and at the same time safeguard their own liberties.[138]

To do so, the celebrations focused on the corporation's successful development of the city to emphasize Manchester's progression and showed 'the rise and progress of the various municipal services during the century'.[139]

The Town Hall Special Committee oversaw the organization of the celebrations for the centenary anniversary of Manchester's incorporation and approved the decision to build a permanent exhibition hall in the Deansgate area of the city centre and decided to host a Civic Day, inviting all lord mayors from leading cities to attend.[140] The committee struggled to gain support for the celebrations from local businesses, however. When the Town Hall clerk sent a letter to leading commercial organizations regarding the proposal to build an exhibition hall, only four of these responded favourably; thirteen were unfavourable or neutral and forty did not reply at all.[141] Nevertheless, the Town Hall committee pressed on, although the 1938 celebrations were not as extensive, exotic or as dramatic and did not turn the city into an exhibition as in Manchester's Civic Week of 1926. There was a historical pageant that portrayed 'important events in the development of Manchester's municipal government' and illustrated its successful investment in the Library, Ship Canal and University.[142] Most of the festivities, however, centred in the Exhibition Hall, used by the corporation to demonstrate the corporation's effectiveness as a municipal power. The hall represented all municipal departments and the Department of Waterworks, for example, showed models of the public baths, 'complete with filtering, aerating and chlorinating plant'.[143] Departments relating to transport, gas and electricity also had displays in the exhibition, suggesting the celebrations were also a way for municipal leaders to advertise and promote their recent investment in urban infrastructure to their own citizens.

The festivities within the Exhibition Hall deliberately aimed to chart the city's evolution and emphasized progress and it asked citizens to compare the Manchester of 1838 with the Manchester of 1938. It described the library provisions in the city, for instance, as products of Manchester's constant progression under the corporation. 'From the small library at Campfield in 1832 to the great circular building in St Peter's Square', declared the handbook to the Exhibition Hall, 'is to move from modest beginnings to the centre of a system of libraries.'[144] Manchester Corporation used the celebrations to claim responsibility for the city's evolution over the century. Publicity material published by the corporation as part of the celebrations highlighted improvements in public health and one promotional publication reported epidemics of 'cholera, typhus, and smallpox, which used to rage among the people, have been stamped out ... from the cradle to the grave the City Council looks after the Welfare of its citizens.'[145] The publication suggested the corporation took an all-encompassing responsibility for its citizens, using rhetoric more closely related to the foundation of the Welfare State in 1945. These narratives helped to influence post-1945 rhetoric from the corporation in relation to the new role of the state.[146]

Similarly, the exhibition informed citizens that schools in nineteenth-century Manchester were 'a small room, not always clean and often dark, where an old dame knowing little more than her pupils would teach them their letters and simple sums',[147] whereas 'today each of Manchester's 90,000 children can attend the school most suited to his needs and a high balance of physical, mental and social education as possible.'[148] The handbook to the corporation's centenary celebrations directly contrasted the provisions made by municipal leaders in

1838 with those made in 1938, including comparisons of bath houses, food markets, roads and housing. Again, like the 1926 Civic Week, public transport was central to depictions of Manchester's modernity. For example, there was a large article in the special centenary edition of the *Manchester Guardian* produced to accompany the events. The article, 'From Horse Bus to Motor Bus', described Manchester's first omnibus, which arrived in 1824, as 'a relatively exclusive conveyance', which was 'narrow and cramped', in comparison to the sophisticated and comfortable public transport in the Manchester of 1938.[149] Similarly, the guide to the Exhibition Hall also strongly contrasted old and new forms of public wash houses recreated by the Baths and Wash Houses Department in the Exhibition Hall.[150] Citizens could therefore make clear comparisons between the provisions of 1838 and those of 1938: they could recognize 'modern Manchester' for themselves. This strategy of comparing the city over a hundred-year period allowed Manchester Corporation to ask citizens of Manchester to trust their municipal leaders and, in the handbook to the celebrations, told citizens that once they voted they 'must leave it to his councillor to support or oppose measures as he thinks fit'.[151] Municipal leaders in Manchester therefore used the celebrations and the narrative of progress to define good citizenship as an individual's willingness to obey civic leaders.

Propaganda produced to promote the celebrations linked the recognition of the city's progress and attendance at the Exhibition Hall with good citizenship. The Lord Mayor Joseph Crookes Grime proclaimed, 'I urge all citizens to attend the Exhibition.'[152] A publication by Manchester Corporation went further and compared the role of the citizen with being a football supporter. It emphasized the need for the citizen to trust in their municipal rulers,

> When the citizen has voted he must leave it to his councillor to support or oppose measures as he thinks fit. The councillor will have a greater opportunity of thinking out each problem because he has many books, reports and debates on these subjects to guide him.[153]

The extract is striking because the citizen is defined as 'he' and the celebrations made no direct references to women citizens, despite their enfranchisement. According to Manchester Corporation, citizens were required to pay their rates, vote, and obey the law, in return for the right to vote and use of civic services. 'The citizen should be just, law-abiding and public spirited. He should remember that he is part of a great civic community, and should know how the city is managed and try to do his duty intelligently,' they explained.[154] Again, the corporation defined the citizen as masculine. Manchester's civic celebrations of

1938 therefore suggest local citizenship as a concept was still in negotiation by the later 1930s. Although class divisions seem less evident within the rhetoric of local politics, it seems citizenship remained gendered and Manchester Corporation defined women's citizenship through their role as consumers, as we saw through the importance of shopping to civic celebrations in both Liverpool and Manchester. In contrast, men's citizenship appears to have remained linked to the public realm of politics and women remained marginalized from this official political language.

The 1938 celebrations also took place at a time when Manchester Corporation was not short of criticism, whether in the form of the local branch of the Communist Party or hunger marchers.[155] Lady Sheena Simon (who published several works on citizenship and the role of local government in the interwar years) criticized what she considered as a lack of vision and imagination from within the city during the 1930s. 'Perhaps the centenary year', wrote Lady Simon hopefully, 'with rateable value again on the up-grade, will inspire citizens with courage to go ahead with the task of re-moulding Manchester nearer to their hearts' desire.'[156] Unlike the celebrations of the 1920s, Manchester's Centenary festivities failed to attract the enthusiasm of local inhabitants and Lady Simon's hopes for a closer relationship between civic leaders and citizens were probably left unsatisfied. Manchester's press included only a few pictures of the festivities and failed to show the eagerness it possessed in its coverage of the 1926 Civic Week. Manchester Corporation described the celebrations as a great success and estimated 100,000 people attended.[157] Yet this was around a tenth of the number of visitors to the 1926 Civic Week. The British Empire Exhibition in Glasgow overshadowed Manchester's centenary celebrations, which opened in the same week, and 100,000 people were expected to travel from Manchester to visit the Empire Exhibition.[158] 'Despite the supposed dullness of some of the subjects, each Department had something interesting to show', claimed Manchester Corporation in its relatively meagre coverage of Manchester's centenary exhibition.[159] It is unlikely, however, that models of sewage works or exhibitions explaining corporation expenditure and instructions in citizenship were as exotic, fun or exciting as what was on offer on Glasgow.

Conclusion

The 1938 celebrations may have been less successful than the spectacular, grandiose Civic Weeks that preceded it, but the vitality of civic celebrations remains striking. Liverpool and Manchester's civic celebrations, especially those hosted within the cities during the late 1920s, turned the cities into exhibitions. As Vanessa Schwartz writes, the great Parisian expositions of the nineteenth century transformed observers' impressions of the city itself, turning Paris itself into an exhibition.[160] Liverpool and Manchester's celebrations mirrored this impact and they helped to promote specific urban images around the cities, as described in Chapter 1. Important features of urban redevelopment in both cities, like the new architecture and public transport, were central to the festivities. Liverpool's Civic Weeks celebrated the city's past in order to emphasize commercial and economic stability in the 1920s and also presented the city as an exciting and outward-looking city. Manchester's civic celebrations emphasized the city as a place of progress and their organizers used the festivities as an opportunity to demonstrate the city's evolution since the Victorian era. Manchester's cosmopolitanism was emphasized and the exhibitions highlighted the range and variety of the city's commercial and industrial endeavours. Local inhabitants could buy into these urban images and act out citizenship by participating in the civic celebrations and purchasing locally produced goods and services. By the 1930s, the nature of the celebrations changed and Manchester Corporation defined citizenship more directly through loyalty and duty to the local government. The city centres were important to local culture and became the focal point of leisure and consumer practices for inhabitants in both Liverpool and Manchester. Chapter 3 shows that just as municipal leaders promoted exciting and positive images of Liverpool and Manchester, retailers and shop owners sought to turn the cities into sites where shopping and consumer practices dominated.

These civic celebrations encompassed consumer culture and civic pride. In similar ways to the Empire Day celebrations in early-twentieth-century Britain, they sought to nurture a sense of collective identity that transcended class barriers.[161] The civic culture fostered by these celebrations reflected a shift towards a more inclusive and demotic civic pride, which reflected the new mass democratic age. These civic celebrations helped local politicians navigate the severe challenges Liverpool and Manchester faced between the two world wars by functioning as powerful exercises in boosterism that had dual aims of attracting investment and encouraging civic patriotism among inhabitants. Thus, post-1918 civic pride reflected the unique conditions of the interwar period and reflected the new cross-class culture of politics but there is evidence to suggest that it remained gendered.

It is, of course, challenging to assess how far citizens accepted the spectacular images of their cities as they enjoyed the civic celebrations. As we have seen, there were dissenting voices and those who enjoyed their visits emphasized the experience in terms of leisure and pleasure. Perhaps the relative lack of interest in Manchester's centenary celebrations indicates that the masses were less interested in learning about citizenship in favour of a 'good day out'. We do, however, know that local politicians and men of commerce were confident about the success of the Civic Week celebrations.[162] We also know that the celebrations were a part of a much wider attempt by municipal politicians to invest in transforming how citizens saw their cities and the proliferation of images and publicity material that accompanied interwar urban transformation. As we shall see in Chapter 3, urban transformation revitalized shopping and consumer culture, and the transformed city became strongly associated with retail and commercialism, which would have important implications for the way that women, in particular, experienced the city.

Part Two

Consumer Culture

'For Profit or Pleasure': New Cultures of Retail, Shopping and Consumer Culture

Urban redevelopment and the manifestation of a rich civic culture that emerged in interwar Liverpool and Manchester also changed local shopping, retail and consumer cultures. In an article titled 'The Renaissance of Bold Street', local periodical the *Liverpolitan* offered a vivid depiction of the rise of a new culture of shopping in Liverpool by highlighting the revitalization of one of the city's most important shopping streets by the late 1930s. 'Bold Street is therefore itself again,' the article proclaimed,

> And what a delight it is: to a woman supreme. ... Some of the shops with their novel and artistic frontages invite you irresistibly to look first and then almost magnetise you to go in. Inside they are like elegant parlours with an intimate air that makes the purchasing of articles more a matter of friendliness than a blunt commercial transaction.[1]

As the article shows, Liverpool's shops became sights of enjoyment in their own right and the city centre became more closely associated with shopping and consumer practices, especially for women who enjoyed the practice of shopping as a form of leisure.

The new shopping culture presented a distinct shift in urban retail practices after 1918, particularly in terms of the role of the department store. Whereas scholarship shows the role of the department store in shaping the late Victorian city and in providing a place of leisure and consumption for women, it is strongly emphasized as an exclusive space for the middle and upper classes.[2] In contrast, historians stress working-class women remained excluded from this consumer culture, except as workers.[3] More particularly, the post-1918 period is seen as a turning point in the fortunes of Britain's department stores, and the general consensus is that department stores declined in importance as a site of retail experience. Rather, the rise of chain stores and co-operatives dominated shopping culture in Britain.[4] At the same time, historians tend to characterize British retailers in general as being unable to respond to the challenges of a wider consumer and shopping revolution wherein American forms of retail thrived. The prevailing image therefore is one of decline for Britain's once-dazzling department stores and an overall lacklustre culture of retailing between the two world wars.[5]

American retailers pioneered innovative trends between the two world wars. Innovations transformed department stores in Depression-era America and focused on the 'building, organizing, decorating, and systemizing the store'.[6] This revitalization extended to all shops and the modernization of store fronts was especially transformative and 'served as a visual harbinger of imminent prosperity to inspire public confidence, stimulate consumption, and provide a focus for the redirection of civic self-representation'.[7] There are notable similarities between accounts of the modernization of American shop fronts in response to interwar economic depression with reactions by retailers in interwar Liverpool and Manchester. This chapter highlights the ways in which shops in these cities, led by department stores, responded with imagination and ambition to both economic depression and wider urban transformation. As Asa Briggs argues of Lewis's department stores, which were modernized and dramatically expanded in the interwar period and had large branches in both Liverpool and Manchester, 'there was no suggestion of retrenchment ... not even in times when several owners of department stores faced imminent collapse'.[8] We need to know more about how stores responded to the challenges they faced after 1918, particularly in light of the material in Chapters 1 and 2 that shows that Liverpool and Manchester saw the emergence of a rich civic culture and vibrant modern urbanism. Stores in Liverpool and Manchester did embrace these new strategies as they made the most out of the wider programmes of urban transformation. The innovations of department stores had important implications for shops and shopping culture throughout both cities and beyond.

Liverpool's most glamorous department stores, Bon Marché and George Henry Lee's, were under the ownership of the visionary American businessman and retail pioneer Harry Gordon Selfridge, who rose to fame in Chicago and whose creative team 'was part of the swelling army of copywriters and image engineers who helped to build an ideology of consumerism' in 1920s Britain.[9] Selfridge was himself renowned for his ostentatious tastes and ambitious investments in expanding his Oxford Street store and although his 'personal vanity and pride' was criticized by Frederick Marquis, director of Lewis's and chairman of Liverpool Organization, they shared a commitment to revitalizing consumer culture and shopping practices.[10] On his appointment to Lewis's in 1920, Marquis quickly realized that retailers were considered to possess a lower social standing in local civic and political life; they were excluded from certain clubs and were absent from boards of large banks, insurance companies and the railways. Marquis sought to reverse this trend and, in doing so, became a vital link between business and local politics, which was essential for permitting the revitalization of local shopping and retail culture to occur.[11] Most notably, Marquis purposefully altered retail practices to improve wages and improve the condition of the working classes, emphasizing the shopkeeper's role 'in social improvement and national well-being'.[12]

The impact of these new techniques and approaches on shopping practices in Liverpool and Manchester, led by the stores run by Selfridge and Marquis, was profound. First, this chapter charts the geographical shift in the location of shops, and shows how interwar urban transformation caused Liverpool and Manchester's city centres to become increasingly associated with shops and consumer culture. Led by department stores, retailers dramatically altered the visual appearance of their shop fronts and interiors, transforming shopping experience. The marketing strategies of department stores, particularly through their careful use of the popular local press, show that the stores became places to see and be seen within; they increasingly aimed their appeal towards the many, rather than the few, and were transformed into populist and cross-class sites of leisure and pleasure. Smaller shops imitated the marketing strategies of department stores, and they altered the urban experience by transforming city centres into exciting sites of consumer culture.

Urban transformation, economic depression and shopping culture

Liverpool and Manchester's transformation and the investment in redevelopment, as seen in Chapter 1, reshaped shopping practices significantly in these cities and the surrounding areas. Data from contemporary trade records reveal the direct relationship between economic depression, urban redevelopment and the emergence of a revitalized consumer culture in Liverpool and Manchester's city centres.[13] A selection of Kelly's trade directories (chosen for their comprehensive and detailed information on shops and businessmen in both cities) across the interwar years shows the distinct connections between urban redevelopment, economic depression and shopping practices over the period. By focusing on shops labelled as Boots and Shoe Sellers, Clothiers, Clothing Clubs, Costumiers, Drapers, Dressmakers, Hosiers and Glovers, Milliners, Tailors, Outfitters, Ladies Outfitters (listed as Ladies and Children's Outfitters in the Liverpool Directory) and co-operatives, the analysis permitted a clear numerical and locational comparison over the interwar years.[14] By constructing a comparison of the inner and outer areas of Liverpool and Manchester, it was possible to make a spatial comparison of shopping practices over the period. Inner Area describes the comparatively small geographical area of the city centre, meaning the area that held the central business area, transport terminus, department stores and civic buildings of the city, whereas Outer Area describes the area beyond the city centre and older suburbs.[15]

The material from trade directories illustrates a notable shift in the location of clothing and clothing-related retailers between 1922 and 1938. More precisely, the ratio of shops in the inner and outer areas of Liverpool effectively reversed in proportion: in 1922, inner Liverpool housed 35 per cent of shops, but by 1938 the proportion nearly reached 60 per cent, whereas the percentage of shops in outer Liverpool fell from 64 per cent to just 40 per cent across the same period. Together, the table and graph show the proportion of shops in the inner and outer areas of Liverpool underwent a significant locational shift interwar. In 1922, there were 1,109 clothing shops listed in inner Liverpool and 2,025 listed in outer Liverpool. Conversely, by 1938, there were 1,209 clothing shops listed in inner Liverpool and just 830 in outer Liverpool. Clothing-related shops were therefore more likely found in Liverpool city centre, rather than the outer area, by the end of the interwar period.

The shift in the location of shops makes sense in light of the material offered in Chapters 1 and 2. As we saw, the investment in public transport and architecture placed the city at the centre of shared communication network and commercial culture. At the same time, department stores got larger and visually more impressive, particularly Lewis's following several phases of expansion in the 1920s and 1930s while under the management of Marquis.[16] In this context, it made better commercial sense for business owners to have shops in Liverpool city centre than in the outer area because, quite simply, they would attract more customers. The need to attract more customers was particularly pressing due to Liverpool's difficult economic circumstances as its port trade was especially vulnerable to the world depression of 1929–32. In 1932, one in three workers in Liverpool was unemployed as economic depression hit the city's shipping industry particularly hard.[17] By 1939, Merseyside's unemployment rate was 18.8 per cent, compared to a national rate of 9.6 per cent.[18] The statistics

Table 3.1 Clothing shops, Liverpool 1922–38

	1922	1932	1938
Percentage of shops in inner Liverpool	35.38	36.72	59.29
Percentage of shops in outer Liverpool	64.61	63.27	40.70

Source: Kelly's Trade Directories, Liverpool 1922, 1932, 1938.

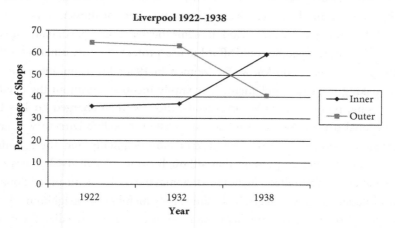

Figure 3.1 Proportion of shops in Liverpool expressed as percentages, 1922–38
Source: Kelly's Trade Directories, Liverpool 1922, 1932, 1938.

from Kelly's suggest the combination of Liverpool's economic problems and the city's redevelopment, particularly the corporation's investment in public transport and the emergence of impressive commercial architecture in the city centre, ensured that shops were more profitable in the city centre than in the surrounding geographical area. Clothing and clothing-related shops were less likely to survive commercially if they were outside the city centre, particularly following the 1929–32 slump.

Redevelopment helped to produce important shifts in the nature of retail culture and encouraged retailers to focus their trade in the city centre. One of the most striking aspects of Liverpool's interwar geographical redistribution of clothing and clothing-related shops was how far it affected particular kinds of shops and signalled broader changes in the nature of retailing. This data shows that shops in the city centre moved away from being shopkeepers who had only one premise or building, as the chain stores and multi-business owners moved into the centres of Liverpool and Manchester. The numbers of drapers and dressmakers, for instance, changed sharply across the period. According to the information from Kelly's, in inner Liverpool the number of drapers rose, from 314 in 1922 to 393 in 1938 and in contrast, the amount of drapers fell in outer Liverpool, from 455 in 1922 to just 128 by 1938. The substantial shift suggests that, as the period progressed, draper shops were more profitable in the city centre and fewer people bought material from local shops in the outer area. Interestingly, the number of dressmakers fell sharply in both areas of Liverpool: there were 149 dressmakers listed in Kelly's in outer Liverpool in 1922, and just 38 by 1938. Similarly, inner Liverpool saw numbers of dressmakers also fall, from 158 to 106 in the same period. It seems the depression particularly affected dressmakers as few people could afford to use 'professional' dressmakers. While, at the same time, we do know that women in 1930s Liverpool often took on dressmaking tasks to supplement their family income.[19] Without the need for advertising, premises or other overheads, these women charged far less than professional dressmakers and remained unlisted in Kelly's Directory. Chapter 4 examines women's use of dressmakers more explicitly and these findings support the chapter's argument that although some women used professional dressmakers, many relied on home dressmaking skills, semi-professional or non-professional dressmakers, including family members or neighbours. Urban transformation and economic depression do seem to have signalled the demise of the 'professional' dressmaker in Liverpool as part of a wider process of democratization of glamour and fashion.

The demise of the professional dressmaker allows us to trace the emergence of the modern shopping 'high street' between the two world wars. For example, the number of shops listed as hosiers and glovers remained fairly steady within inner Liverpool across the period, with twenty-one in 1922 and twenty in 1938. Outer Liverpool was markedly different, however, and hosiers and glovers fell dramatically in numbers, from seventy-two in 1920, to only eighteen in 1938. These statistics further suggest Liverpool city centre became the focus of local consumer experience during the interwar period, since hosiers and glovers survived the depression in the city centre but struggled in the city's outer area. Taken together, from these examples it seems that not only did shoppers in Liverpool increasingly visit the city centre for clothes and clothing-related shopping but, while in the city, they were also more likely to purchase materials for home dressmaking (drapers but not professional dressmakers) or items they could not easily make themselves (hosiers and glovers). Again, the material presented here illuminates the findings of Chapter 4, which show women were more likely to purchase token items like hosiery or items relating to home dressmaking, rather than actual dresses.

The data collected from Manchester's trade directories do not immediately present such a clear picture of change as in Liverpool. Overall, the statistics suggest the proportion of clothes-related shops in the inner area remained relatively unchanged over the period, shown in Table 3.2. Yet Manchester possessed some distinct features that may explain the lack of change. First, the legacy of Manchester's cotton trade probably ensured that cheap cloth remained available throughout Manchester and allowed drapers or dressmakers to set up easily and semi-officially, therefore making them less vulnerable to broader economic and structural changes. Second, Manchester covered a greater geographical area than Liverpool and contained several significant satellite towns with their own concentration of clothing shops. Towns like Stockport (famous for its own hat industry), Oldham, Bolton and Salford acted as shopping centres for the areas immediately surrounding them and so might have developed their own thriving shopping centres. These factors may therefore obscure the relationship between economic depression and retail practices in Manchester.

A closer and more detailed examination of the data taken from Manchester's trade directories does reveal some striking trends in retail culture that also suggest that we can see the emergence of the modern shopping 'high street'. Interestingly, there was an average of 1,200 drapers in outer Manchester throughout the period, but only ever around thirty in the inner city area. Inhabitants of the outer Manchester area may well have visited the city centre more often and made use of the expansion in public transport to peruse clothes shops but they may have also still purchased items nearer to home, which probably cost less due to the ease of access to cloth suppliers.[20] A decline in the numbers of clothing-related shops in the outer area of Manchester, does seem to have taken place, however, which suggests redevelopment and economic decline reshaped shopping practices. For example, the quantity of boot and shoe sellers

Table 3.2 Clothing shops, Manchester 1922–38

	1922	1932	1938
Percentage of shops in inner Manchester	12.5	11.4	10.99
Percentage of shops in outer Manchester	87.49	88.57	89

Source: Kelly's Trade Directories, Manchester 1922, 1932, 1938.

in outer Manchester halved over the period, from 426 in 1922 to 218 in 1936, and tailors also fell significantly in number within Manchester's outer area, from 563 in 1922 to 390 in 1938. These statistics suggest the economic change and urban transformation did impact clothing-related shops in outer Manchester as redevelopment ensured shops were increasingly located in the city centre.

Further inspection suggests the redistribution of Manchester's clothing-related shops also caused its city centre to become increasingly associated with retail experience. The numbers of dressmakers in inner Manchester fluctuated between twenty-one in 1922, ten in 1932 and eighteen in 1938. In the outer area they numbered 348 in 1922, falling to 290 in 1932, and by 1938, there were only 232. These numbers suggest that, as in Liverpool, dressmakers left the city centre in response to urban redevelopment. As the statistics for Liverpool indicate, there is evidence to suggest that shoppers in Manchester also increasingly frequented clothing-related shops for items they could not make at home and, at the same time, tended to rely on shops in inner Manchester to purchase these items. There were twenty-eight Hosiers and Glovers in inner Manchester and seventy-seven in outer Manchester during 1922: by 1938, the numbers were nineteen for inner Manchester and only thirty for the outer area. Similarly, there were nineteen milliners in 1922 within inner Manchester, falling to fifteen by 1938, whereas the number of milliners in outer Manchester fell much more significantly, from 304 in 1922 to just 198 in 1938. The data compiled from trade directories show retailers left the outer area as a consequence of urban redevelopment.

Manchester's fluctuating interwar economy helps to explain the nature of the city's distribution of clothing and clothing-related shops, and the complicated fortunes of its local economy mirror the ambiguities of the statistics produced by the analysis of the trade directories. For instance, Manchester's cotton industry suffered an irreversible crash, creating substantial unemployment throughout Lancashire, yet Manchester's official unemployment levels never met the national rate. Poverty and unemployment spread unevenly throughout the Greater Manchester area.[21] The area around Trafford Park, to the west of the city, for example, saw increased prosperity after Ford set up a factory in 1910 (although the company departed for Dagenham in 1931 to be nearer the European market); Kemp's biscuit factory began production there in 1923, followed by Kellogg's in 1938. 'Trafford Park firms generally survived the Crash of 1929/31 without bankruptcies, which was not the case elsewhere in Lancashire.'[22] Trafford Park was part of a wider attempt to broaden the city's economy and investment centred on the area's factories, the Manchester Ship Canal and Manchester

Airport, although pockets of poverty and unemployment persisted, particularly in the areas of Miles Platting, Chorlton-on-Medlock, Hulme, Ancoats, Angel Meadow and Redbank.[23]

Manchester's cotton collapse, and the subsequent unemployment of mill workers and warehouse staff, may help explain why clothing-related shops left the outer area during the interwar years. It is possible to speculate that the decline of the export market left a glut of cotton in and around Manchester, explaining the survival of drapers, whereas other types of retailers faced far harder times. Conversely, the diversification of the city's economy and the concentration of unemployment in particular areas imply the depression did not affect clothing and clothing-related shops in outer Manchester as extensively as were their Liverpool counterparts. Manchester's particular commercial, geographical size and number of satellite towns, each with its own micro-economy, make it difficult to place the city within a particular model of economic growth or decline. Nevertheless, as the next part of the chapter shows, both city centres became increasingly associated with shopping practices as the interwar period progressed.

Shops as 'the poetry of the streets'

The statistics suggest a link between urban redevelopment and shifts in retail culture. Urban commentators recognized the significant changes in both cities' fabric and appearance from the mid-1920s and highlighted the important visual role of shops in shaping these changes. The *Manchester Guardian Yearbook* of 1925, for example, described two developments in the city during the previous year. 'One has been a very striking improvement in the window display,' claimed the *Yearbook*, 'and the other – and a very remarkable one in view of the general depression in trade – a rapid growth in the number of shops for women's clothes and footwear.'[24] Similarly, in 1928, architectural expert Sir Charles Reilly wrote that behind Liverpool's office quarter 'will spread the shopping and amusement area, ever brighter and gayer.'[25] Department stores were responsible for this development, as they both exploited and contributed to the ongoing urban redevelopment and investment in infrastructure to attract greater numbers of customers.

Shop windows, in particular, became increasingly important as selling tools during the 1920s, and shop managers created exotic window displays to draw shoppers to their stores. Department stores pioneered these fantastical window displays, as a journalist recognized in 1927, 'The window displays at the Bon Marché are always good and at times so good that to alter them seems a pity. The colour schemes are especially outstanding. The general character of the advertising ... attains novelty.'[26] Influenced by innovative trends from Paris and New York, which pioneered the 'cult of window-dressing', shop windows in Manchester and Liverpool became increasingly decorative and filled elaborately with items for sale.[27] Shop windows helped to transform the visual experience of shopping and drew in visitors from the surrounding areas, as the *Manchester Guardian* noted in 1926: 'Shopping in Manchester appeals to thousands of people outside the city's boundaries', key were shop windows, which were part of the shops' aims to 'encourage sightseers and visitors'.[28] Urban commentators credited the new culture of shop windows with changing the nature and role of shopping as shopping became 'a joy as well as a necessity, and part of the pleasure arises from the contemplation of beautiful articles artistically arranged in the spacious windows'.[29] As we shall see in Chapter 4, women's engagement with retail culture in Liverpool and Manchester did change between the two world wars and the rich culture of window-dressing was fundamental to the new demotic culture of shopping that women from a range of class backgrounds could enjoy.

As larger shops' window displays became more exotic and elaborate, smaller retailers began to imitate them to attract customers. Mass Observation, a social research movement that established an anthropological study of Bolton, a town to the north of Manchester, in the late 1930s, noted the emphasis shop owners placed on the aesthetics of their windows.[30] A young female draper admitted to imitating larger shops: 'For ideas I go to the big shops and note the best displays, I started with the cardboard displays and as I increased my stock I tried to show the different goods I had.'[31] Another female draper reported something similar in a separate interview with Mass Observation: 'I do my own window dressing and I try to change the windows once a week', stating she used her newest stock and most fashionable items for the displays.[32] For shop owners in Bolton, windows were essential selling techniques and smaller retailers were directly inspired by larger city centre shops.

The fantastical shop windows also contributed to the increased marginalization of the poorest street sellers from the revitalized cultures of shopping. Not only could street sellers not compete with the strategies pursued by these shop owners, but became perceived as unwanted and incompatible with new retail forms. In 1924, for example, Councillor John Nield brought the plight of the 'extreme poverty and distress' of street sellers to Liverpool Corporation. Nield declared:

> The motorcars of the idle rich are permitted to obstruct the busy thoroughfares, also the window displays of the shops (in particular large business concerns) causing the sidewalks to be blocked, this Council expresses its disapproval at the officious and despotic treatment inflicted on the hawkers and pedlars by the Police and Magistrates, in so far the hawkers and pedlars are 'hustled', 'moved on', and fined, and thus prevented from selling the goods ... they persecute a woman if she happens to stop within view of certain shops with her barrow of goods.[33]

Interestingly, the Council immediately dismissed Nield's complaints and the message was clear: there was no room for hawkers or pedlars in the transformed city.[34]

Department stores contributed to urban culture more generally in the late Victorian and Edwardian years.[35] This process continued into the interwar period, but department store style changed and window displays in the 1930s followed a particular aesthetic of abundance, which reflected the interwar economic depression. Rather than fetishizing single objects through a minimalist aesthetic, objects for sale overloaded shop windows. One report by Mass Observation noted the packed displays: 'Magnificent displays in five shops just off and around Deansgate. They are all, without exception, pink. In one window fifty-seven pairs, then forty-five, thirty-eights, twenty-five and fifteen. They are mostly exceedingly complicated with bones running vertically and slopingly and intricate lacing.'[36] Similarly, the revitalized storefronts in America were central to a new form of retailing and included overcrowded displays that offered 'an image of modernity that was deliberately at odds with the dismal present because it symbolised a hopeful future'.[37] Images of abundance dominated shop windows in Liverpool and Manchester also and offered an enticing image of consumer culture that was contradictory to the economic context of the period. For instance, one window for Woolworths in 1931 displayed numerous items for 'Household Week', which overwhelmingly packed out the window making it difficult to focus on any one item. Ordinary household objects like saws and hammers were organized so they formed a scene of entertainment and spectacle. Nurturing an image of abundance, Woolworth's window projected a fantastical and other-worldly representation of the objects.[38] Similarly, the *Manchester Guardian* described the particularly decorative displays the shops invested in during the Civic Week and highlighted their use of light to maintain their appeal into the evening, when 'the pavements are crowded with little groups of tired women and babies gazing into the brilliant caves of bright stuffs and colours where exquisite wax ladies are gowned for balls or theatres or for study tramps through heathery moors'.[39] There are parallels between the cultures of shopping that emerged in interwar Liverpool and Manchester and with Walter Benjamin's insights relating to phantasmagorical experiences of the modern city. For Benjamin, shop windows made objects other-worldly and department stores and the way they displayed their goods meant, 'the circus-like and theatrical element of commerce is quite extraordinarily heightened.'[40]

The phantasmagorical role of shop windows also shaped the visual experience of city centres. From the mid-1920s, Manchester's visual transformation led by shop managers in their desire to attract greater numbers of customers struck local urban commentators. In 1926, the *Manchester Guardian* wrote, 'Nowadays the shop windows are the poetry of the streets. On melancholy autumn days, they are like bright, enchanted caves edging the pavements.'[41] The newspaper also made grander claims about the changes in the city during the 1920s, which helped to feed into the images of Manchester disseminated through corporation-produced publicity material and the local press. The *Manchester Guardian* Yearbook of 1925 proclaimed,

> Within the past twelve months the buildings which first ousted residentialism from Manchester are being effaced and reconstructed. In their stead have risen expansive and imposing showrooms for the display and accommodation of clothing, drapery. ... Gradually, Manchester is taking a bigger toll of the county's shoppers. ... No opportunity is being neglected to increase the attractiveness of the shops, and just as Manchester is informally treated as the capital of the North of England, so it is destined by the solidarity, worth and value of its service, to become the shopping centre of the North of England.[42]

According to the *Manchester Guardian*, the new shopping culture changed the city centre during the mid-1920s and this contributed to Manchester's marketed image – a shopping destination. As the extract suggests, Manchester's role as the 'shopping centre of the North of England' was a product of the economic depression. As one shop owner in Bolton told Mass Observation, he lost customers to the larger city shops, who could sell goods more cheaply: 'A woman will take a penny bus ride ... and thereby save 6d or 1/ as it is worth it.'[43] The experiences of the shop manager and his customers again support the findings of the statistics collated from Kelly's directories, which suggested shops in the outer areas of Manchester were more vulnerable to the economic depression of the 1930s, particularly in light of the advances in public transport that made access to city centres easier, cheaper and faster. By implication, shops and a more glamorous retail culture increasingly became associated with Manchester's urban centre.

Similar changes also occurred to the culture of shopping in Liverpool city centre. In 1921, Liverpool architectural expert Charles Reilly complained about Bold Street and urged shopkeepers to form a league 'to maintain and improve the character and standard of what might be. ... On gala days they should beflag it as New York does Fifth Avenue.'[44] By 1935, consumer culture visibly transformed the city's streets. 'Lime Street at night is now a favourite rendezvous for numerous visitors, on account of its numerous electric signs, while the majority of our modern cinemas and music halls have their frontages outlined with neon tubing,' wrote one journalist in the *Liverpolitan*, in an affectionately named article, 'The City is getting Gayer!'[45] Technological developments were important as they allowed department stores to produce fantastical visual displays and ensured the buildings themselves were a form of entertainment. Department store historiography emphasizes not only the 'urban monumentality' of their architecture, but also their decline in the interwar period.[46] In contrast, department stores and smaller shops in cities such as Manchester and Liverpool seem to have increased their investment in technology to enhance the appearance and visual spectacle of their stores.

American department stores pioneered developments in technologies of light during the early twentieth century, in the belief that it led to increased sales. 'Between 1911 and 1936 the intensity of illumination in the typical store tripled', writes historian Susan Porter Benson, 'with indirect lighting and accent spotlights replacing older direct lighting.'[47] Smaller shops in Liverpool borrowed department stores' use of light to attract customers. 'The glamour and variety of modern lighting must be reckoned in the renaissance of Bold Street', wrote *Liverpolitan*, in a description of the impact of the technologically advanced lights on the shop fronts.[48] In 1938, the Liverpool Gas Company bought premises on Bold Street to create a 'great new "temple of gas" ... a lavish display amid spacious and ornate appointments'.[49] There was a link between interwar investment in infrastructure, technological developments and urban consumer culture after the mid-1920s, turning the streets into objects of spectacle and entertainment. A poem published in the *Liverpolitan* in 1937 described Bold Street as a place of leisure in itself:

> Straight as an arrow, slim as any girl,
> Of roadway narrow, disapproving whirl,
> It seems a sacrilege to speed your car
> Amidst a mart that's just one long bazaar.[50]

The author encapsulates how the shops' new selling techniques turned Bold Street into a place of amusement as the redeveloped city provided the infrastructure for a popular urban consumer culture to manifest. Department store managers and shopkeepers invested in enhancing the visual experience of shopping in response to economic depression and Liverpool and Manchester's interwar transformation. Yet they did not stop there and, as the next section examines, the use of advertisements further reshaped consumer culture and shopping practices in both cities.

Advertisements

The material presented above shows how shopping culture changed as a result of Liverpool and Manchester's interwar redevelopment. At the same time, department stores were in no way immune from the pressures of economic depression and the interwar years were especially challenging. Chain stores and wider fluctuations in the economy and income levels threatened the very existence of department stores.[51] Department stores' advertisements and promotional strategies in Liverpool and Manchester reveal how they survived and prospered between the wars. Generally understood as exclusive sites of consumption for upper- and middle-class shoppers, they needed to broaden their customer base in response to economic depression, alongside wider changes such as suburbanization, which took the middle-class consumer further away from the city centre, and the rise of working-class 'affluence'.[52] An analysis of the quantity and content of advertisements placed by the main department stores in Liverpool and Manchester reveals the stores' change in approach. Briggs suggests Lewis's department stores (a chain of department stores found throughout the country but with considerable autonomy and influence of store managers) were highly innovative in their advertising campaigns interwar and followed methods 'as far removed from the sensational advertising of the middle of the nineteenth century as they could have been'.[53] In Liverpool, Lewis's led a clear shift in their approach to marketing and advertising and their leadership was in part to the contribution of Marquis, who as chairman of Liverpool Organization represented a key point of collaboration between the council and private business. Marquis transformed the way Lewis's was run and combined his expertise as an economist with his passion for social responsibility, turning Lewis's into a slick, organized machine with increased productivity and turnover, which was used to improve workers' wages and conditions. In his own memoirs, Marquis claimed, 'Efficiency in management and capital risk-taking were producing better conditions of employment and improving the standard of living of the general public.'[54] By implication of the vision and innovation shown by businessmen such as Marquis, department stores in Liverpool and Manchester purposefully reinvented themselves as populist sites of leisure and consumer culture which offered crucial protection from interwar economic depression.

By counting and analysing the number of advertisements placed by Liverpool's key stores, which were Bon Marché, George Henry Lee's and Lewis's, in comparison to Manchester's Affleck and Brown, Lewis's and Kendal's in the local press (the *Manchester Evening News* – hereafter *MEN*, *Manchester Guardian*, *Liverpool Echo*, and *Liverpolitan*), it is possible to chart their change in marketing strategies in response to economic depression and urban transformation.[55] Liverpool and Manchester's press targeted different spending groups, as defined by Seebohm Rowntree's second poverty survey, which identified four groups with A as the highest and D the lowest: the *MEN* and *Echo* each cost one penny and focused on local interest stories, sensational murder reports, cinema and sport and spending groups C and D were more likely to make up their readership.[56] Both newspapers mirrored developments in the national popular press, led by Northcliffe's *Daily Mail*, which demoted politics and parliament from the front pages in favour of human interest stories and advertisements, aiming to attract a more female audience.[57] Northcliffe's strategies implemented in the *Daily Mail* and *Daily Express* also incorporated some features of women's magazines, such as fashion and retail advertisements, and the local press also took up these additions and innovations.[58] Conversely, *Manchester Guardian* (which cost three halfpence in 1919 and two pence in 1939) focused on national and international political events and economics. *Manchester Guardian* was both a national and local newspaper from the later nineteenth century (despite not dropping 'Manchester' from its title until 1959). Yet the newspaper experienced a period of 'Manchesterisation' from the late 1920s and the introduction in 1928 of a regular 'Manchester Letter' in opposition to the newspaper's London Letter, was part of a wider return to a focus on Manchester issues. As we saw in Chapter 1, the newspaper did include many features promoting the council's investment in urban transformation.[59] *Liverpolitan* (which cost three pence) was a monthly periodical that dealt with local and national politics and current affairs. People from spending groups A and B were therefore more likely to be readers of the *Manchester Guardian* and *Liverpolitan*. Nevertheless, these newspapers were not immune from the broader changes sweeping through press culture after the First World War and, for example, in 1922 the *Manchester Guardian* introduced a regular women's page.[60]

This use of the local press reveals the regional-specific marketing approaches employed by Liverpool and Manchester's main department stores. Advertisements are especially illuminating because they provide a form of communication between the capitalist and the consumer that aims to persuade the consumer to make particular choices about certain products.[61] Studies of American advertisements suggests their message, content, attitudes and values remained constant during the 1920s and 1930s, even throughout the economic crash.[62] Department stores in Liverpool and Manchester continued to advertise through the depression years, although their message, content and attitudes did change as the stores altered their marketing approach to attract a wider customer base. There were also broader technological changes in Europe that shaped department stores' ability to advertise differently: in 1919, the typical department store advert was small, consisting of a frame surrounding the logo and perhaps some prices. A decade later, 'the breakthrough of graphic representations in advertising becomes apparent, as both illustrations and a variety of fonts are added to the earlier concept thereby setting a standard which has persisted until the present day.'[63] These broader changes show the importance of the press in permitting department stores to nurture a spectacular culture of shopping that reached a broad, cross-class audience.

Department stores did not just change their style of advertisements but also altered where they placed their advertisements to reflect the new customer base that they sought to attract. Figure 3.2 shows the number of advertisements placed by department stores in the popular press increased significantly over the interwar period. As the graph shows, there was an appreciable rise in those placed by the main department stores in the newspapers most likely read by those from spending groups C and D. For instance, between 1920 and 1938,

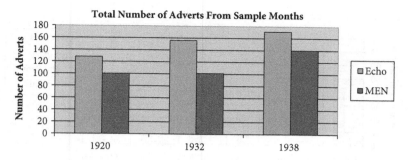

Figure 3.2 Numbers of advertisements placed by department stores, 1920–38
Source: Liverpool Echo and *Manchester Evening News*, 1920, 1932, 1938.

the number of advertisements placed in the *Manchester Evening News* (*MEN*) rose by 40 per cent. This was all the more significant considering they also grew in size and were increasingly decorative and eye-catching. The statistics suggest department stores had a growing presence in the popular press, which may have been a national trend, and drapery and department store advertising constituted the single largest category of promotional expenditure in the press in 1935.[64] The quantity of department store advertisements in the popular press within Liverpool and Manchester certainly rose markedly: During January and February 1920, Lewis's, Lee's and Bon Marché placed a total of sixty-four advertisements in the *Echo* and one hundred in the same months of 1938, an increase of over 50 per cent. Similarly, Kendal's, Affleck and Brown, and Lewis's placed a total of twenty-six advertisements in the *MEN* during October and November of 1920, and seventy-four in the same period of 1938, meaning the quantity in the *MEN* nearly trebled over the period. These statistics illustrate department stores advertised more heavily in the later 1930s in comparison to the early 1920s. They also promoted their goods and services within newspapers more likely read by those in the lower spending groups.

The statistics above illustrate the increased number of advertisements placed in the popular press in Liverpool and Manchester across the interwar years. Looking at the more elite press, however, offers a different story. As Figure 3.3 shows, far fewer department store advertisements appeared in the *Manchester Guardian* as the period progressed. The number placed by Kendal's fell especially sharply over the period: in January and February of 1920, the store placed seventy-seven advertisements, falling to just seven during January and February of 1938. Contrastingly, the store chose to place fourteen in the *MEN* during the same period of 1920, and twelve in 1938, albeit much larger and more illustrative advertisements. The shift in Kendal's marketing practices suggests

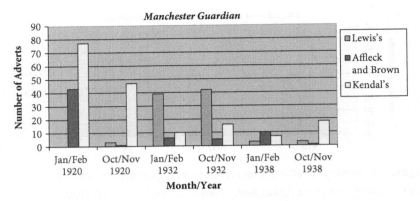

Figure 3.3 Number of department store advertisements in the *Manchester Guardian*, 1920–38

Source: Manchester Guardian, 1920–38.

the store turned away from focusing on attracting customers from spending groups A and B. Advertisements placed by Affleck and Brown follow a more complex pattern but also point to a similar shift: Affleck and Brown placed over forty advertisements in each of the *MEN* and the *Manchester Guardian* during January and February 1920. During the October and November period of 1938, the store placed only one advertisement in the *Manchester Guardian* and fourteen in the *MEN*. It seems that if Affleck and Brown did choose to advertise in the press during the late 1930s, they did so within a newspaper more likely read by those from the lower spending groups.

The decline in the quantity of department store advertisements placed in the *Manchester Guardian* after 1932 reflected the 'catastrophic' decade faced by the newspaper, which, in turn, reflected in a decline in advertising revenue throughout the 1930s.[65] Fortunately, the company bought the *MEN* in 1930, which continued to attract significant advertising revenue and helped the *Manchester Guardian* survive a difficult decade. Department store advertisements provided an important source of revenue for the *MEN* and contributed to the newspaper's success. In 1931, Lewis's booked a record advertising contract with the paper, placing a full-page advertisement for three days a week over an extended period.[66] In contrast, the *Manchester Guardian*'s fortunes followed those of the city's cotton industry, which severely limited the wealth and prosperity of businessmen (and thus advertisers) in the Manchester area and the newspaper earned £300,000 a year in advertising revenue until the Slump. The newspaper's annual income from advertisements fell to £230,000 in the late 1920s, decreasing by a further £40,000 in the year after March 1930, and again by £40,000 during the following year.[67] Despite these damaging figures, the collapse of the cotton industry was not the newspaper's most pressing concern. 'More lasting, and therefore more damaging', however, was the 'diversion of display advertising to the "popular" papers which could offer the mass audience needed for the marketing of mass-produced consumer goods.'[68] The *Manchester Guardian* lost advertising to newspapers like the *MEN* because there was a wider shift among advertisers to target those who read the popular press.

Statistics relating to the number of advertisements placed by stores in Manchester suggest that by the end of the interwar period all three stores focused on attracting customers from lower spending groups. In January and February of 1920, Lewis's, Lee's, and Affleck and Brown placed nineteen, forty-one and fourteen advertisements each in the *MEN*, and none, forty-three and seventy-seven each in the *Manchester Guardian*. By the same period of 1938, the number placed in the *MEN* stood at thirty-five for Lewis's, nineteen for Affleck and Brown, and twelve for Kendal's. In the *Manchester Guardian*, there were three, ten and seven respectively. There are parallels here with findings on British cigarette advertisements, which emphasize a shift away from Victorian styles of advertisements (which appealed to specific individuals) as interwar cigarette manufacturers sought 'to capture as wide a market as possible for each branded commodity'.[69] Department store managers, like cigarette companies, attempted to attract a wider market reflected by the changing nature of their advertisements over the course of the interwar period. The choice made by department stores to advertise in the *MEN* rather than the *Manchester Guardian* was reflective of this shift. The marketing strategy of department store managers in Liverpool and Manchester related to a wider populist and demotic consumer culture that developed in 1930s Britain.

In Liverpool, a more populist marketing approach also emerged in direct response to economic depression and the number of department store advertisements in the *Echo* increased when the city experienced its most challenging economic problems, as Figure 3.4 illustrates. During the November and October period of 1920, Lewis's placed thirty-five advertisements in the *Echo*, Lee's placed sixteen and Bon Marché thirteen. By the same period of 1932, the numbers reached fifty-seven, twenty-one and twenty-four, respectively and, in 1938, stood at thirty-six, fourteen and twenty. These numbers suggest that during times of economic hardship department stores in Liverpool were enthusiastic to invest in advertising within a newspaper more likely read by those from lower

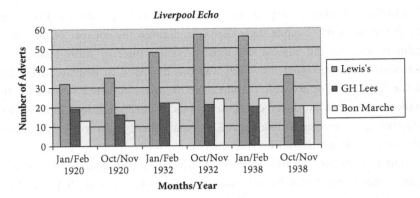

Figure 3.4 Department store advertisements in the *Liverpool Echo*, 1920–38
Source: Liverpool Echo, 1920–38.

spending groups. Taken in conjunction with the earlier material on the locational redistribution of clothing-related shops in Liverpool, it seems the emerging shopping culture in the city centre intensified a sense of competition between the department stores. The number of advertisements placed by department stores in both Liverpool and Manchester indicates they sought to attract customers from lower spending groups and chose not to focus on attracting a smaller number of customers from the higher spending groups. There were important implications following this change in department stores' advertising practices in Manchester and Liverpool. They cultivated a shopping revival, drawing clothing-related shops into the city centre, changed the way women shopped, and encouraged a further link between the city and consumer practices.

'The modern store can be a social centre as well as a shop': Department stores as demotic sites of leisure and pleasure

The changes in advertisements and the new approach of department store managers towards their customers reflected wider developments in the nature of retail culture. In the immediate post-war years and early 1920s, department stores placed very small advertisements that typically acted as an announcement to declare special in-store events.[70] Department stores seemed only to advertise during special promotional events, like the sales, when their customer base changed temporarily. For instance, the only advertisements placed by Affleck and Brown and Kendal's in both the *MEN* and the *Manchester Guardian* during

January and February 1920 promoted their January sales.[71] As a consequence of developments in technology, advertisements placed by department stores in interwar Liverpool and Manchester not only increased in number but also became larger and more eye-catching. Department store managers also expanded their promotional tactics to appeal to an increasingly broad audience. Stores focused their promotional activities around several important sales strategies during the 1930s: themed weeks, amenities, aspirational fashion, glamour and the lure of Hollywood, promotional activities and entertainment. They indicate a significant shift in the marketing and promotional tactics employed by department stores.

Department stores originally aimed to attract middle- and upper-class women shoppers only.[72] Designed for the comfort and leisure of women from the higher spending groups, advertisements presented stores as exclusive sites for these social groups. For instance, one promotional poster for G. H. Lee's in 1919 depicted shopping as a very small aspect of the services provided and portrays the store primarily as a meeting place for ladies:

> All the Facilities of a Ladies' Town Club ... newspapers and periodicals of the day may be perused, correspondence conducted, and your letters received and posted. ... Every amenity, in fact, usually associated with a Ladies' Town Club may be enjoyed.[73]

The poster invited wealthier women to spend their social and leisure time within the store and indicates department stores were exclusive in the women they sought to attract and promoted a clear notion of middle- and upper-class femininity. Department store managers used women's clubs to lure in shoppers from the Edwardian period, when 'clubs were no longer seen as socially daring, dangerous or even feminist'.[74] In contrast, by the later 1930s, stores maintained their role as a social centre but embraced a wider clientele. An advert placed by Lewis's in *Liverpolitan* in 1937 also suggested the store saw itself as a demotic leisure space; it claimed: 'The larger Lewis's will show how the modern store can be a social centre as well as a shop' and marketed itself explicitly to all classes.[75] By the later 1930s therefore, the new marketing strategies presented department stores as sites of leisure and pleasure, rather than just somewhere to make purchases and, crucially, at the same time moved away from their elitist associations. This shift is also illustrated by statistics from G. H. Lee's which show the most popular department in 1933 was the Restaurant, which had had 7,954 recorded customers in 1933, whereas the next most popular department was the Haberdashery with 4,396 recorded customers. The popularity of the restaurant suggested that it, too, had moved towards becoming a site of leisure and pleasure as well as aiming to be a shop for all classes by the early 1930s.[76]

In the immediate post-war years, advertisements for department stores emphasized the exclusivity of the clothes they sold and clearly sought to encourage potential customers from the higher spending groups, as the women they depicted tended to be well dressed but not particularly glamorous or fashionable.[77] During the 1920s, department stores in Liverpool appear to have only invited women from lower spending groups on specific terms. In 1920, Lee's promoted the season's new fashion collection to wealthy women, by describing it in exclusive terms. The collection was made up of 'dainty examples of New Season's goods have the charm of distinction', claimed the advert.[78] Contrastingly, Lewis's in Liverpool sought to attract a different kind of customer during its 'Household Bargain's Week' in February 1920. 'Housewives! You know what this means! Low prices on prodigious quantities of all kinds of usable things, household draperies and linens for the home.'[79] Similarly, Bon Marché held a 'Stocking Week' with 'six days of stocking value which you will not meet again for many months' and, in the same advert, urged 'thrifty women' to also buy fabric for their spring dresses.[80] Advertisements in the early 1920s appear to have identified specific moments when women from particular spending groups were invited to the stores.

By the early 1930s, Manchester's department stores used themed promotional weeks to encourage customers from lower spending groups by presenting their stores as places to find bargains. An advert placed by Affleck and Brown in 1932 to promote 'Household bargains' informed the housewife: 'These prices cannot be maintained when the stock is cleared' and claimed 'the goods were bought when the market was at its lowest in preparation for the Annual Sale ... wise folk will replenish their future needs now as it is a rising market.'[81] At a time of economic difficulty, department stores in Manchester used these advertisements to create a sense of urgency. They implied it was the housewife's only opportunity to purchase goods in a store normally beyond their budgets. Lewis's set up a Central Buying Office in 1923, which allowed the company to buy in bulk and enabled them to provide goods to customers at lower prices.[82] In the 1920s and 1930s therefore, stores deliberately targeted customers with less spending power and this marked a clear shift in their marketing practices from the period before 1918 and reflected a wider democratization of glamour, which we will explore in more detail in Chapter 4.

Themed sales weeks continued in Manchester's department stores, but advertisements targeted a broader range of customers. For example, one advert placed by Lewis's suggests that by the early 1930s, themed weeks also began to attract shoppers as a mass market, rather than isolating and targeting specific spending groups at certain times. Significantly, there were no pictures of women or women's clothing as this prevented the store from alienating anyone, either from lower or higher spending groups. Promising 'New 5/merchandise to the store', the advert recreated the images of abundance that were apparent in shop windows. The advert, and the many others like it, presented the store as having inexpensive and useful items, like bedspreads and curtains, as well as more fashionable and more frivolous items, like stockings and dresses.[83] Interestingly, the store placed a very different advertisement for the 'Million Pound Sale' in the *Manchester Guardian,* in order to target women from higher spending groups and actually depicted a wealthy woman waited upon by a shop assistant in Lewis's during the 'Million Pound Sale'.[84] The advertisement explicitly invited women from wealthier spending groups to attend the sale but promised a very difference consumer experience to those who read the *MEN.* The two differing advertisements illustrate how department stores in Manchester targeted customers with different spending power to attend the same promotional events.

Department stores employed aspirational images of fashion during the later 1930s, which represented an important shift in department store advertising strategy because they were able to appeal to women as a mass market. Rather than using different advertisements to target different groups of shoppers, stores began to use glamorous, fashionable images, which women could aspire to emulate. These aspirational fashions were not necessarily out of the reach of women from the lower spending groups. George Orwell described the nature of trade in the 1930s, which meant it was cheaper to buy luxury items than necessities: 'One pair of plain solid shoes costs as much as two ultra-smart pair'.[85] By implication, aspirational (rather than essential) items of clothing, such as fur coats, could actually be affordable and accessible for women from lower spending groups.[86] An advert placed by Lewis's in October 1938 set out how the modern woman should dress. '5 fundamentals for the well-dressed woman' informed women from all spending groups, '"YOU MUST HAVE" a fur stroller, a good coat, a simple daytime dress, a smart "dressy" dress, a dramatic evening dress.'[87] The advertisement appealed to women generally, by focusing on an aspirational model of womanhood and fashion.

Liverpool's department stores also used images of aspirational glamour to encourage a broad customer base in the late 1930s. Bon Marché promoted a fur sale in 1938 that offered a variety of furs and the advert emphasized glamour. From the 'Delightful Box Coat' and 'Elegant Cape', to the 'Dashing Swagger', prices ranged from as little as seven guineas to as much as £400, with squirrel being the cheapest fur and accessible to many working-class women if they saved carefully. The advertisement indicates the store sought to cater for the budgets of all women and used fur as an iconic item of clothing to unite all women customers. Similarly, Lee's asked *Liverpolitan's* readers, 'Cruising this year?' The advert included depictions of glamorous women on a cruise ship, but the products listed aimed to encompass a range of spending abilities: 'Swim costumes are priced from 15/11 to 49/6 – Wraps from 7/11 to 49/.'[88] Cruising is a glamorous image, but not necessarily divisive or alienating to women with little spending power: the range of products allowed women with less spending power to access the aspirational images these advertisements promoted. By the late 1930s, department stores used aspirational glamour to attract women consumers from all spending groups because its appeal crossed class divisions.

Popular images of feminine identities in the 1930s closely related to the glamour of Hollywood and the centrality of the cinema to working-class leisure.[89] Department stores used the appeal of Hollywood and the popularity of the cinema to attract women shoppers and this strategy allowed managers to promote stores as places of glamour and amusement, which was particularly common in Liverpool from the early 1930s onwards.[90] In August 1932, echoing the successful publicity trick of the 1926 Civic Week that saw West End actress Gladys Cooper create a near-riot in a Liverpool department store, film star Gracie Fields became a shop assistant at Bon Marché as a publicity stunt.[91] Gracie's appearance was incredibly popular and very large crowds of women competed for her service. All the local newspapers reported Gracie's visit and the *Post* described the spectacle: 'Hundreds of women were convulsed with laughter at the antics of Miss Gracie Fields who for an hour yesterday took on the job of shop assistant.'[92] Gracie Fields (1898–1979) began her career as a music hall star in Rochdale and became one of Britain's greatest film stars in the 1930s. From 1936 to 1939, she was the top female star at the British cinema box office. Her most famous films included *Shipyard Sally*, *Sing As We Go* and *Looking on the Bright Side*, allowing Gracie Fields to play characters who were cheerful in the face of misfortune and 'recreated her own rise from mill girl to star, a "rags to riches" saga which demonstrated the continuing validity of the doctrine of self-help'.[93] Gracie was 'evidently something of a national treasure' during the 1930s and was a very different figure to that of Jessie Matthews, Britain's other leading female cinematic star in the 1930s, who was very glamorous and more sexual.[94] Film historian Andrew Higson describes Gracie Fields as 'the unglamorous star, the ordinary person'.[95] Perhaps it was not just Gracie's fame that drew crowds to Bon Marché. Shoppers with little spending money, who wished to participate in the more glamorous and exotic world of the department store, may have seen something of themselves in Gracie Fields because she offered an attainable image of cinematic femininity.

Gracie Fields was not the only movie star used by department stores used to draw in female shoppers. Bon Marché certainly wished to promote the store through the appeal of the cinema and a year later it held a fashion show for clothes imitated from the latest films. 'Just like Marlene's: Film star's coat in a fashion parade. Fans of Marlene Dietrich can now buy a coat exactly like the one the famous actress is to wear in her latest film', reported the *Echo*.[96] Department stores exploited women's desires to imitate their favourite film stars during the 1930s and turned the department store into a form of pleasure in itself, perhaps even as an extension of the cinema. Glamour remained an effective selling tactic into the later 1930s. An invitation placed in the *Echo*, for example, summoned its readers to watch a mannequin parade in Bon Marché. 'A Symphony of Fashion', promised the advert: 'The lovely clothes, the clever grouping, and the graceful movement of the girls, combines to make this a really beautiful performance'.[97] These parades became very important because they offered women the opportunity to participate in the culture of the department store, without having to make a purchase. The emphasis was on fashion, described in this advert as 'a really beautiful performance'. Mannequin parades and similar events helped influence the link between shopping and leisure, and they also allowed women to appropriate fashionable identities through their participation.[98]

Cultures of glamour contributed to wider changes in retailing. Briggs argues 'a new retailing came into existence' between 1922 and 1939, and highlights Lewis's innovative policy of giving store managers the independence to run their own publicity campaigns after 1922.[99] Department stores in Liverpool and Manchester were certainly innovative, as they pursued energetic promotional campaigns that drew people into the city centre for leisure and pleasure. Bon Marché and George Henry Lee's benefited from ownership by Selfridges after 1918, and Harrods bought Kendal Milne in 1919, providing invaluable cash injections to the stores' marketing campaigns. All the stores were ambitious and their in-store events were very imaginative and inventive. 'Many changes were made' in George Henry Lee's, 'special events were run, which were opened by famous actors or actresses. Even bands were brought into the store to attract customers, and mannequin parades were another great attraction'.[100] Department store attractions aimed to bring customers through the shop doors. 'There is a lot of free entertainment to be had in the big shops', wrote a *Liverpolitan* journalist in 1935, 'demonstrations of this and that, a new way to make your hair curl ... an ingenious gadget for mending your stockings or your china.'[101] These descriptions suggest the stores were exciting and became places of amusement and pleasure in their own right without any explicit pressure to make purchases.

G. H. Lee's was notable for its extravagant in-store activities, which is perhaps unsurprising considering it was under Selfridge's ownership between the two world wars.[102] One former employee recalled, 'Advertising was carried out on a large scale, and considerable areas would be given over to the Advertising Department to present attractions of all kinds', including a bread-wrapping machine installed by a local bakery when free loaves were given away.[103] One Easter saw a menagerie of animals installed in the store, bringing chaos and amusement, as one of the penguins got lost in the store and because 'two lion clubs were frequently taken for walks around the store'.[104] Illusionists and magicians were also a regular feature in Lee's and another publicity event saw one hundred monkeys in a 'Monkey Village' set up in the store, 'Here the inhabitants played about on swings, and all the usual apparatus, to the delight of thousands of visitors and probably the customers.'[105] Interestingly, the promotional activities offered fun and pleasure but did not necessarily pressurize people into making purchases. Although the zoo did not promote the sale of clothes, it attracted people into the store and it seems department stores became popular sites of leisure interwar and the stores became something to consume in their own right, almost like a trip to the cinema. In their desire to draw large numbers of people into the stores, department store managers focused on attention-seeking, rather than product-selling, events and attractions. Interestingly, they chose attractions that appealed to the masses, rather than the wealthier classes. Marquis claimed that, at the same time, department stores moved towards protecting the interests of the working classes and one of his innovations was to introduce the Lewis's Bank in their stores. Motivated both by wanting to protect cash-carrying customers from pickpockets and by his dislike of hire-purchase, Marquis 'created a system of hire-purchase in reverse', which would offer customers far better value than any hire-purchase firm: 'I created a Bank and urged people to use it to save money and to gain interest on their savings, both of which they could, if they wished, use for purchases in the store.' Lewis's pioneered the use of female bank clerks and 'grew beyond my (Marquis) dreams and proved much value to our customers and gave a good profit to our firm'.[106] These innovations may also have been a strategy to counter the growth of the co-operative movement, which focused its appeal on working-class shoppers and aimed to provide a comprehensive service to its customers, including consumer protection and financial assistance.[107]

Although Marquis led the innovations in Liverpool, department stores in Manchester also used special promotional events in an attempt to draw in customers from a range of spending groups. During Civic Week, Kendal's department store hosted a mannequin parade that included the 'interesting innovation' of inexpensive items of clothing,

> To the woman of good taste but shallow purse a mannequin parade is often tantalising. She may delight in the frocks shown, but knows she cannot buy them. For once her needs were met. Some very charming day and evening frocks, neat costumes, and winter coats were shown which, if they did not rank as equals with the models, did not at any rate look like their poor relations.[108]

Later, in 1938, Kendal's staged a 'North Country Home' exhibition in their 'furnishing galleries' department. The event recreated a home within the store to advertise the store's collection of furnishings, including a 'wonderful exhibition of Modern Floral Decoration'.[109] Significantly, no advert appeared in the *Manchester Guardian* for the event and it seems the exhibition aimed its appeal at those from the lower spending groups. The event may have particularly targeted those who moved into the new municipal suburbs, like Wythenshawe, because it encouraged customers from lower spending groups to buy home furnishings. Kendal's marketing of the 'North Country Home' exhibition also drew on the image of the *Daily Mail's* Ideal Home Exhibition in the 1930s. Deborah Ryan argues the popularity of the Ideal Home Exhibition was born out of the aspirations of an emerging lower middle class, and reflected an age when 'class divisions were eroding, shifting and re-formulating'.[110] The new suburban dwellers helped shape a new mass customer market within Manchester by the later 1930s.

Conclusion

Kendal's 'North Country Home' event was typical of the new strategies employed by department stores in interwar Liverpool and Manchester. Their department stores increasingly presented themselves as cross-class sites of leisure and consumer culture through their shift in marketing strategies, which were a response to economic depression and urban transformation. For instance, an advertisement for Lewis's in 1932 claimed the store's appeal crossed social boundaries: 'LEWIS'S began by taking care of the needs of the working-classes – LEWIS'S is now a great popular Shopping Centre for all classes of the community', proclaimed the advert.[111] Similarly, Reece's guidebook to Manchester, published in 1939, also told all shoppers to go to Lewis's:

> A mecca to shoppers all over the country, is the city's most complete example of the modern store; for a generation the builders have never been long of the doorstep and the result is seen in a host of pioneer 'gadgets' and ideas, from moving staircases to cafeterias.[112]

Department store managers, particularly due to the pioneering work of Marquis at Lewis's and Selfridge as owner of Lee's and Bon Marché, pursued a deliberately populist marketing strategy by the late 1930s and sought to attract a broad customer base. By the late 1930s, shoppers from the highest spending groups no longer dominated the department stores in England's urban north and reflected a broader shift towards mass consumer culture.

The emergence of a populist culture of shopping was partly an implication of the investments made by municipal leaders in slum clearance, suburbanization, public transport, architecture and in disseminating new urban images. This investment provided the infrastructure for consumer culture to dominate the city centre and ensured more shoppers could travel easily into the city centre. Department store advertisements, their use of light and technology, fantastical and overcrowded shop windows all nurtured a consumer urban fantasy around the city centres. By the later 1930s, the city centres were closely associated with shopping and perceived as a place to consume and consume within, becoming important sites of leisure. Shops could not survive outside of the city centre due to the redevelopment of Liverpool and Manchester and, at the same time, department store managers need to broaden their customer base because of challenging economic conditions of the period. These developments contributed to the emergence of a modern shopping 'high street' that came to dominate Britain's retail culture for nearly a century.

The change in attitudes by department store managers towards potential customers also mirrored the shift in attitudes by municipal leaders to their electorate. Charles McGovern argues mass suffrage shaped consumer culture in America. 'If advertisers portrayed themselves as politicians then they saw consumers as citizens', argues McGovern, 'advertisers equated the consumer's dollars with the franchised citizens' vote. Purchasing was like voting, an expression of free and individual choice, a form of social and (usually) political activity.'[113] There are parallels with McGovern's analysis and the material offered here: just as local and national politicians sought to appeal to their new mass electorate, store managers also sought to attract customers in ways that transcended spending barriers.[114] As we shall see, Chapter 4 develops these themes and illustrates the impact of the new urban consumer culture for women, for whom the city became a site for the public performance of status and fashionable identities.

Performing Fashionable Selfhoods
in the Transformed City

Urban redevelopment contributed to the emergence of a vibrant culture of shopping in interwar Liverpool and Manchester. Their city centres became more closely associated with retail culture; however, due to the combination of economic pressures, the energy and innovation of those in charge of the larger department stores, and the new urban infrastructure, shops in the outer areas of the cities simply could not survive. At the same time, there was a more general democratization of glamour that contributed to the populist marketing strategies pursued by department stores. As George Orwell's *Road to Wigan Pier* famously depicted, on the whole, working-class people possessed greater access to consumer and cinematic culture during the decades following the First World War. He wrote,

> The two things that have probably made the greatest difference of all are the movies and the mass-production of cheap smart clothes since the war. ... You may have three halfpence in your pocket and not a prospect in the world, and only the corner of a leaky bedroom to go home to; but in your new clothes you can stand on the street corner, indulging in a private daydream of yourself as Clark Gable of Greta Garbo, which compensates you for a great deal. ... Whole sections of the working class who have been plundered of all they need are being compensated, in part, by cheap luxuries which mitigate the surface of life.[1]

Orwell's description of interwar cultures of fashion and glamour reflected wider shifts in retail culture. As Chapter 3 demonstrated, businessmen and shop owners in Liverpool and Manchester pursued deliberately populist marketing strategies in response to economic depression. The process was part of a wider democratization of consumer and leisure culture that seemed to fascinate and frustrate contemporary observers, such as Orwell, in equal measure.[2] More recently, historians have acknowledged the positive role that consumer culture and the democratization of glamour played in the lives of working-class women, offering them agency and self-fulfilment.[3] Glamour signalled a new form of femininity that stressed independence and confidence, which challenged traditional models of womanhood.[4] Yet glamour also represented rebellion and the fashionably dressed working-class woman could be a problematic figure who embodied wider anxieties about gender and consumer culture in interwar Britain.[5]

Women's access to cultures of glamour emerged hand in hand alongside new employment opportunities for working-class women, particularly.[6] These changes coincided with important technological developments that aided a democratization of glamour and, perhaps most notably, the mass availability of sewing machine permitted women with little spending power to obtain fashionable clothes, especially through home dressmaking.[7] At the same time, popular culture offered women new, glamorous and aspirational images, which, 'playing on fantasy and desire, enabled women to *imagine* an end to domestic drudgery and chronic want'.[8] The transformed cityscapes of Liverpool and Manchester gave women opportunities to perform the aspirational images that they saw in the cinema, in novels and in advertisements. There are similarities with studies of working-class women in New York, where 'putting on finery, promenading the streets, and staying late at amusement resorts became an important cultural style for many working women'.[9] The transformed city centres of Liverpool and Manchester provided women with opportunities to perform fashionable identities in ways that obscured class divisions, which reflected a wider culture of using the streets for leisure in nineteenth- and twentieth-century urban communities.[10] However, a key feature of the localized urban modernities in these cities lay in the way the local state valued women's roles as shoppers, and celebrated and encouraged women's engagement in shopping culture. Urban transformation contributed to a populist, cross-class space for women, where shopping and being fashionable was a public and performative act that had implications for self-identity.

Here, historical material from the Mass Observation Archive, alongside material from the local press and department store archives, is used to provide a case study through which to explore women's engagement with the transformed urban environment. Although much of the Mass Observation material focuses on Bolton, a town north-west of Manchester, it illuminates the relationship between Liverpool and Manchester's urban transformation and consumer culture in a number of ways. First, it shows how the redevelopment of Liverpool and Manchester shaped the consumer and retail culture of smaller towns. Second, it reveals how women from Bolton travelled to larger cities, especially

Manchester, for the experience of shopping in more glamorous shops, even if that did not involve making purchases and focused on the enjoyment of shop windows. Finally, the rich material from Mass Observation offers a detailed insight into the meanings of shopping and fashion to both younger and older working-class women. Used in conjunction with an analysis of Liverpool and Manchester's press, it permits a re-evaluation of women's engagement with urban space and places working-class women at the centre of accounts of the modern provincial city.

An 'anthropology of ourselves': The Mass Observation Archive

Women's interest in shopping and retail culture intrigued Mass Observation so much that it dedicated a great deal of research attempting to understand the culture, particularly in Manchester and the surrounding Lancashire towns. Mass Observation was a social research movement, which existed in its original form from 1937 to 1949. Established in 1937 by Charles Madge, a poet and journalist, Humphrey Jennings, a poet and documentary film-maker, and Tom Harrisson, an ornithologist and anthropologist, Mass Observation intended to create an 'anthropology of ourselves'. There were two main centres of research: a study of 'Worktown' and a national panel. Worktown provided a very detailed study of the Lancashire town of Bolton, fifteen miles north-west of Manchester. It covered several aspects of working-class life, including leisure, food, budgets, shopping, superstition and religious faith, most of which were researched in 1937–40. Mass Observation chose Bolton because of the town's significant level of unemployment and high proportion of working-class inhabitants. Bolton was a town in decline: in 1939, its population was 170,000, decreasing by 1,000 a year; 11 per cent of registered workers were unemployed; and half of its population were employed in the cotton industry.[11] Researchers undertook the Worktown study through a combination of observations, photographs and interviews, and by 'following' subjects, although this was not without problems as they faced hostility and ridicule from local inhabitants. The researchers complained they had been thrown out of pubs, made to blush by flirtatious mill girls and chastised by suspicious housewives.[12] Despite the challenges faced by researchers, the material offers a rich insight into working-class culture. As a town in the Greater Manchester area, Mass Observation's study of Bolton is unrivalled in depicting the impact of Manchester's transformation in the wider area and illuminates how women's shopping practices were shaped by the revitalized shopping and consumer cultures. Alongside the Worktown materials, the national panels also provide rich and revealing material as they allowed Mass Observation to dispatch questionnaires on subjects of their choice, including clothes and personal appearance, and attitudes to war, or to ask them to keep diaries for a particular day: a total of 2,847 individuals replied to at least one directive during the period 1937–45. In addition, two hundred of these people kept diaries, and Mass Observation had a total of five hundred diarists during the Second World War.[13]

Like Orwell's extended stay in Wigan, Bolton attracted Mass Observation's researchers for political reasons. They 'were motivated by curiosity about the proletarian North, as well as by guilt over mass unemployment. It was not a *very* political way of expressing social concern, and its context was general unease about where modern society was heading, as Hitler, Franco and Mussolini strode on.'[14] Their researchers tended to be Oxbridge-educated and politically left of centre.[15] These political concerns shaped the movement's choice of research subjects and the researchers' interpretations of what they observed. The expectations and social identities of middle-class observers influenced the findings of Mass Observation's investigations, particularly in Bolton and Blackpool (also part of the Worktown study). As Peter Gurney's study of working-class sexuality asserts for example, they 'largely misunderstood the sexual activities and rituals that they mapped out so assiduously'.[16] There are similarities between Gurney's findings on Mass Observation's misrepresentation of working-class sexuality and their attitude towards consumer culture. For example, when researchers visited Blackpool, they were bemused by holiday-makers' behaviour – writing 'whatever they get away from it is not shops and shopping'.[17] Mass Observation was surprised as over 50 per cent of inhabitants only earned between £2.10 and £5 a week and 35 per cent earned less than £2.10 a week, but shopping played a substantial role in the lives of those who lived in Bolton.[18] Mass Observation's findings in Blackpool inspired the researchers' return to Bolton in order to look at shopping habits more closely and 'see what part shops play there in communal life'.[19]

The upper-middle-class backgrounds and political allegiances of Mass Observation often meant that they did not understand what they found, particularly in their Worktown study. By implication, Mass Observation 'failed to take working-class selfhood seriously … alternative identities and subjectivities were either ignored or simply observed, with varying degrees of empathy'.[20] Mass Observers seemed particularly baffled by the role of fashionable dress in their subjects' lives and in 1941, their study of clothes rationing argued the majority of the British public felt pressured to be fashionably dressed before the Second World War, which was 'something of a strain … both psychologically and economically'.[21] The report claimed, 'A good deal of clothes spending is not determined by *necessity* so much as by prestige and social pressure motives. "Fashion" is only the most obvious example of the general tendency to dress for the benefit of others'.[22] Mass Observation's attitude towards fashion, glamour and consumer culture mirrored that of Orwell, Walter Greenwood and other leftist intellectuals who particularly condemned young women's attempts to dress glamorously on small incomes.[23] Women did devote a great deal of time and effort to shopping and fashion, alongside significant financial and emotional investment. However, this tells us far more about women's ability to define and negotiate their own forms of identity and social status than Mass Observation or other contemporary critics recognized: it is through consumer culture that 'the everyday lives of large numbers of ordinary women were most deeply affected by the process of modernity'.[24]

Fashionable women as agents of economic regeneration

Interwar consumer culture appealed to women of all ages and classes through a variety of mediums but especially the press.[25] The press increasingly catered for women specifically and there was explosion in articles and magazines aimed at women and girls. Notable titles such as *Woman* (1937), *Woman's Own* (1932) and *Good Housekeeping* (1922) emerged, alongside the more working-class titles such as *Peg's Paper* (1919). With a focus on glamour, fashion and the cinema, 'women's pages' and the women's press told young girls and women of all ages how to dress, wear cosmetics, what to wear to impersonate their favourite movie stars and, perhaps most importantly, how to use these skills to find and keep a male admirer.[26] As Chapter 3 demonstrated, shopping and consumer culture permeated the press in Liverpool and Manchester. Alongside the proliferation of department store advertisements in the local press, there also emerged a greater interest in fashion and dress that mirrored broader national trends and the rise of the 'women's press'.

There was a significant shift in attitudes from the local press towards shops and the women who used them, which seemed to appear hand in hand both with the rise of the 'women's press' more generally and Liverpool and Manchester's new retail culture. In Manchester, attitudes towards shopping moved from being ambiguous to celebratory as the press understood its role in economic regeneration. In 1925, for example, the *Manchester Guardian Yearbook* depicted the vitality of Manchester's shops but claimed, 'Manchester never consciously attempted to become a shopping centre.'[27] Similarly, the Civic Week Handbook of 1926 highlighted Manchester's vibrant shopping culture but emphasized its hierarchical nature, describing the city 'as carefully divided into shopping districts as it is into Council wards. Each district has its own speciality and its own following.' Stretford Road, for example, was 'for people who have to ponder over every penny spent', whereas Deansgate was home to the exclusive shops for wealthier shoppers.[28] That said, shops and the women who shopped in them were an integral part of Manchester's Civic Week in 1926 and, as we have already seen, shops hosted special events. The press not only helped to promote these events but the *Manchester Guardian* also included an article in all its issues during Civic Week titled 'Civic Week Shopping', which focused on the changing fashions and women's remarkable ability to keep up with them.[29] The articles also carried an important message, which stressed women's role as consumer-citizen. 'No Manchester woman', the *Manchester Guardian* explained, 'need set out to buy a particular article and come home without it.'[30]

Manchester's Civic Week appears to have triggered a greater interest in shopping and retail culture. Urban commentators increasingly began to recognize women's specific role within the emerging consumer landscapes: The *Manchester Guardian Yearbook* of 1927 portrayed the Manchester woman, who

> comes in from the suburbs ... not necessarily to buy, but only to stroll round admiring the window displays and the splendid collections of goods inside. She knows, as she looks, that she is seeing the very best that the season can offer her and that, whether her wants are ambitious or modest, she will find as wide as selection and good value as could be given anywhere in the country. ... The prosperous woman can buy everything she or her household needs, whether it be a Chinese lacquer bird-cage, a bottle of wine or a Paris hat. Here all the beautiful produce of other countries is gathered together and every new fancy and luxury is displayed.[31]

The extract's enthusiasm towards the women who travelled in to the city centre from the suburbs but 'not necessarily to buy' is striking. It represents these shoppers as symbols of Manchester's cosmopolitanism, where a woman could find goods from around the world. Similarly, the *Yearbook of 1928* described a woman returning from a round-the-world trip, bringing goods back from every place she visited. On her return to the city, 'refreshed and sunburnt, sets out to look patronisingly at the shops. By the end of an hour she has found in their windows all the foreign novelties that she has brought laboriously home with her.'[32] By the late 1920s therefore, the local press depicted Manchester as a cosmopolitan city in the sense it was international in the diversity of goods available for women (and seemingly only women) to buy.

Women shopping were also a source of fun and amusement within the press, which at times masked anxieties about the role of consumer culture in women's lives. Liverpool's monthly magazine, *Liverpolitan*, epitomized this ambiguous attitude through a semi-regular column called 'Lucille of Liverpool'. Penned by an anonymous author, the tongue-in-cheek column reveals both the centrality of shopping and consumer culture in women's lives by the early 1930s and also the duality of gender identity as women could move between the roles of housewife at home and fashionable girl-about-town:

> **November 10th** Receive brochure from George Henry Lee's, assuring me that this is the time to shop, as prices were at the lowest and bargains could never be repeated ... suggest to David that 'this is the time to shop' who looks unmoved, and says he must be going. Am aware of certain unwifely thoughts, and viciously decide to take the wherewithal out of the housekeeping money, which means dealing at Irwin's, shepherd's pie every Wednesday ... but am undeterred.
>
> **November 12th** Spend highly pleasurable morning at Lee's ... I buy horribly expensive gown. Visualise the effect on David of (a) the gown; (b) its price.
>
> **November 13th** Ring up butcher and cancel order for meat on Wednesday, also MacSymous, to say that we shall be out of town for the rest of the month. Transfer order to Irwin's. [33]

Lucille's diary was a light-hearted, satirical representation of women's attitude towards shopping and the extract above suggests women would reduce their spending on their husband's food in favour of gowns from department stores. Yet its sense of mockery and anxiety indicates that the press perceived women as losing all sense of wifely responsibilities when they entered the city and lured into making purchases.[34]

Stories like Lucille's diary, which depicted women's extreme enthusiasm for shopping, may not be an extreme exaggeration. A 2006 exhibition at the

Liverpool Walker Art Gallery, 'A Liverpool Lady's Wardrobe', suggested fashion was central to at least one woman's experiences of the interwar city. The gallery received a donation of seven hundred items of clothing (many of which were unworn and still with price tags attached), owned by Emily Tinne, a doctor's wife who lived in Liverpool from 1906 until her death in 1966. The curators stress the donation 'does not reflect the true nature of Emily's buying', as many items were unsuitable for exhibition.[35] Much of the collection consisted of clothes Emily bought in the 1920s and 1930s, particularly from the department stores Bon Marché and Owen Owen. Emily Tinne was almost certainly exceptional in that she kept her clothes until her death and could afford to own numerous fur coats and a 'huge collection of hats', many that remained unworn.[36] Nevertheless, since purchases were not always necessary, Emily may well not have been exceptional in her love of shopping and fashion. Her daughters remember 'their mother going shopping almost every afternoon, much as one pursues a hobby'.[37] Although shopping as a hobby required time, it did not necessarily require spending power, and, as we shall see, enjoyed by women without Emily Tinne's disposable income. Emily Tinne and Lucille of Liverpool suggest that compulsive shopping habits were not unimportant issues in the 1930s transformed city.

The influence of America and of Hollywood in particular was also evident in the local press. In 1937, the *Liverpolitan* published an article titled 'Oh Miss 1937, Please Stop Trying to Look Like a Film Star!', which called for women in the city to stop copying Greta Garbo and Ginger Rodgers. 'Do you suppose … that they achieved world-wide fame through looking like anyone else? Of course they didn't. They dramatized their own styles.'[38] The *Liverpolitan* called on women to make the most of their own features and find their own glamorous look, arguing it would save them from changing their appearance every time a new film star appeared. At the same time, however, local discourse around women who enjoyed shopping and glamour contributed to new images of Liverpool more generally. As we saw in Chapter 1, the Lord Mayor of Liverpool made an important civic visit to New York in 1931. During the visit, the Lord Mayor's wife declared the similarities between the two cities when it came to women and shopping, although she conceded that the women of New York were 'more glamorous' than those in Liverpool.[39] Images of women shopping and enjoying fashion were important because they helped to forge a close association between the city centres, the new retail culture and women's local citizenship, turned shopping into a public and performative act.

'One of the most tantalising and engrossing pastimes known to women':[40] Shopping as a public and performative act

Women's apparent preoccupation with shopping was not confined to the pages of the local press and Mass Observation was especially struck by the centrality of shopping and consumer culture to the lives of the women they studied in Bolton and Manchester. In 1939, while undertaking a study of shopping habits in Manchester, one middle-aged woman caught the eye of a Mass Observation researcher. Described as dressed neatly in black with a hat with veil, grey stockings, black gloves and black handbag and considered by the researcher to be working class, the woman, the researcher noted, 'looks very distinguished', and her activities were recorded as she moved around the city centre:

> [She] glimpses at Nasby's Draper, Market St. Has a look at Johnson summer frocks. … Looks at Marks and Spencer window handbags and in Marks and Spencer looks at all stalls in passing … goes to stockings, short look at them, then slips, takes some of the artificial silk vests in her hands, opens them … goes on, interested in blouses and comes to frocks, goes on … looks at blue shoes and goes to exit, looking once more at stockings.[41]

According to the observations made by the researcher, despite spending several hours in (mainly clothes) shops, the woman only bought some buttons, toilet roll and boot polish. It seems the public role of shopping lay in its appearance, rather than the act itself, and women could participate without making actual purchases. Mass Observation made similar observations in Bolton and, in a study of Woolworths, one researcher noted there was 'little actual buying. People just wander round, looking'.[42]

Statistics from George Henry Lee's in Liverpool support these findings by Mass Observation. Table 4.1 illustrates the growing difference between the numbers of actual sales and the numbers of people who came into the store in the period 1925–36. For the period of 1925/26, the difference between sales and customers stood at 168,748 and, by the period 1934/35, this difference increased to 445,106. The number of visitors rose steadily over the period but the actual sales fell. A graph best illustrates the increasing difference between visitors and customers, shown in Figure 4.1.

Table 4.1 G. H. Lee's sales and customers, 1925–36

Year	Sales	Customers
1925/6	596,375	765,123
1928/9	561,802	783,450
1932/33	436,755	858,104
1934/35	452,639	897,745
1935/36	448,548	853,757

Source: John Lewis Archive Box 180/3/a.

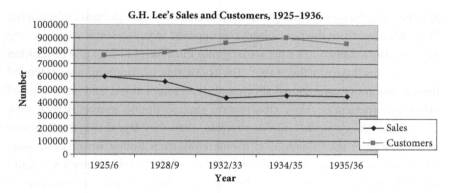

Figure 4.1 Graph depicting gap between customers and sales at G. H. Lee's, 1925–36
Source: John Lewis Archive Box 180/3/a.

According to the *Manchester Guardian*, the idea of a woman looking, but not buying, was a common one and supported by the shops themselves;

> The large, modern shop is furnished like a palace. It is light and airy, with wide rooms and thick, soft carpets. It has lifts and comfortable stairs, restaurants, writing-rooms, and lounges, the woman coming in from the country or suburbs may use it as a club if she wishes. ... That in the course of the day she buys only a card of darning wool or even nothing at all does not worry the people who own the shop. They like her to feel that she can stroll in at her pleasure and see the pretty things they have collected there.[43]

Alongside the statistics from G. H. Lees, this extract suggests that the broader technological and marketing developments outlined in Chapter 3 transformed retail experience in Liverpool and Manchester, which helped to manifest the public and performative nature of shopping for women. The smartly dressed working-class woman who 'looks very distinguished', as noted by Mass

Observation in Manchester, was typical of the new identities women could perform within the transformed urban centres.

Mass Observation identified the important social role shopping had for women:

> The working-class wife's activities outside her own home are not very many. ... So that when the wife does go out of the house, coming into contact with people outside home-circles, it represents a means of social intercourse for her, and it is this significance that the journey to the shop, whether one in the next street or in the centre of the town, assumes.[44]

Significantly, the report highlighted the particular social importance of shopping for housewives from the new suburbs, as opposed to young single wage-earning girls, usually assumed to be the social group most likely to engage with fashion and shopping between the wars.[45] The social role of shopping also extended beyond the more aspirational shops and department stores and encompassed everyday experiences. Mass Observation studied Bolton market, which took place three times a week, and was shocked when they found two-thirds of one hundred houses they visited over a mile away from Bolton town centre were empty on market day. Mass Observation concluded that the market 'cannot simply be regarded as a place for buying and selling. People meet each other, chat, stroll about looking at and fingering, and listen to the talk of the barkers, particularly those selling cures, or dealing in magic'.[46]

Shopping without making actual purchases was fundamental to the performative nature and social role of shopping by the 1930s. One woman showed a Mass Observation researcher her shopping list, which included tea towels, sheets and other household goods. The researcher noted that the women said 'she would need a coat, but does not want to buy it but only have a look round.'[47] A Day Survey completed by a housewife in Burnley, Lancashire, in 1937, shows the centrality of 'just looking' and she explained how a typical Saturday would involve two trips to the town shopping centre (returning at lunch to cook for the family). The survey also shows that the Saturday trip to the shops gave her valuable opportunities for eavesdropping, which was, surprisingly, fundamental to her enjoyment of the day. First of all she listened to two ladies in conversation as she travelled on the bus to town and told Mass Observation they were talking about leaving their 'new houses which were a disappointment'. Later that morning,

> Went shop-gazing in main-streets. Returned 10.45 to market-square now busier – smartly dressed people came in cars and bought vegetables, fruit etc. ...

Listened to what conversation possible whilst shopping. ... Went into Public
Reading room (deserted) to look at magazines.[48]

Her testimony is revealing because it shows that the act of shopping was about
seeing, being seen and listening, as both an active and a passive actor. In 1939,
one Mass Observer noted similar findings when they joined a housewife (listed
as 'M') in Bolton on her Saturday shopping trip. The researcher was bemused by
the amount of looking, touching and talking that the day involved:

M said now we should have coffee at Collinson's what is the usual proceeding.
What we did. But we did not talk very much about the coat or other purchases,
besides one or two remark that we did quite well and had a satisfied feeling.[49]

Interestingly, the researcher notes that the performative aspect of shopping did
not end when the housewife returned home and that she was excited about
leaving the café:

After 30 minutes we went home, looking forward to unpack, and see how things
looked. What we did with great pleasure showing out thing to the people at
home. M. says that she always likes unpacking and to show things at home.[50]

The material from Mass Observation thus shows how shopping gave women
not only pleasure but also status and agency. For the housewife joined on her
Saturday shopping trip by a Mass Observer, returning home to show family the
goods and, perhaps most importantly, receiving their admiration and praise, was
an important aspect of the day itself.

The public and performative role of shopping meant that women took extra
care and attention towards the way they dressed on days when they visited the
shops. As Mass Observation noted, the weekly trip to town was a special occasion
for women: 'Women have usually two shopping baskets, one for every day and one
for town shopping. On Friday the weaver comes out with very nice baskets to the
mill because they go shopping in the afternoon.'[51] Women wore their finest and
most fashionable clothes when shopping, which was one of the most important
aspects of the performative role of shopping. One female respondent told Mass
Observation that it was the opinion of strangers that mattered most: '"Other
people" are basically "strangers." It doesn't matter so much at home.'[52] Returning
to the earlier extract, the Mass Observation researcher noted the working-class
woman who walked around Manchester's shops was dressed in black, including
a hat and veil, grey stockings, black gloves and black handbag, suggesting the
woman had taken great care in dressing for her afternoon at the shops.[53] The

Burnley housewife's Day Survey for Mass Observation also noted that when she went to look at the shops on Saturday afternoon, 'the market square was now busy with work people (half-holiday) in best clothes doing shopping.'[54] Responses to Mass Observation's national Directive Response on personal appearance show how seriously women took dressing for a shopping trip to town. One young teacher from Liverpool, for example, told Mass Observation that she dressed carefully for her shopping trips to the city. She went 'wearing my best – (on) Saturday mornings when I shop with friends' and claimed, 'I generally wear my second best for theatres etc. and important visits.'[55] Although the respondent does not explain why she felt the need to wear her finest clothing, it seems it was a way to become absorbed into the exotic culture of retail the young teacher and her friends ostensibly consumed.

It seems that by dressing up in their finest clothing for a weekly trip into town, these women sought to see and be seen within the transformed city centres. As we saw in Chapter 3, shop windows became increasingly extravagant and shop window gazing became an essential part of women's shopping experience. Mass Observation's study of Bolton offers some sense of just how much shop window-gazing took place. After a period of observation of shop windows in Bolton, Mass Observation researchers recorded forty-nine people staring into shop windows and not making a purchase, fifteen people staring into windows and making a purchase, and only ten going into a shop to make a purchase without first window gazing.[56] On one level, shop windows were significant because they allowed those who felt too poor and shabby to enter the stores and gave 'pleasure to those who love beauty whether they have money to buy it or whether they can only look and pass on.'[57] Mass Observation noted that women window-shopped in places where they could not afford to make purchases, such as Mrs Jackson, the wife of a mill worker, 'keen on fashions, and looks around in shop windows' and 'likes looking in Manchester shops, but prefers to shop in Bolton.'[58] For Mrs Jackson, the shops in Manchester gave her pleasure and enjoyment but she made her actual purchases in Bolton, which was probably cheaper but did not have the grandiose department stores as cities such as Manchester did.

It is also apparent that for the fashionably dressed shopper, shop windows had an active role in permitting access to the new consumer culture. For many women, shop windows directly informed their shopping choices. One housewife told Mass Observation that she and her daughter 'will go round the shop windows and compare, a week or two before they buy', allowing them to think carefully about what to purchase.[59] The depth of research and careful consideration over which purchases to make is particularly striking among middle-aged housewives, for whom shop windows was one of the key ways they assessed what they would buy. As the Burnley housewife, aged forty-eight, reported to Mass Observation,

> I always study fashion articles, advertisements and women's magazines to keep my ideas up to date. I never discuss with friends, but I take notes on what well-to-do people wear, and notice … of the Queen or Duchess of Kent as naturally the fashion houses who dress these people know what is coming in. I take every chance of studying the displays in the best shops, though I could not afford to patronize them. The fashion in this locality lags behind the fashion in a large city like Manchester so I like to see the shops there.[60]

As the housewife reveals, the costs of fashion meant that it took careful consideration and research when choosing what to buy and that the larger city stores were the most useful in informing her spending choices. Significantly, their use of shop windows in Manchester shows that cultures of fashion and consumerism that emerged in the two decades following 1918, which historians tend to associate with young, single women, did not necessarily exclude older housewives.[61] As the material from Mass Observation shows, shop windows opened cultures of fashion up to these women because they could spend time, perhaps between buying household items and undertaking more practical tasks, informing their decisions about what to buy but often making their purchases in cheaper shops. Crucially, as both the Burnley housewife and Mrs Jackson from Bolton both tell us, the spectacular shop window displays in Manchester city centre influenced what they bought back in the own town centres, which were likely to be far cheaper. For housewives, therefore, shop windows were key in permitting them to balance their desire to be fashionable with their need to be frugal, and they may be able to incorporate window-shopping into other housewifely duties.

For younger women with fewer responsibilities, shop windows were even more central in influencing their shopping decisions. As one housewife informed Mass Observation, her daughters 'didn't bother to read any women's papers or women's pages, but got most of their ideas by looking in the shops'.[62] Even for the young Liverpool teacher with a rather generous budget of £25 a year, her purchasing decisions strongly relied on what she saw in shop windows:

> Decision as to what to buy – this needs a great deal of thought and review of the current contents of my wardrobe. I must choose something suitable in colour and style. I then study shop windows – Bold St here is the poshest shopping street and Bon Marché the best shop. I study the windows carefully for style and

price etc. I also watch the magazines – notable *Good Housekeeping, Woman's Fair* and *Woman and Beauty.* If these occur conveniently I attend mannequin parades. I balance my accounts and count up my assets and decide how much I can spend. … I take a friend (trusted and tasteful) to tell me about back fits etc. My friend is a great help for buying clothes as she has good taste. I discuss styles and prices with her and my mother and other friends.[63]

At the same time, it seems that shop windows also allowed women to imagine another identity for themselves, as one article on Liverpool's shopping culture revealed:

Shop window gazing is one of the most tantalising and engrossing pastimes known to women … we, in imagination, don the gowns, the ravishing hats and the luxurious underwear that drape the lay figures. … We enjoy vicariously all the pleasures of possession.[64]

Shop windows thus shared similarities with the appeal of the cinema, magazines and novels, which all thrived between the two world wars and offered women new opportunities to imagine and perform different selfhoods.[65] Figure 4.2 depicts men and women staring intently at one of the window displays in Manchester's Kendal Milne department store. The display seems to have

Figure 4.2 Window shoppers outside Messrs Kendal, Milne & Co in Deansgate, Manchester, 27 August 1931
Source: Getty Editorial Image 99174504.

attracted more men than most windows, because it contained sitting room furniture and more likely to have been a joint-purchase than just fashion or smaller decorative items. The image gives some sense of the size of the windows and their popularity among shoppers as they appear to scrutinize the display closely and deliberate with their companion, if they have one. For women, shop windows and the department stores that were home to them offered the images of glamorous femininity that they sought to obtain through cheaper means, which had important implications for the forms of selfhood that they performed within the transformed urban centres.

Fashion and status in the transformed city

Dressing fashionably was closely associated with the public and performative importance of shopping. Women's investment in their physical appearance contributed to their status by the 1930s and, more importantly, represented a form of self-identity defined by women themselves. Respondents to Mass Observation on their 1939 Directive on Personal Appearance revealed the ambivalent feelings women had towards fashion and dress, often claiming not to care and showing that they did indeed care very much. One 25-year-old typist from Liverpool admitted, 'I have two distinct moods with regard to personal appearance. Sometimes I want to be smart and well turned out, and then on the other occasions I see no virtue of being dressed up. ... Why can't everyone just dress for comfort?'[66] Yet she also admitted how much time and investment she made in her personal appearance and accepted how much she thought it mattered:

> I think that one's appearance does matter. People, unconsciously, judge one by appearance. ... Personally, I spend as much as I can afford on clothes and make up but, to my mind, it is not one spends on these things as much as what one chooses ... I go to any amount of trouble to match accessories etc., and spend lots of my spare time going round the shops to see where I can get exactly what I want. This is where the rub comes in. I know what I want, but I cannot always afford to pay for it.[67]

The typist herself was shocked when she realized just how much time and expense she invested in her personal appearance. She confessed,

> Since the beginning of this year I have kept a record of the amount I have spent on make-up, and it averages (much to my astonishment) at 2/- per week, which

seems quite an appreciable amount reckoned over the whole year. So far as time is concerned, I estimate I spend about half an hour three times a day over my face.[68]

The testimony gives some sense of just how much time and effort women invested in their appearance by the late 1930s.

Testimony from older women echoed the young typist's confessions and ambivalent attitudes towards personal appearance. A 47-year-old single teacher from the Wirral, near Liverpool, also began her answer to Mass Observation's questionnaire on personal appearance denying that it had any bearing on her life at all. 'I take the minimum trouble and expense to achieve' a well-groomed look, she explained, because of

> Lack of means and also because I do not find my personal appearance at all engrossing, whereas many other things are. Lack of means make it difficult to maintain the standard I would prefer ... I do not use cosmetics – I haven't time for what I regard as a trifle. It simply never occurs to me to make up an artificial appearance.[69]

The teacher claimed that her mind was too preoccupied with work to think much about her appearance, yet further on in the questionnaire she admitted to spending an increasing amount of time on her hair:

> A well-groomed head of hair I think is an asset socially. The appearance of the hair and the dressing of it makes for a pleasant or unpleasant appearance of face and whole head, and thus it is a factor in sex appeal. A well-groomed head is certainly a more comfortable one and the feel comfortable and well-groomed does add to ones sense of self-respect.[70]

The testimony is revealing because it shows that women who deemed themselves beyond the realm of fashion and glamour were still anxious about their personal appearance. The middle-aged teacher was able to find status by participating in some form of fashion, in this case by focusing on her hair, rather than the more showy fashions of dress and make-up. The reference to 'sex appeal' is interesting because although she is aware of looking appealing to the opposite sex, it seems her own self-respect is the most important factor in caring about her appearance. As the Burnley housewife we encountered earlier explained, she found 'clothes have a slight tonic effect but I do not trouble much about their effect on others so long as I am satisfied with them'.[71] For older women therefore, clothing and personal appearance were more about self-fulfilment but they were reluctant to admit any concerns about the ways in which others thought about the way they dressed or looked.

Although the testimony of younger women showed that they admitted to being more concerned about the approval of others, they did not confess that that they sought the approval of men. The young Liverpool typist was explicit in her explanation: 'Personally I don't dress to please the male sex, because my experience is that men never know precisely what you are wearing. They get the general idea – you either look nice or you don't, but can't say why.'[72] Although the typist did admit she knew what to wear to attract male attention if needed and confessed to wearing a white collar to tease her male colleagues:

> They don't notice the dress – the collar does the trick: give me a white collar! The same thing applies to a transparent blouse – although perhaps in this case it's easier to analyse the reaction. A transparent blouse will keep you busy all morning, dealing with the visitors to your desk.'[73]

Despite this mischievous confession, the typist explained that male attention was not the motivation behind her dedication to her personal appearance: 'No, I confess I dress to please myself and annoy other women. They are such catty creatures, most of them.'[74] The young Liverpool teacher responded similarly to the same directive:

> I love wearing new clothes because I feel smart and confident in their good taste. A new outfit generally acts as a tonic, because if I still feel fed up I don't think about it in the interest of choosing make-up and accessories. ... When dressed I hold a sort of mannequin parade, I say it is to prove if my slip shows but really it is for approval. *(On Prize Day at her school there was great competition with other teachers over clothes)*, an occasion for much mutual admiration and some veiled sarcasm. Prize Day was also an occasion for trying clothes and their effect on men. Most of them pretend to be oblivious to them but it's surprising how much nicer they are when they approve of your outfit.[75]

As both young women acknowledged, dressing to gain the attention of men was amusing and a source of entertainment but dressing for the attention of women was serious and took considerable time and effort. The young typist's concern about her appearance was driven, in part, to 'annoy other women' because she recognized people were judged by what they looked like. Likewise, the young teacher enjoyed investing in her appearance both because it made her feel better about herself and because of the approval of others it attracted.

Both the typist and young teacher were part of a generation of women who accessed consumer culture through their experiences of employment: 69 per cent of women and girls aged fifteen to twenty-four years were in paid employment in the 1930s.[76] Although representations of interwar Britain often stress a north–south divide, there is evidence to suggest that there 'was also a sexual division', as men experienced unemployment and women enjoyed employment and the new consumer culture it permitted.[77] Helena Forrester's autobiographical writings about life in Liverpool in the 1930s described girls working from the age of fourteen who enjoyed a few crucial years of affluence. Helena was excluded from the consumer culture other girls accessed as teenage workers and consumers:

> They were cheap labour and at the age of sixteen they would often be unemployed, like their elder sisters, but in the meantime they were frequently the most affluent members of their household, with money to spend in Woolworth's on cosmetics and rhinestone jewellery. I envied them their neat, black, work dresses and, even more, their best Sunday coats and hats and high-heeled shoes. They never spoke to me, except sometimes to jeer at my rags.[78]

Forrester was atypical because she had been born a middle-class girl, whose family went bankrupt and were plunged into poverty, yet Forrester's articulation of her social alienation and her exclusion from being able to dress fashionably like her peers is revealing. Forrester's experience supports recent historical research that emphasizes the social isolation felt by young women who could not afford new clothes or trips to the cinema.[79]

As the evidence from older women to Mass Observation showed, the interest in fashion and appearance was by no means limited to young women. It seems that many women were competitive in finding and wearing the most fashionable clothes that they could. The owner of a clothes shop in Bolton told Mass Observation that most women in the town worked hard to be fashionable because it enhanced their social status:

> If you sold a customer something and they were well satisfied once upon a time they would tell their neighbours. Not today. They would exaggerate the price and say that they got it from somewhere else. A woman bought an overcoat here at 7/6. She told me that a friend asked her where she had got it from and she said she had got it from the Co-op and paid 30- for it.[80]

The shop owner suggests women were competitive in their quest to be fashionable, going so far as to deceiving others over where and how they obtained their clothes. They perhaps did not want to be imitated, or may have wanted others to perceive their clothes as being more expensive than they actually were. Such competitive, and almost duplicitous strategies, were typical in the ways in which women of modest means successfully imitated the glamorous images of fashionable women that they saw inside department stores and within shop window displays.

Becoming a fashionable woman

In Liverpool, Manchester and the surrounding towns, women's significant concern when choosing clothes, thinking about their personal appearance or balancing their budgets, was fashion. The young Liverpool teacher told Mass Observation: 'Am I well dressed? I consider I am because my clothes are good, fashionable and carefully chosen to match each other without being in the extremes of fashion.'[81] Although the Burnley housewife told Mass Observation, 'I do *not* think myself well-dressed', she explained her priorities when choosing clothes to purchase focused on fashion: 'I spend a *little* on a few things and have frequent changes. If one buys an expensive thing to make it last, the length of coats and skirts changes or something else in fashion alters so it is no use spending much on any article.'[82] These women did not mention respectability or smartness as something they looked for in clothes, rather fashion and being fashionably dressed was their paramount concern.

The concern with being fashionable very clearly shaped where and how these women acquired their clothes. Perhaps surprisingly, the concern with being fashionable turned women away from making any significant purchases in the annual sales periods shops held, the largest being in January. Mass Observation's survey on the January sales in Bolton, undertaken in 1939, showed that people did not perceive them as useful opportunities to obtain clothes cheaply. In contrast, respondents to the Mass Observation questionnaire claimed the Sales were occasions for curiosity and leisure, but considered the clothes on sale unfashionable and therefore undesirable. The questionnaire asked three questions:

- Did you save money in order to shop at the sales?
- Did you go to sales to pick up bargains, without knowing exactly what?
- Did you wait for the sales to buy any particular thing?[83]

Mass Observation's archived material show the overwhelming response to all questions was no.[84] At the same time, Mass Observation found 62.4 per cent of shops with Sales in January were clothing and shoe shops, and the Sales were very much concentrated in the city centre.[85] The January Sales may, therefore, have been part of the broader culture of shopping as a leisure pursuit, rather than as a rational strategy of purchase.

Mass Observation's report on the Sales concluded: 'Trading at Sales time has developed into a combat between the experience of the woman shopper and the knowledge of the shopkeeper. The woman will rarely admit that she has been beaten.'[86] Mass Observation's findings undermine the stereotypical image of the ruthless and duplicitous shopkeeper, who seduced gullible women into making unnecessary and exploitative purchases, most famously portrayed in the character Octave Mouret, department store owner in Emile Zola's 1883 novel *Au Bonheur des Dames*. In contrast, the evidence from Bolton shows women were not lured into the Sales and seduced into spending by promises made by shopkeepers, but were rational and measured in their approach to spending. Nor did women make purchases for the sake of it. One interviewee told Mass Observation the Sales disrupted her enjoyment of shopping, complaining, 'I'm always quite glad when they are over. All the shops seem to look too untidy and some are rather like junk shops.'[87] Those who complained about the Sales believed they were an opportunity for shopkeepers to sell unfashionable items of stock. One respondent admitted: 'Curiosity plays a part. But I would not always feel it was wise to buy goods at a sale. They may be going out of fashion'. Another commented, 'The trouble with January sales is that most of the fashions are from the year before.'[88] Visitors were suspicious of the Sales as they were not an opportunity to obtain fashionable clothes, although it is likely that shoppers still made purchases in the Sales but, like the shoppers who refused to admit they used the Co-operative, did not admit doing so. Mass Observation's findings revealed that those who did confess to making purchases during the Sales only admitted to buying items that could not easily go out of fashion like gloves, stockings and underwear, but never hats, dresses or coats. 'I think the sales are a good opportunity to purchase garments which do not vary much in style from one year to the next', one respondent confided.[89] As the respondents to Mass Observation's questionnaire testify, the Sales were a period in which women shoppers were particularly astute and cautious in their purchases because they could not be guaranteed to find the fashionable clothes that they most wanted.

The focus on fashion exceeded far beyond the Sales period and was a startlingly important focus of women's lives. Mass Observation's interviews with housewives are striking, in that they reveal the centrality that fashion and dress occupied within the weekly effort to make ends meet, and both the passion women had for fashionable clothes and the innovation they displayed in order to obtain the clothes they wanted are apparent. 'If we want any clothes I'll try an' get 'em', confided one housewife to a Mass Observer, 'I made this blue one I'm wearing now, last year, it cost me 6/10 wholesale – you see I get it wholesale – the wool, an' knit myself a dress. That was the price with the buttons, everything.'[90] In similar ways to the shopper who proudly displayed her purchases to her family once she had returned home, this housewife's enthusiasm to divulge her achievement in obtaining a woollen dress illustrates the sense of pride she felt about her ability to obtain new clothes through inexpensive methods. The same housewife was particularly pleased with her determined efforts to obtain a fur coat. As Chapter 3 noted, the fur coat was the most aspirational of all fashionable and glamorous clothes for women in 1930s Britain and the housewife interviewed by Mass Observation had taken on an extra job specifically in order to be able to purchase one: 'She pointed out that she had got a fur coat by going out and cleaning at her sister's every Friday at 3/ a time.'[91] The fur coat was an iconic item of clothing during the 1930s: the housewife's investment was not only financial, but an emotional one too and a fur coat gave her a sense of fulfilment and achievement, as well as enhanced status. Mass Observation continually noted the sacrifices women made for fashionable clothes; for example, a housewife with two adult daughters said: 'Last year family sacrificed their holiday in June, to buy clothes', revealing the priority clothes occupied when it came to making choices about spending.[92] Mass Observation also cites a discussion one researcher witnessed between another housewife, who worked as a weaver, and her adult daughters, who received unemployment allowance, over whether or not to take a short holiday to London. The mother stated: 'It is a choice whether new clothes or the trip', before deciding, 'I think we shall have new clothes.'[93] These women prioritized spending on clothing, over other forms of leisure or expenditure, because of the social and emotional investment they placed in fashionable dress.

Even after forgoing holidays and taking extra paid work, affording fashionable clothes was difficult for many women and required careful spending choices. Dressmaking (whether at home or by semi-professional dressmakers) was an essential part of the rational culture of clothing acquisition for women, which allowed those with little spending power to dress fashionably. As the women quoted above testified to Mass Observation, department stores and shop windows were crucial in shaping how they wanted to dress but the sewing machine was absolutely fundamental in helping them achieve what they saw. As the young Liverpool teacher testified, she researched what clothes she wanted carefully through department stores but her best dress was made by a local dressmaker with material she had bought herself costing 45 shillings; the same dressmaker also made her a coat for 45 shillings, which 'would have cost 45 guineas in a shop'.[94] Dressmaking was thus an affordable method to obtain the clothes on display in department stores. The practice seemed to be commonplace and the young teacher reported, 'My own friend buys her clothes by buying material and getting the dress made. She plans an outfit before buying anything'.[95] The young Liverpool typist also used the same method:

> I just tell my tailor what I want and choose the material, he measures me, I have a couple of fittings, and then it's all over. … Sometimes I choose suit materials entirely by myself, and in that case I have a good idea what I want by looking in various shops. This process also tells me what to avoid.[96]

Women in Bolton also relied on home dressmaking skills to obtain fashionable clothes. An interview by Mass Observation with one young women reported she 'makes all of her clothes herself, if one buys a reliable pattern and good material things look very nice', and through this method, 'she likes to get every season something new'.[97] The interviewee clearly desired to maintain a fashionable appearance, despite the seasonal variations, and reveals the importance of the pattern industry (widely available to women by the 1930s and often provided for free in women's magazines) in allowing women to imitate changing fashions.[98] Home dressmaking allowed women to access the changing world of fashion and glamour, permitting women with little spending power to imitate the clothes they saw in fashion pages and in department stores.

Women chose home dressmaking against the rise of chain stores and the increasing availability of off-the-peg clothes. Clothing chain stores increased significantly in numbers over the interwar period, rising from 5,957 nationally in 1920, to 9,814 in 1939.[99] Nevertheless, until the Second World War many women considered the ready-to-wear women's clothes offered by chain stores to be of poor quality and higher cost and lacking in style and fashion.[100] Although access to sewing machines is difficult to quantify, often handed down through generations and even affordable to skilled workers by the late nineteenth century, it seems fair to assume that most families could access one by 1918.[101] The interwar period witnessed a further expansion in the availability of the sewing machine: the number of Singer retail outlets rose by 50 per cent, from 600 in 1920, to 900 by 1938.[102] There was also the opportunity to obtain a sewing machine on hire-purchase between the two world wars.[103] These developments indicate that most women could access a sewing machine, in some form or other, by the 1920s and 1930s. The sewing machine was thus fundamental to the interwar democratization of fashion and, through home dressmaking, women could become fashionable women and imitate the styles they had gazed at in shop windows or at department store mannequin parades.

Women overcame limited spending power through the sewing machine; this was especially important because not only were ready-made clothes inadequate, but co-operative societies failed to provide women with the materials they required to become fashionable. Superficially, it seems co-operative stores were also part of the interwar democratization of fashion: there were over 2,000 co-operative draperies by 1938 and 97 per cent of members belonged to societies with drapery departments.[104] By implication, 'virtually all members of Co-operative Societies were able, if they so wished, to purchase women's and girls' wear and drapery from their local Society'.[105] Yet, like their left-wing allies such as Orwell, the leaders of the co-operative movement distrusted the glamorous mass consumer culture that emerged between the two world wars. Rather,

> Co-operators underestimated the allure of the new commodity culture and they also failed to think seriously about fantasy more generally ... many co-operators regarded the showy extravagance of these palaces of consumption as both wasteful and immoral; and in the hostile interwar climate the puritanical voice of the local leadership became shriller ... the mode of consumption in the 1930s was very different to that envisioned by the co-op.[106]

Furthermore, it seems that the movement struggled to recover from the economic crash of 1929–31. Mass Observation noted that 'although the Bolton Co-operative Society has held for many years a strong position in the retail trade of the town, it has been badly hit by the depression and does not seem able to adjust itself very readily to changing economic circumstance'. The researchers found that membership to Bolton's Co-operative had stalled with 54,214 members in 1929 and 55,398 in 1932.[107]

Other retailers in Bolton informed Mass Observation of the Co-operative's lacklustre marketing effort and reluctance to follow the broader trends in consumer culture that were emerging elsewhere. One retailer told a researcher that 'when new brands of goods, new materials or processes were offered to the public, the private trader took the risk of first introducing it and when it was established as a favourite, the Co-op shop started to stock it'.[108] The Co-op was literally left behind: 'It was also suggested by some of the retailers interviewed that the Co-op. had serious disadvantages in that it appeared to lack imagination in selling policy, had little initiative, and was liable to miss the best trade because of this'.[109] The drapery department of Bolton's co-operative experienced crushing falls in sales across the interwar period: in 1925 sales stood at £113,810, falling to £102,033 in 1927, before falling again to £99,455 in 1931 and to just £68,995 in 1934.[110] The demise in fortunes of the Co-op drapery department is especially surprising considering the rise in popularity of home dressmaking between the two world wars. In the words of one retailer in Bolton however, 'if a girl wants a new blouse for Blackpool, she doesn't go to the Co-op'.[111]

The demise of Bolton's Co-operative drapery department was a response to the movement's reluctance to participate in the emerging consumer culture. As Mass Observation reported, 'The general impression is that while it deals in good solid quality goods, it cannot meet the demand for "fashion goods"'.[112] Women were indeed reluctant to shop in co-operatives because it denied them access to the exotic and glamorous consumer culture they associated with department stores. Although women were generally sympathetic to the co-operative ideology, they understood the movement to be oppositional to the particular identity they sought to appropriate through fashionable dress. 'The co-operative is a good movement', admitted one Bolton woman to a Mass Observation, 'but I don't like their goods'.[113] Again, women in Bolton emphasised the importance of fashion to Mass Observation researchers. One interviewee conceded the co-operative often provided 'genuine bargains', but admitted she was reluctant to shop there as it 'is not encouraging to see the same dance dress displayed sale after sale'.[114] This woman made it clear that fashion came second to price. Women like her, despite restricted spending power, publicly rejected the co-operative store because it did not provide the status they sought through fashionable dress.

As well as home dressmaking and a rejection of chain stores and co-operatives, women were very careful about the kinds of items they purchased. More specifically, they deliberately used token items to help their homemade clothes look appropriately fashionable. It seems this trend emerged in response to the broader shifts in retail and consumer culture illustrated in Chapter 3. At the start of the period for instance, women (largely middle and upper class) visited department stores for their entire outfits: in April 1920 Liverpool's Bon Marché's dress department took £1,070, whereas the glove department took just £176.[115] By the early 1930s however, department stores reported a different pattern of spending. Table 4.2 illustrates small items of dress and adornment, particularly hosiery and haberdashery, attracted the most customers in Liverpool's G. H. Lee's in 1933. These items allowed women access to the culture of the department store through the purchase of fashionable inexpensive items. As the statistics show, Lee's most popular feature in 1933 was the Restaurant, which further

Table 4.2 G. H. Lee's number of customers in relation to department, 1933

Department	Number of Customers (making purchases)
Dressmaking	49
Fur	50
Millinery	948
Hosiery	2,949
Gloves	1,139
Haberdashery	4,396
Gowns	564
Laces and Ribbons	3,588
Restaurant	7,954

Source: John Lewis Archive Box 180/3/a.

suggests department stores became demotic sites of leisure and pleasure: women could enjoy the stores without making actual purchases. Haberdashery, Laces and Ribbons, and Hosiery were, following the Restaurant, the most popular departments and sold items that helped homemade clothes to look like the fashionable clothes sold by department stores. By the 1930s therefore, when department stores became more popular sites of leisure and pleasure, women bought smaller, less expensive items, as part of their enjoyment of department stores. They provided a key role in women's rational purchasing strategies to obtain fashionable clothes.

Testimony by women to Mass Observation further reveals the ways in which women used inexpensive items from department stores to ensure homemade clothes looked fashionable and up to date. For the young Liverpool teacher, dresses could be cheap but she invested more money on items not easily copied or imitated. She described hats as a necessary expense and justified the cost: 'To be fashionable I have to buy an expensive one because the cheap ones are too tight and just look silly.' Similarly, she admitted she could spend up to 10 shillings on gloves as 'they have to last until the outfit they match is discarded', which could be six months to two years.[116] The local press also acknowledged the importance of appropriate accessories: 'Today, to be chic, accessories must be correct, not only in colour, but in style and fabric, and they must definitely link up with the costume with which they are worn,' wrote a journalist in the *Liverpolitan*.[117] Interestingly, although not actually rationed, Mass Observation reported that people stopped buying hats following the outbreak of the Second World War and the introduction of clothes rationing. Mass Observation argued that this was because hats provided the finishing touch to an outfit and with rationing women lacked new outfits to accessorise.[118] By the 1930s, therefore, accessories were an important aspect of self-adornment and its implications for women's public demonstrations of status and fashionable selfhoods.

Conclusion

Dressing fashionably was central to the lives of women in Liverpool, Manchester and Bolton, despite the very modest means many of them possessed. Department stores gave these women glamorous images of fashionable femininity and through determination and rational spending choices, women were able to imitate the images they saw. The fashionably dressed shopper became an important aspect of the new images of Liverpool and Manchester promoted in the press as the local state valued women's roles as shoppers. However, she was in many ways a mirage: these women made few purchases and probably possessed less spending power than the journalists or urban commentators who wrote about them realized. They were not 'silly girls with their synthetic Hollywood dreams,' or a 'prosperous woman' looking for 'a Chinese lacquer bird-cage, a bottle of wine or a Paris hat'.[119] Rather, these women were probably mill girls, working-class housewives or the young single typist or teacher, looking to spend their small disposable incomes carefully on items of dress and adornment or merely staring intently at department store windows, planning their next hard-won dress.

This new culture of shopping and glamour offered working-class women the opportunity to take on new identities. Matt Houlbrook suggests that interwar Britain represented a distinct shift in the nature of selfhood, and 'rather than authentic, stable, and immediately discernible, identity was increasingly presented as something fashioned through a careful engagement with consumer culture'.[120] As the writings of Orwell show, the working-class woman dressed like a film star epitomized this emerging culture. By implication, the fashionably dressed woman seeing and being seen and shopping but not buying ensured that the transformed urban centres transcended class divisions. For example, Mass Observation found it frustratingly challenging to judge a person's class by his or her appearance in the 'Follows' part of their study. Researchers who undertook the Follows often had to examine what items shoppers bought, if they bought anything at all, to define their class. One Follow included the description of a woman who, the researcher presumed, was aged about twenty-five who went into Woolworths with her 3-year-old daughter. Described in the Follow's notes as being 'very well got up, camel coat, silk stockings, good shoes', the woman, the researcher observed, bought a toothpaste for 6d., and on seeing the child's balloon burst, she quickly replaced it with a new one costing 1d. From this exchange, the Mass Observer classified the woman as middle class.[121] In contrast, a woman assumed to be nineteen years old, wearing a 'short grey fur coat, light stockings', looked around the shop but made no purchase, and so was classified as 'good working-class'.[122] 'Black coat – Astrathan collar, black dress, black hat, stockings, snakeskin shoes, bad at heels' was the description of one woman who was defined as being working class because she 'has a look round doesn't [but] buy'.[123] Mass Observers relied on making judgements about shoppers' apparent spending power to define class because their fashionable dress obscured other divisions.

The Follows undertaken by Mass Observation also indicate that the majority of women used dress to portray their apparent respectability and those who could not dress fashionably experienced poor status. Mass Observation described one couple which was observed in Woolworths where the woman was heavily pregnant, with 'old brown-fawn coat, old brown hat, rather frayed on back of head, dirty face. Cotton socks, greyish old black shoes, heels (worn) down, bought biscuits for 3d after deliberation'.[124] For Mass Observation, the poor dress and 'deliberation' over the purchase of biscuits led them to describe the woman as 'poor, unemployed'. Mass Observers also suggested poorly dressed shoppers were ashamed of their appearance and felt alienated. A report described one woman as, 'dressed in faded, shabby brown coat, with a dirty flowered frock underneath … her husband is unemployed – she is embarrassed about this.'[125] 'Shabby ill-fitting coat glasses, with boy, 12, blue coat, glasses, weedy', was the description of another woman deemed by Mass Observation to be 'poor working class'.[126]

Mass Observation's anthropological study of Bolton and Manchester can be criticised for maintaining middle-class expectations of working-class culture and people. Mass Observation 'rendered them quaint, harmless, slightly peculiar and comic, as were Malekulan (tribe studied by Harrisson) cannibals'.[127] What the Follows do reveal, however, is the social isolation experienced by those who could not participate within consumer culture or obtain fashionable clothes. Thus, dressing fashionably was important because it publicly displayed status and the rational culture of spending practised by women to obtain clothes meant even those with limited spending power could access fashionable clothes, through careful and measured methods of acquisition. Although the cultures of fashion and glamour that suffused women's lives by the 1930s required some money and certainly a great deal of time, commitment and passion, the implications meant that it offered women new forms of selfhood that transcended class divisions. What Mass Observation and their contemporaries misunderstood, therefore, was the potentially liberating and transformative power of this new consumer culture: the transformed city offered opportunities for new glamorous identities that took women nearer to Hollywood and to the lives of the movie stars they sought to imitate. As a case study, it uncovers the ways in which women experienced the redeveloped city centres. It also shows how Liverpool and Manchester's transformation shaped consumer and retail culture more generally in the surrounding region. By implication, the material stresses women's experiences were central to the redeveloped city centres. As we shall move on to see, women's roles as shoppers and consumers became no less important when Catholic leaders turned their attentions to urban transformation.

Part Three

Catholic Urban Culture

Gender and Religious Selfhoods
in Manchester

As we have seen, Liverpool and Manchester's transformation ensured that their urban centres became increasingly associated with consumer culture. By implication, shopping had become fundamental to women's experiences of the city and their public demonstrations of status. Many historians have argued that the rise of modern consumer culture went hand in hand with a decline in religious belief and see the interwar years as key in the secularization of Britain.[1] Yet, more recently, secularization has been described as 'a broken concept, inapplicable to the British experience'. By implication, historians need to employ a 'more sophisticated and contextualised methodology for the study of religion, which takes religion seriously in the sense of recognizing the sophistication, complexity, and generative power of the values, practices, and ideas of the people of the past'.[2] These concerns pave the way for a more imaginative methodological approach to the scholarly analysis of religiosity and a greater interest in regional variations in popular worship to understand the role of religion in Britain more fully.

Indeed, historians of modern Britain have much to learn from the influential work of anthropologist Anthony Orsi, who demonstrates the importance of religion to Italian migrants in New York City but draws out the complexities around their religious beliefs and identities. For example, Orsi shows that Italian-Catholic women in New York City were able to balance their religious selfhoods with the emerging opportunities in consumer culture, leisure and employment that were increasingly becoming available to them.[3] Most significant is Orsi's study of the festival of the Madonna of Mount Carmel in New York City as it offers a more flexible understanding of religion, its role in women's lives and its importance in shaping community and shared identities. His ethnographic approach reveals that during the festa, 'the community on these days was given the opportunity to see itself acting as a community. The essential and complex structures of the social life of a community in transition were bodied forth in a highly visible manner, in the people's relations with each other and with the Madonna. … Everyone who talks about the devotion to the Madonna of 115th Street takes care to mention that even those people who would not set foot in church faithfully attended the festa.'[4] Orsi's approach suggests that historians of Britain need to rethink how religious worship connected and intersected with other aspects of modern life, especially for women.

Manchester was also home to colourful Catholic processions, which is the focus of this chapter. Its processions first emerged in the nineteenth century, but, as this chapter argues, by the interwar period, they too had become crucial for nurturing and performing shared identities. Focusing on Manchester's annual Whit processions, the chapter shows their importance and significance peaked between the two world wars and was a product of the investment made in urban transformation, which not only revitalized civic and consumer cultures in Manchester but had significant implications for cultures of religion. The chapter first shows that one implication of housing reform ensured Catholic communities were broken up and widely dispersed throughout the new suburbs, making it necessary to find new ways to articulate their shared identity. Second, the new forms of commercial and municipal architecture and the revitalized culture of shopping that were emerging caused the city centre to become an increasingly important and emotive site to express religious collectivity. Third, the city centre became a stage for the performance of public, yet episodic, forms of Catholic identity by the 1930s, which allowed women to balance their religious identities with their interests in shopping, consumer culture and leisure. Like Orsi's study of Italian women in New York City, women's involvement in Manchester's Catholic Whit processions shows the centrality of religion to migrant women's expressions of belonging and shared identity in their adopted city. As a case study, the Whit processions reveal important details about the cultural meanings of the interwar city and contribute to an emerging field of cultural geography that explores the relationship between space and faith.[5] At the same time, they offer an important contribution to the ongoing secularization debate in twentieth-century British history by demonstrating the central role of religion in urban culture between the two world wars.[6]

Manchester's Whit processions reflected a broader tradition of using public spaces for individuals to 'put themselves on display to others'.[7] The Whit celebrations necessitated putting the self on display but to demonstrate a community identity, which is best understood through an analysis of how religious collectivity was itself constructed through the processions. The materiality of processions 'create(s) a rich and varied field of symbols, ideal for semiotic investigation'.[8] Thus, we can read shifts in the articulation of a Catholic shared identity through the changes in the icons and religious symbols in Manchester's Whit celebrations, which exposes the connections between the ritualistic nature of the processions and their relationship with collective identities. As anthropologist Anthony Cohen suggests, ritual 'confirms and strengthens social identity and people's sense of social location: it is an important means through which people experience community'.[9] Cohen's analysis helps explain why and how Catholics increasingly relied on the ritual of Whit processions while Manchester's redevelopment disrupted their parish-based communities.

Existing accounts of the Catholic Whit processions draw on the local press and autobiographies to emphasize continuity in their role and expression over the period 1880–1939.[10] In contrast, visual sources permit an anthropological reading of the shifting signs and symbols within the processions, which uncovers their changing cultural role. Around 40 per cent of available photographs of the Whit processions (both Catholic and Protestant) donated to local archives are used here, alongside film footage held by the British Film Institute and Pathé. Although not without limitations, these visual sources in conjunction with published sources and personal testimony offer some sense of how religious selfhoods were displayed through the Whit processions.[11] As recent scholarship on photographs emphasizes, they are constructed representations and are key as a way for individuals or groups to structure memory and signal the significance of their own lives.[12] Photographs reveal the emotional significance processions had in the lives of Catholics in Manchester. An analysis of such images in conjunction with other sources shows the form and expression of the Catholic processions became more distinct and exotic in comparison to their Protestant counterparts over the period. By implication, religious iconography became a much more prominent feature as the interwar period progressed. However, the nature of Catholic collectivity was episodic, which related closely to the specific form of Catholicism in interwar Manchester and the contribution of its migrant constituents.

Catholicism and urban redevelopment in the interwar city

Manchester's redevelopment had a profound impact on Catholic inhabitants throughout Lancashire, which the revitalization of the annual Whit processions came to reflect. Salford Diocese (which covered Manchester, Stockport in the south, Preston in the north-east, Clithoroe to the north and Todmorden on the eastern edge of the Pennines) estimated there were 300,000 Catholics in 1936, within Greater Manchester's population of just over 2,700,000.[13] Although the myths of 'Little Ireland' persist, there was no such thing as a Catholic ghetto in Manchester by 1918. Catholics did tend to be concentrated in the poorest working-class districts around the city centre, including Angel Meadow, Collyhurst, Hulme, Ancoats and Miles Platting.[14] The Catholic population was also diverse and multiracial and not limited to Irish migrants. Significant numbers of non-Irish Catholics settled in the city during the decades prior to the First World War, notably from Italy and Eastern European countries including Poland and Hungary.[15] Clusters of Catholics formed on a localized and parish (rather than ghettoized) level throughout the Greater Manchester area, in Ancoats, Oldham, Rochdale, Hulme, Plymouth Grove and Salford.[16] Catholic migrants imported their own culture of religious celebration and had a significant impact on the Catholic community, shaping shared identity from within.

Catholicism remained strongly linked with poverty in interwar British cities such as Manchester. As noted earlier, overall unemployment rates in Manchester never met the national rate, but some parts of the city were particularly badly affected, which included the districts more heavily populated with Catholics.[17] Ancoats was one of the most famous Catholic areas, known as 'Little Italy' because of its especially high number of Italians. These Italian migrants had a strong and visual and aural presence in the city as they sold ice cream, played traditional music and sung the Tarantella, a southern Italian folk song and dance, on street corners. Ancoats encapsulated the link between poverty and Catholicism in post-First World War Manchester. As one survey undertaken by Manchester University in the 1930s noted, around 35 per cent of Ancoats' inhabitants was Roman Catholic; 70 per cent of men earned less than £3 a week, and 53 per cent of households lived below the poverty line.[18] Yet, the study also noted the longevity and stability of the Ancoats community, where over 40 per cent of inhabitants lived in the same house for over twenty years and some for over thirty years.[19] Subsequently, the report concluded, 'Ancoats people have a great deal of pride and are attached to their neighbourhood through long association.'[20] Although the title suggests the survey was undertaken in 1937 and 1938, the introduction states the 'study occurred as Ancoats was scheduled for clearance in 1934'.[21] The researchers were concerned about the future of the community as the Corporation targeted Ancoats for clearance, along with other Catholic areas.

As we saw in Chapter 1, housing reform was a priority for local politicians after 1918. Crucially for Manchester's Catholics, clearance focused on built-up areas adjacent to the city centre and especially affected their communities: whereas 40 per cent of all Catholics lived in seven parishes close to the city centre in 1890, the proportion had fallen to less than 25 per cent by 1939.[22] Clearance destroyed traditional parish networks. For example, despite the cohesiveness of the Ancoats communities, the number of Catholics in the area halved during the 1930s, which ruined its micro-economy and forced local tradesmen (particularly the ice-cream sellers) to relocate.[23] Catholic churches near the city centre struggled to survive: the Corporation rehoused 2,000 parishioners of St Anne's Church in Ancoats by 1939, and the church nearly closed.[24] Salford Diocese was alarmed, particularly because Manchester Corporation ignored the Diocese's requests for members of Catholic parishes to be rehoused together.[25] The Diocese embarked on a building programme in those suburbs within its jurisdiction: in 1928 alone, Irlam, Bolton, Didsbury, Burnley and Blackley established new parishes.[26] Forty-one new churches were built and fifteen new parishes were formed during the episcopate of Thomas Henshaw, Bishop of Salford (1925–38).[27] However, other dioceses governed some of Manchester's larger housing estates, including Wythenshawe, which was part of Shrewsbury Diocese, and did not witness significant building programmes until the 1960s.

Despite Salford Diocese's best efforts, the splintering and dislocating effects of housing reform on communities were profound and, by implication, the Catholic population had to change the way in which their sense of community was expressed. Catholic identity in Manchester was traditionally flexible by nature and linked to class and ethnicity. Manchester's Catholics were 'neither simply Irish, Catholic or working class, but an amalgam of all three'. By implication, it 'was an extremely malleable identity, defined by ambiguity and equivocation, with vague boundaries and a viable character'.[28] Manchester's redevelopment caused Catholics to develop a less ambiguous, yet episodic, form of community. Cohen argues communities respond to change by asserting a stronger sense of collectivity, suggesting 'societies undergoing rapid, and, therefore, de-stabilizing processes of change often generate atavistically some apparently traditional forms, but import meaning to contemporary circumstance'.[29] Cohen's analysis helps explain why Manchester's Catholic population used the traditions of the Whit processions to assert a stronger sense of collectivity following Manchester's redevelopment and became important in displaying and performing community in similar ways to Orsi's analysis of Italian-Catholic festivals in New York.[30] To understand this more clearly, the nature and significance of the Whit processions need a more direct examination alongside a consideration of why the city centre also became more important as a stage to perform shared identity.

Redefining the city as a spiritual space

Held annually from the early nineteenth century, Whit processions took place throughout Lancashire and provided the most dazzling and extensive religious celebrations in the country. Whit weekend (usually the last weekend in May) saw Catholics process on the Friday and Protestants on a Monday and they each competed for the most impressive celebrations, carrying banners, statues and flowers. The tradition probably originated from the arrival of migrants to Lancashire's new industrialized centres, bringing with them folkloric countryside celebrations of springtime. Catholics began to take part during the mid-nineteenth century, following the influx of Irish and Italian immigrants to the city and imbued the celebrations with a sense of religious difference.[31] Although they took place throughout Lancashire, Manchester city centre drew the largest processions and crowds. Howard Spring's 1934 novel, *Shabby Tiger*, described the Catholic procession starting from Albert Square in front of the city's Town Hall:

> The square was a huge black reservoir, and into it bright tributary streams were flowing from all the streets that had it as its centre. ... Soon the square was awash with the agitation of all that youth and colour, the wind taking the banners and filling them out like bellied sails. ... On the pavements wedged tight as they could be, the citizens had assembled behind the police barriers that guarded the sacred roads ... the heart of Manchester was sealed and impassable.[32]

The processions were a unique moment when the religious difference was articulated and expressed collectively and publicly in a city largely untroubled by sectarian divisions and tensions, particularly in comparison to elsewhere in Britain.[33]

Whit weekend traditionally represented a key moment when religious celebration took Manchester city centre over. Nevertheless, the impact of the processions became more emotive and significant as the city centre itself underwent notable change. As we saw in Chapters 1 and 2, significant investment in municipal architecture, public transport, civic celebrations and the publicity campaigns that accompanied such investment transformed and revitalized Manchester's civic culture. Most notably, a more clearly defined civic area emerged following the great investment made by municipal leaders, which expanded the Town Hall and built a Central Library adjacent to it. As Chapters 3 and 4 demonstrated, urban transformation contributed to rich and innovative cultures of retail and the city centres became closely associated with shops and consumer culture. The Whit processions sought to subvert these powerful civic and commercial cultures that had emerged in Manchester city centre. The celebrations therefore represent an example of 'the attempted reimagination of a civic community by citizens of multiple races, ethnicities, religions, genders, and ages'.[34]

The impact of the Whit processions became more emotive as the new civic and commercial architecture emerged. The Catholic procession started from Albert Square in front of the Town Hall and finished at Portland Street, beginning at 10 o'clock in the morning with the hymn 'Faith of Our Fathers', which told the story of Catholic persecution and subsequent triumph.[35] The route first took the Catholic procession along Deansgate, the most fashionable shopping district, and past Kendal's department store. Then, it followed on through Peter Street, alongside the Town Hall and the new extension, as well as the newly built Central Library, before moving up along Market Street and past the city's other shops and department stores, including Lewis's and Woolworth's. Finally, the walkers reached Piccadilly Gardens, the city's main transport terminus. Thus, the procession utilized the very areas of the city that underwent significant changes between the wars: Catholic walkers took advantage of the developing city centre and appropriated the space for themselves.

The importance of the Whit procession also increased with the involvement of Bishop Henshaw, who made a clear attempt to invest the celebrations with a more explicitly religious meaning. In 1927, for example, Henshaw compared the impact of the Catholic procession to that of the previous year's General Strike. During Whit, he wrote,

> Commercial Manchester rests for a spell from its task of making money. The stock exchange is deserted; the shops are shut ... the real wealth of the nation comes out into the sunshine. ... The children of the poor invade the centre of Commerce.[36]

As Henshaw's address suggests, Manchester's Whit celebrations disrupted the day-to-day workings of the city and there was a striking contrast between the commercial buzz of the city and the hymns, colour and religiosity of the Whit ceremonies. Yet the Whit processions also offered a form of amusement and leisure. Street hawkers sold orange boxes for people to stand on, as well as flowers and unofficial handbooks that covered the day's events. Photographers and newsreel companies set out to record the events, women did no cooking that day and many combined it with a day in a public house. For many it was a leisure activity and remembered Whit was 'as good as going to Blackpool'.[37] Nostalgic representations emphasized the importance of Whit weekend for children; many of them remembered it because they received new clothes and considered it as a time of excitement and fun. The nature of the processions as a form of leisure suggests similarities with Italian-Catholic celebrations in New York, since Orsi also emphasizes the mix of the sacred and the profane, particularly due to the amount of gambling that took place during and in conjunction with the festa.[38] Nevertheless, although the role of Manchester's Whit celebrations in providing leisure and amusement is important, it has overshadowed the procession's importance as a religious ceremony and its role as a form of leisure was by no means incompatible with its spiritual significance. Furthermore, the emphasis on leisure is symptomatic of the broader neglect of religion in existing historical accounts of twentieth-century Britain.[39]

Catholic processions actually became more popular after 1918, as the sheer quantity of photographs donated to local history archives indicates: sixty Whit photographs are from the period before 1918, nearly two hundred are from the period 1918–39, and just forty-one are from the post-1945 period.[40] Many of these photographs carry stamps from private photographic firms and it seems there was a significant market for Whit photographs interwar. Moreover, the desire to have photographs is a testimony to the importance assigned to the Whit celebrations because they provided a reminder of the emotional and financial investment associated with taking part. The number of available Pathé films of the event also illustrates the popularity of the Whit processions between the wars: of the seventeen films available on the British Pathé online archive, all but two are from the 1918–39 period.[41] Their existence also testifies to the importance of the Whit processions, as Andrew Prescott's discussion scholarship on the Mitchell and Kenyon films explains:

> For those who had been stuck behind an umbrella trying to watch the parade and had barely glimpsed a daughter in her hard-won costume, the film provided an important record of a major family event which went beyond the simple pleasure of recognising a face on the screen. In this way, there was a symbiotic relationship between the film and the social message of the procession, which was to grow increasingly intimate.[42]

That so many families wished to have a photographic or cinematographic memento of the processions is indicative of the emotional and financial investment Catholics made in the celebrations and that this investment peaked in importance during the interwar period.

As Figure 5.1 illustrates, the rise in photographs of the celebrations was mirrored by a significant increase in the number of official participants in the Catholic processions between the two world wars: 16,000 people took part in 1903, but in 1929 (the centenary year of Catholic Emancipation) this rose to nearly 22,000 participants, and settled at around 20,000 into the 1930s. Nevertheless, although participation in the Whit processions became more important as an assertion of Catholic identity as the interwar period developed, this remained an episodic form of public selfhood and continued to be a rare moment in Manchester when sectarian divisions were clearly asserted. People expressed their allegiance through small, but highly emotive, acts such as refusing to wash their front step or by preventing their children from watching the procession.[43] Ivy Bolton and Edie Smythe (born in Manchester in the 1920s) recalled that when the sun shone on Whit Friday Catholics would say 'God knows his own'.[44] Whit weekend drew out tensions and issues regarding collective identity and community, not normally witnessed in Manchester and the surrounding area. However, the shared religious identity that emerged during Whit remained flexible. Steven Fielding highlights the importance of Irishness in processions, writing 'what emerged on Whit Friday was a collectivity defined by Catholic and Irish ideas and sentiments founded upon a past largely distinct from the rest of society'.[45] Although these aspects of identity and articulations of religious difference that

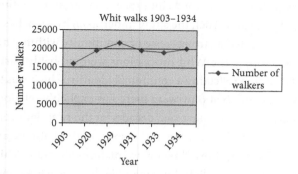

Figure 5.1 Number of participants in the Catholic processions, 1903–34
Source: Salford Catholic Diocese. *The Authorised Official Programme of the Catholic Whit-Friday Procession* (Manchester), 1895–1934.

emerged were traditionally associated with Manchester's Whit processions, the context of urban redevelopment combined with a greater involvement of non-Irish Catholics altered their expression between the two world wars. Differences between Catholic and Protestant forms of expression during Whit were limited at the start of the interwar period. As Catholic parishes were broken up, shared identity increasingly relied on the annual processions and their forms of expression became more exotic and overtly Catholic in iconography.

Parish identities and processional culture

Although the tradition of separate Catholic and Protestant processions existed throughout Lancashire since the mid-nineteenth century, there was little in their display or expression that offered a clear sense of religious difference. Indeed, at the start of the twentieth century they reflected a parish identity foremost. Figure 5.2 depicts a Catholic parish from Ancoats (home to many Italian migrants) in a Whit procession at around the time of the First World War. Despite the poverty of the area, women appear to be in their best dresses and are wearing hats, yet there is nothing about the walk that suggests that it is actually Catholic and the women do not carry any icons, just a banner which is probably for the parish. As we shall see, even Catholics from the poorest areas attempted to obtain white costumes in the later interwar years, suggesting poverty was not the reason these women did not wear matching white costumes. This scene is also echoed in a picture of St Paul's Methodist Church (also from Ancoats) taking part in the Whit procession of 1920, and indicates they were typical of the Whit processions around the time of the First World War.[46] As we saw earlier, the study undertaken by Manchester University in the 1930s highlighted a strong sense of community within Ancoats.[47] These images therefore imply the Whit processions were probably part of a broader processional tradition reflecting a communal identity, which was to evolve later in the interwar period. Not only were there few explicitly religious symbols in the Whit processions in the first two decades of the twentieth century, but the similarities between the expression and display of the Catholic and Protestant celebrations were strong. The following two pictures illustrate Whit celebrations from around 1918 and highlight little tangible difference between the Catholic and Protestant processions. Figure 5.3 depicts a Catholic walk as it left Albert Square to traverse through Market Street, Manchester's main shopping district. It shows girls wearing white dresses, they carry flowers and a banner that spells

Figure 5.2 St Michael's Roman Catholic parish, Ancoats, c. 1910s
Source: MCL LIC Ref m69150.

Figure 5.3 Roman Catholic walk, c. 1918
Source: MCL LIC Ref 1313026.

out 'JESU', but as in Figure 5.2, no part of the iconography of costume suggests the walk is Catholic. The large crowds are an important feature of the picture with observers six or seven deep leaning out of the windows, showing it was an important local event but not necessarily a proclamation of Catholic difference. Similarly, the *MEN*'s description of the scene in 1920 shows references to religion in the Catholic procession perceived it as 'picturesque', rather than spiritual.

> Record crowds witnessed the arrival of the Roman Catholic Guilds, which, for splendour and pageantry and attention of detail, are unexcelled outside Rome. This morning, many beautiful floral tableaux were portrayed. Youths dressed as Roman martyrs and gladiators lent a picturesque touch, while hundreds of banners were carried.[48]

The article indicates that in 1920 the Whit celebrations were a time of celebration and festivity, but the form of Catholic expression was not narrowly prescribed: children were dressed as both martyrs and gladiators and banners were an important part of the processional culture.

There are difficulties in detecting visible differences between the Catholic and Protestant Whit processions in the first two decades of the twentieth century. Images of Protestant group of walkers depict girls wearing white dresses and flowers, which are very similar to those in the Catholic procession shown in Figure 5.3 and, again, there is little overtly religious iconography and the emphasis seems to have been on young girls in white dresses, carrying flowers, perhaps, in part, a celebration of springtime.[49] The theme also appears in newsreel footage of the processions, which indicates Catholic and Protestant Whit walks related to a broader processional culture in England during the early 1920s. Pathé newsreel shows both the Protestant and Catholic processions of 1921 composed of girls wearing white dresses, as they were in Figure 5.3, and they are also shown carrying shepherd's crooks and flowers. The film footage, like the photographs, portrays few men in the Catholic procession (unlike the Protestant procession, the Catholic celebrations took place on a working day and few men were unable to participate because of work) with the exception of those holding the statues, which were very large and heavy. Pathé certainly perceived little difference between the processions in 1921 and gave the different newsreels similar titles, which again emphasized the scenic and decorative qualities of the processions. The Catholic procession was described as 'Whit Friday Procession, Picturesque Scenes at Annual Parade'.[50] Similarly, Pathé titled the Protestant procession as 'Protestant Procession, Picturesque Scenes at Annual Parade'. In both processions, the participants carried parish banners and the only explicitly religious icons were the Italian's crucifix and a statue of the Madonna in the Catholic procession.[51] Both the Protestant and Catholic processions seem to have been strongly related to traditional celebrations of springtime, related to a nostalgic vision of the countryside. The ribbons and banners carried are notably similar to a Maypole, which is perhaps unsurprising considering the popularity of these traditions during the two decades prior to the First World War.[52]

As the photographs and newsreel footage show, there were few prominent religious icons in either Protestant or Catholic Whit processions around the time of the First World War and this contributed to the similarities between their form and expression. It seems that not only did the celebrations not then articulate a narrowly religious identity, but that the collective identity was itself malleable in nature. For instance, during the Boer War, the Catholic parishes of St Johns and Holy Name dressed boys as soldiers and girls as nurses and marched them behind the Union Jack.[53] There were complaints about the lack of Irish music after the Manchester Catholic procession of 1904 and the musical bands were often non-Catholic, including the Primitive Methodist Prize Band, and by 1912 Catholic groups hoped to improve matters by introducing hymns to the procession.[54] Nevertheless, little had changed by the early 1920s and, in 1922, the *Manchester Guardian* reported the Italians brought a cross and the Madonna, 'the only religious emblems, beyond the processional cross and the banners'.[55] The absence of many explicitly Catholic icons may have reflected the problematic nature of Irishness in the first decades of the twentieth century. Catholic priests dissuaded Irish Catholics from promoting their identity in the Whit celebrations because feared the inflammatory nature of Irish nationalism. As a result, 'when Irish Catholics took to the streets it was usually to ostensibly express their Catholic faith rather than their Irish nationality'.[56] Irish nationalism was especially problematic in the years 1920–2, with several violent attacks on Manchester by the IRA.[57] Perhaps only the influence of other Catholic nationalities, alongside a decline in IRA terrorism, made Irish involvement and symbols associated with Irish nationality more acceptable in the Whit celebrations by the 1930s.

The relative sobriety of the costume worn by women and in Catholic processions such as in Figure 5.2 and the focus on children as seen in Figure 5.3 also coincided with a period of anxiety about religious women's roles in the wider world. As peace finally fell throughout Europe, the Catholic Church was one of many institutions that looked to reassert traditional gender relations in response to the chaos and destruction of the First World War.[58] In 1919, Pope Benedict XV outlined his perceived evils of the modern world in an address titled 'Women's Mission in Modern Society'. Pope Benedict specifically warned women against 'those exaggerations of fashions', declaring, 'We are filled with amazement at seeing those who communicate the poison seem not to realise its malignant action, and those that set the house on fire seem to ignore the destructive force of the fire.'[59] According to Rome, women's interest in fashion made them agents of immorality and invested them with the 'poison' of corruption. In response to this apparent problem, Pope Benedict called on all Catholic women to form leagues promoting decent fashions and to 'fulfil the strict duty of not giving scandal, and of not becoming a stumbling block to others in the path of virtue'.[60] The Pope's association between fashion, the emerging consumer culture and women's ability to manifest moral corruption was to have important consequences for the way Catholic leaders considered women's place in the post-war world. Manchester was no exception.

Pope Benedict's assertion led a group of women in Ireland to form an official league against 'Immodest dress'. Their oath pledged to avoid 'all impropriety in the matter of dress and to maintain and hand down the traditional purity, and modesty of Irish womanhood'.[61] There was also a meeting in Ireland in opposition to 'the introduction of new forms of dancing into the city of Dublin', and an association was formed 'to place on record its apprehension that nightclubs such as exist in other places may be introduced into the city, and respectfully urges the citizens to take strenuous measures to prevent such an evil'.[62] In Ireland, the association between the emerging consumer cultures, fashion and leisure with immorality was clear. These ideas also affected a large number of Irish immigrants and their descendants in North West England.[63] Opposition to women's interest in leisure and consumerism was not limited to the Catholic Church and Penny Tinkler argues secular concerns and discourse over women's leisure peaked during the Second World War.[64] Within specifically Catholic discourse, however, these fears were very prominent during the immediate post-war years.

Events in Ireland and Rome could not fail to influence Salford Diocese. In his Christmas pastoral letter to his diocese in 1919 the Bishop of Salford, then Louis Charles, called on women of the diocese to form a league 'against the evils of fashion'.[65] During the immediate post-war years, the perceived link between fashion and corruption was strong within Salford Diocese. In 1921, Bishop Charles's command was repeated through the Lenten pastoral letter: 'It has been reported to us on credible authority that at some of the dances among Catholics certain of these young people have appeared in costumes utterly repugnant to Christian modesty'.[66] Bishop Charles went even further and claimed that the modern world was in opposition to the Catholic idea of womanhood:

> there is the matter of amusement, frivolity, worldliness … there is an excess, resulting in a craving for constant, daily amusement, which grows like a taste for alcohol and drugs, and leads to a frivolous and dissipated state of mind, to extravagance and religious carelessness.[67]

The Bishop advised women to abstain from attending the theatre, cinema, and dances during Lent and, in doing so, articulated the ways in which Catholic leaders elsewhere attempted to deal with the 'problem' of women's modernity.[68]

Becoming a modern Catholic woman

These anxieties about femininity also shaped and influenced the nature and meaning of the Whit celebrations. In particular, the role of adult women, rather than predominantly children, grew in importance as the role of the Catholic Whit processions began to change in the 1920s, once the redevelopment of Manchester took hold. In particular, 1925 marked an important turning point as Thomas Henshaw become Bishop of Salford and was instrumental in transforming the celebrations into a vital spiritual event in Manchester's Catholic calendar. For instance, he renamed the celebrations as the 'Annual Catholic Procession', which distanced it from the Protestant Whit celebrations. Henshaw also introduced a personal address, published in the *Official Programme*, to directly invest the processions with a more overtly spiritual role. In his first address, he proclaimed the Whit celebrations were a symbol of Catholic rejuvenation and represented 'a noble and striking demonstration of the strength and power of the Church which is rebuilding itself in England upon the ashes of its martyred self'.[69] By 1932, Henshaw claimed that the annual celebrations permitted Catholic families of Manchester to 'feel that at least one right of citizenship is theirs equally with the rich, the right to parade the street of their own city'.[70] The Whit processions allowed Catholic leaders to nurture an alternative image of Manchester than that created by municipal leaders or businessmen through the new civic architecture or shops and businesses.

Just as Bishop Henshaw asserted the specifically religious role of the Catholic Whit celebrations from the mid-1920s, so the icons and items of dress used within the processions also changed. Figure 5.4 shows a Whit procession from a Catholic parish in Angel Meadow and illustrates how girls still wore white dresses and carried flowers in the mid-1920s, but there is a much stronger presence of Catholic iconography in comparison to the earlier Whit processions.[71] For example, the image depicts a boy holding a crucifix and the two banners in the background portray religious icons. Salford Diocese prohibited non-Catholic symbols from the procession during the later 1920s and, in 1931, explicitly forbade the use of non-Catholic flags and emblems.[72] The ruling suggests Catholic leaders were eager to clearly define the Catholic

Figure 5.4 St William's procession, Angel Meadow, Salford, 1926
Source: MCL LIC Ref N4101.

procession and made a conscious decision to make it different in expression than the Protestant Whit procession. Yet, it is clear that from the 1920s Catholic women were instrumental in negotiating the way the Catholic processions looked. Figure 5.3 illustrated it was very common for children to wear white dresses during Whit, but by the mid-1920s more adult women took part in the Catholic processions and wore costumes to emulate the Virgin Mary. Figure 5.5 illustrates a group of women dressed to participate in the Catholic procession of 1927 as 'The Children of Mary', which was a semi-formal religious group in Manchester. These women set themselves apart by wearing veils and emphasized their close relationship with the Virgin Mary. The tradition continued throughout the late 1930s as it became increasingly common for women to cover their heads during the procession. Salford Diocese even began a tradition of crowning a young girl 'Mary' during Whit from the mid-1920s. Margaret Kierman, born in Manchester during the 1920s, remembered the Diocese ceased the crowning of Mary for a period because it caused so many problems within the Catholic community as the honour was so great.[73] This was a clear link to Mary, Mother of God and a Catholic oppositional figure to the Rose Queen, who was crowned during the Protestant Whit celebrations. Newsreel footage from 1928 shows the crowning of a Rose Queen in Lancashire, the emphasis (as in the early Whit processions) was on springtime and many girls wore white dresses, some children wore Scout and Guide uniforms, and many carried flowers.[74] Thus, the iconography of the Rose Queen celebrations

Figure 5.5 Children of Mary, Catholic Whit procession, 1927
Source: MCL LIC Ref 905039.

mirrored some elements of the early Whit processions and, by the mid-1920s, the Whit processions incorporated English traditions with Catholic iconography to nurture a localized form of religious expression and imitating Mary was a strong expression of Catholic difference.

Catholics seem to have been especially concerned about the importance of obtaining specific costumes as the interwar period progressed, despite the poverty many families found themselves in. One Anglican cleric, who worked in Manchester in the early 1930s, recalled people falling into debt in their desire to provide the necessary costumes for the Whit processions, claiming 'our Roman Catholic friends were more guilty of this sort of thing' as 'they made greater demands'.[75] His criticism reflects the complexities around the expressions of Catholic selfhood during the Whit processions by the late 1920s and early 1930s. On the one hand, the pressure to have the necessary items of dress and adornment was difficult for many families, but at the same time, participation in the processions was fulfilling and offered Catholics public and visible demonstrations of status and respectability. Nostalgic recollections of those who participated in the Catholic walks as children during the late 1920s often draw attention to the importance of clothing: children were 'dressed up really nicely' for Whit, recalled Winifred Kelly, herself Catholic, and noted the clothes were sometimes kept for a couple of Sundays 'before they go into the pawn shop'.[76] Similarly, Edith professed her mother 'did always try to buy you a bit of something', remembering slippers cost 4s. 11d. and socks 1s. 3d., and these small token items meant 'at least you'd got a bit of something new'.[77] In an essay on dress and identity, Carolyn Steedman questions the concept of 'the other' as an analytical tool in understanding collective identity. 'This other is a very big thing, and undetailed', writes Steedman, 'Littleness, on the other hand, is the something tiny that can be held, and appropriated and incorporated *into* the idea of who you are'.[78] 'Little things', like the socks and shoes, helped articulate an increasingly stronger sense of difference between Catholics and Protestants during Whit. Protestants and Catholics not only defined their collective identity in opposition to each other, but also constructed a shared identity from within and performed publicly in the city centre during the Whit celebrations.

In order to participate in the Whit processions and obtain the 'little things' they needed, women found themselves obtaining clothes for Whit in the same imaginative and frugal ways they obtained more fashionable clothes, including home dressmaking made possible by wide access to the sewing machine.[79] These methods became essential as the period developed and participation within the processions was increasingly important as an assertion of collective Catholic identity while at the same time, problems of unemployment and poverty made it especially challenging for women to obtain the specific items of dress and adornment needed to take part. The Whit celebrations of 1926 were badly hit by the General Strike, but Winifred Kelly recalls how the Catholic community came together to ensure everyone could take part. Winifred remembered that her mother convinced Elworth's, a drapers on the corner of Deansgate and Market Street in the city centre, to sell her some dress material cheaply. As a skilled dressmaker, Winifred's mother used it to make matching Whit costumes for six or seven children.[80] Other oral testimonies echo this experience: Margaret Kierman remembered her mother saving in clubs all year to pay for Whit outfits, and Ivy recalled, 'My mother would save every penny she had to get our dresses … mum used to save hard to make you look nice for the Whit Walk.'[81] In 1934, the *Catholic Herald* celebrated the effort Catholics made to obtain the costumes needed for the procession, 'I cannot, and shall not, attempt to describe the overwhelming detail of this cavalcade of Catholicity … I applaud the courage and sacrifice that had been obviously made in thousands of homes.'[82] Yet not all families could afford to take part and many undoubtedly had to miss out. Andrew Davies' study of leisure and poverty in Manchester and

Salford includes the testimony of Mrs Phelan, whose father was unemployed during the 1930s and who spent much of his unemployment allowance on betting. Mrs Phelan recalled, 'We never had any Whit week clothes. We used to just look through the parlour window and see everybody else dressed up.'[83] That Mrs Phelan and her sister remained indoors and did not join the huge crowds outside is revealing of the isolation and marginalization they must have felt at not having the correct outfits. Manchester's Whit celebrations were clearly a moment of both emotional and financial investment for Catholics by the late 1920s and early 1930s but represented a difficult moment for those unable to participate.

Catholic women's appropriation of modern consumer culture for a religious event reflected the importance of Whit as a method of bolstering shared identity as the community underwent a period of change. Cohen's anthropological study of Whalsay, in the Shetland Isles, suggested inhabitants used change to boost their own sense of uniqueness and harden their collective identity. When threatened by change, inhabitants 'nurture a view of their own eccentric modernity'.[84] Again, there are parallels with the interwar Catholic Whit processions, which occurred within a background of broader social and cultural change. As we saw in Chapter 5, a populist culture of glamour and consumer culture emerged after the First World War and attracted the attention of young, working-class women, which alarmed the Catholic Church. Salford Diocese pursued its own campaign against fashionable dress and women's 'craving for constant, daily amusement', particularly the cinema and dances.[85] Yet by the late 1920s and early 1930s, Salford Diocese (particularly under Henshaw's leadership) became noticeably more relaxed about modern forms of consumer culture and, as shown above, Catholic women incorporated them into the Whit processions to stress a stronger sense of difference from their Protestant counterparts and, as Cohen's inhabitants of Whalsay, fostered their own form of modernity.

Catholic women's greater autonomy in shaping the form and expression of the celebrations marked the Whit processions of the later 1920s and early 1930s. In around 1930 Salford Diocese, in recognition of the poverty so many Catholic families experienced, ruled against a stipulation for Whit costumes. The ruling meant white dresses were not compulsory and aimed to alleviate financial burdens, yet this caused a great outcry among Catholic women. Margaret Kierman recalls, the 'mothers all said "we want them to wear white dresses"' and the white costumes remained.[86] There was a mutual relationship between church leaders and Catholic women: they negotiated the form of expression taken by the Whit walks and the façade of appearance offered Catholic women status and became increasingly specific to the Catholic processions into the later 1930s.

Adult women were also far more involved in the Catholic processions in comparison to Protestant women by the 1930s. Newsreel footage of the 1934 procession depicts greater numbers of statues and icons, larger and more ornate than in the earlier years. Rather than spelling out generically Christian inspired words such as 'PURITY', as the Protestant walkers did, flowers spelt out 'AVE MARIE' to accompany a large statue of the Madonna, also covered in flowers. Many girls were also dressed as peasants with their heads covered and young boys wore Eastern European satin suits with pointed slippers. Thus Catholic procession members in the later 1930s reflected a more exotic, and certainly non-English, expression of Catholicism because of the influence of immigrants to Manchester.[87] Those who were children in Manchester during the mid and late 1930s emphasized the impact of immigrant Catholics on the form and expression of the Catholic walks. Essie and Ronnie Strul, themselves both Jewish, recalled watching the walks in Manchester when they were children and remarked the Catholic processions were considered to be an especially great occasion because of the exotic costumes.[88] Alma Todhill remembered the Catholic walks were 'very colourful', particularly the Hungarian participants in national dress, whereas Ivy insisted the Irish in their national colours were the most noteworthy members of the procession.[89] In contrast, the Protestant processions were then dominated by patriotic banners and flags, with children in Scout and Guide uniforms and few white dresses or flowers.[90] By the later 1930s, the Catholic Whit processions were noticeably different to the Protestant procession and this was reflective of internally constructed forms of shared identity and of a popular and exotic urban religious culture.

The active role Catholic women played in shaping the form and expression of the Whit processions and their ability to incorporate contemporary cultures of fashion and shopping into the celebrations reflected the church's broader confidence in Catholic women's ability to navigate the modern world by the 1930s. As the Catholic Church in Manchester became more relaxed about women's perceived vulnerability to modernity, Catholic women were increasingly able to balance their religious identities with more secular endeavours, outside of the Whit processions. For example, Catholic leaders recognized the popularity of home dressmaking and sought to channel women's interest in fashion towards charitable Catholic endeavours. The Catholic Needlework Guild (which made clothes for poor people) was especially popular as Catholic leaders believed it allowed Catholic women the opportunity to combine their interest in modern consumer culture with religious duties and principles. Salford Diocese engaged with the emerging spectacular consumer culture to provoke excitement and support for the Guild's achievements. In January 1932, *Harvest* (the monthly periodical for Catholics in Salford Diocese) reported the Guild's collection of garments: Maine Road, Manchester City's football stadium, 'was not far away, but even the crush of City would not rival the thrill of a "close up" of over 16,000 garments'.[91] Leisure pursuits that allowed Catholic women to spend time together were also encouraged. *Harvest* described a tea party for Catholic Mothers in 1932 as a 'demonstration that Catholic faith is as strong and vigorous – that Catholic morals are still gloriously upheld'.[92] The church saw these women-only pursuits as ways for women to enjoy modern forms of leisure but that also promoted Catholicism.

Manchester's Catholic leaders also recognized young women were entering formal employment in growing numbers.[93] Rather than condemn women's paid work, Salford Diocese encouraged Catholic women to choose professions that extended women's roles as nurturers. Catholic leaders directly persuaded women to become nurses or teachers because these jobs allowed women access to the public world through paid employment, but also considered as roles that promoted values Catholic femininity. One article in *Harvest* encouraged women's vocations to the nursing professions by stating, 'What a joy to every priest who has a hospital to look after to find a Catholic nurse in charge ... a Catholic nurse is beyond words of appreciation.'[94] By the early 1930s, the Catholic leaders in Manchester engaged with wider debates relating to growing work opportunities for women. They did not discourage or condemn women's work but offered a specifically Catholic feminine identity in the public sphere. Nor were Catholic women alienated from public issues and the Catholic Women's League was especially active during the 1930s to promote Catholic women's role in society and, in particular, campaigned to broaden women's knowledge about the modern world. They were adamant Catholic women should not be kept ignorant of the key debates relating to modern society, including birth control and social issues. In 1934, one of the Catholic Women's League leaders explained to Bishop Henshaw why it was essential to allow Catholic women to debate all issues:

[Imagine] a good Catholic, intelligent, but her only distraction the local co-operative women's guild. Some controversial subject comes up, and by a little strategy she manages to get the matter held over for a meeting or two. Meantime she learns (or should learn) from the CWL (Catholic Women's League) magazine that 'such a' Diocese is discussing the matter and appeals for us to help.[95]

Again, this shows there was a negotiation between Catholic women and Catholic leaders. It was surely no coincidence that Salford Diocese took on a more conciliatory attitude towards the opportunities arising for women in the modern world from the early 1930s.

Conclusion

In 1939, Salford Diocese reported to the Vatican,

> From a spiritual point of view the state of the diocese is very satisfactory. Despite the fact that many Catholics have been moved to building estates just beyond the borders of our jurisdiction, and many others have been forced by circumstances to seek employment in the South, the number of Catholics in the diocese has increased.[96]

Thus, Catholicism thrived in the face of some potentially crippling social changes and, for Salford Diocese, was a period of confidence: 'The Catholic community is recognised as an integral part of the city's life', the Diocesan weekly magazine declared in 1938.[97] Manchester's interwar redevelopment disrupted parish communities and widely dispersed the Catholic population. Many moved to the new municipal suburbs, such as Wythenshawe, which was beyond the jurisdiction of Salford Diocese. Salford Diocese's confidence was reflected in the ability of the Whit processions to allow the Catholic community to maintain an episodic, yet powerful, possession of the city centre. In the early twentieth century, a celebration of a parish and religious identity characterized the processions. By the 1930s, however, the parish identity had been diminished and Catholic shared identity dominated. The celebrations ensured Manchester's Catholic population retained a strong presence in local culture, when their sense of community was marginalized and under threat.

The importance of the Whit processions peaked interwar, which supports Cohen's understanding of the role of ritual in strengthening shared identity, particularly in times of change.[98] Nevertheless, the peculiarities of the Whit celebrations need further consideration. Manchester was, of course, not the only city to witness important religious or secular processions in the early twentieth century and marching was an important aspect to cultures of Catholicism around the world and to sectarianism in Ireland and Britain.[99] The presence of Italian and Eastern European Catholics, alongside Irish Catholics was important: the diversity permitted a more fluid Catholic shared identity and ensured the Whit processions became more exotic in their expression as the period progressed. Thus, the changes to the Whit processions related closely to the nature of the Catholic community and the pressures it experienced between the two world wars.

Catholic processions were also noteworthy because they included greater numbers of adult women during the 1930s. At a time of great debate about Catholic women's role in the changing world, they offered women agency and fulfilment, despite the financial pressures, and some of the key turning points in the evolution of the Catholic processions interwar were products of assertions by women, particularly on dress. Whit walks allowed women to combine popular forms of consumer culture and spending, particularly in terms of dress, for more explicitly spiritual roles. Catholic women could forge their own form of 'eccentric modernity', which contrasted with their counterparts elsewhere.[100] Callum Brown's secularization thesis argues the loss of women from churches in the 1960s was crucial in the de-Christianisation of Britain and may explain both the strength of the Catholic processions interwar and their subsequent decline. Brown suggests, 'British women secularized the construction of their identity, and the church started to lose them. ... The key to understanding secularization in Britain is the simultaneous de-pietisation of femininity and the de-feminisation of piety from the 1960s.'[101] Thus, the relative strength of the processions between the two world wars lay in Catholic women's pietisation of femininity, which was to be lost by the 1960s.

The Whit processions never again reached the popularity of the 1930s. They declined significantly during the 1950s and collective Catholic identity tended to be expressed through St Patrick's Day celebrations, rather than more explicitly spiritual processions.[102] The context of the interwar period and particularly the impact of Manchester's redevelopment can explain the popularity of the Whit processions and the changes in the expression of the Catholic celebrations. Thus, the Whit processions peaked at the same time as politicians' and planners' investment in the city. What made the city centre a powerful stage for the performance of a religious identity related closely to broader cultural meanings invested in the urban environment. Perhaps the best way to understand the relationship between urban space and religious identity is to look at the multiple cultural appropriations of the urban environment: maybe the real power of the Whit processions lay in the commercial and civic urban cultures that the Catholics wished to overcome, even for just one day of the year. Nevertheless, as Chapter 6 explores, the Catholic Church in Liverpool invested in the transformed city centre in a very different, and arguably even more dramatic, way.

The Cathedral That Never Was?

The Catholic Church in Liverpool also responded to urban redevelopment with ambition and innovation. As architectural expert Charles Reilly announced to readers of the *New York Times* in 1930, 'Liverpool is starting to build a second and even greater cathedral. Her new project, indeed, calls for the greatest cathedral in the world next to St Peter's at Rome.'[1] Designed by Edwin Lutyens, 'arguably the greatest British architect of the twentieth century,' the planned Catholic cathedral, named the Metropolitan Cathedral of Christ, was intended to be second largest in the world and expected to cost £3 million.[2] The impact of the cathedral on the city and beyond was highly anticipated: 'I see the cathedral then, like a rainbow across the skies radiating the true and the good', wrote one prominent member of Liverpool Archdiocese.[3] For the Archdiocese and, in particular for the cathedral's pioneer, Archbishop of Liverpool Richard Downey (1881–1953), it represented an opportunity to transform the way in which Catholicism was seen both in Britain and beyond. Catholic leaders embraced the opportunity presented by Liverpool's wider programme of redevelopment and, using a grandiose building project of their own, sought to market Liverpool as a centre of Catholicism with international significance.

The cathedral project began in 1929 and in just one decade the Archdiocese's energetic fundraising campaign raised nearly £1 million, one-third of the money needed. This total was no small achievement since there was no financial help from Rome or even from Catholic leaders in Westminster.[4] The cathedral's fortunes were short-lived, however, as the Second World War and its demands for labour and material halted progress, leaving only the crypt completed. Postwar inflation rates saw costs soar to nearly £30 million and the Archdiocese eventually abandoned Lutyens' cathedral in 1954, and it remains known as 'the very greatest building that was never built'[5]. In 1962, Sir Frederick Gibberd's pioneering design replaced Lutyens' cathedral, although it is roughly only half the size of Lutyens' intended design.[6] Despite the grandiosity of Lutyens' and

Downey's planned cathedral, historians have neglected this rather unusual episode in the history of early-twentieth-century Britain. Although references to Lutyens' and Downey's Catholic cathedral project do exist, they tend to be limited to architectural historians' interest either in the cathedral's aesthetic form or as part of Lutyens' career and life more generally.[7] As a case study, however, it reveals the ways in which religious leaders such as Downey responded to wider processes of modernity, embraced Liverpool's redevelopment and used the built environment to strengthen Catholic power and influence.

There are important similarities between the cathedral project and broader innovations in planning and urban design between the two world wars. As we saw in Chapter 1, Liverpool was at the forefront of trends in urban planning due to its international links and influences and through the energetic work of Charles Reilly and the Liverpool School of Architecture. Like urban transformation more generally, the planned Catholic cathedral emerged within a wider international culture of cathedral-building and reflected the remarkable power, influence and ambition of Catholic leaders in a provincial city. Using the cathedral project as a case study, this chapter argues that its extensive fundraising campaign created a powerful Catholic image of the city, in which Catholics, both in Liverpool and beyond, were able to invest. The language and rhetoric of the cathedral campaign sought both to impose the power and authority of the Catholic Church and to nurture a strong sense of Catholic shared identity. As with the emerging civic and consumer culture we saw in earlier chapters, the Archdiocese aimed to foster a populist and demotic culture of Catholicism. The cathedral project therefore reveals the similarities between Catholic leaders and the investment in urban transformation made by local politicians and businessmen. By implication, a vision of an assertive and dynamic culture of Catholicism emerges, that was in no way marginalized from (and indeed embraced) broader cultural and social changes.

A tale of two cathedrals

Described by one inhabitant in the 1930s as 'the most Irish city in the world outside of Ireland,' it is perhaps unsurprising that of all British cities, the attempt to build the largest Catholic cathedral outside of Rome occurred in Liverpool.[8] Liverpool was already famous for its large Catholic population following the influx of Irish immigrants in the decades after the famine of 1846–51.[9]

Nevertheless, Irish immigration to Liverpool nearly trebled over the interwar period, from 3,200 migrants in 1924 to 8,200 in 1936, as emigration to America became increasingly difficult.[10] Liverpool Diocese (founded in 1850) was reorganized in response to increased Irish migration after the First World War. In 1924, the newly created Diocese of Lancaster took forty-six of Liverpool's parishes leaving Liverpool Archdiocese with an official population of 183,811, but this figure ignored Catholics living beyond the immediate city centre area.[11] One estimate counted 249,000 Catholics living in the 3- to 4-mile radius surrounding Liverpool Town Hall in 1925, whereas a separate survey suggested Liverpool was home to 400,000 Catholics in 1934.[12] Within a general population of around 750,000, therefore, Liverpool's Catholic community encompassed at least a third and possibly over a half of the city's overall population between the two world wars. Liverpool's other majority religion was Protestantism, and there were notable numbers of Presbyterians, Methodists, and a significant Jewish community.

The city's Catholic population loomed large in the concerns of local politicians and urban planners, not merely because of its size but also because of its geographical segregation. Scotland Road, a large area between the docks and the city centre, was home to 75,000 Catholics in 1924, which was then larger than the Dioceses of Cardiff, Shrewsbury, Portsmouth and Middlesbrough combined.[13] Scotland Road had long been considered the 'black spot on the Mersey', but many Irish migrants chose to live there because of the support network offered.[14] It is more accurate to understand the area as a micro-society, with an independent form of hierarchy and social stratification. As Pat O'Mara's *Autobiography of a Liverpool Irish Slummy* testifies, the lowest social groups lived in Scotland Road's 'Courts', narrow alleys home to twenty-five families with two shared toilets. The Courts were home to the poorest-paid labourers and underemployed: frequented by the 'cheaper elderly whores' and where 'screams often rent the air at night. ... Huge cats continually stalked the place, their eyes an eerie phosphorescence in the darkness.'[15] If inhabitants of the Courts were the bottom of Scotland Road's micro-society, O'Mara shows that residence outside the Courts, regular work and a strong devotion to Catholicism, placed other families nearer the top.

Inhabitants of Scotland Road remained largely unaffected by Liverpool's interwar redevelopment and Catholics (usually employed in lower paid occupations such as dock work) were often unable to move to the new 1930s suburbs because of the high rental costs, although this was not always lamented.[16] The size, stability and cohesiveness of the Catholic community were not only crucial for the Archdiocese's ability to even conceive of such a large cathedral, but also helped to fuel the fantasy around the cathedral of Liverpool as a Catholic city. To the local state, the Catholic population loomed large and threatened rebellion, instability and violence. Sectarian divisions had always been strong in Liverpool and the year 1909 was particularly bloody. Tensions continued to shape local culture – Liverpool did not unveil a civic memorial to the fallen of the First World War until 1930 because of sectarian tensions and divisions over its form and design.[17] The influence of religion on local politics in Liverpool is well documented and, for instance, one commentator in the 1920s, 'likened the monthly Labour meetings to "a lesson in apartheid", where members segregated themselves according to religion and politics.[18] Anti-Catholic and anti-Irish sentiments did seem to intensify in Britain more generally after 1918, particularly in light of economic decline. In 1931, the *Manchester Guardian* blamed Irish migrants for the burden they placed on the country. It argued that 'the national government and the civic authorities ought to take steps to find out the full charges upon the Exchequer and the local rates caused by our Irish invaders.[19] Irish migrants also found themselves to be the focus of blame for similar problems in Liverpool: in 1936, a survey suggested that 86 per cent of public assistance in Liverpool went to people of Irish extraction and the St Vincent de Paul society asked its Irish branches not to send any more job seekers to the city.[20] Conceived within such a culture of suspicion and scrutiny of Irish Catholics, the cathedral project's ambition and scope reflected Downey's desire to transform the negative reputation of Catholics in Britain and to counteract their marginalizsation from official civic and political cultures.

Although ambitions for a Catholic cathedral first emerged in the 1850s, it gained real momentum only under the energetic and ambitious leadership of Doctor Richard Downey. Appointed Archbishop of Liverpool in 1928, aged forty-seven, Downey was then the youngest Roman Catholic Archbishop in the world, and became 'the most powerful figure in the English Church.[21] Downey preferred to work without the cooperation of England's other Catholic bishops and experienced particular tension with Bishop Bourne (Bishop of Westminster, 1903–35, Cardinal from 1911) and with Cardinal Griffin (who became Archbishop of Westminster in 1943). Reflecting their rivalry and his own arrogance, Downey famously reminded Cardinal Griffin, 'I rule the North.[22] The sheer scale and form of Lutyens' plan reflected Downey's grand agenda for Catholicism both in Liverpool and beyond. Downey never saw himself as the leader of a parochial Catholic Church in the northern environs of England and never in any way felt or behaved as if he was further down the hierarchy than Cardinal Griffin. In fact, he seemed to see Northern England as the heart and power of Catholicism and above Westminster. Downey's aims and objectives through the cathedral project reflected his rather ambitious belief that Liverpool was an internationally important centre of Catholicism, second only to Rome.

The choice of Edwin Lutyens (1869–1944) as the architect of the Catholic cathedral was a deliberately audacious and noteworthy one. Lutyens built his career on English country houses, imperial architecture in New Delhi, the Whitehall Cenotaph and the Memorial to the Missing of the Somme at Thiepval.[23] Lutyens' mother was an Irish Catholic who converted to Anglicanism on marriage, making him acceptable to Downey and the Catholic Church. Lutyens possessed some sort of religious faith himself and confessed to his friend, long before he commissioned to build the cathedral, 'I am horribly religious, yet cannot speak it and this saves my work.'[24] Lutyens certainly developed a strong emotional investment in the project, requesting drawings of the cathedral around the room as he lay dying.[25] For Lutyens' son, the cathedral 'could and should have been built. It may well have been the final affirmation of his faith in the eternal thing that so transcends mere building.'[26] As the most prominent architect in the British Empire between the wars, Downey's commissioning of Lutyens reflected both Downey's ambition for the cathedral and his wider belief that Catholicism was not a marginal or foreign presence in Britain and that Liverpool was no parochial outpost. Downey's choice of Lutyens sent a clear message to the rest of the country and the world, and by choosing the most famous architect of the time, who had created some of the most iconic buildings and monuments of the period, he ensured the cathedral project achieved credibility and respect from contemporaries.

Alongside the choice of Lutyens as the architect, Downey was aware that the cathedral site could contribute to the gravitas he hoped the cathedral would have. Following the Poor Law revisions, Downey pounced on the opportunity to seize Liverpool Workhouse, which stood a hill overlooking the city centre. The purchase eventually completed following a period of difficult negotiations with both the council and the Ministry of Health and protests by Protestants.[27] Nevertheless, Liverpool Archdiocese obtained the 'finest site in the city' eventually and the council agreed to its sale by passing 'a majority which would have been unbelievable a few years ago.'[28] Their achievement in obtaining the site suggests Downey and Lutyens' shared vision and ambition for the city even persuaded a reluctant Liverpool Corporation to cooperate with the project. Crucially, the land was above the city centre and in direct opposition to the Anglican cathedral. After consulting plans of Liverpool in 1929, Lutyens wrote to Downey to say, 'The Ordnance Survey Map of Liverpool gives your site as being some thirty feet higher than that of the Anglican Cathedral – which is good',[29] which Downey highlighted and annotated with a '!'. Catholic publicity material used the cathedral site to create a distant Catholic fantasy image of Liverpool and reveals how the old Workhouse site allowed the Archdiocese to re-imagine the city in dramatic ways. Typical images of the cathedral produced by the fundraising campaign emphasized that it would be larger than the city's Anglican cathedral (begun in 1910) and, by connotation, larger in status also. Furthermore, Lutyens' design tended to dominate the landscape in the images, dwarfing the city's famous buildings including the municipal buildings, Liver Building, Dock Offices and even St George's Hall. Such images give a strong indication that the cathedral intended to marginalize any other buildings in the city and dwarf the skyline, even from beyond the River Mersey.[30]

Representations of the cathedral in publicity material reflected Lutyens' recognition that the Catholic cathedral needed to be visually impressive and larger in opposition to the Anglican cathedral. 'How ridiculous it would be to have two similar churches, as though Liverpool had brought two from a trayful', remarked Lutyens in 1929.[31] Liverpool's Anglican cathedral is gothic in style and made from sandstone, whereas Lutyens' design used Irish granite (which may have been a way to gain support from Irish Catholics), was Byzantine in style and designed around Romanesque triumphal arches. Figure 6.1 depicts a scale model of the cathedral, currently on display at the Museum of Liverpool. It shows Lutyens' design was a strong visual contrast to the Anglican cathedral, which reflected the sense of religious difference that they wished to manifest through the cathedral. There are aesthetic similarities between Lutyens' cathedral design and his Memorial to the Missing of the Somme. Stamp writes, 'Something of the grandeur and originality of the (cathedral's) conception can be grasped when standing under the high vault of the Arch at Thiepval.'[32] Like the monument at Thiepval, the cathedral was to be imposing and influenced by Roman triumphal style and made up of complex interconnections. Stamp's description of Thiepval could almost be of Lutyens' cathedral design: 'Arches are placed centrally in each block – except on the principal elevations to east and west where the lower, flanking blocks are extended outwards to create a buttressing effect. The Thiepval Memorial is not an arch but a tower of arches.'[33]

Figure 6.1 Image of scale model of Liverpool Catholic Cathedral, designed by Edwin Lutyens, at Museum of Liverpool. Copyright, Mike Peel

Lutyens and Downey intended the cathedral to be the largest outside Rome, far larger than the Catholic cathedral finally built in Liverpool during the 1960s. Crucially, Liverpool Archdiocese wanted the cathedral to be larger and more imposing than the rival Anglican cathedral, designed by Giles Gilbert Scott. The Anglican cathedral is 104,275 square feet in area with a tower 331 feet in height.[34] Lutyens' cathedral was to be 216,500 square feet in area and over 500 feet in height and would have been closer in comparison to St Peter's in Rome, which is 227,000 square feet in area.[35] Lutyens' cathedral was to have the largest congregation space in the world with room for 10,000 worshippers, over double the area of the Anglican cathedral.[36] There were also plans for a façade surmounted by a figure of Christ that would be visible from sea and from the Scotland Road area.[37] Like Liverpool's urban planners more generally, American architectural trends and innovations influenced Downey's ambitions for the cathedral. In particular, he wanted the cathedral to mirror the impact of New York's skyline on those arriving into the city by boat. 'In years to come ships travelling from the West to England, will see as their first glimpse of that supposedly Protestant land the towering catholic cathedral of Christ the King', anticipated one publicity pamphlet for the cathedral.[38] David Gilbert and Claire Hancock's analysis of representations of the New York skyline highlights the importance of its visual impact in encouraging tourists to the city. They argue 'the rituals of arrival in early-twentieth-century New York helped turn the immediate process of immigration itself into a tourist spectacle,' as passengers sailed past the Statue of Liberty and then onto Ellis Island, a 'working' tourist attraction from its opening in 1894.[39] Downey wanted the cathedral to dominate the Liverpool skyline and, influenced by American trends, provide a striking religious image that dominated the built environment, particularly for those arriving into the city by ship, who would most likely be arriving from Ireland or from America.

Lutyens and Downey rejected the tradition of designing cathedrals in the gothic style, as the Anglican cathedral was, and wanted to promote Catholic difference visually. Downey explained to the readers of the *New York Times*:

'We do not want something Gothic', said the Archbishop. 'The time has gone by when the church should be content with a weak imitation of the medieval architecture. On the other hand, we want nothing "Epsteinish". Our own age is worthy of interpretation now and there could be no finer place than a great seaport like Liverpool. ... Hitherto all cathedrals have been dedicated to saints. I hope this one with be dedicated to Christ himself with a great figure surmounted on the cathedral visible for many a mile out at sea.'[40]

Lutyens therefore designed the cathedral in Byzantine style (associated with the pre-Reformation era), in keeping with the style that other Catholic cathedrals built in the early twentieth century. Again, like urban transformation more generally, this choice of architectural style reflected the influence of a wider culture of internationalism on the cathedral's design, such as Westminster Cathedral (1895–1910); the Basilica of the National Shrine of the Immaculate Conception, Washington DC (1920–59); and the Cathedral Basilica of Saint Louis (1907–28), all built in the Byzantine tradition. Lutyens and Downey's decision to build the cathedral in Byzantine style also reflected the Catholic Church's desire to use architecture to create a sense of longevity, survival, and perseverance and Liverpool's Catholic cathedral intended to 'give outward expression to the majesty of the Catholic religion'.[41] Lutyens and Downey believed a Byzantine style of architecture created this image of permanence and power. Liverpool Archdiocese was also keen to ensure the new cathedral would overshadow the emerging commercial and municipal buildings. It was 'in competition with adjacent "sky-scrapers" that the new cathedral at Liverpool has been designed on so vast a scale', claimed one publication in 1933.[42] The cathedral's aesthetic style and internationally influenced design was fundamental to Downey's plans to remarket Liverpool as an important focus of Catholicism and to boost the religion's profile and reputation within Britain.

Rebranding Catholicism

Downey's ambitions for Liverpool's cathedral project was illustrative of a broader period of confidence among the Catholic Church in England and America.[43] Such confidence was particularly apparent around the centenary celebrations of Catholic Emancipation in 1929, relating to the repeal of controversial legislation in 1829 that saw the removal of most of the restrictive legislation against Catholics and permitted them to gain seats in Parliament. Celebrations in London focused around a National Catholic Congress, which included open-air masses near Westminster Cathedral and a Procession of Youth, where 12,000 children marched in celebration.[44] Yet Liverpool saw the largest celebrations and 400,000 Catholics gathered in jubilation.[45] There, 'rich and poor, young and old, the educated and ill, stood shoulder to shoulder'.[46] These celebrations and the sense of confidence they fuelled within the church shaped the rhetoric of the cathedral campaign. Propaganda argued the cathedral project was indicative of 'a time when other religions are deploring their empty churches, Catholics are building for numbers with whose increase they can hardly keep pace'.[47]

Such confidence encouraged Downey to attempt a broader remarketing of Catholicism. The preparations for the consecration ceremony for the cathedral site in 1933 reveal Downey's ambitions were to elevate its standing both within Britain and beyond. For example, in 1933 Downey wrote to the British Legation to the Holy See to discuss which Papal representative would attend the cathedral's consecration service and was reluctant towards the idea of an Irish Cardinal in order to distance the Catholic Church from Ireland.[48] Rather, like urban planners, civic politicians and businessmen, Downey looked to forge international links and requested the attendance of Cardinal Hayes of New York at the ceremony, arguing 'there are ... many links between Liverpool and New York'.[49] Downey's plans were by no means impossible since prominent Catholic, Lady Armstrong, wife of Harry Gloster Armstrong who, as we saw in Chapter 1, assisted civic politicians in making trade links in America, was very close to Cardinal Hayes due to her work with the Catholic Church in New York City.[50] These links, alongside the connections and energy of architectural expert Charles Reilly, might help to explain why the *New York Times* covered Downey's cathedral project relatively heavily and positively. Its support was notable in comparison to the relative lack of coverage in the British national press and boosted the cathedral's fundraising campaign.[51] The attempts of civic politicians to boost Liverpool's reputation and promote the city internationally therefore helped to improve the power and strength of the Catholic Church and advertised Liverpool's image as a Catholic city to a wider audience.

The idea of a shared Catholic community permeated the rhetorical approach of the cathedral's publicity campaign. Lutyens claimed to be 'resolved to turn this soil, once sacrificed to sorrow and despair, into one given up to praise, prayer and *great* thanksgiving – into a *"true* refuge,"' for the weary and the heavy-laden'.[52] In the context of economic depression, this language served to support the Archdiocese's investment into the ambitious cathedral project. When the Papal Legate, Cardinal McRory, visited the site in 1933, he declared it was 'sanctified by the tears of the widow and the prayers and holy resignation of the poor'.[53] This concept of a communal sacrifice was echoed by Downey's sermon in 1937: 'The poor who dwelt here, were the forerunners, preparing the way for Christ's coming by their prayers, their mortifications, their sufferings, their conformality to the will of God.'[54] The language of sacrifice placed the cathedral within broader Catholic narratives of martyrdom and redemption. For instance, Downey claimed the cathedral would 'become a great centre of public prayer, praise and sacrifice'.[55] At the same time, this populist rhetoric used by the Archdiocese mirrored Liverpool Corporation's approach to their citizens and for Liverpool Archdiocese, this language of classlessness was an effective way of drawing support for the cathedral project. One publicity brochure for the cathedral claimed the Workhouse had been there in the years 1771–1928 and therefore had 'one hundred and fifty-seven years of history closely connected with the Catholic Church', as three-fifths of inmates were Catholic.[56] Such rhetoric promoted a form of Catholic ownership of Brownlow Hill and presented the cathedral as a reward for the Catholic population's devotion to the church, even in times of poverty. The use of a deliberately populist rhetoric was particularly important as Catholic leaders grew increasingly concerned about the threat of Communism and other forms of political extremism.

The language used in the funding campaign aimed to mobilize Catholic support at a time of potential upheaval and rebellion against the church. By implication, Liverpool Archdiocese presented the cathedral project as a spiritual campaign that relied on Liverpool's Catholics coming together, even in the earlier days of the campaign. A pastoral letter written by Bishop Keating in 1922 argued,

> *No one has a right to stand out.* Whether you recognise the need for a cathedral or not ... whether you belong to the Archdiocese by birth, or by adoption; whether you live in Liverpool, or the more remote parts of Lancashire ... whether you are wealthy or one of the labouring poor ... your co-operation is sought and expected.[57]

Similarly, the *Liverpool Catholic Parishioner* declared: 'All classes of people are asked to help build the Metropolitan Cathedral of Liverpool.'[58] When Downey renewed the cathedral campaign, this rhetoric of a shared spiritual responsibility reappeared but became more important as the Catholic Church grew increasingly concerned about growing support for Communism in England. These fears were not unwarranted: the Communist Party of Great Britain attempted to attract Catholic membership from cities like Glasgow and Liverpool, as Catholics were often working class and many experienced unemployment.[59] In the Liverpool docks particularly, 'the Communists made amongst the despised and ill-treated dock labourers'.[60] Downey made the church's position on Communism very clear. An Advent Pastoral Letter of 1932, written by Downey and read in all churches in the Liverpool Archdiocese declared, 'Between Catholicism and Communism there can be no compromise. A Catholic cannot be a Communist; a Communist cannot be a Catholic.'[61] Liverpool's cathedral project aimed to unite the Catholic community against the spread of Communism. Although it is difficult to assess how far the Archdiocese was successful in promoting unity, the cathedral project reveals how they sought to nurture a stronger sense of shared identity against the rise of such political extremism.

The need to foster a sense of unity against extremism was essential at a time of political, economic and social upheaval throughout Europe. Liverpool Archdiocese was criticized for its ambitious cathedral project at a time of high unemployment and poverty in the city. One letter to the *Evening Express* in April 1930s asked, in a poem, 'Why all the Fuss' at a time of economic depression:

> One letter read, the sum to be spent
> To the poor should be given, or perhaps lent,
> And yet I've got a strange recollection
> Of another cathedral in course of erection.
> Would that money also do
> To ease the poor, and needy too?[62]

Such condemnation was threatening because the Archdiocese asked the poor of the city to donate money. Helen Forrester's autobiographical novel of life in 1930s Liverpool complained that, as 'city health officials looked in despair at horrifying infant mortality rates and at a general death rate nearly the highest in the country. ... The Roman Catholic Church and the Church of England continued to build themselves a cathedral apiece and solicited donations.'[63] The Archdiocese responded to criticism by presenting the cathedral as a possession of the poor, with the aim of uniting the poor behind the project. 'If we were to deduct from our Cathedral funds all the big donations which we have ever received, the bulk of the money would remain intact, made up of the offerings, I might say the blood-offerings, of the poor', claimed Downey in 1933.[64] This claim may not be an accurate estimation of the money donated, but Downey shows the Archdiocese consciously sought to unite the Catholic community and engage the poorest Catholics in the cathedral project. The Archdiocese again claimed: 'It is the poor, precisely, who *want* their cathedral, who are determined to have it; who would be shocked if you told them that they must abandon the idea of their Cathedral, and get themselves better rooms.'[65] Publicity material continued to claim the poor were the true cathedral builders, even going as far as claiming that 'most of the money which reaches the Cathedral is in copper!'[66] The building fund accounts do not reveal whether the poor did donate the most amount of money.[67] Yet the Archdiocese's desire for the poor to be seen as the *real* cathedral builders is important and highlights how they sought to use the cathedral project to strengthen Catholic collectivity.

The Vatican were confident that the cathedral would help protect Catholics against Communism. Downey travelled to Rome in 1931 and received the Vatican's formal approval for the cathedral, which Pope Pius XI described as 'a bulwark against Bolshevism.'[68] Publicity material presented the cathedral as benefiting the lives of the poor, both physically and spiritually. Lutyens' plan included a heated narthex, which was to be open day and night for anyone who needed the warmth, which Downey described as 'a spiritual sanctuary for the cold and destitute.'[69] At the same time, richer donors were rewarded spiritually and the Archdiocese established a reward system on a sliding scale, the lowest being those who gave £100 and were given the title 'Memorial Benefactors.'[70] Those who gave £1,000 earned the title 'Founders' and were rewarded with weekly Masses, and an annual individual Mass for every £1,000 donated. Nevertheless, although the reward system was hierarchical in nature and rewarded those who gave the most money, the scheme also reinforced traditional Catholic doctrines regarding the equality of all men in God's eyes. This populist understanding of the Catholic community was emphasized through visual representations of the cathedral and the Catholic urban fantasy the propaganda fostered.

Catholic urban fantasies

Reilly, Liverpool's leading architectural expert of the interwar period, was confident that Lutyens' cathedral would 'change everything'. Reilly was sure the Cathedral would dominate the city, arguing 'we will all be humbler ... our ordinary buildings will be simpler ... for having in our midst this noble expression of the power and beauty of fine architecture.'[71] While remaining unbuilt, Lutyens' cathedral design changed how Catholics perceived Liverpool. Catholic propaganda re-imagined the city to portray this particular form of urban fantasy and, for example, some images show Lutyens' cathedral superimposed to depict it towering over Liverpool's most famous civic and commercial architecture, such as the Pierhead buildings, which were symbolic of the city's power and prestige as a port.[72] Such pictures served to promote the cathedral project and to attract money for the campaign but also contributed to helping Catholics envision the power and prestige of the church in Liverpool, despite the cathedral remaining incomplete.

Images that depicted the cathedral towering over Liverpool's best-known buildings were common propaganda techniques used by the Archdiocese in the cathedral project and aimed to impress Catholics and encourage donations to the building fund. Depicting the cathedral this way belittled the existing architecture in the city, as well as the powers (civic and commercial) that created them. In one image, the Archdiocese sought to justify the £3 million cost of the cathedral by showing it in comparison to HMS *Hood*, which cost the same amount. Downey's caption to an illustration of the building superimposed on *Hood* stated the Cathedral's 'colossal proportions simply dwarf this great battleship'.[73] Publicity material made several comparisons between the cathedral and HMS *Hood*, as it gave a vivid depiction of the scale of Lutyens' cathedral and laid claim to the Archdiocese's power and status. The choice of HMS *Hood* was significant as the ship became a national symbol in the post-First World War years, 'embodying the material reality of empire; for native populations her presence underlined both the power and the beneficence of the imperial overlord, while for British officials and "white" citizens of the empire she symbolized and made real a remote and intangible homeland.'[74] Liverpool Archdiocese's depiction of the cathedral dwarfing HMS *Hood* intended to show the church's power and status, but also sought to help contextualize the money being spent and showed potential donors that the £3 million cost was warranted and worthwhile as it would lead to a building which was even more impressive than the popular HMS *Hood*. This comparison also gave some indication of the impact Catholic leaders hoped the cathedral would have. What *Hood* was for the Empire, the Cathedral promised to be for the Catholic Church more generally and the representations of *Hood* and the cathedral reflected a wider attempt to encourage Catholics to see the cathedral's visual impact, while it remained unbuilt.

Downey was ambitious for the 1933 foundation stone ceremony, describing it in private correspondence as the 'greatest event in the ecclesiastical history of England since the Reformation'.[75] The cathedral project shaped perceptions of the city, even without being built and this was a key part of Downey's plans for the ceremony. Along with Downey, the ceremony included a Papal Legate, Lutyens, the Archbishops of Galway, Cardiff, Birmingham and Edinburgh (representing each of the four British countries), thirty-two bishops and six abbots, at considerable expense.[76] One commentator claimed there were 1,000 priests in attendance and 'every kind of dignitary of the Roman Catholic Church'.[77] Never one to be outshone, Downey would undoubtedly be pleased that the Liverpool celebrations drew over twice the number of clerics than did the consecration of the St Louis Catholic cathedral in 1926, which attracted five hundred cardinals, bishops and priests.[78] Downey also attempted to secure the presence of delegates from the British armed services in order to invest the occasion with gravitas and to try and avoid perceptions of provincial Catholic celebrations as parochial or marginalized from mainstream British culture. However, this objective was to prove difficult to achieve and the Office of the Admiralty refused Downey's invitation, explaining, 'I can trace no record of the Admiralty ever having been represented at a religious ceremony such as the present.'[79] Similarly, the Air Ministry and the War Office also refused invitations from Downey and both claimed that there was no precedent for their attendance. Indeed, it seems no representatives from the armed services attended any of the celebrations on the Cathedral site.[80] The British army appeared to resent the status given to the Pope following the Roman-Vatican settlement of 1929, as they did not wish to grant the pope or papal representatives the status of a chief of state.[81] There were also widespread calls for the army to abolish church parades, although the Secretary of State appeased the situation in 1930 by declaring 'no man was ever made to go to Church'.[82] Downey may have been unfortunate to have made the request during a moment of debate about the relationship between the armed services and religious groups, or there may have been a more general reluctance within the armed services to establish a formal professional relationship with the Roman Catholic Church.[83]

Despite such setbacks, Downey persisted with grandiose plans for the celebrations. Lutyens built a vast temporary altar intended to be the focus of the site for pilgrimages until the cathedral's completion and Downey argued the temporary altar 'will give us a concrete example of the genius of our architect and a foretaste of the beauty and magnificence of the cathedral-to-be'.[84] As Figure 6.2 illustrates, the plain altar was not dissimilar in style to Lutyens' Cenotaph in Whitehall.[85] The altar also helped to change the urban landscape through its great size and bright white colour, ensuring it was visible from some distance away. Downey explained the foundation stone celebration was to 'give satisfaction

Figure 6.2 Temporary altar during the ceremonial laying of the foundation stone, 1933.

Source: Stuart Bale Archive, National Museums and Galleries on Merseyside, 1613–114.

to those thousands of our people who have so generously subscribed to the cathedral and who will not live to see its completion'.[86] The ceremony was clearly an attempt to invest the cathedral site with sacred meaning. Again, we can see the influence of other cathedrals around the world, especially the Sacré-Coeur in Paris (constructed 1874–1910), which attracted 115,000 pilgrims during the first year of the project alone.[87] Saint John's Cathedral in New York also witnessed numerous religious celebrations taking place on the unbuilt cathedral site, especially around the feast of St John, investing the area with spiritual meaning and maintaining motivation for the fundraising campaign.[88] These influences show Liverpool Catholic Cathedral emerged within a wider international culture of cathedral-building and drew on broader trends and innovations.

Just as the celebrations on the site of the Sacré-Coeur attracted devoted pilgrims who redefined a building site as a spiritual space, so did Liverpool's foundation stone celebrations of June 1933. On Friday 2 June 1933, a procession of children left St George's Hall (Liverpool's greatest civic building and main public transport terminus), walked through the city's shopping area and past the department stores, and along Mount Pleasant to the cathedral site. Although Downey could not secure the attendance of the British military, it seems he was determined to invest Liverpool's civic and commercial symbols with spiritual meaning and there are similarities with the impact of Manchester's Catholic processions, as we saw in Chapter 5. The celebrations included special masses and continued over the weekend, culminating in the laying of the foundation stone on the Sunday. Pathé captured the scene in a newsreel entitled *Solemn Blessing and Laying of the Foundation Stone of Liverpool Metropolitan Cathedral of Christ the King to be the Second Largest in the World*. The footage of the service focuses on the great crowds of people who came into the city to see the celebrations. Although the cathedral site had seated accommodation for 30,000, an estimated 95,000 arrived.[89] Film footage shows people leaning out of windows to see the ceremony and cramming into every available space to get a view.[90] 'Every window, roof, and many of the chimney-stacks that I can see, are swarming with yet more (people)', described the event's radio commentator.[91] One estimate suggested that half a million people came into Liverpool for the celebrations.[92] The radio commentary explained the cathedral belonged to the ordinary Catholics of Liverpool

> Dear poorer people of Liverpool, who are crowding the streets that you were (I know) decorating up to 3 o'clock this morning, but who can't get into this space – so large, yet far too narrow to hold anything like all of you – don't think you are all forgotten.[93]

The ceremony drew large numbers of people into the city centre, which illustrates the way in which religion was a source of enjoyment and fulfilment for people in Liverpool in the 1930s. At the same time, it also suggests that many found some kind of connection with the cathedral project. After the 1933 foundation stone ceremony, numerous Catholic celebrations took place on the site, including a mass to celebrate the completion of the crypt in 1937. In 1937, 30,000 people came to watch the internment of Archbishop Whiteside (Bishop of Liverpool, 1894–1911) and on 4 November 1937, 100,000 people came to an outdoor mass on the cathedral site.[94] Following the example of the Sacré-Coeur, Downey actively encouraged people to visit Brownlow Hill for religious ceremonies, even though it still largely remained a building site.

The celebrations of 1933 also intensified sectarian tensions in Liverpool and Protestants interpreted the cathedral project as part of the Catholic Church's desire to take greater control both in Liverpool and beyond. Consequently, suspicion of Catholic power aroused 'Protestant warhorses' in the early 1930s.[95] The locally published *Protestant Times* regularly attacked what it perceived as the growing influence of the Catholic Church. In just one edition of the magazine in January 1935, there were several articles attacking the growth of the church's power. One article, 'Rome's Grip on the Press, Screen, Radio', claimed the pope spent over twenty million lire to build a radio station. A further report was titled '"Betrayed" Influence of Roman Church in High Positions of State, Menace to British Nation'.[96] Protestants claimed the cathedral was a further financial burden on the city caused by Irish Catholics, alongside slums and prisons. One cartoon suggested that for Protestants, the Catholic cathedral was one of many concerns about the church's financial exploitation of Liverpool. Captioned 'The Man with a Load of Mischief', it depicted a cartoon Irishman burdening the council with unemployment, Catholic schools and the planned cathedral. Next to the Irishman, the Liverpool Citizen asks, 'I wonder why the burden never grows lighter?'[97] Protestants portrayed the cathedral as opposing the investment of municipal leaders and men of commerce in Liverpool's redevelopment, representing Catholics as non-citizens because of their support for the cathedral.

Protestant groups certainly unleashed their warhorses during the weekend of the foundation stone ceremony. There were large demonstrations by Orangemen during the weekend of the ceremony, including a protest in Shiel Park in Liverpool that attracted an estimated crowd of 8,000. A speech made at the demonstration accused the planned cathedral of being 'a spectacular display made in an effort to recapture England for Romanism'.[98] A total of 20,000 Protestants attempted to disrupt the foundation stone ceremony, trying to hold up the cars taking priests and representatives to the site. A local newspaper reported that protesters broke car windows and attempted to prevent traffic from getting through the city centre.[99] These attacks followed sporadic but not uncommon spates of religious violence in Liverpool during the early 1930s, including attacks on Downey.[100] Despite remaining unbuilt, therefore, the cathedral project seems to have intensified sectarian divisions in Liverpool. It cemented the city's reputation at home and abroad as a centre of religious tensions, with attacks by Orangemen on the cathedral on 15 July 1932 attracting notable press attention.[101]

'Hands, hearts, souls across the sea': Catholic shared identity

A stronger sense of Catholic collectivity emerged around the cathedral project but it was not restricted to Liverpool, particularly as the Archdiocese's propagandist efforts were global in their reach. A report written by the Archdiocese in 1953 shows that between 1928 and 1936 the great majority of funds came from Liverpool, after which the campaign took on a greater international perspective.[102] One key approach by Downey was to use iconography to market Liverpool as an internationally important centre of Catholicism and so attempted to create an icon, 'Our Lady of the Sea'. This title would permit the creation of statues and other ephemera inside the cathedral that depicted Mary, Mother of Jesus and the River Mersey, in the same way there are icons for Our Lady of Lourdes or Our Lady of Fatima. Rome refused permission since there were no known visitations by Mary to Liverpool. The Archdiocese received a rather curt response that reflected the audacity of their request: 'If every small place or large city were to create their own Our Lady would that not detract from solid devotion to authenticated shrines?'[103]

Undeterred by his defeat over the use of Mary, Downey instead attempted to present the cathedral as the 'Cathedral of the North' to bring together all the Catholics in Northern England. Such an approach was not unproblematic however and Downey's ambition riled (and likely threatened) other Catholic leaders, who perceived the cathedral project as a form of megalomania. In 1931 for example, the Bishop Henshaw of Salford wrote an angry letter to Downey, complaining he had not given permission for Catholics in Salford to have collection boxes for Liverpool Cathedral. Henshaw argued it was the 'committing of trespass and infliction of damage … [I] forbid you to collect either by means of boxes or any other way from the diocese of Salford.'[104] Correspondence between Downey's office and the *MEN* in 1936 also reveals tensions between Downey and

Henshaw. A journalist for the *MEN* agreed an article on the cathedral would be written and published in the newspaper, but would be presented as if it had been undertaken without Liverpool's knowledge or cooperation, 'So you (Downey) could always blame "one of those blank reporters" in case Salford raised an eyebrow.'[105] Since Salford Diocese faced pressing concerns relating to church and school building interwar, it seems Henshaw feared Lutyens' cathedral project distracted money away from his own causes. What is more, Downey and Henshaw's rivalry mirrored that between municipal leaders and businessmen in Liverpool and Manchester. It may be that the Catholic building projects contributed to a wider sense of civic pride, which, as we saw in earlier chapters, flourished interwar when competition between the two cities was especially intense. Tensions were not limited to the north-west of England, however, and Downey also received a negative response from the Archbishop of Cardiff, who told Downey he was preoccupied with building churches. He wrote that he was 'astonished that you should ask permission to beg in this Diocese. I do not possess a magnificent cathedral in my own Diocese,' and forbade Downey from fundraising in the diocese.[106] These responses suggest Downey's aggressive attempts to assert Catholic power alienated other Catholic leaders, who were also perhaps envious of his ambitious cathedral plan.

Despite these conflicts, Downey's fundraising rhetoric presented the cathedral as a way to unite all Catholics and did not limit his ambitions to the north of England. In some ways, especially due to the conflicts with other bishops, it was easier to fundraise outside of Britain. Downey's ambitions were global: 'Men of all nations will unite under one roof, in one common worship', Downey wrote in 1933, 'It will lift the city to a higher plane than that of nationalism in religion ... it will echo the universal language of the church.'[107] Downey specifically aimed to use the cathedral to connect Catholics all around the world, claiming 'hands, hearts, souls across the sea ... the hearts of those who, dwelling across the seas, are linked to us by bonds of blood and kinship.'[108] In particular, the support from the *New York Times* was invaluable, which regularly hailed the cathedral as 'the great edifice' and proclaimed 'the great cathedral ... will be four times as big as Westminster cathedral and be surpassed in size only by St Peter's in Rome.'[109] The fundraising campaign was certainly successful in attracting support from all around the world and in 1936, the *Liverpool Post and Mercury* claimed that, with the exception of Russia, there had been donations to the cathedral fund from every country in the world, including Iraq, India and North Borneo.[110]

The reach of the fundraising campaign is perhaps less surprising once we understand its scale and innovation. The campaign effort focused on generating support through public rallies from 1928 and this shifted to the 'Golden Book' campaign in the early 1930s, which raised £167,000 by 1953 by asking individuals to make subscriptions.[111] Yet the campaign was active in far more innovative ways and marked a new approach of the church towards consumer culture. Downey's predecessor, Bishop Keating, for example, saw the cathedral as an opportunity to curb the spending and leisure habits of the Catholic community, as his declaration shows:

> If a new Catholic Cathedral means that amongst Catholics there has been deliberately brought about less drinking and betting, less luxury and more self-denial, a football match foregone one week, a packet of cigarettes the next, a new jumper sacrificed without a feminine sigh ... then will the projected cathedral be well and nobly built.[112]

But Downey did not tell Catholics not to spend money on consumer goods. In contrast, he sought to provide ways for Catholics to enjoy these things in a way that benefited the cathedral project. One of the most ostentatious forms of Catholic acts of consumption was the production of 'Cathedral Cigarettes', which allowed Catholics the opportunity to fund the building of the cathedral as they smoked. Their advertisement declared, 'At last ... Liverpool's *own* Cigarette. **"Cathedrals."** A fine Cigarette for the City of finest Cathedrals. Worthy of the City that builds for the future.'[113] The cigarette company licensed the use of the cathedral from the Archdiocese, submitting a minimum of £250 a quarter to the cathedral fund.[114] Decorated with a large image of the cathedral, the cigarettes offered a direct link with the cathedral project and were a way for Catholics to demonstrate their support for the project through the purchase of these cigarettes.

Smoking was not the only way in which the cathedral project shaped consumer culture in Liverpool. One company produced 'Cathedral Tea', promoted as 'The tea with double the appeal. ... Every quarter sold adds to the Metropolitan Cathedral Appeal.'[115] In July 1933, 5,000 pounds of Cathedral Tea was sold every week and sales were expected to double in volume over the following months.[116] There was also the opportunity to subscribe to the 'Golden Book': 'As builders of the Sanctuary and Blessed Sacrament Chapel your name and the names of your relatives or friends, living or dead, would be inscribed therein **FOR EVER.**'[117] The Archdiocese also established a scheme that gave people a replica model of the cathedral in return for collection boxes. 'Be a leader. ... Say with pride in years to come: "I helped to raise this, the second *largest* of all Cathedrals,"' proclaimed the advert for collection boxes.[118] These collection boxes alone raised over £600 between 1 March and 30 June 1933.[119] The range of products and spending opportunities allowed Catholics to demonstrate their Catholic identity through their purchases. Chapter 4 emphasized importance of women placed on particular acts of spending and in similar ways, Catholic items for consumption allowed Catholic to obtain alternative forms of fulfilment and status. Advertisements for these products appealed directly to Catholics through the *Liverpool Cathedral Record*, but were not placed in the mainstream press such as the *Liverpolitan* or the *Liverpool Echo* or the national press.

Catholic women seem to have reacted enthusiastically to the role of cathedral builders. From the mid-1930s, it was popular for women to bequest donations to the Cathedral fund on their death, and, in 1934, a Miss A. G. M. Standish left her entire jewellery to the fund, and she was not a rare case.[120] As the *Manchester Guardian* reported in 1930, just one year into the fundraising campaign, the amount of jewellery donated was impressive:

> Diamond cuff-links and gold coins are among the articles being received in aid of the fund for building a Roman Catholic cathedral at Liverpool. Other gifts include watches, diamond rings, snuff-boxes, crucifixes, cigarette cases, silver spoons, and a golden chalice.[121]

The opportunity to become Cathedral builders was not limited to the wealthy. In 1935, the *Daily Mail* reported a woman from Scotland Road raised £200 by collecting and selling jam jars.[122] There are no comparable references to money made raised by (lay) men for the Cathedral. Archived accounts also show that of the different chapels in the cathedral, most of the subscriptions were by women to chapels that reflected their identity. For example, the Union of Catholic Mothers subscribed £144 10s. to the Lady's Chapel.[123] Subscriptions were available for several of the chapels, including St Patrick's Chapel (very popular with Irish subscribers), Teacher's Chapel, Children's Chapel, St Joseph's Chapel and the Seamen's Chapel. The Lady's Chapel received the most donations and attracted £60,000 in donations by 1953, whereas St Joseph's Chapel received £4,600 and the Children's Chapel only £3,300.[124] Catholic women possessed a clear role within the Archdiocese's vision of religious modernity and their role as cathedral builders within the cathedral project was symbolic of this. There are parallels with Catholic women's citizenship – defined through their fundraising efforts for the cathedral – and wider female citizenship between the wars, in which women in organizations, such as the Women's Institute, raised money for good causes as a way to demonstrate their citizenship without challenging gender norms.[125] The energy and commitment shown by Catholic women does, however, highlight their important role in Liverpool's civic life more generally and illuminates their wider contribution to the city's public culture.

Conclusion

The enthusiasm of Catholic women towards the cathedral reflected a wider culture of popular religiosity. It is perhaps not surprising the Catholic Church felt confident enough to embark on such an ambitious building project in the 1930s, as the immediate post-war years experienced a general revival in Christian religious belief in Britain and beyond.[126] Mass attendance records suggest a growth in popular Catholicism in interwar Liverpool: in 1908 the average Catholic in Liverpool attended mass ten times a year and during the period 1915–24, it had increased to twenty-five times a year.[127] The cathedral project seems to have both fuelled, and been fuelled by, this flourishing culture of Catholicism in Liverpool. In the early 1920s, for instance, there were sixty-four convents in Liverpool Archdiocese and eighty-two by 1940.[128] 'Dominic's Day', which was a time of pilgrimage for a popular saint, saw 2,500 people take to the city's streets in 1925 and 10,000 in 1939.[129] As a case study, therefore, the cathedral project not only reveals the vitality of urban Catholicism in interwar Liverpool but also demonstrates the ambition and dynamism of Catholic leaders, especially Downey. The cathedral project strengthened Catholic shared identity and collectivity but in a way that embraced the processes of modernity. 'Cathedral Cigarettes' may best encapsulate how the planned cathedral offered individuals a way to embrace their religious and their modern selves to create a form of modernity similar to that produced in Manchester's Whit processions as we saw in Chapter 5.

The fundraising campaign and the opportunity to purchase items such as Cathedral Cigarettes seems to have been successful and by 1939, the cathedral fund stood at £934,786.[130] Yet the Second World War took away the manpower needed for building the cathedral. With Lutyens' death in 1944 and Downey's following in 1953, the two leading personalities of the building project were lost. Money continued to trickle though to the campaign, usually from those who had bequeathed the cathedral fund in their wills or had taken out life insurance in its honour.[131] As Liverpool received significant bomb damage, cathedral-building was certainly not a priority in the decade following 1945.[132] Eventually, in 1954, an Architect's Report reviewed Lutyens' design and progress. The report concluded that Lutyens' design would actually have seated just 2,500 people and a large proportion of these would 'see nothing of the Celebrant or the ceremonies around the Altar owing to the great height of the Sanctuary above the Congregation seating floor'.[133] More critically, the cost of Lutyens' design soared due to post-war inflation rates: rather than the initial estimated cost of £3 million, by the 1950s, its estimated cost stood at £27,370,438.[134] The unmanageable cost forced the Archdiocese to abandon Lutyens' and Downey's dream cathedral and the money raised went towards a more modest design. Ironically, Gilbert Scott, brother of Giles Gilbert Scott (architect of the Anglican cathedral), took over the planning of the Cathedral in August 1957, but this too was abandoned and a new competition for a Cathedral design was launched in 1960. Liverpool finally got its Catholic cathedral in 1967 when Sir Frederick Gibberd's pioneering design was completed over one hundred years after plans were first raised.

Architectural historian David Watkins suggests that the planned cathedral 'would have been the greatest church in the world'.[135] John Summerson argues that despite remaining unbuilt, Lutyens' design 'is a landmark in the architectural history of its time'[136] Although the cathedral was never completed, the propaganda nurtured a competing urban fantasy around Liverpool city centre, which emphasizsed Catholicism in the city, challenged the religion's marginalization in wider civic culture and boosted Liverpool's status as a provincial city. For example, during the formal opening of Gibberd's cathedral, the accompanying publicity pamphlet highlighted Downey's role in fuelling the project and proclaimed, 'He destroyed the legend that Catholics were undignified, unacceptable people.'[137] Lutyens' and Downey's cathedral was a symbol of the Catholic modernity Liverpool Archdiocese sought to promote. Although Lutyens' design is known as the 'the cathedral that never was', Liverpool's planned Catholic cathedral still had a profound impact on the city and its inhabitants, before the Second World War halted Downey and Lutyens' shared dream.[138]

Conclusion: The Second World War and the Challenge to Interwar Urban Culture

Liverpool's Catholic cathedral, although incomplete, reflected the wider culture of ambitious urban design in interwar Liverpool and Manchester. Like local politicians' investment in housing, transport, civic architecture and civic celebrations, and shop owners' new approach to marketing and shopping culture, Catholic leaders also attempted to create new images of urban modernity. Political, economic and social turmoil motivated these ambitious programmes of urban transformation and shaped the accompanying urban images. In particular, local politicians in Liverpool and Manchester invested in significant programmes of redevelopment in response to instability and the press and municipal publications promoted urban transformation heavily to disseminate new urban images and to communicate with the new, cross-class electorate. There was, at times, a fantasy element to the way these publications presented urban redevelopment as local politicians attempted to guide the citizen's guise away from ongoing problems and the persistent spectre of unemployment proved especially problematic. Redevelopment remained uneven in its success and characterized by incompleteness, as the inability of either Liverpool or Manchester Corporation to deliver on their goals for housing reform by 1939 testified.[1] Although it is difficult to gauge how far citizens accepted or even rejected these images of the transformed cities, their pervasiveness, the popularity of the civic celebrations and the corporations' relative ability to quell dissenting voices, suggests that redevelopment and the accompanying publicity campaign possessed some impact on inhabitants.

The outbreak of war in 1939 interrupted the work of urban planners, local politicians, businessmen, and Catholic leaders in Liverpool and Manchester. The building of Liverpool's Catholic cathedral staggered on through the early days of war due to the dedication of a small number of labourers, until conscription finally caught up with them.[2] Manchester held no religious processions during the war, leaving uncelebrated Whit Weeks the 'strangest in the memory of Manchester'.[3] Tenacious as ever, Lewis's department store attempted to make the most of wartime conditions, announcing in September 1939 that they 'urge their customers to buy now from present stocks', before prices increased.[4] Of course, clothes rationing and supply problems proved straightened conditions even for the most dynamic of department stores.[5] The war also removed the attention of Frederick Marquis, who, as the Earl of Woolton, became Minister of Food in 1940, overseeing rationing and ensuring the British population had adequate nutrition.[6] The war also brought new challenges and new responsibilities for local politicians, who had to shift their focus away from housing and prestige projects towards preparing their cities for war and their priority became building air raid shelters, rather than new civic monuments.[7]

Unfortunately, German bombing raids damaged both Liverpool and Manchester's city centres. Its role as a port made Liverpool particularly vulnerable to air raids, and with 4,000 casualties, saw the highest civilian deaths outside of London. There were severe damages to the overhead railway, Anglican cathedral, Blacklers and Lewis's department stores and most of the buildings on Lord Street required repairs or rebuilding. The bombs destroyed the Customs and Excise building on Canning Place, alongside many cinemas, the central telephone exchange, the corn exchange and the Rotunda Theatre. Liverpool was not the only casualty in the North, however, and the Germans also recognized Manchester's commercial importance and marked it as a target. The bombing focused on the city centre, particularly during the 'Christmas Blitz' in 1940 when nearly seven hundred people died during heavy fire. Although Manchester did not suffer as much as Liverpool did, it affected the city centre badly. 'Familiar landmarks ... are now blackened shells, or ... heaps of rubble,' reported the *Manchester Guardian*: the Free Trade Hall, Victoria Buildings, Rates Office, Cross Street Chapel, Manchester Cathedral, Chetham's Hospital, Masonic Temple, Corn Exchange, St Anne's Church, City Hall, Smithfield Market, Gaiety Theatre, Piccadilly Gardens and Deansgate were all badly hit.[8]

The war wiped the slate clean, if only metaphorically, for planners and local politicians throughout the country who did not wait for war to end before they devised large-scale plans of urban redesign. Planners seized upon the chance to re-imagine the city in new ways and, for example, Plymouth's destruction in the war 'represented an exceptional opportunity to create a new and modern city'.[9] Urban fantasies reappeared in these new plans and post-war urban reconstruction was 'characterized by a marked gap between the rhetoric and reality'.[10] Indeed, during the war, many cities and towns invested in ambitious plans that were never completed, such as Edwin Lutyens and Patrick Abercrombie's 1945 plan for Hull or Charles Reilly's 1944 plan for Birkenhead. Frank Mort draws parallels between the 1943 *Country of London Plan* and the Beveridge Report, suggesting they both offered 'a rhetoric of popular democracy that worked by condensing policy into nuggets of graspable meaning'.[11] Like pre-war urban images therefore, the replanning and reimagining of cities both during and after the war reflected the particular social and economic context of the period. There are clear continuities in cultures of urban planning in the pre- and post-war era and the roots of post-war 'reconstruction' are evident in Liverpool and Manchester's interwar redevelopment.

In Liverpool and Manchester, as more generally in Britain, the impetus for planning continued during and after the war. In 1941, for example, Alfred Shennan, leader of the Conservative Party in Liverpool announced plans to create an inner ring road and a more clearly defined civic centre as soon as war ended. The Mersey Tunnel entrance was to be at the heart of the new civic centre and plans also extended to wide avenues around both cathedrals, suggesting that post-war plans for Liverpool reflected a continuation of interwar redevelopment.[12] Nevertheless, planners in the city embraced new technologies and ideas about urban modernity into the 1950s and attempted an unrealized scheme to build a heliport in Liverpool as a way to improve congestion and urban mobility.[13] In Manchester, the Corporation published the City of Manchester plan in 1945, a glossy, comprehensive book that considered a complete redesign of the city centre and demolishment of the Town Hall.[14] Yet, rather than an example of post-war 'reconstruction', the Manchester plan was relatively conservative and 'the intention of the Corporation was to control the right to plan the city, rather than completely reshape it'.[15] By implication, it seems planning historians exaggerate post-war differences in urban planning, and Liverpool and Manchester's experience supports the idea of continuities between interwar and post-war cultures of planning and civic design.

The continued focus on planning was not an easy one for the local state as Liverpool and Manchester, in common with other provincial cities, faced a challenging post-Second World War period. Local and civic identities are considered to have been overshadowed by the unifying rhetoric of the 'People's War', for instance.[16] The growth of the power of central government both during and after the Second World War is also strongly associated with finally ending municipal autonomy.[17] Nevertheless, there is evidence to suggest that the central government considered local authorities able to take on the new tasks associated with the foundation of the Welfare State and 'reconstruction'.[18] As I have shown elsewhere, in Manchester politicians responded to these challenges again with great confidence and innovation, and invested in a civic film, made by the leading documentary film-maker Paul Rotha. The film, called *A City Speaks*, promoted Manchester's interwar urban transformation but was a continuation of the promotional work to engage with citizens that we saw in Chapters 1 and 2. Rather than offering a new image of Manchester to reflect the post-war period, the film disseminated an image of Manchester that reflected 1930s urban redevelopment, which seemed outdated by 1947. In contrast to local politicians' efforts between the two world wars therefore, the film was poorly received by citizens and reflected inhabitants' lack of confidence in local government to deal with the challenges of the post-war era.[19] Yet, Selina Todd's research on post-war planning in Liverpool and Coventry stresses the centrality of working-class people to the local state's vision of civic life.[20] This research is important because it suggests that urban planning as a method to engage with a cross-class electorate, as we have seen here, continued after 1945 and with an even greater focus on the working-class population. It also suggests that scholarship needs to move away from looking at post-war plans and towards a greater concern with how inhabitants experience and respond to redevelopment.

Paying greater attention to the impact of post-war urban planning on inhabitants will also help to reconsider entrenched stereotypes about British urban experience after 1945. Liverpool and Manchester in particular, have become strongly associated with urban decay and social deprivation after 1945 due to significant population loss and dramatic economic decline. Manchester's population fell to 404,861 in 1991, barely half the 1931 peak, and unemployment rates reached 58 per cent in some parts of the city during the 1980s.[21] Liverpool's economy also struggled and by the 1970s and 1980s, Liverpool 'assumed the status of a post-industrial pariah'.[22] However, we need to think more carefully about responses to these urban problems and particularly in relation to the investment made by the local state and energetic civic patriots after 1945.

The other aspects of Liverpool and Manchester's interwar redevelopment covered here also faced a challenging post-war period. The vibrant shopping cultures that emerged interwar were fundamental to Liverpool and Manchester and department stores were instrumental in transforming shopping practices and making stores enticing sites to see and be seen within. Of course, rationing and shortages ensured it was impossible for stores to maintain interwar practices, although Lewis's attempted to maintain its practices as far as possible and the Central Buying Office spent time in both Liverpool and Manchester, as a pre-emptive strategy to deal with wartime disruption. Yet department stores never regained their influence or presence within provincial consumer culture and shopping practices after 1945, until the expansion into Northern England by Selfridges and Harvey Nichols during the past decade. Liverpool's Lewis's was rebuilt after the Blitz but department stores were not expanded or developed in either city as they were before 1939 and many seem to have faded into obscurity. Of all the stores featured here, Lewis's recently closed, leaving only Kendal's to remain in business. Local consumer culture did remain focused around the city centre, but the rise of chain stores, supermarkets, and out-of-town shopping malls characterized mass consumer culture in the second half of the twentieth century and represented a very different type of retail culture.[23] Historians may need to reconsider their approach to understanding retail culture and, for example, recent research on the location of shops highlights the importance of retail space in the neighbourhood unit principle after 1944.[24] Shopping does seem key to later twentieth-century regeneration however, and Manchester's Arndale Centre and Trafford Centre and the recent Liverpool One development are examples of important consumer and shopping developments that represent wider programmes of investment in urban redevelopment.

The new shopping culture appealed to women especially, who were recognized as agents of regeneration and important as individuals shaping interwar urban culture. Glamour and fashion offered important methods of self-fashioning and fulfilment, although not without pressures. Again, the Second World War disrupted interwar cultures of fashion and appearance, as Mass Observation reported in 1941.[25] Nevertheless, clothing and appearance remained important to women's lives, despite the material shortages, but reflected the specific climate of the Second World War and looking attractive was part of women's wartime duties.[26] At the same time, historical scholarship on women's engagement with fashion and consumer culture tends to emphasise a general backlash against cultures of glamour in the 1950s and stress the valued and idealized role of the housewife, rather than fashionable shopper.[27] Perhaps historians need to think more imaginatively about retail culture, glamour and women's urban experiences in post-war Britain to understand how far there may be continuities with the interwar period.

Yet shopping culture was not incompatible with the vibrant cultures of religion that thrived following Liverpool and Manchester's redevelopment. My approach towards urban religious cultures supports work that argues we should not study the history of religion by looking at church attendance or baptism records, but by thinking more about how individuals and communities experienced, perceived and articulated religious belief and practice.[28] Offering a more nuanced and sensitive approach to analysing religiosity can complicate established narratives around secularization. For instance, although war halted the cathedral project in Liverpool, it did not hold back the Catholic Church who mobilized their infrastructure for the war effort. In 1940 for instance, Downey established a Temporary Diocesan Board of Union Catholic Women Board that brought together all the Catholic women's societies with the aim to mobilize their presence in the Home Front, to continue contributions to civic culture and, in particular, to influence programmes of evacuation and ensure Catholic children stayed with other Catholics.[29] The great involvement of the Catholic Church in urban life in both cities highlights the continued role of organized religion in shaping urban experience in the twentieth-century city and illuminates the intersections between civic culture and religious groups.

The findings here also add to Callum Brown's claims that Britain did not experience secularization until the 1960s and that the continued strength of the Christian Church relied upon women and the role of Christian femininity.[30] Manchester's Whit processions reappeared after war ended but they never reached the same popularity as before 1939, although there are currently attempts to revive the tradition. Liverpool finally got its Catholic cathedral in 1967 but Sir Frederick Gibberd's design is notably smaller than the one Lutyens and Downey dreamed of. We can read the demise of the Whit processions and the downsizing of Liverpool's cathedral as symbols of Brown's secularization thesis but, again, more current research suggests that the role of the Catholic Church might remain important in post-war Britain.[31] In 1982 for example, the visit of Pope John Paul to Liverpool drew a million people to the city and it maintains a strong culture of Catholicism around the cathedral. Manchester might not have the same strong link with Catholicism in popular consciousness as Liverpool, but in 2009, when the relics of St Thérèse of Lisieux toured Britain, Salford Cathedral attracted the largest crowds outside of London: 30,000 visitors in comparison to 17,000 in Liverpool.[32] Certainly, religious belief does not seem incompatible with urban life.

Modernity and exceptionalism

The impact of religious leaders in shaping urban culture in Liverpool and Manchester contributed to a wider culture of modernity that did not marginalize Catholicism. Whereas Liverpool and Manchester are often deemed 'exceptional' cities and depicted as existing outside of more mainstream cultures of modernity, scholarship places London as both the epitome of British modernity and as the 'flagship' of civic culture and powerful local government.[33] Liverpool and Manchester's redevelopment shows they did experience modernity in ways that were in common with broader cultures of modernity, notably the rise of consumer culture, the growing public role of women and a rich local political culture that embraced universal suffrage and engaged with the newly enfranchised electorate. Their modernity was also characterized in ways that might be different to more general trends, however, including powerful cultures of urban Catholicism, which also embraced modern consumer cultures. In doing so, it suggests that there was a powerful regional modernity, which supports arguments made in recent publications by cultural historians of modern Britain, which stress the existence of competing modernities.[34]

At the same time, Liverpool and Manchester's interwar experience suggests we might wish to reconsider the very definition and meaning of what it meant to be modern. The important role of religion and the agency and centrality of working-class women in Liverpool and Manchester's modernity suggests that British modernity itself might be less secular and less focused around elite spaces than many existing studies suggest. For example, Ross McKibbin argues the Protestant Church declined between 1918 and 1951 because it 'had to cope with the obvious manifestations of the secular', whereas 'the comparative introversion of the Roman Catholic community permitted the Catholic Church to escape them until the 1960s'.[35] Yet, the Catholic Church could not and did not isolate itself from the secular forces of the interwar period. In contrast, Catholic leaders reshaped and remodelled these forces to promote a Catholic vision of modernity and their negotiated approach to modernity successfully strengthened Catholic belief and shared identity. In particular, Liverpool and Manchester's experience evokes Joshua Landy and Michael Saler's argument about re-enchantment, which challenges the perceived incompatibility between modernity and the sacred. As they write, 'Modernity is messy'.[36]

Modernity in Liverpool and Manchester was also outward-facing. The programmes of redevelopment that were key to Liverpool and Manchester's modernity were not only ambitious and innovative but also influenced by international trends and emerged within a wider culture of international exchange. By implication, urban redevelopment not only drew on cutting-edge strategies of civic design, especially in Liverpool, but the influence of architects and planners abroad ensured the emerging urban culture was by no means inward-looking or parochial. Although social and cultural historians of early-twentieth-century Britain stress the cultural suspicion towards 'Americanization', Liverpool and Manchester's redevelopment created an outward-looking modernity that incorporated American influences in a productive manner.[37] Liverpool, in particular, aimed to draw comparisons with American cities and its innovations in civic design caused *The Times* to give the city the accolade of naming it 'the Chicago of Great Britain' in 1931.[38] The intellectual and academic exchanges between Charles Reilly and his students the Liverpool School of Architecture with architects and planners in America were fundamental in encouraging an outward-looking approach to civic design in Liverpool. Although Reilly's influence was notably less strong in Manchester, we have seen that planners and architects in both cities were by no means shielded from or hostile towards international trends in civic design. Thinking more carefully about the international connections and exchanges between experts, such as architects, offers a different perspective than that which emphasises economic and cultural isolationism.

Individuals such as Reilly were key in driving and shaping Liverpool's and Manchester's interwar redevelopment. Local politicians, businessmen and Catholic leaders were active in shaping urban culture but, at the same time, local inhabitants also contributed to the cultures of modernity that emerged. Inhabitants were not necessarily passive consumers but important actors within the modern urban culture that emerged. However, we need to know more about the longevity and temporality of regional modernity. Between the 1940s and 1960s, many of the key cultural changes that occurred in England centred on London 'but this was not the result of some natural metropolitan dominance nor of capital city chauvinism' and can be explained as 'the product of time and circumstance'.[39] Modernity was not therefore 'made' in the metropolis, but the post-war dominance of London may have overshadowed regional cultures of modernity and the vibrancy of Britain's provincial cities.

Liverpool and Manchester's modernity shared both commonalities and differences with the metropolitan model. By implication, the material presented here challenges their image of 'exceptional' cities and suggests that such a framework is not necessarily a productive one for urban historians to utilise. Certainly there is evidence to suggest civic culture flourished throughout Britain's towns and cities interwar. Municipal leaders in 1930s Coventry were also ambitious and farsighted in their civic investment between the wars.[40] Other cities, some also experiencing challenging economic conditions in the 1920s and 1930s, appear to have made similar investments in civic pride. As Chapter 2 noted, Salford, Cardiff, Hull, Bristol and Derby all hosted Civic Weeks at the British Empire Exhibition Hall at Wembley in the 1920s, perhaps also with the aims of attracting investment and nurturing stronger civic patriotism among citizens. Urban redevelopment was also at work on a grand scale in other cities: 'The First World War was the biggest turning point in London architecture since the fire at the Palace of Westminster in 1834', evidenced by the 'sheer size and number of projects for office blocks, town halls, power stations, housing estates and flats'.[41] Liverpool was not the only city that developed and promoted its Victorian civic architecture. Birmingham council renovated the city's Town Hall, originally built 1832–4, in 1927 and increased its capacity by the addition of a double gallery.[42] Other industrial towns and cities invested in impressive and ambitious civic buildings: Sheffield City Hall, built 1929–32 (costing £500,000); Birkenhead Library, completed 1934; and Leeds Civic Hall, built 1931–3. Investment in public transport and suburbanisation on a grand scale was not limited to Liverpool and Manchester either and impressive housing estates and tram and bus networks appeared throughout the country.[43] Although more research is needed to understand if politicians in other cities publicised and promoted their investment in urban redevelopment to their populations in similar ways to that seen in Liverpool and Manchester, these examples suggest there may be commonalities in the motivations and approaches towards interwar programmes of redevelopment.

Urban redevelopment revitalized retail culture and caused the fashionably dressed working-class woman to become a symbol of British modernity in cities like Liverpool and Manchester. By highlighting the important contribution made by department stores in producing a demotic shopping culture and the perceived relationship between women's citizenship and shopping, the relationship between shopping and urban redevelopment between the two world wars emerges. The rise of the new culture of retailing did not inhibit popular religious belief however, and cultures of Catholicism flourished in Liverpool and Manchester. Other towns and cities might not have witnessed Catholic building plans on the scale of the Liverpool cathedral or celebrations as large as Manchester's Whit processions; the interwar period was a confident one for the Catholic Church more generally.[44] Such confidence was evident in the ambitious plans at Prinknash Abbey to outsize the nearby Gloucestershire cathedral, and Benedictine monks at Douai Abbey (near Reading) planned a church which, if completed, would have equalled the scale of Liverpool cathedral. The strength and dynamism of Catholicism indicates there are similarities between cultures of Catholicism in Liverpool and Manchester with those outside of Britain, particularly North America, and it might be fruitful for historians to address connections and similarities between Catholic communities in ways that cross national divisions.[45]

Experiencing modernity in interwar Liverpool and Manchester

Vibrant cultures of Catholicism, a dynamic retail culture and innovative civic pride emerged in response to the ambitious programmes of urban redevelopment that politicians in Liverpool and Manchester invested in as a response to economic, social and political turbulence. The ambition and scale of redevelopment, the ways in which it was communicated to local inhabitants and its implications for a range of urban cultures and for women's urban experience are striking. The local press was fundamental in working with the council to promote urban transformation and suggests historians of twentieth-century Britain should pay more attention to the continuing influence and power of the provincial press after 1918.[46] The local press helped a rich visual culture emerge in accompaniment to redevelopment as urban transformation, both real and imagined, appeared in image-form the press, in municipal publications, and through civic celebrations and exhibitions. This promotional material functioned as a way to engage with inhabitants and to encourage them to absorb and accept the new urban images. Since great crowds attended Civic Week celebrations, women embraced the new retail culture and enjoyed the transformed cityscapes as shoppers, it seems these images and promotional material had some impact. Similarly, the great enthusiasm and investment made by women for the Whit processions and the striking popular support for Liverpool's planned Catholic cathedral attracted, demonstrated by the Archdiocese's ability to raise £1 million by 1939, a third of its total goal, is revealing of the emotional role these projects possessed for Catholics in both cities. Such evidence offers some sense of how inhabitants responded to the new urban images and provides some insights into how individuals experienced modernity in these provincial cities.

The notion of citizenship was central to these urban images and it lay at the heart of Liverpool and Manchester's redevelopment. It was no coincidence that local politicians invested in urban transformation at a time of political turbulence and social upheaval and the accompanying publicity material emphasised the relationship between the revitalized urban environment and the need for good citizenship. As Margaret Beaven, Liverpool's first female Lord Mayor and affectionately nicknamed 'the little mother of Liverpool', announced to huge crowds at the city's Civic Week in 1927 that 'Civic pride is good citizenship.'[47] At a time of social and political change therefore, the local state aimed to shape and define citizenship on a civic level. Yet the discourse around citizenship shaped the nature of urban cultures that emerged following redevelopment as civic, consumer and Catholic cultures disseminated a populist rhetoric of citizenship that aimed to transcend class barriers. Although these notions of citizenship aimed to be classless, however, they remained gendered. Local politicians and businessmen saw the female shopper as an agent of regeneration and women's civic duty became defined through their role as consumers, while Catholic women's role as shoppers was key to popular forms of worship and religiosity. These narratives and concepts therefore show that locally produced ideas of citizenship flourished interwar and that there could be competing models of citizenship, which individuals could perform episodically. Nevertheless, women's roles as consumer-citizens suggests similarities with national trends, wherein women's political enfranchisement and subsequence political activities stressed their domestic role and did not subvert gender norms.[48]

Of course the inhabitants of both Liverpool and Manchester were by no means passive recipients to the work of local politicians and planners, businessmen or Catholic leaders and an important dialectical relationship between selfhood and urban space existed. It would be wrong however to suggest that inhabitants were always in favour of the Corporations' programmes of redevelopment. Civic Weeks attracted criticisms because of their costs and the Catholic cathedral stirred up more than a little resistance, especially from Protestants. Nor did redevelopment quell dissatisfaction more generally in either city as both witnessed a number of riots and disturbances through the period.[49] However, the scale and depth of these problems may look less significant in comparison to economically depressed areas such as Glasgow or South Wales. Glasgow experienced a particularly acute problem with gang violence interwar, explained as a product of the city's sectarian divisions combined with high levels of poverty and unemployment as its shipbuilding industry experienced significant decline.[50] Although Glasgow and Liverpool shared some similarities therefore, it is interesting to note that Liverpool does not appear to have possessed a comparable gang culture. It may well be that urban transformation did inspire greater confidence in local government and its ability to deal effectively with the problems Liverpool and Manchester faced and contributed to inhibit the kinds of social tensions and revolutionary change that we see elsewhere in Europe between the two world wars.

Redevelopment did not eradicate problems of poverty or unemployment in Liverpool and Manchester and despite the impact of investment in urban transformation, both cities economies faced extreme challenges. Poverty maintained a clear presence in many people's lives and a new library or Town Hall extension may well have done little to aid someone struggling with unemployment. Urban transformation also remained incomplete. Manchester Corporation continued to struggle to fulfil their aims for Wythenshawe after war ended and in 1947 the Secretary for Wythenshawe Community Council claimed publicly that many residents wished to move because of the lack of amenities and sociability.[51] Wythenshawe only got a civic centre in the 1960s and, described 'as an extreme pocket of social deprivation and alienation' by the *New York Times* in 2007, it remains a problematic estate for Manchester Council.[52] Nevertheless, although interwar urban transformation and the vibrant urban cultures that emerged did not solve all of Liverpool and Manchester's problems, the innovation and ambition displayed by local politicians, businessmen and Catholic leaders challenges both cities' reputations as sites of urban decay.

Finally, the revitalised city centres were demotic and populist sites where individuals performed a range of identities that obscured class differences. Although class remained the most important organising category throughout the interwar period, the new forms of civic, consumer and religious cultures that emerged in response to Liverpool and Manchester's transformation offered opportunities for selfhood and shared identity that transcended class divisions. Thus, although the body of work that utilises class as the key analytical category with which to analyse interwar Britain is important, other identities also mattered in the transformed urban environment. Some forms of shared identity were episodic or co-existed with other seemingly contradictory ones: a working-class woman might be a fashionable shopper who enjoyed the Civic Week exhibitions, but she might also participate in the Whit processions or the cathedral fundraising campaign. Perhaps these kinds of experiences in the transformed urban environment best summarise what modernity meant in interwar Liverpool and Manchester. McKibbin concludes that in the first half of the twentieth century, 'England had no common culture, rather a set of overlapping cultures.'[53] Looking at the regional city, however, we can see how culture overlapped much more closely.

Appendix

Corporation income and expenditure

Liverpool, 1924–35

	1924	1926	1927	1934	1935
Income from Rates	2,753,508	2,624,279	2,730,396	4,451,766	4,367,220
Total income	5,366,155	5,385,086	5,727,315	9,349,273	9,400,589
Total expenditure	5,257,316	5,500,919	5,736,605	9,167,280	9,901,259

Manchester, 1924–35

	1924	1926	1927	1934	1935
Income from Rates	2,872,912	2,913,929	3,188,843	4,614,255	4,623,801
Total income	4,947,920	5,165,854	5,576,928	8,312,642	8,621,477
Total expenditure	4,886,402	5,314,373	5,577,214	8,132,590	8,610,392

Electricity

LIVERPOOL	1924	1926	1927	1934	1935
EXPENDITURE	523,134	634,599	896,119	962,497	985,219
INCOME	979,470	N/A	1,269,230	1,733,826	1,770,062

MANCHESTER	1924	1926	1927	1934	1935
EXPENDITURE	770,917	878,619	1,031,319	1,064,352	1,266,481
INCOME	1,474,007	N/A	1,636,600	1,877,343	1,972,065

Trams 1935

	LIVERPOOL	MANCHESTER
EXPENDITURE	1,278,245	1,783,948
INCOME	1,582,003	2,315,308

Corporation expenditure: Liverpool

	1924	1926	1927	1934	1935
Elementary Education	1,288,304	1,290,416	1,298,393	1,412,268	1,506,199
Higher Education	289,176	315,512	313,315	365,261	380,628
Public Arts	84,069	73,775	72,109	85,652	91,193
Police Force	688,540	739,527	799,562	733,335	758,793
Fire Brigade	60,091	59,767	60,695	65,271	66,796
Sewage	63,342	62,086	61,182	57,736	48,254
Refuse	295,806	303,237	288,286	217,944	215,097
Maternity/Child Welfare	77,626	83,558	89,978	116,321	122,796
Baths/Washhouses	59,640	57,463	64,901	84,040	85,287
Housing (assisted schemes)	109,525	39,733	109,637	92,372	78,550
Streets/Highways	223,112	229,027	139,188	N/A	N/A
Lighting	100,166	111,986	122,454	132,790	143,149
Electricity Supply	523,134	634,599	896,119	962,497	985,219

Corporation expenditure: Manchester

	1924	1926	1927	1934	1935
Elementary Education	1,187,387	1,246,659	1,233,389	1,295,792	1,359,392
Higher Education	361,256	381,753	399,652	438,644	461,311
Public Arts	92,428	102,192	109,205	109,047	126,864
Police Force	415,045	473,919	484,745	506,953	533,171
Fire Brigade	42,898	41,411	42,979	48,780	51,761
Sewage	135,913	147,789	142,772	105,989	100,864
Refuse	197,390	208,008	218,457	225,240	217,047
Maternity/Child Welfare	54,220	62,250	66,594	86,263	83,732
Baths/Washhouses	75,330	86,366	87,930	100,825	100,273
Housing (assisted schemes)	81,267	15,383	101,922	105,020	107,281
Streets/Highways	424,439	450,528	355,017	N/A	N/A
Lighting	149,657	1,593,913	172,881	195,635	192,022
Electricity Supply	770,917	878,619	1,031,319	1,064,352	1,266,481

Source: Ministry of Health, *Local Taxation Returns, England and Wales* (London: Her Majesty's Stationary Office, 1926–36).

Spatial redistribution in clothing and clothing-related shops, 1922–38

Shops in inner and outer Liverpool and Manchester, 1922–38

Liverpool - Inner	1922	1932	1938
Boot and Shoe Sellers	194	133	128
Clothiers	33	33	29
Costumiers	24	38	54
Drapers	314	283	393
Dressmakers	158	95	106
Hosiers and Glovers	21	19	20
Milliners	113	112	N/A
Tailors	124	96	190
Outfitters	23	30	59
Ladies Outfitters	55	52	102
Co-operatives	50	101	128

Liverpool - Outer	1922	1932	1938
Boot and Shoe Sellers	273	174	94
Clothiers	62	52	18
Costumiers	51	88	36
Drapers	455	360	128
Dressmakers	149	106	38
Hosiers and Glovers	72	46	18
Milliners	135	92	N/A
Tailors	591	556	353
Outfitters	120	97	68
Ladies Outfitters	46	48	15
Co-operatives	71	90	62

Manchester - Inner	1922	1932	1938
Boot and Shoe Sellers	51	47	47
Clothiers	76	15	3
Clothing Clubs	0	1	1
Costumiers	N/A	22	24
Drapers	23	34	24
Dressmakers	21	10	18
Milliners	19	16	15
Tailors	229	242	156
Outfitters	6	18	21
Ladies Outfitters	9	11	17
Co-operatives	N/A	1	7

Manchester - Outer	1922	1932	1938
Boot and Shoe Sellers	426	306	218
Clothiers	259	144	91
Clothing Clubs	0	14	24
Costumiers	N/A	87	75
Drapers	1,120	1,257	1,059
Dressmakers	348	290	232
Hosiers and Glovers	77	46	30
Milliners	304	281	198
Tailors	563	598	390
Outfitters	46	118	143
Ladies Outfitters	67	92	151
Co-operatives	22	185	239

Source: Kelly's Directories, 1922, 1932, 1938.

Department store advertisements

Advertisements placed by selected department stores in the local press, Liverpool and Manchester, 1920–38

Liverpool Echo

	Jan/Feb 1920	Oct/Nov 1920	Jan/Feb 1932	Oct/Nov 1932	Jan/Feb 1938	Oct/Nov 1938
Lewis's	32	35	48	57	56	36
GH Lees	19	16	22	21	20	14
Bon Marché	13	13	22	24	24	20

Liverpolitan

	May–Dec 1932	1938
Lewis's	7	1
GH Lees	2	10
Bon Marché		8

Manchester Evening News

	Jan/Feb 1920	Oct/Nov 1920	Jan/Feb 1932	Oct/Nov 1932	Jan/Feb 1938	Oct/Nov 1938
Lewis's	19	23	42	32	35	57
Affleck and Brown	41	1	18	10	19	14
Kendal's	14	2	15	2	12	3

Manchester Guardian

	Jan/Feb 1920	Oct/Nov 1920	Jan/Feb 1932	Oct/Nov 1932	Jan/Feb 1938	Oct/Nov 1938
Lewis's	0	3	39	42	3	3
Affleck and Brown	43	1	6	5	10	1
Kendal's	77	47	10	16	7	18

Total number of adverts (for sample months combined)

	1920	1932	1938
Echo	128	156	171
MEN	100	101	140
M. Guardian	171	106	41

Source: Liverpool Echo, Liverpolitan, Manchester Guardian, Manchester Evening News, 1920–38.

Notes

Introduction

1 *Liverpool, The Mart of Nations*, Promotional Map, 1924, Manchester Central Library Local Studies Collection (MCL LSC).

2 'Manchester's Civic Week', *Manchester Guardian (MG)*, 9 June 1926, 13.

3 'Liverpool's Slums', *Daily Mail*, 4 October 1930, 9.

4 'Liverpool's Poor Law Beneficiaries', *MG*, 6 April 1929, 6

5 'Overcrowding in Liverpool', *MG*, 21 December 1931, 2.

6 'Grave Position in Cotton Area', *The Times*, 17 March 1921, 17.

7 'Unemployment Distress in Manchester', *MG*, 18 December 1926, 13.

8 Andrew Davies, *Leisure, Gender and Poverty: Working-Class Culture in Salford and Manchester, 1900-1939* (Buckinghamshire: Open University Press, 1992), 23.

9 'Manchester's Worst Slum', *MG*, 2 May 1923, 13.

10 Sheila Marriner, *The Economic and Social Development of Merseyside* (London: Croom Helm, 1982), 1.

11 Dave Haslam, *Manchester, England: The Story of a Pop Cult City* (London: Fourth Estate, 2000), viii–ix.

12 A. J. P. Taylor, *English History: 1914–1945* (Oxford: Clarendon Press, 1965), 317.

13 Walter Greenwood, *Love on the Dole* (London: Vintage, 2004), 42.

14 J. B. Priestley, *English Journey: Being a Rambling but Truthful Account of what One Man Saw and Heard and Felt and Thought during a Journey through England during the Autumn of the Year 1933* (London: Penguin, 1977), 375.

15 Derek Aldcroft, *The Inter-War Economy: Britain, 1919–1939* (London: B.T. Batsford, 1970), 79–94; John Stevenson and Chris Cook, *The Slump: Society and Politics during the Depression* (London: Quartet, 1977), 48–50; Tim Hatton, 'Unemployment and the Labour Market in Inter-War Britain', in *The Economic History of Britain since 1700. Volume 2: 1860–1939*, eds. Roderick Floud and Deirdre McCloskey (3 vols., Cambridge: Cambridge University Press, 1994), 359–85.

16 George Orwell, *The Road to Wigan Pier* (London: Penguin, 1989), 46. Originally published 1937.

17 Nick Hubble, *Mass-Observation and Everyday Life: Culture, History, Theory* (Hampshire: Palgrave MacMillan, 2006).

18 Helen Forrester, *Tuppence to Cross the Mersey* (London: Harper Collins, 1993), 9.

19 Peter Fearon, 'A "Social Evil": Liverpool Moneylenders 1920s–1940s', *Urban History* 42, no. 3 (2015): 445.

20 Pat O'Mara, *The Autobiography of a Liverpool Irish Slummy* (London: Martin Hopkinson Ltd, 1934), 21.

21 Alan Kidd, *Manchester* (Edinburgh: Edinburgh University Press, 2002), 13.

22 Ibid., 187.

23 David Ayerst, *Guardian: Biography of a Newspaper* (London: Collins, 1991), Graph, 'Cottonopolis, 1820–1955', 436–7.

24 Greenwood, *Love on the Dole*, 12–13.

25 Howard Spring, *Shabby Tiger* (Manchester: Memories, 1999), 21.

26 See for instance, Ross McKibbin, *Classes and Cultures: England, 1918–1951* (Oxford: Oxford University Press, 1998); Davies, *Leisure, Gender and Poverty*; Andrew Davies and Steven Fielding (eds), *Workers' Worlds: Cultures and Communities in Manchester and Salford, 1880–1939* (Manchester: Manchester University Press, 1992); Judy Giles, *Women, Identity and Private Life in Britain, 1900–50* (Basingstoke: MacMillan, 1995); Paul Johnson, *Saving and Spending: The Working-Class Economy in Britain, 1870–1939* (Oxford: Clarendon Press, 1985); Alan Kidd and David Nichols (eds), *Gender, Civic Culture and Consumerism: Middle – Class Identity in Britain, 1800–1940* (Manchester: Manchester University Press, 1999); Elizabeth Roberts, *A Woman's Place: An Oral History of Working-Class Women, 1890–1940* (Oxford: Blackwell, 1984); Steven Fielding, *Class and Ethnicity: Irish Catholics in England, 1880–1939* (Buckingham: Open University Press, 1993); John Bohstedt, 'More than One Working Class: Protestant-Catholic Riots in Edwardian Liverpool', in *Popular Politics, Riot and Labour: Essays in Liverpool History, 1790–1940*, ed. John Belchem (Liverpool: Liverpool University Press, 1992), 173–216; Nick Hayes '"Calculating Class": Housing, Lifestyle and Status in the Provincial English City, 1900–50', *Urban History* 36, no. 1 (2009): 113–40; Selina Todd, 'Domestic Service and Class Relations in Britain 1900–50', *Past and Present* 203 (2009): 181–204; Helen McCarthy, 'Service Clubs, Citizenship and Equality: Gender Relations and Middle-Class Associations in Britain between the Wars', *Historical Research* 81, no. 213 (2008): 531–52; Martin Johnes, 'Pigeon Racing and Working-Class Culture in Britain, c. 1870–950', *Cultural and Social History* 4, no. 3 (2007): 361–83; Lucy Noakes, 'Demobilising the Military Woman: Constructions of Class and Gender in Britain after the First World War', *Gender and History* 19, no. 1 (2007): 143–62.

27 Stevenson and Cook, *The Slump*, 5; Aldcroft, *The Interwar Economy*, 350.

28 Margaret Mitchell, 'The Effects of Unemployment on the Social Condition of Women and Children in the 1930s', *History Workshop Journal* 19, no. 1 (1985): 106. See also Charles Webster, 'Healthy or Hungry Thirties?', *History Workshop Journal* 13, no. 1 (1982): 110–29.

29 Davies and Fielding (eds), *Workers' Worlds*.

30 Davies, *Leisure, Gender and Poverty*, 14.

31 Fielding, *Class and Ethnicity*.

32 Selina Todd, *The People: The Rise and Fall of the Working Class* (London: John Murray, 2015), 62–3. See also: Selina Todd, 'Class, Experience and Britain's Twentieth Century', *Social History* 39, no. 4 (2014): 489–508; Selina Todd, 'Affluence, Class and Crown Street: Reinvestigating the Post-War Working Class', *Social History* 22, no. 4 (2008): 501–18.

33 McKibbin, *Classes and Cultures*, 529–33. On interwar culture, see Alison Light, *Forever England: Femininity, Literature and Conservatism between the Wars* (London: Routledge, 1991).

34 Jon Lawrence, 'Class, "Affluence" and the Study of Everyday Life in Britain, c. 1930–64', *Cultural and Social History* 10, no. 2 (2013): 273–99.

35 Francis Mulhern, *Culture/Metaculture* (London: Routledge, 2000), 13; Matthew Grimley, *Citizenship, Community, and the Church of England: Liberal Anglican Theories of the State between the Wars* (Oxford: Clarendon Press, 2004).

36 Liz Conor, *The Spectacular Modern Woman: Feminine Visibility in the 1920s* (Bloomington: Indiana University Press, 2004), 7.

37 The Modern Girl around the World Research Group, Alys Eve Weinbaum, Lynn M. Thomas, Priti Ramamurthy, Uta G. Poiger, Madeleine Yue Dong and Tani E. Barlow, *The Modern Girl Around the World: Consumption, Modernity, and Globalization* (London: Duke University Press, 2008), 2.

38 Colin G. Pooley and Jean Turnbull, 'Commuting, Transport and Urban Form: Manchester and Glasgow in the Mid–Twentieth Century', *Urban History* 27, no. 3 (2000): 360–83; Colin Divall and Winstan Bond (eds), *Suburbanizing the Masses: Public Transport and Urban Development in Historical Perspective* (Aldershot: Ashgate, 2003); Bill Luckin, 'Pollution in the City', in *The Cambridge Urban History of Britain, Volume III 1840–1950*, ed. Martin J. Daunton (Cambridge: Cambridge University Press, 2000), 207–28; Robert Millward, 'The Political Economy of Urban Utilities', in *The Cambridge Urban History of Britain, Vol. III*, ed. Daunton, 315–50; John Sheldrake, *Municipal Socialism* (Aldershot: Avebury, 1989); Barry M. Doyle, 'The Changing Functions of Urban Government: Councillors, Officials and Pressure Groups', in *The Cambridge Urban History of Britain, Volume III*, ed. Daunton, 287–314.

39 Simon Gunn, 'The Spatial Turn: Changing Histories of Space and Place', in *Identities in Space: Contested Terrains in the Western City since 1850*, eds. Simon Gunn and Robert J. Morris (Aldershot: Ashgate, 2001), 1–14.

40 Michel de Certeau, *The Practice of Everyday Life*, trans. Steven Rendall (Berkeley: University of California Press, 1984); David Harvey, 'From Space to Place and Back Again: Reflections on the Condition of Postmodernity', in *Mapping the Futures*, eds. Jon Bird, Barry Curtis, Tim Putnam, George Robertson and Lisa Tickner (London: Routledge, 1993), 3–29; Denis Cosgrove, *Social Formation and the Symbolic Landscape* (Madison: University of Wisconsin Press, 1998). For a

recent analysis of these debates, see Leif Jerram, 'Space: A Useless Category for Historical Analysis?', *History and Theory* 52, no. 3 (2013): 400–19.

41 Michel Foucault, 'Of Other Spaces', *Diacritics* 16, no. 1 (1986): 22–7. Uses of governmentality include. Christopher Otter, *The Victorian Eye: A Political History of Light and Vision in Britain, 1800–1910* (Bristol: University of Chicago Press, 2008); Peter C. Baldwin, *In the Watches of the Night: Life in the Nocturnal City, 1820–1930* (Chicago: University of Chicago Press, 2012); Patrick Joyce, *The Rule of Freedom: Liberalism and the Modern City* (London: Verso, 2003); and Simon Gunn, *The Public Culture of the Victorian Middle Class: Ritual and Authority and the English Industrial City, 1840–1914* (Manchester: Manchester University Press, 2000).

42 Henri Lefebvre, *The Production of Space*, trans. Donald Nicholson-Smith (Oxford: Basil Blackwell, 1974).

43 Frank Mort, *Capital Affairs: London and the Making of the Permissive Society* (London: Yale University Press, 2010); Lynda Nead, *Victorian Babylon: People, Streets and Images in Nineteenth-Century London* (London: Yale University Press, 2000); Judith Walkowitz, *Nights Out: Life in Cosmopolitan London* (London: Yale University Press, 2012); Matt Houlbrook, *Queer London: Perils and Pleasures in the Sexual Metropolis, 1918-1957* (Bristol: Chicago University Press, 2005).

44 Houlbrook, *Queer London*, 4.

45 Peter J. Larkham and Keith D. Lilley, 'Plans, Planners and City Images: Place Promotion and Civic Boosterism in British Reconstruction Planning', *Urban History* 30, no. 2 (2003): 184–205; Peter Shapely, 'Civic Pride and Redevelopment in the Post-War British City', *Urban History* 39, no. 2 (2012): 310–28.

46 Peter J. Larkham and John Pendlebury, 'Reconstruction Planning and the Small Town in Early Post-War Britain', *Planning Perspectives* 23, no. 3 (2008): 291–321; Junichi Hasegawa, 'The Rise and Fall of Radical Reconstruction in 1940s Britain', *Twentieth Century British History* 10, no. 2 (1999): 137–61; Nick Tiratsoo, 'The Reconstruction of Blitzed British Cities, 1945–55: Myths and Reality', *Contemporary British History* 14, no. 1 (2000): 27–44; Mark Clapson and Peter J. Larkham (eds), *The Blitz and its Legacy: Wartime Destruction to Post-War Reconstruction* (Farnham: Ashgate, 2013).

47 For an important account of the impact of Americanization on British urban planning after 1945, see Mark Clapson, *Anglo-American Crossroads: Urban Planning and Research in Britain, 1940-2010* (London: Bloomsbury, 2012).

48 William Whyte, 'The 1910 Royal Institute of British Architects' Conference: A Focus for International Town Planning?', *Urban History* 39, no. 1 (2012): 151.

49 Royal Institute of British Architects, *Town Planning Conference, London, 10–15 October 1910: Transactions* (London: Royal Institute of British Architects, 1911), 107.

50 Whyte, 'The 1910 Royal Institute of British Architects' Conference', 155 and 157.

51 Peter Hall, *Cities of Tomorrow: An Intellectual History of Urban Planning and Design in the Twentieth Century* (Oxford: Blackwell, 1996), 164–5.

52 Sian Nicholas, 'The Construction of National Identity: Stanley Baldwin, "Englishness" and the Mass Media in Inter-War Britain', in *The Conservatives and British Society, 1880–1990*, eds. Ina Zweiniger-Bargielowska and Martin Francis (Cardiff: University of Wales Press, 1996), 127–46.

53 Gunn, *The Public Culture of the Victorian Middle Class*, 190–1.

54 R. J. Morris, 'Structure, Culture and Society in British Towns', in *The Cambridge Urban History of Britain, Volume III*, ed. Daunton, 417 and 426. See also Barry Doyle, 'The Structure of Elite Power in the Early Twentieth-Century City: Norwich, 1900–35', *Urban History* 24, no. 2 (1997): 179–99; John Smith, 'Urban Elites and Urban History', *Urban History* 27, no. 2 (2000): 269–74.

55 Nick Hayes, 'Counting Civil Society: Deconstructing Elite Participation in the Provincial English City, 1900–50', *Urban History* 40, no. 2 (2013): 287–314. See also Lucy E. Hewitt, 'Associational Culture and the Shaping of Urban Space: Civic Societies in Britain before 1960', *Urban History* 39, no. 4 (2012): 590–606.

56 Tom Hulme, 'Putting the City Back into Citizenship: Civics Education and Local Government in Britain, 1918-1945', *Twentieth Century British History* 26, no. 1 (2015): 26–51; Charlotte Wildman, 'Urban Transformation in Liverpool and Manchester, 1918–39', *The Historical Journal* 55, no. 1 (2012): 119–43; Helen Smith, *Masculinity, Class and Same-Sex Desire in Industrial England, 1895–1957* (London: Palgrave Macmillan, 2015); Rebecca Conway, 'Making the Mill Girl Modern?: Beauty, Industry, and the Popular Newspaper in 1930s' England', *Twentieth Century British History* 24, no. 4 (2013): 518–54.

57 Hulme, 'Putting the City Back into Citizenship', 29. For an examination of the role of civics in shaping and motivating the General Post Office Film Unit, see Scott Anthony and James G. Mansell (eds), *The Projection of Britain: A History of the GPO Film Unit* (Basingstoke: Palgrave Macmillan, 2011).

58 There is a thriving market for popular accounts of the north and on by journalists and broadcasters. See Paul Morley, *The North (And Almost Everything In It)* (London: Bloomsbury, 2013); Martin Wainwright, *True North: In Praise of England's Better Half* (London: Guardian Books, 2009); Stuart Maconie, *Pies and Prejudice: In Search of the North* (London: Ebury Press, 2007) and *The Pie At Night: In Search of the North at Play* (London: Ebury Press, 2015). For specific accounts of recent programmes of regeneration in Liverpool and Manchester, see Chris Couch, *City of Change and Challenge: Urban Planning and Regeneration in Liverpool* (Aldershot: Ashgate, 2003); Jamie Peck and Kevin Ward (eds), *City of Revolution: Restructuring Manchester* (Manchester: Manchester University Press, 2002).

59 John Belchem, *Merseypride: Essays in Liverpool Exceptionalism* (Liverpool: Liverpool University Press, 2000), 29.

60   John Belchem (ed.), *Liverpool 800: Culture, Character and History* (Liverpool: Liverpool University Press, 2006). See also Laura Balderstone, Graeme Milne and Rachel Mulhearn, 'Memory and Place on the Liverpool Waterfront in the Mid-Twentieth Century', *Urban History* 41, no. 3 (2014): 478–96; Martin Dodge and Richard Brook, 'Dreams of Helicopter Travel in the 1950s and Liverpool's Undeveloped Plans for a City Centre Heliport', *Transactions of the Royal Historic Society of Lancashire and Cheshire* 163 (2014): 111–25.

61   Kidd, *Manchester*, 235.

62   John Parkinson-Bailey, *Manchester: An Architectural History* (Manchester: Manchester University Press, 2000); Viv Caruana and Colin Simmons, 'The Promotion and Development of Manchester Airport, 1929–74: The Local Authority Initiative', *The Local Historian* 30, no. 3 (2000): 165–77; Richard Brook and Martin Dodge, *Infra_MANC: Post-War Infrastructures of Manchester* (Manchester: Bauprint, 2012).

63   The debates have flourished over the past decade, following the publication of Callum Brown, *The Death of Christian Britain: Understanding Secularisation, 1800–2000* (London: Routledge, 2000). For an overview of these continuing debates, see Jeremy Morris, 'Secularization and Religious Experience: Arguments in the Historiography of Modern British Religion', *Historical Journal* 55, no. 1 (2012): 195–219; David Nash, 'Reconnecting Religion with Social and Cultural History: Secularization's Failure as a Master Narrative', *Cultural and Social History* 1, no. 3 (2002): 302–25.

64   Daunton (ed.), *Cambridge Urban History of Britain, Volume III 1840–1950*.

65   Leonore Davidoff and Catherine Hall, *Family Fortunes: Men and Women of the English Middle Class, 1780–1850* (London: Hutchinson, 1987). For an account of its impact and reception, see Kathryn Gleadle, 'Revisiting Family Fortunes: Reflections on the Twentieth Anniversary of the Publication of L. Davidoff and C. Hall (1987) *Family Fortunes: Men and Women of the English Middle Class, 1780–1850*', *Women's History Review* 16, no. 5 (2007): 773–82.

66   Judith Walkowitz, *Prostitution and Victorian Society Women, Class, and the State* (Cambridge: Cambridge University Press, 1980); Judith Walkowitz, *City of Dreadful Delight: Narratives of Sexual Danger in Late-Victorian London* (London: Chicago University Press, 1992); Samantha Caslin, ' "One Can Only Guess What Might Have Happened if the Worker Had Not Intervened in Time": The Liverpool Vigilance Association, Moral Vulnerability and Irish Girls in Early- to Mid-Twentieth-Century Liverpool', *Women's History Review* 25, no. 2 (2016): 254–73; Philippa Levine, ' "Walking the Streets in a Way No Decent Woman Should": Women Police in World War I', *The Journal of Modern History* 66, no. 1 (1994): 34–78.

67   Mark Clapson, 'The Rise and Fall of Monica Felton, British Town Planner and Peace Activist, 1930s to 1950s', *Planning Perspectives* 30, no. 2 (2015): 211–29;

Elizabeth Darling, '"The Star in the Profession She Invented for Herself": A Brief Biography of Elizabeth Denby, Housing Consultant', *Planning Perspectives* 20, no. 3 (2005): 271–300; Jill Seddon, '"Part-Time Practice as Before": The Career of Sadie Speight, Architect', in *Women and the Making of Built Space in England, 1870–1950*, eds. Elizabeth Darling and Lesley Whitworth (Aldershot: Ashgate, 2007), 143–62.

68 Darling and Whitworth (eds), *Women and the Making of Built Space in England, 1870–1950*. See also Rosemary Sweet and Penelope Lane, *Women and Urban Life in Eighteenth-Century England: 'On the Town'* (Aldershot: Ashgate, 2003).

69 Helen Meller, 'Gender, Citizenship and the Making of the Modern Environment', in *Women and the Making of Built Space in England*, eds. Darling and Whitworth, 13–32.

70 For a quintessential example, see Mica Nava, 'Modernity's Disavowal: Women, the City and the Department Store', in *Modern Times: Reflections on a Century of English Modernity*, eds. Mica Nava and Alan O'Shea (London: Routledge, 1996), 38–76.

71 See Martin J. Daunton and Bernhard Rieger, 'Introduction', in *Meanings of Modernity: Britain from the Late Victorian Era to World War II*, eds. Martin J. Daunton and Bernhard Rieger (Oxford: Berg, 2001), 1–21; Nava and O'Shea (eds), *Modern Times*; Bernhard Rieger, *Technology and the Culture of Modernity in Britain and Germany, 1890–1945* (Cambridge: Cambridge University Press, 2005); Becky Conekin, Chris Waters and Frank Mort, *Moments of Modernity: Reconstructing Britain, 1945–1964* (London: Rivers Oram Press, 1999).

72 Belchem, *Merseypride*, xi.

73 Kidd, *Manchester*, 13.

74 James Vernon, *Distant Strangers: How Britain Became Modern* (Berkeley: University of California Press, 2014).

75 Daunton and Reiger, 'Introduction', 3.

76 David Harvey, *Paris, Capital of Modernity* (London: Routledge, 2004); David Ward and Oliver Zunz (eds), *The Landscape of Modernity: New York City, 1900–1940* (Baltimore: Johns Hopkins, 1997); Vanessa R. Schwartz, *Spectacular Realities: Early Mass Culture in fin-de-siècle Paris* (London: University of California Press, 1998).

77 David Gilbert, '*London of the Future*: The Metropolis Reimagined after the Great War', *Journal of British Studies* 43, no. 1 (2004): 92.

78 Frank Mort, 'Fantasies of Metropolitan Life: Planning London in the 1940s', *Journal of British Studies* 43, no. 1 (2004): 124.

79 Ibid.

80 Adrian Bingham, *Gender, Modernity, and the Popular Press in Inter-War Britain* (Oxford: Clarendon Press, 2004); Adrian Bingham, *Family Newspapers? Sex, Private Life, and the British Popular Press 1918–1978* (Oxford: Oxford University Press, 2009).

81 For a recent example of an analysis of the press in the Georgian era, see Hannah Barker, 'Medical Advertising and Trust in Late Georgian England', *Urban History* 36, no. 3 (2009): 379–98. On the national press, see Adrian Bingham, 'The British Popular Press and Venereal Disease during the Second World War', The *Historical Journal* 48, no. 4 (2005): 1055–76; Clive Emsley, 'Violent Crime in England in 1919: Post-War Anxieties and Press Narratives', *Continuity and Change* 23, no. 1 (2008): 173–95.

82 Andrew J. H. Jackson, 'Civic Identity, Municipal Governance and Provincial Newspapers: The Lincoln of Bernard Gilbert, Poet, Critic and "Booster," 1914', *Urban History* 42, no. 1 (2015): 113–29; Michael Bromley and Nick Hayes, 'Campaigner, Watchdog or Municipal Lackey: Reflections on the Inter-War Provincial Press, Local Identity and Civic Welfarism', *Media History* 8, no. 2 (2002): 197–212.

Chapter 1

1 There is a significant body of literature that addresses the impact of First World War on Britain and Europe, in particular see: Jon Lawrence, 'Forging a Peaceable Kingdom: War, Violence, and Fear of Brutalization in Post–First World War Britain', *Journal of Modern History* 75, no. 3 (2003): 557–89; Jay Winter, *Sites of Memory, Sites of Mourning: The Great War in European Cultural History* (Cambridge: Cambridge University Press, 1995); Michael Roper, *The Secret Battle: Emotional Survival in the Great War* (Manchester: University of Manchester Press, 2009); Samuel Hynes, *A War Imagined: The First World War and English Culture* (London: The Bodley Head, 1990). On disruptions to Peace Day specifically, see Brad Beaven, 'Challenges to Civic Governance in Post-War England: The Peace Day Disturbances of 1919', *Urban History* 33, no. 3 (2006): 369–92.

2 Lucy Bland, 'White Women and Men of Colour: Miscegenation Fears in Britain after the Great War', *Gender and History* 17, no. 1 (2005): 29–61.

3 Michael Rowe, 'Sex, "Race" and Riot in Liverpool, 1919', *Immigrants and Minorities* 19, no. 2 (2000): 55.

4 Ron Bean, 'Police Unrest, Unionization and the 1919 Strike in Liverpool', *Journal of Contemporary History* 15, no. 4 (1980): 633–53.

5 Pat O'Mara, *The Autobiography of a Liverpool Irish Slummy* (London: Martin Hopkinson Ltd, 1934), 134.

6 'Start of Strike in Manchester', *MG*, 4 May 1926, 9; 'Distress Caused by General Strike', *MG*, 30 November 1926, 14. For an account and explanation of the General Strike, see Selina Todd, *The People: The Rise and Fall of the Working Class* (London: John Murray, 2015), 46–60. In terms of IRA violence, 1920–2, in particular, witnessed a period of violent attacks on Manchester by the IRA. Michael Herbert,

The Wearing of the Green: A Political History of the Irish in Manchester (London: Irish Representation Group, 2001), 108–15.

7 Tim Hatton, 'Unemployment and the Labour Market in Inter-War Britain', in *The Economic History of Britain since 1700. Volume 2: 1860-1939*, eds. Roderick Floud and Deirdre McCloskey (3 vols., Cambridge: Cambridge University Press, 1994), 374.

8 See John Stevenson and Chris Cook, *Britain in the Depression: Society and Politics, 1929-39* (London: Longman, 1994).

9 Paul Rotha, *Documentary Diary: An Informal History of the British Documentary Film, 1928-1939* (London: Martin Secker & Warburg Ltd, 1973), 103.

10 Duncan Tanner, 'Electing the Governors/the Governance of the Elect', in *The British Isles, 1901–1951*, ed. Keith Robbins (Oxford: Oxford University Press, 2002), 43–71; Jon Lawrence, 'The Transformation of British Public Politics after the First World War', *Past and Present* 190, no. 1 (2006): 186–216.

11 Laura Beers, 'Education or Manipulation? Labour, Democracy and the Popular Press in Inter-War Britain', *Journal of British Studies* 48, no. 1 (2009): 129–52; David Jarvis, 'Mrs Maggs and Betty: the Conservative Appeal to Women Voters in the 1920s', *20th Century British History* 5, no. 2 (1994): 129–52; David Thackeray, *Conservatism for the Democratic Age: Conservative Cultures and the Challenge of Mass Politics in Early Twentieth Century England* (Manchester: Manchester University Press, 2013); Jon Lawrence, *Electing Our Masters: The Hustings in British Politics from Hogarth to Blair* (Oxford: Oxford University Press, 2009).

12 R. J. Morris, 'Structure, Culture and Society in British Towns', in *The Cambridge Urban History of Britain, Volume III 1840-1950*, ed. Martin J. Daunton (Cambridge: Cambridge University Press, 2000), 417 and 426; Simon Gunn, *The Public Culture of the Victorian Middle Class: Ritual and Authority and the English Industrial City, 1840-1914* (Manchester: Manchester University Press, 2000), 190–1.

13 Richard Trainor, 'The "Decline" of British Urban Governance since 1850: A Reassessment', in *Urban Governance: Britain and Beyond since 1750*, eds. Robert J. Morris and Richard H. Trainor (Aldershot: Ashgate, 2000), 37.

14 Ibid.

15 Patrick Joyce, *The Rule of Freedom: Liberalism and the Modern City* (London: Verso, 2003), 167–8.

16 Frank Mort, 'Fantasies of Metropolitan Life: Planning London in the 1940s', *Journal of British Studies* 43, no. 1 (2004): 120–52; Peter J. Larkham and Keith D. Lilley, 'Plans, Planners and City Images: Place Promotion and Civic Boosterism in British Reconstruction Planning', *Urban History* 30, no. 3 (2003): 184–205; Nick Bullock, *Building the Post-War World: Modern Architecture and Reconstruction in Britain* (London: Routledge, 2002).

17 John Stevenson and Chris Cook, *The Slump: Britain in the Great Depression* (Harlow: Longman, 2010), 67–9.

18 H. G. Gentleman, 'Merseyside and Its Region', in *Merseyside: Social and Economic Studies,* eds. Richard Lawton and Catherine M. Cunningham (London: Longman, 1970), 47–8.

19 Dudley Baines, 'Merseyside in the British Economy: The 1930s and the Second World War', in *Merseyside: Social and Economic Studies,* eds. Lawton and Cunningham, 62.

20 Sam Davies, Pete Gill, Linda Grant, Martin Nightingale, Ron Noon and Andy Shallice, *Genuinely Seeking Work: Mass Unemployment on Merseyside in the 1930s* (Birkenhead: Liver Press, 1992), 13.

21 *Liverpolitan,* July 1932, 1 and 19.

22 Marriner suggests that Liverpool maintained its relative position as a port in the UK. Sheila Marriner, *The Economic and Social Development of Merseyside* (London: Croom Helm, 1982), 99.

23 Alan Kidd *Manchester* (Edinburgh: Edinburgh University Press, 2002), 187.

24 Derek Aldcroft, *The Inter-War Economy: Britain, 1919–1939* (London: B.T. Batsford, 1970), 95.

25 Kidd, *Manchester,* 219.

26 Ibid., 188.

27 Sian Nicholas, 'The Construction of National Identity: Stanley Baldwin, "Englishness" and the Mass Media in Inter-War Britain', in *The Conservatives and British Society, 1880-1990,* eds. Ina Zweiniger-Bargielowska and Martin Francis (Cardiff: University of Wales Press, 1996), 127–46.

28 P. J. Waller, *Democracy and Sectarianism: A Political and Social History of Liverpool, 1868–1939* (Liverpool: Liverpool University Press, 1981), 325; John Belchem, *Irish, Catholic and Scouse: The History of the Liverpool Irish, 1800–1939* (Liverpool: Liverpool University Press, 2007), 297.

29 For example, in the early 1920s, around ninety council members in Liverpool were Conservatives plus twenty-five each of Liberals and Independents, and around six members of the Labour Party. By the mid-1930s, there were a greater proportion of Labour council members and, in 1936, there were seventy-eight Conservatives, fourteen Liberals, seven Independents, twelve Protestants, and fifty-three Labour. For an overview of these developments in national politics, see John Davis, *A History of Britain, 1885–1939* (Basingstoke: MacMillan, 1999).

30 Ross McKibbin, *The Ideologies of Class: Social Relations in Britain, 1880-1950* (Oxford: Clarendon Press, 1990) and *Parties and People: England 1914-1951* (Oxford: Oxford University Press. 2010); Lawrence, 'The Transformation of British Public Politics after the First World War'; David Jarvis, 'British Conservatism and Class Politics in the 1920s', *The English Historical Review* 111 (1996): 59–84.

31 Carl Smith, *The Plan of Chicago: Daniel Burnham and the Remaking of the American City* (Chicago: University of Chicago Press 2006), 9.

32 Town Planning Special Committee, 7 October 1925, MCL LSC.

33 Gunn, *Public Culture*; Joyce, *The Rule of Freedom*.

34 Lord Simon was Liberal Party MP for Withington, 1923–4, and again, 1929–31, and parliamentary secretary for the Ministry of Health in 1931. Simon was also a member of Manchester City Council in 1911–25 and chairman of the housing committee in 1919–23; he became Lord Mayor of Manchester in 1921 and chairman of Manchester University Council from 1941 to 1957. See Brendon Jones, 'Simon, Ernest Emil Darwin, first Baron Simon of Wythenshawe (1879–1960)', *Oxford Dictionary of National Biography*.

35 E. D. Simon, as quoted, *MG*, 4 September 1937.

36 Manchester Council Meetings Minutes, 27 January 1930, Vol. 2, 212 MCL LSC.

37 See Joseph Sharples, Alan Powers and Michael Shippobottom, *Charles Reilly and the Liverpool School of Architecture, 1904-1933* (Liverpool: Liverpool University Press, 1996).

38 Peter Richmond, *Marketing Modernisms: The Architecture and Influence of Charles Reilly* (Liverpool: Liverpool University Press, 2001), 38–9.

39 Reilly wrote that on one trip to America 'hearing that Burnham, the architect mainly responsible for the new plan for Chicago, which was the exciting thing at the moment, was going out West and that I might miss him, I took … a limited express to Chicago from Philadelphia and then back to New York to meet someone else'. Charles Reilly, *Scaffolding in the Sky: A Semi-Architectural Autobiography* (London: Routledge, 1938), 128.

40 Charles Reilly, *Some Liverpool Streets and Buildings in 1921* (Liverpool: The Liverpool Daily Post and Mercury, 1921) and Charles Reilly, *Some Manchester Streets and Buildings* (Liverpool: The Liverpool Daily Post and Mercury, 1924).

41 Abercrombie championed a three-fold approach to planning: urban improvement, external growth of towns and country planning. Patrick Abercrombie, 'Clearance and Planning: The Re-Modelling of Towns and Their External Growth', *The Town Planning Review* 16, no. 3 (1935): 196.

42 'Obituary: John Alexander Brodie', *Minutes of the Proceedings of the Institute of Civil Engineers* 240 (1935): 787–9; Adrian Jarvis, 'Brodie, John Alexander (1858–1934)', *Oxford Dictionary of National Biography*.

43 Waller, *Democracy*, 290–7.

44 Liverpool Conservative Party Conference Minutes, 3 May 1926. Liverpool Local Studies Collection (LCL LSC).

45 Graham Wallas, preface, E. D. Simon, *A City Council from Within* (London: Longmans, 1926), xvi.

46 'Armstrong Quits Consul Club Post: Elected Honorary President for Life', *New York Times* (*NYT*), 26 October 1930, 20; 'Women Pay Tribute to Lady Armstrong', *NYT*, 25 January 1930, 23.

47 'Armstrong becomes Chairman of Manchester Ship Canal', *NYT*, 4 May 1930, 18.

48 'Sir H. G. Armstrong, Ex-consul, is Dead', *NYT*, 7 February 1938, 15.

49 Tim Rooth, *British Protectionism and the International Economy: Overseas Commercial Policy in the 1930s* (Cambridge: Cambridge University Press, 1993).

50 £5,366,155 would have been worth £5,801,349 in 1935, based on a calculation using the GDP. Lawrence H. Officer, 'Five Ways to Compute the Relative Value of a UK Pound Amount, 1830–2005' MeasuringWorth.Com, 2006. www. measuringworth.com calculator (accessed 27 February 2011).

51 £4,947,920 was worth £5,349,195 in 1935, using the GDP.

52 Rates were 8s. 8d. in 1910–15 and 15s. by 1921–22. Arthur Redford, *The History of Local Government in Manchester, Volume 3. The Last Half Century* (London: Longmans, 1940), 359.

53 Statistics collated from the Annual Local Taxation Returns published by the Ministry of Health, 1925–35 editions used.

54 Madeline McKenna, 'The Suburbanisation of the Working-Class Population of Liverpool between the Wars', *Social History* 16, no. 2 (1991): 173–90.

55 See Colin G. Pooley and Sandra Irish, 'Housing and Health in Liverpool, 1870–1940', *Transactions of the Historic Society of Lancashire & Cheshire* 143 (1994): 193–219 and John Parkinson-Bailey, *Manchester: An Architectural History* (Manchester: Manchester University Press, 2000), 39–45.

56 McKenna, 'Suburbanisation', 173.

57 David Caradog Jones (ed.), *The Social Survey of Merseyside* (3 vols., London: University Press of Liverpool, 1934), I, 262. For accounts of suburbanisation, see Mark Swenarton, 'Tudor Walters and Tudorbethan. Reassessing Britain's Inter-War Suburbs', *Planning Perspectives* 17, no. 3 (2002): 267–86; Mark Clapson, *Suburban Century: Social Change and Urban Growth in England and the USA* (Oxford: Berg, 2003); Mark Clapson, *Working-Class Suburb: Social Change on an English Council Estate, 1930–2010* (Manchester: Manchester University Press, 2012).

58 Liverpool Housing Committee (LHC) Minutes, 19 July 1928, 352 MIN/HOU 1/10, LCL LSC.

59 Scotland Road was 'inhabited by the very lowest and worst population in the whole city. Disorder is perpetual, and disease is never absent'. As quoted in Belchem, *Irish*, 63.

60 Madeline McKenna, 'Municipal Suburbia in Liverpool, 1919-1939', *The Town Planning Review* 60, no. 3 (1989): 298–9. For an alternative interpretation, see Mark Clapson, 'The Suburban Aspiration in England since 1919', *Contemporary British History* 14, no. 1 (2000): 151–74.

61 In 1934, a large number of shopkeepers in the Walton, Norris green and Dovecot Estates applied for a reduction in rent because of affordability problems. LHC Minutes 13 September 1934, 352 MIN/HOU 1/10, LCL LSC.

McKenna suggests that some suburban dwellers preferred to return to town for their shopping, and as we will see in Chapter 3, shops tended to struggle for business outside of the city centre. McKenna, 'Municipal suburbia', 310. The corporation did not always facilitate retail provisions in the suburbs and in 1935 the housing committee rejected Woolworth's second application to open in Norris Green due to restrictions on the kinds of trades shops could have; however, they accepted that some tenants believed it would bring more customers to the area. LHC Minutes 11 February 1935, 352 MIN/HOU 1/10, LCL LSC.

62 Liverpool promotional map, Civic Week, 18–25 September 1924, LCL LSC.

63 Edwin Thompson, 'Merseyside and Its Industrial Potentialities', *Liverpool Post and Mercury (LPM)*, 1 June 1931, 1.

64 William Morrison, 'Liverpool's Architectural Development', *LPM*, 1 June 1931, 23.

65 'Liverpool Soon to Build Dwellings for 40,000', *NYT*, 1 September 1933, 2. See also: 'Liverpool Housing: Convene Special Court to Push City's Building Program,' *NYT*, 11 September 1921, 100; 'Housing in Liverpool', *NYT*, 18 March 1934, xxiii.

66 'State Credit Aids Housing Problems: Mrs. Helen H. Hanning Tells of its Good Effects in English Cities', *NYT*, 1 February 1925, 9.

67 Manchester Corporation, *How Manchester Is Managed: A Record of Municipal Activities* (Manchester: Manchester Corporation, 1933), 138 and 140–1. This number excludes those in area beyond the corporation's jurisdiction including Sale and Stockport, and Manchester Corporation's boundary was extended in 1926 to include Wythenshawe, and again in 1931 to include Northenden and Baguley.

68 Financial burden was expressed by a significant proportion of a survey undertaken of 304 families living in housing estates in Manchester by the *Manchester Evening News (MEN)* in 1935. *MEN*, 16 November 1935, MCL LSC Cuttings 421 *Architecture: Housing, Planning, Manchester Corporation*.

69 Parkinson-Bailey, *Manchester*, 158.

70 *MG*, 16 May 1938, 15.

71 Wesley Dougill, 'Wythenshawe: A Modern Satellite Town', *The Town Planning Review* 16, no. 3 (1935): 214.

72 Ibid., 212. See also W. Russell Tylor, 'The Neighbourhood Unit Principle in Town Planning', *The Town Planning Review* 18, no. 3 (1939): 174–86.

73 Brian Rodgers, 'Manchester: Metropolitan Planning by Collaboration and Consent; or Civic Hope Frustrated', in *Regional Cities in the UK, 1890-1980*, ed. George Gordon (London: Harper and Row, 1986), 44.

74 William Barker (ed.), *Your City: Manchester, 1838-1938* (Manchester: Manchester Corporation, 1938), 8 and 16.

75 For further examples, see also Manchester Corporation, *How Manchester Is Managed: A Record of Municipal Activities* (Manchester: Manchester Corporation, 1935), 7. Progress from the Victorian era was also the key theme to the 1938 centenary celebrations of the city's incorporation; see Manchester City Council, *Centenary Celebration of Manchester's Incorporation, May 2-7 1938* (Manchester: Manchester Corporation, 1938).

76 'Hulme Vs Wilbraham Estate', *Manchester City News*, 26 October 1933, MCL LSC Cuttings: Box 421.

77 Manchester Corporation Housing Committee Minutes, 1930–1, 481, MCL LSC.

78 'The Housing Problem in Manchester: Facts and Figures, 1931', Report for Manchester and Salford Housing Week, 18–25 October 1931, M383/8 2/5, MCL LSC.

79 Manchester Corporation Minutes, 1932–3, Vol. 2, 652, MCL LSC.

80 Manchester, Salford and Counties Property Owners' Association, 'The Hulme Clearance Area. Memorandum on the Treatment of the Area, 1932', MCL LSC.

81 Ibid.

82 Architect's Report on the City of Manchester Hulme clearance area, 1932, MCL LSC.

83 Liverpool Corporation, *City of Liverpool Official Handbook 1924* (Liverpool Corporation: Liverpool, 1924), 25.

84 Liverpool Corporation, *City of Liverpool Official Handbook 1939* (Liverpool Corporation: Liverpool, 1939), 95.

85 Peter de Figueiredo, 'Symbols of Empire: The Buildings of the Liverpool Waterfront', *Architectural History* 46 (2003): 249.

86 Liverpool Corporation, *Liverpool 1924*, 61.

87 Reilly, *Scaffolding in the Sky*, 18.

88 For a detailed account of the design and aesthetic style of St George's Hall, see Frank Salmon and Peter De Figueiredo, 'The South Front of St George's Hall, Liverpool', *Architectural History* 43 (2000): 195–218.

89 Sharples, *Liverpool*, 50.

90 Eugène Hénard, *Carrefour a Giration des Grands Boulevards* (1910), in *Plan of Chicago*, ed. Daniel Burnham (New York: Da Capo Press 1970), 89.

91 Royal Institute of British Architects, *Town Planning Conference, London, 10–15 October 1910: Transactions* (London: Royal Institute of British Architects, 1911), 345–67.

92 John A. Brodie, 'The Development of Liverpool and Its Circumferential Boulevard', *The Town Planning Review* 1, no. 2 (1910): 102.

93 John A. Brodie, 'Some Notes on the Development of Wide Roads for Cities', *The Town Planning Review* 5, no. 4 (1915): 296.

94 Brodie, 'The Development of Liverpool and Its Circumferential Boulevard', 102. See also Charles Reilly and Patrick Abercrombie, 'Town Planning Schemes in America', *The Town Planning Review* 1, no. 1 (1910): 54–65.

95 Reilly, *Scaffolding in the Sky*, 250.

96 Waller, *Democracy and Sectarianism*, 290–7.

97 Stanley Salvidge, *Salvidge of Liverpool: Behind the Political Scene, 1890–1928* (London: Hodder & Stoughton, 1934), 283.

98 Thomas White, *Memorandum of the Chairman of the Mersey Tunnel Joint Committee on the Present Financial Position* (Liverpool: Liverpool Corporation, 1932).

99 Sir Thomas White, Chairman, Mersey Tunnel Committee, 'The Ambassador of Merseyside's Industry and Commerce', *Liverpool Daily Post* Supplement, 1 June 1931,

100 *The Times*, 19 July 1934, 9.

101 John Belchem, 'Celebrating Liverpool', in *Liverpool 800: Culture, Character and History*, ed. John Belchem (Liverpool: Liverpool University Press, 2006), 36.

102 *LPM*, 1 June 1931, 1.

103 Ian Yearsley and Philip Graves, *The Manchester Tramways* (Glossop: Transport Publishing Company, 1988), 98 and 108.

104 Manchester Council Records, 1928–9, 15 August 1929, 547, MCL LSC.

105 Manchester Guardian, *Commercial Yearbook 1925* (Manchester: Manchester Guardian, 1925), 19.

106 Manchester Corporation Transport Department, *A Hundred Years of Road Passenger Transport in Manchester* (Manchester: Manchester Corporation, 1935), 25–6.

107 Ibid., 31.

108 *MG*, 16 May 1938, 25.

109 See R. Stuart Pilcher, *Road Passenger Transport: Survey and Development* (London: Sir Isaac Pitman and Sons Ltd., 1937).

110 'Town-planning on the Grand Scale', *MG*, 29 June 1925, 11.

111 Manchester Corporation Transport Department, *General Statistical Information and Descriptions of Depots* (Manchester: Manchester Corporation, 1928), 11.

112 'The New Central Library. Easily Reached By Tram or Bus', Central Library promotional poster 1934, http://manchestertransport.files.wordpress. com/2011/02/central-library-tram-bus.jpg (accessed 23 April 2014).

113 Manchester Guardian, *Commercial Yearbook 1921* (Manchester: Manchester Guardian, 1921), 3 and 213. See also Reilly, *Some Manchester Streets and Buildings*.

114 Manchester Town Hall Committee Council Minutes (TH CM) 1924–5, Vol. 2, 439, MCL LSC.

115 *Development of Manchester*, Report of Town Hall Clerk on Regional Planning Conference, New York City 20–5 April 1925. TH CM 1924-5 E, 766, MCL LSC.

116 TH CM 1924–5, Vol. 2, 439, MCL LSC.

117 TH CM 1930–1 *E*, 766, MCL LSC.

118 Parkinson-Bailey, *Manchester*, 148–9.

119 In 1937, the council claimed the library had received 7,407,910 visitors and had issued 4,609,872 books. Manchester City Council, *Centenary*, 71.

120 Manchester Corporation, *Manchester 1939*, 113.

121 'Annual dinner of Manchester Society of Architects', *MG*, 30 November 1930, 17.

122 Charles Reilly, 'New Buildings in Manchester: An Appreciation', *MG*, 16 June 1932, 7.

123 Anne Clendinning, *Demons of Domesticity: Women and the English Gas Industry, 1889–1939* (Aldershot: Ashgate, 2004), 230.

124 Advertisements produced by the corporation promoting their gas and electricity targeted the housewife particularly. For example, see 'Install the Sunshine of Electricity in your Home', in Manchester Guardian, *Manchester Handy Book* (Manchester: Manchester Guardian, 1928), 43.

125 TH CM 1924–5, Vol. 2, 444, MCL LSC.

126 Manchester Corporation, *How Manchester Is Managed: A Record of Municipal Activities* (Manchester: Manchester Corporation, 1932), 39.

127 Manchester Corporation, *Manchester 1933*, 46 and Manchester Corporation, *How Manchester Is Managed: A Record of Municipal Activities* (Manchester: Manchester Corporation, 1939), 41.

128 For an insightful examination of the relationship between the city and the middle class in Britain, see Simon Gunn, 'Class, Identity and the Urban: The Middle Class in England, 1800-1950', *Urban History* 31, no. 1 (2004): 29–47.

129 Charles Reilly, 'The New Architecture in New York', *MG*, 14 April 1923, 9.

130 British Medical Association, *The Book of Manchester and Salford* (Manchester: British Medical Association, 1929), 14.

131 Parkinson-Bailey, *Manchester*, 143.

132 Ibid., 144.

133 Charles Reilly, 'Manchester's New Office Buildings: Height and Simplicity The Case for a Few Skyscrapers', *MG*, 6 August 1928, 9.

134 *MG*, 8 November 1927, 14. *Daily Dispatch*, 4 October 1926, MCL LSC: *Civic Week, 1926, Volume 1*.

135 The newspaper claimed the unnamed building would be 70 feet higher than the Ship Canal Building. *MG*, 8 March 1928, 9. For further examples, see *MG*, 1 March 1926, 7; *MG*, 28 February 1933, 11; *MG*, 18 November 1937, 13.

136 *MG*, 9 December 1927, 14.

137 *MG*, 31 October 1930, 4.

138 *MG*, 18 November 1937, 13.

139 Reilly, *Scaffolding in the Sky*, 128.

140 *MG*, 7 January 1923, 10.

141 'Professor Reilly Resigns: Strain of Overwork', *MG*, 8 February 1933, 11.

142 Reilly, *Scaffolding in the Sky*, 216.

143 Richmond, *Marketing Modernisms*, 39.

144 Sharples, *Liverpool*, 31.

145 Harry Stuart Goodhart-Rendel, *English Architecture since the Regency* (London: Constable, 1953), 236.

146 *Liverpool, the Mart of Nations*, Promotional Map, 1924, LCL LSC.

147 'Liverpool and New York', *The Observer*, 19 April 1931, 11.

148 'Relay from Liner', *MG*, 15 April 1931, 10.

149 'Commercial Delegates for Washington: Last Night's Broadcast from the Britannic', *MG*, 25 April 1931, 14.

150 'Walker to Welcome Mayor of Liverpool', *NYT*, 2 May 1931, 14.

151 'Liverpool's Mayor Greeted by Walker', *NYT*, 6 May 1931, 25.

152 *LPM* 6 May 1931, LCL LSC Cuttings: *Visit of the Lord Mayor of Liverpool to the Mayor of New York City, May 1931*.

153 'Liverpool's Mayor Greeted by Walker', *NYT*, 6 May 1931, 25.

154 Although the city remained linked with gang warfare and police corruption, the city's pioneering advances in civic design made it an appealing ally for Liverpool politicians and businessmen. On the image of Chicago in relation to gangster culture, see Andrew Davies, 'The Scottish Chicago: From "Hooligans" to "Gangsters" in Interwar Glasgow', *Cultural and Social History* 4, no. 4 (2007): 511–27.

155 'Liverpool Link with Chicago: Greetings Flashed Over 4,000 Miles', *MG*, 10 June 1930, 16.

156 'Lord Mayor Speaks to New York: A Radio Speech', *MG*, 26 September 1931, 16.

157 'Lord Mayor of Manchester: The visit to America Party Sails in the Baltic', *MG*, 28 September 1931, 11.

158 'Manchester Mayor Sails', *NYT*, 27 September 1931, 23.

159 'British Lord Mayor Due Here Tomorrow', *NYT*, 4 October 1931, 20.

160 'The Lord Mayor in New York', *MG*, 16 October 1931, 4.

161 'Manchester Chief Coming', *NYT*, 10 September 1931, 10.

162 'The Lord Mayor's Return: American Visit a Big Success at a Strenuous Time', *MG*, 28 October 1931, 5.

163 Reilly, *Scaffolding in the Sky*, 120, 218, 220. As architectural historian Peter Richmond points out, however, readers need to take some of Reilly's claims to success in his autobiography, *Scaffolding in the Sky*, with a large dose of salt. Richmond, *Marketing Modernisms*, 130.

164 For a small selection, see 'The New Spirit in Architecture: A Break with the Past', *MG*, 29 June 1932, 7; 'Cities of the Future: Architect's Forecast: "Skyscraper Offices and Tenements"', *MG*, 13 March 1934, 5; Modern expression in architecture: the cinema', *MG*, 20 June 1934, 9.

165 'British Laud Work of H. G. Armstrong', *NYT*, 18 February 1931, 7.

166 Francis Mulhern, *Culture/Metaculture* (London: Routledge, 2000), 13.

Chapter 2

1 *Daily Courier (DC)*, 20 September 1924, LCL LSC Cuttings: *Liverpool Civic Week, Wembley 1924*.

2 *Evening Express*, 1 October 1924, LCL LSC Cuttings: *Liverpool Civic Week, Wembley, 1924*.

3 Jeffrey Auerbach, 'The Great Exhibition and Historical Memory', *Journal of Victorian Culture* 6, no. 1 (2001): 91 and 99.

4 Simon Gunn, *The Public Culture of the Victorian Middle Class: Ritual and Authority and the English Industrial City, 1840–1914* (Manchester: Manchester University Press, 2000), 163.

5 Ibid., 182.

6 Ibid.

7 Daniel Mark Stephen, ' "The White Man's Grave": British West Africa and the British Empire Exhibition of 1924–25', *Journal of British Studies* 48, no. 1 (2009): 102. Stephen argues elsewhere that supporters of the Exhibition hoped it would aid Britain 'to retain a global position made uncertain by the war and increasing international competition'. Daniel Mark Stephen, ' "Brothers of the Empire?": India and the British Empire Exhibition of 1924–25', *Twentieth Century British History* 22, no. 2 (2011): 165.

8 Sarah Britton, 'Urban Futures/Rural Pasts: Representing Scotland in the 1938 Glasgow Empire Exhibition', *Cultural and Social History* 8, no. 2 (2011): 213.

9 Becky E. Conekin, *'The Autobiography of a Nation': The 1951 Festival of Britain* (Manchester: Manchester University Press, 2003).

10 Graeme J. Milne, 'Liverpool, Manchester and Market Power: The Ship Canal and the North West Business Landscape in the Late Nineteenth Century', *Transactions of the Historic Society of Lancashire & Cheshire* 157 (2008): 125–48.

11 Brad Beaven and John Griffiths, 'Creating the Exemplary Citizen: The Changing Notion of Citizenship in Britain 1870–1939', *Contemporary British History* 22, no. 2 (2008): 203–25; Jim English, 'Empire Day in Britain, 1904–1958', *Historical Journal* 49, no. 1 (2006): 247–76.

12 See also Charlotte Wildman, 'A City Speaks: The Projection of Civic Identity in Manchester', *Twentieth Century British History* 23, no. 1 (2012): 80–99; Tom Hulme, 'Putting the City Back into Citizenship: Civics Education and Local Government in Britain, 1918–1945', *Twentieth Century British History* 26, no. 1 (2015): 26–51.

13 Wider scholarship on women's citizenship emphasises the role of domesticity, especially in women's political participation. See Catriona Beaumont, *Housewives and Citizens: Domesticity and the Women's Movement in England, 1928-1964* (Manchester: Manchester University Press, 2013).

14 Report of Lord Mayor on the visit to the British Empire Exhibition, 28 December 1928. Finance Committee Minutes, Liverpool Corporation, September 1923–April 1925. 352 MIN/FIN/II/1/71.

15 Ibid.

16 Ibid.

17 The meeting also committed a grant of £2,000 for the costs. British Empire Exhibition Meeting, 16 January 1924. Finance Committee Minutes, Liverpool Corporation, September 1923–April 1925, 352 MIN/FIN/II/1/71, 208.

18 Manchester Corporation Minutes, 24 February 1924.

19 Letter from British Empire Exhibition Board to Town Hall Committee, 6 September 1924. Manchester TH CM, 10 September 1924, Vol. 22.

20 TH CM, 14 January 1925. Manchester Corporation Records, 1924–5 *Epitome*, 233.

21 Manchester Council Records, 26 October 1926.

22 TH CM, 14 January 1925. Manchester Corporation Records, 1924–5 *Epitome*, 234–5.

23 Ibid.

24 Manchester Council Records, 1925–6, Vol. II, 182.

25 *DC*, 1 September 1924, LCL LSC Cuttings: *Liverpool Civic Week, Wembley 1924*.

26 Interestingly, neither Liverpool nor Manchester acknowledged that other cities might have a claim on this title and promotional material and the press never mentioned Glasgow, Belfast or Birmingham as rivals.

27 *Liverpool Post*, n.d. August 1926, MCL LSC, Cuttings: *Civic Week 1926, Volume 2*.

28 'Manchester Vs Liverpool', *Manchester Dispatch*, 29 September 1926, MCL LSC Cuttings: *Civic Week 1926, Volume 1*.

29 *DC*, 1 September 1924, LCL LSC, Cuttings: *Liverpool Civic Week, Wembley 1924*.

30 Ibid.

31 The newspaper claimed Liverpool Corporation was paying £1,000 rent for one week, whereas the newspaper claimed Manchester Corporation received a quote for the same sum for a month. *MG*, 10 April 1924.

32 *DC*, 16 September 1924, LCL LSC, Cuttings: *Liverpool Civic Week, Wembley 1924*.

33 *DC*, 20 September 1924, LCL LSC, Cuttings: *Liverpool Civic Week, Wembley 1924*.

34 'Packing His Trunk for Wembley', *Liverpool Echo*, 11 September 1924, LCL LSC Cuttings: *Liverpool Civic Week, Wembley 1924*.

35 *DC*, 1 September 1924, LCL LSC, Cuttings: *Liverpool Civic Week, Wembley 1924*.

36 *LPM*, 15 September 1924, LCL LSC Cuttings: *Liverpool Civic Week, Wembley, 1924*.

37 'Liverpool Civic Week', *DC*, September 15 1924, LCL LSC Cuttings: *Liverpool Civic Week, Wembley, 1924.*

38 *Liverpool Echo*, 4 September 1924, LCL LSC Cuttings: *Liverpool Civic Week, Wembley, 1924.*

39 *LPM*, 23 September 1924, LCL LSC Cuttings: *Liverpool Civic Week, Wembley, 1924; MG*, 6 May 1925, 4.

40 *LPM*, 23 September 1924, LCL LSC Cuttings: *Liverpool Civic Week, Wembley 1924.*

41 *Evening Express*, 1 October 1924, LCL LSC Cuttings: *Liverpool Civic Week, Wembley, 1924.*

42 Ibid.

43 *MG*, 26 September 1926, 18.

44 *The Times*, 17 November 1934, 12.

45 *MG*, 6 October 1925, 20.

46 Liverpool Corporation, *Liverpool Civic Week Programme 1925* (Liverpool: Liverpool Corporation, 1925), 1.

47 *The Times*, 6 October 1925, 11.

48 Ibid.

49 Frederick James Marquis, first earl of Woolton (1883–1964), *Oxford Dictionary of National Biography*. See also Michael Kandiah, 'Lord Woolton's Chairmanship of the Conservative Party, 1946–1951', Unpublished PhD Thesis, University of Exeter, 1992, 9–18.

50 F. J. Marquis, *Report of the Liverpool Organization*, 29 September 1928 to City of Liverpool Finance Committee, 352 MIN/FIN II 1/73/A.

51 'Liverpool Advertising Itself', *MG*, 29 July 1926, 11.

52 Letter from Liverpool Organization to Liverpool Finance Committee, 13 June 1927. 352 MIN/FIN/ II 1/73, 365.

53 Liverpool Finance Committee, 16 September 1927. 352 MIN/FIN/ II 1/73, 480–1.

54 F. J. Marquis, *Report of the Liverpool Organization*, 4, 29 September 1928 to City of Liverpool Finance Committee. 352 MIN/FIN II 1/73/A.

55 Marquis, *Report of the Liverpool Organization*, 6.

56 Ibid., 3.

57 Ibid.

58 Ibid., 6.

59 Ibid.

60 Ibid.

61 *MG*, 18 September 1927, 20.

62 *MG*, 3 October 1927, 5.

63 Frederick Bowman (ed.), *Liverpool Civic Week Programme and Cinema Souvenir, Profusely Illustrated* (Liverpool: Liverpool Organization, 1928), 3–4.

64 David Gilbert, '"London in All Its Glory – or How to Enjoy London": Guidebook Representations of Imperial London', *Journal of Historical Geography* 25, no. 3 (1999): 280.

65 Liverpool Civic Week 24 September – 1 October 1927, promotional poster LCL LSC.

66 *Liverpool, The Mart of Nations*, Promotional Map, 1924.

67 Bowman, *Liverpool Civic Week*, 3.

68 *MG*, 6 October 1925, 20.

69 *MG*, 9 October 1925, 15.

70 Liverpool Corporation, *Liverpool Civic Week Programme 1925*, 4.

71 *MG*, 7 October 1925, 10.

72 Asa Briggs, *Friends of the People: The Centenary History of Lewis's* (London: B.T. Batsford Ltd, 1956), 147.

73 The quality of the diary itself and Hilda's description of the quality of her life and lack of paid position suggests she was comfortable middle class. Diary of Hilda Baines, aged twenty-one. 25 September 1928. LCL LLSC.

74 *MG*, 19 October 1926, 12.

75 *MG*, 25 October 1926, 13.

76 Ibid.

77 *MG*, 9 October 1925, 15.

78 *MG*, 22 October 1926, 7.

79 Marquis, *Report of the Liverpool Organization*, 6.

80 *Yorkshire Observer*, 29 September 1926, MCL LSC, Cuttings: *Civic Week 1926, Volume 2.*

81 *MG*, 29 September 1927, 12.

82 *MG*, 19 September 1927, 11.

83 Diary of Hilda Baines, aged twenty-one. 25 September 1928. LCL LLSC.

84 *Daily Dispatch* (*DD*) 28 September 1926, MCL LSC Cuttings: *Civic Week 1926, Volume 2*; *Irwin's Weekly Chronicle*, 11 October 1928.

85 Ibid., 18 October 1928.

86 Ibid., 11 October 1928.

87 See James Greenhalgh, '"Till We Hear the Last All Clear": Gender and the Presentation of Self in Young Girls' Writing about the Bombing of Hull during the Second World War', *Gender & History* 26, no. 1 (2014): 167–83.

88 Colonel Stevens, Port of Manchester Warehouses Limited and Dr. Rée, of the Manchester Chamber of Commerce expressed this concern most clearly and publicly. 'A Civic Week for Manchester', *MG*, 29 October 1925, 13.

89 *MG*,16 January 1926, 13.

90 *MG*, 2 October 1926, 24.

91 *MG*, 9 June 1926, 13.

92 As quoted in the *MG*, 23 June 1926, 11.

93 *MG*, 23 September 1926, 24.

94 Manchester Council Records, 26 October 1926.

95 Manchester Council Records, 1925–6, Vol. I, 429–30.

96 Manchester Council Records, 1925–6, Vol. II, 157.

97 Ibid.

98 *MG*, 16 January 1926, 13.

99 *Daily Telegraph*, n.d. MCL LSC Cuttings: *Civic Week 1926, Volume 3*.

100 *MG*, 13 September 1926, MCL LSC Cuttings: *Civic Week, 1926, Volume 1*.

101 Alan Kidd, *Manchester* (Edinburgh: Edinburgh University Press, 2002), 200. As quoted in Tom Hulme, 'Civic Culture and Citizenship: The Nature of Urban Governance in Interwar Manchester and Chicago', Unpublished PhD Thesis, University of Leicester, 2013, 33.

102 'Open Sesame of Civic Week', *MG*, 2 October 1926, 15.

103 Henry Clay and K. Russell Brody (eds), *Manchester at Work: A Survey* (Manchester: Manchester Civic Week Committee, 1929), 1.

104 *MG*, 13 September 1926, MCL LSC Cuttings: *Civic Week, 1926, Volume 1*.

105 *MG*, 14 September 1926, MCL LSC Cuttings: *Civic Week, 1926, Volume 1*.

106 Ibid.

107 Hulme, 'Civic Culture and Citizenship', 100.

108 *Manchester Chronicle*, 1 October 1926, MCL LSC Cuttings: *Civic Week, 1926, Volume 1*.

109 Manchester Civic Week Official Handbook (Manchester: Civic Week Committee, 1926), 23 and 27.

110 *DD*, 1 October 1926, MCL LSC, Cuttings: *Civic Week, 1926, Volume 6*.

111 *MG*, 17 September, 1926, 11.

112 *DD*, 2 October 1926, MCL LSC, Cuttings: *Civic Week, 1926, Volume 1*.

113 *DD*, 9 September 1926, MCL LSC, Cuttings: *Civic Week, 1926, Volume 1*.

114 *MG*, 16 September 1926, 11.

115 Gunn, *Public Culture*, 53.

116 Christopher Otter, 'Making Liberalism Durable: Vision and Civility in the Late Victorian City', *Social History* 27, no. 1 (2002): 5. See also Christopher Otter, *The Victorian Eye: A Political History of Light and Vision in Britain, 1800–1910* (Bristol: University of Chicago Press, 2008).

117 *MG*, 16 September 1926, 11; 'Refuge Tower Illuminated', MCL LSC Image Collection, Ref. M07624; Hulme, 'Civic Culture and Citizenship', 85.

118 *Daily Dispatch*, 4 October 1926, MCL LSC: *Civic Week, 1926, Volume 1*.

119 *MG*, 21 September 1926, MCL LSC Cuttings: *Civic Week, 1926, Volume 1*.

120 *MG*, 1 October 1926, MCL LSC Cuttings: *Civic Week, 1926, Volume 1*.

121 In *Manchester Chronicle*, 1 October 1926, MCL LSC Cuttings: *Civic Week, 1926, Volume 1*.

122 'Civic Week Shopping: The Age of Luxury', *MG*, Saturday 10 October 1926, 9.

123 *MG*, 5 October 1926, 10.

124 *MG*, 2 October 1926, 8.

125 Advert for Affleck and Brown. Source: MCL LSU: Cuttings *Civic Week, 1926, Volume 5.*

126 *MG*, 5 October 1926, 6.

127 *DD*, 4 October 1926, MCL LSC Cuttings: *Civic Week, 1926, Volume 1.*

128 Clay and Brody (eds), *Manchester at Work*, 7.

129 'Civic Week trail of Triumph', *Evening Chronicle*, 8 October 1926, MCL LSC Cuttings: *Civic Week, 1926, Volume 1.*

130 Arnold Maren to the *MG*, 10 September 1926, 11. The debate appeared in several issues of the *Manchester Guardian* but I can find no references to it in the official publications of the organizers.

131 *Northern Voice*, 8 October 1926, II, 22, 2.

132 *MEN*, 1 September 1926, MCL LSC Cuttings: *Civic Week, 1926, Volume 1.*

133 'Civil Link with Empire', by L. S. Amery, Secretary of State for Dominion Affairs, *DD*, 4 October 1926, MCL LSC Cuttings: *Civic Week, 1926, Volume 5.*

134 See Stephen Constantine, ' "Bringing the Empire Alive": The Empire Marketing Board and Imperial Propaganda, 1926–33', in *Imperialism and Popular Culture*, ed. John M. MacKenzie (Manchester: Manchester University Press, 1986), 192–231.

135 *MG*, 10 October 1926, 11.

136 Manchester Council Records, 1925–6, Vol. II, 261. There was some success here and by 1931, Lancashire exported 8,080,000 yards of cotton to China. *MG*, 22 October 1931, 12. However, the success was short-lived due to political instability and an increased tariff in China alongside increased competition from Japan stifled trade. *MG*, 10 January 1934, 5.

137 Kidd, *Manchester*, 187.

138 *MG*, Manchester Corporation Centenary Issue, 16 May 1938.

139 Manchester Corporation, *How Manchester Is Managed: A Record of Municipal Activities, with a Description of the City* (Manchester, 1938), 35.

140 N. D. Manchester Corporation Records, 1936–7 *Epitome*, 666.

141 Ibid.

142 Manchester Corporation, *How Manchester Is Managed* (1938), 40.

143 Manchester City Council, *Centenary Celebration of Manchester's Incorporation. Official Handbook to the Exhibition of Civic Services, City Hall*, Deansgate, 2–7 May 1938 (Manchester: Percy Brothers, 1938), 35.

144 Manchester City Council, *Centenary Celebration*, 71.

145 William Barker (ed.), *Your City: Manchester, 1838–1938* (Manchester: Manchester Corporation, 1938), 16.

146 Wildman, '*A City Speaks*: The Projection of Civic Identity in Manchester'.

147 Barker, *Your City*, 20.

148 Ibid.

149 *MG*, Manchester Corporation Centenary Issue, 16 May 1938, 25.

150 Manchester City Council, *Centenary Celebration*, 28–9.

151 Barker, *Your City*, 44.

152 Manchester City Council, *Centenary Celebration*, 7.

153 Barker, *Your City*, 44.

154 Ibid.

155 Manchester and Salford District Committee of the Communist Party of Great Britain, *This Is Our City: A Programme for a Modern Manchester* (Manchester: Communist Party of Great Britain, Manchester and Salford District Committee, 1937). The local party outlined their grievances with the way the Corporation ran the city in the publication. There were national bi-annual hunger marches throughout the 1930s as a reaction against enduring unemployment and social problems. See Peter Kingsford, *The Hunger Marchers in Britain, 1920–1939* (London: Lawrence and Wishart, 1982).

156 Sheena Simon, *A Century of City Government: Manchester, 1838–1938* (London: George Allen & Unwin, 1938), 405.

157 Manchester Corporation, *How Manchester Is Managed* (1938), 35.

158 *MEN*, 4 May 1938, 1.

159 Manchester Corporation, *How Manchester Is Managed* (1938), 35.

160 Vanessa R. Schwartz, *Spectacular Realities: Early Mass Culture in fin-de-siècle Paris* (London: University of California Press, 1998), 1.

161 English, 'Empire Day in Britain, 1904–1958', 248.

162 See, for example, 'Civic Week Trail of Triumph', *Evening Chronicle*, 8 October 1926, MCL LSC Cuttings: *Civic Week 1926*; *LPM*, 23 September 1924, LCL LSC Cuttings: *Liverpool Civic Week, Wembley 1924*.

Chapter 3

1 'The Renaissance of Bold Street', *Liverpolitan*, January 1938, 17.

2 Erika D. Rappaport, *Shopping for Pleasure: Women in the Making of London's West End* (New Jersey: Princeton University Press, 2000). See also Mica Nava, 'Modernity's Disavowal: Women, the City and the Department Store', in *Modern Times: Reflections on a Century of English Modernity,* eds. Mica Nava and Alan O'Shea (London: Routledge, 1996), 38–76.

3 Pamela Cox and Annabel Hobley, *Shopgirls: The True Story of Life Behind the Counter* (London: Hutchinson, 2015).

4 Geoffrey Crossick and Serge Jaumain, 'The World of the Department Store: Distribution, Culture and Social Change', in *Cathedrals of Consumption: The European Department Store, 1850–1939,* eds. Geoffrey Crossick and Serge Jaumain (Aldershot: Ashgate, 1999), 22. See, James B. Jeffreys, *Retail Trading in Britain,*

1850–1950 (Cambridge: Cambridge University Press, 1954), 335 and Peter
Gurney, *Co-operative Culture and the Politics of Consumption in England, 1870–
1930* (Manchester: Manchester University Press, 1996). See also Janice Winship,
'Culture of Restraint: The British Chain Store 1920–1939', in *Commercial Cultures:
Economies, Practices, Spaces,* eds. Peter Jackson, Michelle Lowe, Daniel Miller and
Frank Mort (Oxford: Berg, 2000), 15–34; Frank Mort, 'Retailing, Commercial
Culture and Masculinity in 1950s Britain: The Case of Montague Burton, the
"Tailor of Taste"', *History Workshop Journal* 323, no. 3 (1994): 106–27.

5 See, Victoria de Grazia, *Irresistible Empire. America's Advance through
20th-Century Europe* (Cambridge, MA: Harvard University Press, 2005).

6 Susan Porter Benson, *Counter Cultures: Saleswomen, Managers, and Customers
in American Department Stores, 1890–1940* (Chicago: University of Illinois Press,
1988), 131.

7 Gabrielle Esperdy, *Modernizing Mainstreet: Architecture and Consumer Culture in
the New Deal* (Chicago: Chicago University Press, 2008), 9.

8 Asa Briggs, *Friends of the People: The Centenary History of Lewis's* (London: B.T.
Batsford Ltd, 1956), 154. Bill Lancaster also suggests that 'by 1939, the department
store could look back over the previous decade with satisfaction. Largely the
product of the Victorian period, the *grand magasin* in Britain continued to
prosper, unlike many of its industrial counterparts that were born in the same
period'. Bill Lancaster, *The Department Store: A Social History* (London: Leicester
University Press, 1995), 105. More recently, Peter Scott and James Walker's
comparative analysis of department stores in Britain and the US found that
although the US stores instigated a retail revolution, the 'US-style service sector
industrialization was rapidly and enthusiastically embraced by British stores …
British stores reaped high returns from investment in these innovations'. Peter
Scott and James Walker, 'The British "Failure" that Never Was? The Anglo-
American "Productivity Gap" in Large-Scale Interwar Retailing – Evidence from
the Department Store Sector', *Economic History Review* 65, no. 1 (2012): 301.

9 Lindy Woodhead, *Shopping, Seduction and Mr Selfridge* (London: Profile Books,
2007), 163.

10 Earl of Woolton, *The Memoirs of the Rt. Hon. The Earl of Woolton* (London:
Cassell, 1959), 104.

11 Woolton, *Memoirs*, 68.

12 Ibid., 108.

13 Kelly's Trade Directories, published from 1845 until the 1970s, offer
comprehensive and detailed information on shops and their locations. Kelly's
listed retailers (including name and business address) by trade, making clothing
and clothing-related retailers relatively simple to geographically locate and
quantify.

14 The extensive information supplied by Kelly's directories raised certain methodological issues. The directories covered many of the satellite and smaller towns that encircle Liverpool and Manchester and they were excluded from this study to avoid a distorted or unclear assessment of the interwar changes.

15 I initially distinguished between Outer Area (a), the area beyond the city centre, encompassing the older suburbs, and Outer Area (b), the new suburbs built in the 1920s and 1930s. The number of shops was so insignificant in the new suburbs, however, that they made a negligible impact on the study and as a spatial category Outer Area (b) became irrelevant.

16 See advert for Lewis's, *Liverpolitan*, May 1937, inside cover.

17 Sam Davies, Pete Gill, Linda Grant, Martin Nightingale, Ron Noon and Andy Shallice, *Genuinely Seeking Work: Mass Unemployment on Merseyside in the 1930s* (Birkenhead: Liver Press, 1992), 13 and 19.

18 Sheila Marriner, *The Economic and Social Development of Merseyside* (London: Croom Helm, 1982), 126.

19 Pat Ayers, 'The Hidden Economy of Dockland Families: Liverpool in the 1930s', in *Women's Work and the Family Economy in Historical Perspective,* eds. Pat Hudson and W. R. Lee (Manchester: Manchester University Press, 1990), 279.

20 A possible avenue for further research would be to re-examine the trade directories and focus on the area immediately surrounding Manchester city centre, including Withington, Cheetham Hill and Ancoats, ignoring its satellite towns.

21 Alan Kidd, *Manchester* (Edinburgh: Edinburgh University Press, 2002), 219.

22 Ibid., 188.

23 Viv Caruana and Colin Simmons, 'The Promotion and Development of Manchester Airport, 1929–74: The Local Authority Initiative', *The Local Historian* 30, no. 3 (2000): 165–77; Kidd, *Manchester*, 219.

24 Manchester Guardian, *Commercial Year-book 1925* (Manchester: Manchester Guardian, 1925), 193.

25 Liverpool Organization, *The Book of Liverpool: Civic Week, 1928* (Liverpool: Liverpool Organization 1928), 14.

26 Jessica Walker Stevens, *Studio*, May 1927, 263, John Lewis Archive (JLA) 208/c45.

27 'The Art of the Shop Window', *The Observer*, 1 February 1931, 17.

28 'Christmas Shopping: Attractions for Women', *MG*, 17 December 1926, 5.

29 'A New Shopping Centre', *MG*, 7 May 1927, 17.

30 For a close analysis of Mass Observation's approach see Penny Summerfield, 'Mass-Observation: Social Research or Social Movement?', *Journal of Contemporary History* 20, no. 3 (1985): 439–52. Chapter 4 undertakes a more detailed examination of Mass Observation's agenda, ideology and research.

31 Mass-Observation Archive (MO A:): Worktown (WT) 29/a Shops and Shop Owners.

32 MO A: WT 29/a Shops and Shop Owners.

33 Liverpool Corporation Council Minutes, 3 September 1924, 352/MIN/COU II.

34 Ibid.

35 Rappaport uses the example of Music Hall culture to illustrate this. Rappaport, *Shopping*, 192.

36 MO A: WT 30e/34, 19 May 1939.

37 Esperdy, *Modernizing Mainstreet*, 3.

38 Woolworth's Household Week Window Display, 1931, Stewart Bale Photographic Archive N8773. A similar aesthetic of abundance also feature in pictures of Ellwoods, Draper's Shop, Manchester, 1935, Manchester Central Library Local Studies Photographic Collection, M55942 and Bon Marché Blouse Department 1930s, JLA Photographic Collection.

39 *MG*, 5 October 1926, 10.

40 Walter Benjamin, *The Arcades Project*, trans. Howard Eiland and Kevin McLaughlin (London: Harvard University Press, 2002). A 4, 1, 43.

41 *MG*, 2 October 1925; Manchester Guardian, *Commercial Yearbook 1925*, 177 and 179.

42 Manchester Guardian, *Commercial Yearbook 1925*, 177 and 179.

43 MO A: WT29/b Shops and Shop Owners.

44 Charles Reilly, *Some Liverpool Streets and Buildings in 1921* (Liverpool: The Liverpool Daily Post and Mercury, 1921), 23.

45 Henry A. Miller, 'The City is getting Gayer!', *Liverpolitan*, August 1935, 26.

46 Crossick and Jaumain, 'The World of the Department Store', 21. See also Rappaport, *Shopping*.

47 Susan Porter Benson, *Counter Cultures*, 39.

48 'The Renaissance of Bold Street', 17.

49 Ibid.

50 A. E. S. *Liverpolitan*, March 1937, 35.

51 Lancaster, *Department Store*, 85.

52 On the emergence of spending power or young working-class people, see David Fowler, *The First Teenagers: the Lifestyle of Young Wage-Earners in Interwar Britain* (London: Woburn Press, 1995).

53 Briggs, *Friends of the People*, 149–50.

54 Woolton, *Memoirs*, 94.

55 Advertisements in the *Liverpool Echo*, *Liverpolitan*, *Manchester Evening News* and *Manchester Guardian* were utilized were counted and analysed for the months of January and February, October and November in 1920, 1932 and 1938. I examined each daily issue of the *MEN*, the *Manchester Guardian* and the *Liverpool Echo* for the sample months and years and I counted advertisements in each issue of *Liverpolitan*, a monthly periodical. Different socio-economic groups read these

publications, so an analysis of the message and quantity of their advertisements needs to address the importance of readership. The appendix provides a complete account of the number of advertisements found.

56 B. Seebohm Rowntree, *Poverty and Progress: A Second Social Survey of York* (London: Kongmans Green and Co., 1942).

57 Adrian Bingham, *Gender, Modernity, and the Popular Press in Inter-War Britain* (Oxford: Clarendon Press, 2004), 26.

58 Ibid., 45.

59 David Ayerst, *Guardian: Biography of a Newspaper* (London: Collins, 1991), 452. No comparative history exists for the *MEN*, or for the Liverpool press, but an engaging history of the press in Manchester during the twentieth century does exist, although it focuses on the national newspapers printed in Manchester: Robert Waterhouse, *The Other Fleet Street: How Manchester Made Newspapers National* (Altrincham: First Edition Limited, 2004).

60 Bingham, *Gender, Modernity, and the Popular Press*, 41.

61 Guy Cook, *The Discourse of Advertising* (Routledge: London, 2001).

62 Roland Marchland, *Advertising the American Dream: Making way for modernity, 1920–1940* (London: University of California Press, 1986), xvi.

63 Donald Weber, 'Selling Dreams: Advertising Strategies from *Grands Magasins* to Supermarkets in Ghent, 1900–1960', in *Cathedrals of Consumption,* eds. Crossick and Jaumain, 177.

64 Bingham, *Gender, Modernity, and the Popular Press*, 148.

65 Ayerst, *Guardian*, 488.

66 'The Best Shop Window: "Manchester Evening News" Record Contract', *MG*, 18 September 1931, 11.

67 Ayerst, *Guardian*, 489.

68 Ibid.

69 Matthew Hilton, *Smoking in British Popular Culture 1800–2000: Perfect Pleasures* (Manchester: Manchester University Press, 2000), 96 and 111.

70 See, for example, Kendal's advert, *MEN*, 7 January 1920; Affleck and Brown advert, *MG*, 1 January 1920.

71 Taken from an analysis of all advertisements placed by Kendal's and Affleck and Brown in the *MEN* and *Manchester Guardian* during January and February 1920.

72 Rachel Bowlby, *Carried Away: The Invention of Modern Shoppin* (New York: Columbia University Press, 2001), 8; Rappaport, *Shopping for Pleasure*, 4.

73 Promotional Poster for G. H. Lee's, Liverpool c.1920, JLA 637/a.

74 Rappaport, *Shopping for Pleasure*, 101.

75 *Liverpolitan*, inside cover, 1937; *Liverpolitan*, May 1932, inside cover.

76 JLA Box 180/3/a.

77 See, for example, Kendal's, *MG*, 10 February 1920.

78 G. H. Lee's, *Liverpool Echo*, 3 February 1920.

79 Lewis's, *Liverpool Echo*, 12 February 1920.

80 Bon Marché, *Liverpool Echo*, 19 January 1920.

81 Affleck and Brown, *MEN*, 3 February 1932.

82 Briggs, *Friends of the People*, 49.

83 'Another 5/Day at Lewis's Million Pound Sale', *MEN*, 16 January 1932.

84 Lewis's, *MG*, 12 January 1932.

85 George Orwell, *The Road to Wigan Pier* (London: Penguin, 1989), 82.

86 Sally Alexander shows how fur was relatively cheap and available for purchase in regular instalments. Sally Alexander, 'Becoming a Woman in London in the 1920s and 1930s', in *Metropolis: London, Histories and Representations*, eds. David Feldman and Gareth Stedman Jones (London: Routledge, 1989), 265.

87 Lewis's, *MEN*, 7 October 1938.

88 G. H. Lees, *Liverpolitan*, July 1938, 32.

89 Annette Kuhn, 'Cinema and Femininity in the 1930s', in *Nationalising Femininity: Culture, Sexuality and British Cinema in the Second World War*, eds. Christine Gledhill and Gillian Swanson (Manchester: Manchester University Press, 1996), 177–92; Andrew Davies, *Leisure, Gender and Poverty: Working-Class Culture in Salford and Manchester, 1900-1939* (Buckinghamshire: Open University Press, 1992).

90 Jeffrey Richards states that in 1934 annual cinema admissions stood at 903 million, rising to 1,027 million in 1940. Jeffrey Richards, *The Age of the Dream Palace: Cinema and Society in Britain 1930-1939* (London: Routledge, 1984), 11.

91 'Gracie Sells Stockings', *Liverpool Post*, 1 September 1932. JLA Cuttings.

92 Ibid.

93 Jeffrey Richards, 'Fields, Dame Gracie (1898-1979)', *Oxford Dictionary of National Biography*.

94 Andrew Higson, *Waving the Flag: Constructing a National Cinema in Britain* (Oxford: Clarendon Press, 1995), 103.

95 Ibid., 160.

96 *Liverpool Echo*, 19 September 1933.

97 'A Symphony of Fashion', *Liverpool Echo*, 18 October 1938, 8.

98 See Kathy Peiss, 'Making UP, Making Over: Cosmetics, Consumer Culture, and Women's Identity', in *The Sex of Things: Gender and Consumption in Historical Perspective*, eds. Victoria de Grazia with Ellen Furlough (London: University of California Press, 1996), 311–36. For a discussion of the mannequin parade and its relationship with modernity see Caroline Evans, 'Multiple, Movement, Model, Mode: The Mannequin Parade', in *Fashion and Modernity*, eds. Christopher Breward and Caroline Evans (Oxford: Berg, 2005), 125–45.

99 Asa Briggs, *Friends of the People*, 22.

100 'A Lifetime in Retailing', *The Gazette*, 29 May 1971, John Lewis Press Cuttings Folder, JLA.

101 Katrine, 'For Profit or Pleasure, do your business in Liverpool', 3.

102 For an account of Selfridge's pioneering role in retail, see Woodhead, *Shopping, Seduction and Mr Selfridge*.

103 'Some Pre-War Reminiscences on Life at G. H. Lee's', G. H. Lee's *Chronicle*, 23 January, 1569, in John Lewis Press Cuttings Folder, JLA.

104 'Some Pre-War Reminiscences', 1570.

105 Ibid.

106 Woolton, *Memoirs*, 100.

107 Nicole Robertson, *The Co-operative Movement and Communities in Britain, 1914-1960: Minding Their Own Business* (Farnham: Ashgate, 2010); Nicole Robertson, 'Collective Strength and Mutual Aid: Financial Provisions for Members of Co-operative Societies in Britain', *Business History* 54, no. 6 (2012): 925–44.

108 *MG*, 5 October 1926, 6.

109 Kendal's, *MEN*, 11 February 1938.

110 Deborah S. Ryan, ' "All the World and Her Husband": The *Daily Mail* Ideal Home Exhibition 1908–39', in *All the World and Her Husband: Women in Twentieth-Century Consumer Culture*, eds. Maggie Andrews and Mary M. Talbot (London: Cassell, 2000), 11.

111 *Liverpolitan*, May 1932, inside cover.

112 S. Reece, *Guide to Manchester and Salford* (Manchester: Sherratt & Hughes, 1939), 52.

113 Charles McGovern, 'Consumption and Citizenship in the United States, 1900–1940', in *Getting and Spending: European and American Consumer Societies in the Twentieth Century*, eds. Susan Strasser, Charles McGovern and Matthias Judt (Cambridge: Cambridge University Press, 1998), 43.

114 See, David Jarvis, 'British Conservatism and Class Politics in the 1920s', *The English Historical Review* 111 (1996): 59–84; Mary Hilson, 'Women Voters and the Rhetoric of Patriotism in the British General Election of 1918', *Women's History Review* 10, no. 2 (2001): 325–47.

Chapter 4

1 George Orwell, *The Road to Wigan Pier* (London: Penguin, 1989), 81 and 82–3.

2 For further examples, see also Walter Greenwood, *Love on the Dole* (London: Vintage, 2004), 42 and John Sommerfield, *May Day* (London: London Books, 1936), 30.

3 Kathy Peiss, *Cheap Amusements: Working Women and Leisure in Turn-of-the-Century New York* (Philadelphia: Temple University Press, 1986), 57; Katharine Milcoy, 'Image and Reality: Working-Class Teenage and Girls' Leisure in Bermondsey during the Interwar Years', Unpublished PhD thesis, University of Sussex, 2001, 159; Brigitte Søland, *Becoming Modern: Young Women and the Reconstruction of Womanhood in the 1920s* (Oxford: Princeton University Press, 2000); Elizabeth Wilson, *Adorned in Dreams: Fashion and Modernity* (London: Virago, 1985).

4 Carol Dyhouse, *Glamour: Women, History, Feminism* (London: Zed Books, 2011), 56.

5 Charlotte Wildman, 'Miss Moriarty, the Adventuress and the Crime Queen: The Rise of the Modern Female Criminal in Britain, 1918–1939', *Contemporary British History* 30, no. 1 (2016): 73–98; Lucy Bland, *Modern Women on Trial: Sexual Transgression in the Age of the Flapper* (Manchester: Manchester University Press, 2013).

6 Selina Todd, 'Young Women, Work, and Leisure in Interwar England', *Historical Journal* 48, no. 3 (2005): 791 and 803.

7 Robert Bruce Davies, *Peacefully Working to Conquer the World: Singer Sewing Machines in Foreign Markets, 1854–1920* (New York: Arno, 1976); Joan Perkin, 'Sewing Machines: Liberation of Drudgery for Women?', *History Today* 52, no. 12 (2002): 35–41; Wendy Gamber, *The Female Economy: The Millinery and Dressmaking Trades, 1860–1930* (Chicago: University of Illinois Press, 1997); Barbara Burman (ed.), *The Culture of Sewing: Gender, Consumption and Home Dressmaking* (Oxford: Berg, 1999); Cheryl Buckley, 'On the Margins: Theorizing the History and Significance of Making and Designing Clothes at Home', *Journal of Design History* 11, no. 2 (1998): 157–71.

8 Sally Alexander, 'Becoming a Woman in London in the 1920s and 1930s', in *Metropolis: London, Histories and Representations*, eds. David Feldman and Gareth Stedman Jones (London: Routledge, 1989), 247.

9 Peiss, *Cheap Amusements*, 57.

10 Andrew Davies, *Leisure, Gender and Poverty: Working-Class Culture in Salford and Manchester, 1900-1939* (Buckinghamshire: Open University Press, 1992).

11 Humphrey Spender, *Worktown People: Photographs from Northern England, 1937–39* (Bristol: Falling Wall Press, 1982), 10.

12 Peter Gurney emphasises the lack of cooperation the Mass Observation researchers met in Bolton and many inhabitants were distrustful of those claiming to work for Mass Observation. One pub, The Vaults, barred Humphrey Spender after the landlord called the police when Spender took photographs of the customers. Peter Gurney, ' "Intersex" and "Dirty Girls": Mass-Observation and Working-Class Sexuality in England in the 1930s', *Journal of the History of Sexuality* 8, no. 3 (1997): 266.

13   Cited in Penny Summerfield, 'Mass-Observation: Social Research or Social Movement?', *Journal of Contemporary History* 20, no. 3 (1985), 441. See also James Hinton, *Nine Wartime Lives: Mass Observation and the Making of the Modern Self* (Oxford: Oxford University Press, 2010). The history of the movement is chronicled in Nick Hubble, *Mass-Observation and Everyday Life: Culture, History, Theory* (Hampshire: Palgrave MacMillan, 2006).

14   Angus Calder, 'Mass-Observation 1937–1949', in *Essays on the History of British Sociological Research*, ed. Martin Blumer (Cambridge: Cambridge University Press, 1985), 127.

15   Summerfield, 'Mass-Observation: Social Research or Social Movement?', 440.

16   Gurney, '"Intersex" and "Dirty Girls"', 260.

17   MO A: WT 30/e 81 Retail in Blackpool.

18   Mass Observation defined four distinct spending groups in Bolton by their income in 1937. Group A (2.1 per cent of Bolton's population) was aid to have an annual income of over £500, Group B (10.6 per cent) with a weekly income of between £5 and £10, Group C (52.3 per cent) with an income of between £2 10s. and £5 a week, and Group C (35 per cent), who earned less than £2 10s. a week. MO WT A 29/a Shopping.

19   MOA WT 30/e 81 Retail in Blackpool.

20   Gurney, '"Intersex" and "Dirty Girls"', 261.

21   Mass Observation, *Change, No. 1 Bulletin of the Advertising Service Guild*, Clothes Rationing Survey, An Interim Report Prepared for The Advertising Guild (London: The Advertising Guild, 1941), 9–10.

22   Mass Observation, *Change*, 9.

23   Again, see John Sommerfield, *May Day*, George Orwell, *Road to Wigan Pier* and Walter Greenwood, *Love on the Dole*.

24   Mica Nava, 'Modernity's Disavowal: Women, the City and the Department Store', in *Modern Times: Reflections on a Century of English Modernity*, eds. Mica Nava and Alan O'Shea (London: Routledge, 1996), 46. See also Bill Lancaster, *The Department Store: A Social History* (London: Leicester University Press, 1995), 171; Susan Porter Benson, *Counter Cultures: Saleswomen, Managers, and Customers in American Department Stores, 1890–1940* (Chicago: University of Illinois Press, 1988), 3.

25   For an important and influential account of gender and the press in interwar Britain, see Adrian Bingham, *Gender, Modernity, and the Popular Press in Inter-War Britain* (Oxford: Clarendon Press, 2004).

26   Penny Tinkler, *Constructing Girlhood: Popular Magazines for Girls Growing up in England, 1920–1950* (London: Taylor and Francis, 1995), 119–50.

27   Manchester Guardian, *Commercial Yearbook 1925* (Manchester Guardian: Manchester 1925), 177.

28 Manchester Civic Week Committee, *Manchester Civic Week Official Handbook* (Manchester: Civic Week Committee, 1926). 55.

29 *MG*, 2 October 1926, 9; *MG*, 4 October 1926, 4; *MG*, 4 October 1926, 5; *MG*, 2 October 1926, 8.

30 *MG*, 2 October 1926, 8.

31 Manchester Guardian, *Commercial Yearbook 1927* (Manchester: Manchester Guardian, 1927), 151.

32 Manchester Guardian, *Commercial Yearbook 1928* (Manchester: Manchester Guardian, 1928), 169.

33 'Lucille of Liverpool … Her Diary', *Liverpolitan*, December 1932, 9.

34 For similar themes see the second instalment, 'Lucille of Liverpool … Her Diary', *Liverpolitan*, January 1933, 7.

35 Pauline Rushton, *Mrs Tinne's Wardrobe: a Liverpool Lady's Clothes, 1900–1940* (Liverpool: The Bluecoat Press, 2006), 27.

36 Ibid., 32.

37 Ibid., 33.

38 'Oh Miss 1937, Please Stop Trying to Look Like a Film Star!', *Liverpolitan*, February 1937, 26.

39 *LPM*, 6 May 1931, LCL LSC, Cuttings: Visit of the Lord Mayor of Liverpool to the Mayor of New York City, May 1931.

40 'These Words Are a Woman's', *Liverpolitan*, March 1933, 14.

41 MO A: WT 30/e, Saturday 9 June 1939.

42 MO A: WT W31/h Shopping and Shop Windows, 15 February 1938.

43 'Civic Week Shopping', *MG*, 2 October 1926, 8.

44 MO A: WT 29/a Shopping.

45 See Alexander, 'Becoming a Woman'; Selina Todd, 'Poverty and Aspiration: Young Women's Entry to Employment in Inter-war England', *Twentieth Century British History* 15, no. 2 (2004): 119–42; David Fowler, *The First Teenagers: the Lifestyle of Young Wage-Earners in Interwar Britain* (London: Woburn Press, 1995).

46 MO A: Shopping Box 29/a Report on Bolton Market c.1939.

47 Report dated 13 March 1937, MO A: WT 29/a Shopping.

48 MO A: Day Survey 53, 12 June 1937.

49 MO A: Shopping Box 29/a Report dated 13 March 1939.

50 MO A: Shopping Box 29/a Report dated 13 March 1939.

51 MO A: WT 29/a Shopping.

52 MO A: FP A17, 9.

53 MO A: WT 30/e Saturday 9 June 1939.

54 MO A: Day Survey 53, 12 June 1937.

55 MO A: Personal Directive on Personal Appearance, 1939. Correspondent 1057. Single b.1912.

56 MO A: WT 30/a, Shopping and Household Budgets.

57 'Civic Week Shopping', *MG*, Saturday 2 October 1926, 10.

58 Interview with Mrs Jackson, Rupert Street. MO A: Topic Collection (TC) 18, Personal Appearance and Clothes, 1/C.

59 MO A: TC 18 1/C, Interview with Mrs Banks, Fairlough Street.

60 MO A: Personal Directive on Personal Appearance. Respondent 1032, 48-year-old married housewife in Burnley.

61 Again see Alexander, 'Becoming a Woman' and Todd, 'Poverty and Aspiration'.

62 MO A: TC 18 1/C, Interview with Mrs Rogerson Grant Street, MO A: TC 18 1/C.

63 MO A: Personal Directive, 1057

64 'These Words Are a Woman's', 14.

65 Matt Houlbrook, ' "A Pin to See the Peepshow": Culture, Fiction and Selfhood in Edith Thompson's Letters, 1921-1922', *Past & Present* 207, no. 1 (2010): 215–49; Annette Kuhn, *An Everyday Magic: Cinema and Cultural Memory* (London: I. B. Tauris, 2002), 215–36.

66 MO A: Replies to April 1939 Personal Directive on personal appearance. Correspondent 1040, female typist aged twenty-five from Liverpool.

67 Ibid.

68 MO A: Replies to April 1939 Personal Directive 1040.

69 MO A: Replies to April 1939 Personal Directive on personal appearance. Correspondent 1052, female Teacher Single b.1892, from the Wirral.

70 Ibid.

71 MO A: Personal Directive on Personal Appearance. Respondent 1032, 48-year-old married housewife in Burnley.

72 MO A: Replies to April 1939 Personal Directive 1040.

73 Ibid.

74 Ibid.

75 MO A: Personal Directive on Appearance, Correspondent 1057.

76 Selina Todd, *Young Women, Work, and Family in England, 1918–1950* (Oxford: Oxford University Press, 2005), 20. For an assessment of the impact of the new industries on women's unemployment rates see also Miriam Glucksmann, *Women Assemble: Women Workers and the New Industries in Inter-War Britain* (London: Routledge, 1990).

77 Alexander, 'Becoming a Woman', 245. See also Sally Alexander, 'Men's Fears and Women's Work: Responses to Unemployment in London between the Wars', *Gender & History* 12, no. 2 (2000): 401–25 and Todd, 'Young Women, Work, and Leisure in Interwar England'.

78 Helen Forrester, *Tuppence to Cross the Mersey* (London: Harper Collins, 1993). 130.

79 Todd, 'Young Women, Work, and Leisure', 806.

80 MO A: WT31/e, The Sales, Interview with Manager of Cash Clothing Company, 15 February 1940.

81 MO A: Personal Directive, 1057.

82 MO A: Personal Directive on Personal Appearance. Respondent 1032, 48-year-old married housewife in Burnley.

83 MO A: WT 31/g, January Sales Questionnaire 1939–40.

84 Ibid.

85 MO A: WT 31/f, The Sales, Report, 6.

86 MO A: WT 31/f, The Sales, Report, 7.

87 MO A: WT 31/g, January Sales Questionnaire 1939–40.

88 Ibid.

89 Ibid.

90 MO A: WT 28/b, Budgets, 3.

91 MO A: WT 28/b, Budgets, 5.

92 MO A:, TC 18 1/C. Interview with Mrs Banks, Fairlough Street.

93 MO A:, TC 18 1/C. Interview, 3 March 1939.

94 MO A: Personal Directive, 1057.

95 Ibid.

96 MO A: Replies to April 1939 Personal Directive 1040.

97 MO A: TC 18 1/C. Interview April 18 1939.

98 See Fiona Hackney, 'Making Modern Women Stitch By Stitch: Home Dressmaking and Women's Magazines in Britain, 1919–1939', in *The Culture of Sewing*, ed. Burman, 76–7; Joy Spanabel Amery, *A History of the Paper Pattern Industry: The Home Dressmaking Fashion Revolution* (London: Bloomsbury, 2014).

99 James B. Jeffreys, *Retail Trading in Britain, 1850–1950* (Cambridge: Cambridge University Press, 1954), 62.

100 Hackney, 'Making Modern Women Stitch By Stitch', 88.

101 Joan Perkin, 'Sewing Machines: Liberation of Drudgery for Women?', 3.

102 Jeffreys, *Retail Trading*, 401.

103 Alexander, 'Becoming a Woman', 221–2.

104 Jeffreys, *Retail Trading*, 335.

105 Ibid.

106 Gurney, *Co-operative*, 234 and 238.

107 MO A: Worktown Box 30 J52.

108 Ibid.

109 Ibid.

110 Ibid.

111 Ibid.

112 Ibid.

113 MO A: WT W30/a, E68 Conversation 27 March 1939.

114 MO A: WT W31/e, The Sales. Interview Working-class woman, over thirty years in age.

115 JLA Box 208/c/34, Bon Marché monthly takings by month 1920–2.

116 MO A: Personal Directive, 1057.

117 Hilda, 'The Little Things of Fashion', *Liverpolitan*, April 1935, 9.

118 Mass-Observation, *Change*, 43.

119 Sommerfield, *May Day*, 30; Manchester Guardian, *Commercial Yearbook 1927* (Manchester: Manchester Guardian, 1927), 151.

120 Matt Houlbrook, '"A Pin to See the Peepshow": Culture, Fiction and Selfhood in Edith Thompson's Letters, 1921-1922', *Past & Present* 207, no. 1 (2010): 223.

121 MO A: WT 30/d Follows.

122 Ibid.

123 Ibid., 12 December 1938.

124 MO A: WT 30/d Follows.

125 MO A: WT 41/b Reports on Opinion Forming.

126 MO A: WT 30/d Follows.

127 Gurney, '"Intersex" and "Dirty Girls"', 262.

Chapter 5

1 Ross McKibbin argues the Anglican and Free churches declined significantly between the wars and claims Roman Catholic Church attendance was bolstered only by high levels of Irish immigrants in Britain. Ross McKibbin, *Classes and Cultures: England, 1918–1951* (Oxford: Oxford University Press, 1998), 276 and 286. See also Adrian Hastings, *A History of English Christianity 1920–1985* (London: Collins, 1985), 193; S. J. D. Green, *The Passing of Protestant England: Secularisation and Social Change, c.1920-1960* (Cambridge: Cambridge University Press, 2011). William Leach claims women's involvement in shopping culture in early-twentieth-century America is illustrated in their autobiographies and diaries, which show 'how far the secularization of thought and behaviour had proceeded in the lives of many women, whose daily activity seems to have been barely touched by religious reflection'. William R. Leach, 'Transformations in a Culture of Consumption: Women and Department Stores, 1890–1925', *The Journal of American History* 71, no. 2 (1984): 336.

2 Jeremy Morris, 'Secularization and Religious Experience: Arguments in the Historiography of Modern British Religion', *Historical Journal* 55, no. 1 (2012): 210 and 211.

3 Robert Orsi, *Thank You, Saint Jude: Women's Devotion to the Patron Saint of Hopeless Causes* (London: Yale University Press, 1996).

4 Robert Anthony Orsi, *The Madonna of the 115th Street: Faith and Community in Italian Harlem, 1880–1950* (London: Yale University Press, 1985), 188.

5 See Lily Kong, 'Religious Landscapes', in *A Companion to Cultural Geography*, eds. J. Duncan, N. Johnson and R. Schein (Oxford: Blackwell Publishing, 2004), 365–81.

6 Morris, 'Secularization and Religious Experience'; Sam Brewitt-Taylor, 'The Invention of a "Secular Society"? Christianity and the Sudden Appearance of Secularization Discourses in the British National Media, 1961–4', *20th Century British History* 24, no. 3 (2013): 327–50; Callum G. Brown, 'Secularization, the Growth of Militancy and the Spiritual Revolution: Religious Change and Gender Power in Britain, 1901-2001', *Historical Research* 80, no. 209 (2007): 393–418.

7 John K. Walton, 'Policing the Alameda: Shared and Contested Leisure Space in San Sebastián, c.1863–1920', in *Identities in Space: Contested Terrains in the Western City since 1850*, eds. Simon Gunn and Robert J. Morris (Aldershot: Ashgate, 2001), 228.

8 Jonathan Sperber, 'Festivals of National Unity in the German Revolution of 1848–1849', *Past and Present* 136 (1992): 116.

9 Anthony P. Cohen, *The Symbolic Construction of Community* (Chichester: Ellis Horwood, 1985), 50.

10 Steven Fielding, *Class and Ethnicity: Irish Catholics in England, 1880–1939* (Buckingham: Open University Press, 1993), 76–7.

11 The study used a collection of oral testimony recording undertaken during the early 1990s by the North-West Sound Archive (NW SA OTC). For an examination of methodological issues and debates regarding oral history see Penny Summerfield, *Reconstructing Women's Wartime Lives: Discourse and Subjectivity in Oral Histories of the Second World War* (Manchester: Manchester University Press, 1998). On the use of photographs, see Jane Hamlett, ' "Nicely Feminine Yet Learned": Student Rooms at Royal Holloway and the Oxford and Cambridge Colleges in Late Nineteenth-Century Britain', *Women's History Review* 15, no. 1 (2006): 137–61.

12 Penny Tinkler, 'Picture Me as a Young Woman: Researching Girls Photo Collections from the 1950s and 1960s', *Photography and Culture* 3, no. 3 (2010): 261–82; Penny Tinkler, *Using Photographs in Social and Historical Research* (London: Sage, 2013).

13 *MG*, 4 December 1936, MCL LSC Cuttings Collection: Box 481 *Religion*.

14 Fielding, *Class and Ethnicity*, 30. In reality, 'Little Ireland', the slum area to the south of the city centre, was only a short-term product of the famine years, 1845–51, and the subsequent influx of Irish immigrants into Manchester. See Colin Pooley, 'Segregation or Integration? The Residential Experience of the Irish in Mid-Victorian Britain', in *The Irish in Britain, 1815–1939*, eds. Roger Swift and Sheridan Gilley (London: Pinter, 1989), 63–83; Donald M. MacRaild, *Irish Migrants in Modern Britain, 1750-1922* (Basingstoke: MacMillan, 1999). For

a specific history of the Irish famine see Frank Neal, *Black '47: Britain and the Famine Irish* (Basingstoke: MacMillan, 1998).

15 See Anthony Rea, *Manchester's Little Italy: Memories of the Italian Colony of Ancoats* (Manchester: Neil Richardson, 1988).

16 Local historian Paul de Felici estimates that Ancoats was home to 600 Italians in 1891 and 2,000 in 1914. De Felici emphasizes that Italians tended to emigrate though kin networks and rebuilt their existing communities when they settled in Manchester. http://www.bbc.co.uk/legacies/immig_emig/england/manchester/index.shtml (accessed 4 July 2012).

17 Alan Kidd, *Manchester* (Edinburgh: Edinburgh University Press, 2002), 219.

18 Manchester University Settlement, *Ancoats: A Study of a Clearance Area. Report of a Survey Made in 1937–1938* (Manchester: Manchester University, 1945) 16, 48 and 61.

19 Ibid., 13.

20 Ibid., 13.

21 Ibid., 4.

22 Fielding, *Class and Ethnicity*, 30.

23 Richard Wright, 'Italian Fascism and the British – Italian Community, 1928–43: Experience and Memory', Unpublished PhD Thesis, University of Manchester, 2005, 8.

24 Charles A. Bolton, *Salford Diocese and its Catholic Past: A Survey* (Manchester, 1950), 6.

25 The provisions of Catholic schools were the other key issue. See Martin Broadley, 'The Episcope of Thomas Henshaw, Bishop of Salford, 1925–1938', Unpublished M.Phil Thesis, University of Manchester, 1998.

26 Ibid., 129.

27 Bolton, *Salford Diocese*, 133.

28 Fielding, *Class and Ethnicity*, 2 and 13.

29 Cohen, *Symbolic Construction*, 46.

30 Orsi, *The Madonna of the 115th Street*, 188.

31 See Steven Fielding, 'The Catholic Whit-Walk in Manchester and Salford, 1890–1939', *Manchester Regional History Review* 1 (1987): 3–10.

32 Howard Spring, *Shabby Tiger* (Manchester: Memories, 1999), 128–9.

33 See P. J. Waller, *Democracy and Sectarianism: A Political and Social History of Liverpool, 1868–1939* (Liverpool: Liverpool University Press, 1981), and Raymond Boyle and Peter Lynch, *Out of the Ghetto? The Catholic Community in Modern Scotland* (Edinburgh: John Donald, 1998).

34 Lynn Hollen Lees, 'Urban Public Space and Imagined Communities in the 1980s and 1990s', *Journal of Urban History* 20, no. 4 (1994): 445.

35 Fielding, *Class and Ethnicity*, 76.

36 *The Authorised Official Programme of the Catholic Whit-Friday Procession 1927* (Manchester: Salford Diocese, 1927), 7.

37 NW SA OTC. Edith, in Alec Greenlaugh, 'Mam, I can hear a band'.

38 Orsi, *The Madonna of the 115th Street*, 221.

39 With the notable exception of Callum Brown, *The Death of Christian Britain: Understanding Secularisation, 1800–2000* (London: Routledge, 2000), 164.

40 It is not always possible to distinguish the Protestant and Catholic processions, particularly in the early 1900s, which is why they have been counted together, rather than separately.

41 http://www.britishpathe.com/search/query/whit+manchester (accessed 11 February 2013).

42 Andrew Prescott, ' "We Had Fine Banners": Street Processions in the Mitchell and Kenyon Films', in *The Lost World of Mitchell and Kenyon: Edwardian Britain on Film*, eds. Vanessa Toulmin, Patrick Russell and Simon Popple (BFI Publishing: London, 2004), 131.

43 Fielding, *Class and Ethnicity*, 76.

44 NW SA OTC. Ivy Bolton b. circa 1925 and Edie Smythe b. c1920.

45 Fielding, 'The Catholic Whit-Walk', 9.

46 St Paul's Ancoats, 1920, Manchester Central Library Local Image Collection (MCL LIC) Ref m69185.

47 Manchester University Settlement, *Ancoats*, 13.

48 *MEN*, 22 May 1920, 2.

49 See St Gabriel's Church, Whit Walk, Manchester 1915 MCL LIC Ref m69199; St Joseph's Roman Catholic Walk, Mossley, GMCRO IC Ref 1036/9; Joynson Memorial Church Whit Walk, Manchester, 1920 MCL LIC Ref m69206.

50 Catholic Procession, Manchester 30 May 1921, Pathé Online Film Archive (POFA), Number 234.41.

51 Protestant Procession, Manchester 19 May 1921, POFA 234.21.

52 R. Judge, 'Merrie England and the Morris, 1881–1910', *Folklore*, 104 (1993): 124–43.

53 Fielding, *Class and Ethnicity*, 76.

54 Prescott, ' "We Had Fine Banners": Street Processions in the Mitchell and Kenyon Films', 127.

55 *MG*, 10 June 1922, 5.

56 Fielding, *Class and Ethnicity*, 73.

57 Michael Herbert, *The Wearing of the Green: A Political History of the Irish in Manchester* (London: Irish Representation Group, 2001), 108–15.

58 Susan Kingsley Kent argues there was an attempt to remedy the havoc caused by world war through a desire to restore 'gender peace' in Britain. Susan Kingsley Kent, *Making Peace: The Reconstruction of Gender in Interwar Britain* (Sussex: Princeton University Press, 1993).

59 Pope Benedict XV, 'Women's Mission in Modern Society', *The Tablet*, 4 January 1919, CXXXIII, 559.

60 Ibid.

61 *Catholic Herald*, 10 January 1920, 1.

62 Ibid., 6.

63 Relations and links between Irish immigrants, their descendants and their home country remained strong. Personal testaments of Irish people living in England stress the maintenance of close connections with their families and communities that remained in Ireland. See, Sharon Lambert, *Irish Women in Lancashire 1922–1960: Their Story* (Lancaster: Centre for North-West Regional studies, University of Lancaster, 2001); Mary Lennon, Marie McAdam and Joanne O'Brien, *Across the Water: Irish Women's Lives in Britain* (London: Virago Press, 1988). Barry Hazley's research illuminates the complexities of Irish migrant women's sense of self in post-war Britain. Barry Hazley, 'Ambivalent Horizons: Competing Narratives of Self in Irish Women's Memories of Pre-Marriage Years in Post-War England', *Twentieth Century British History* 25, no. 2 (2014): 276–304.

64 Penny Tinkler, 'Cause for Concern: Young Women and Leisure, 1930–50', *Women's History Review* 12, no. 2 (2003): 233–62.

65 Louis Charles, Bishop of Salford, '*Regina Pacis*: An Advent Pastoral Letter', *The Acta*, 1919, Salford Diocesan Archive (SDA).

66 Louis Charles, Bishop of Salford, 'Lenten Pastoral Letter', *The Acta*, 1921, SDA.

67 Ibid.

68 On Ireland, see Maryann Valiulis, 'The Politics of Gender in the Irish Free State, 1922–1937', *Women's History Review* 20, no. 4 (2011): 569–78, and on Italy, see Victoria de Grazia, *How Fascism Ruled Women: Italy, 1922–1945* (London: University of California Press, 1992).

69 *The Authorised Official Programme of the Catholic Whit-Friday Procession 1925*, 15. SDA.

70 *The Authorised Official Programme of the Catholic Whit-Friday Procession 1932*, 13. SDA.

71 See also St Williams Catholic Whit processions 1926, MCL LIC Ref m69219 and m69220.

72 *The Authorised Official Programme of the Catholic Whit-Friday Procession 1931*, 19. SDA.

73 NW SA OTC. Margaret Kierman b.7.3.1925.

74 *Procession and Crowning of the Rose Queen*, 1928, 35mm St. B/W POS 606487A.

75 NW SA OTC. Alec Greenhalgh, 'Mam I can hear a band'.

76 NW SA OTC. Winifred Kelly b.1913.

77 NW SA OTC. Edith in Alec Greenlaugh, 'Mam, I can hear a band'.

78 Carolyn Steedman, 'Englishness, Clothes and Little Things', in *The Englishness of English Dress,* eds. Christopher Breward, Becky Conekin and Nancy Cox (Oxford: Berg, 2002), 35.

79 Sally Alexander, 'Becoming a Woman in London in the 1920s and 1930s', in *Metropolis: London, Histories and Representations,* eds. David Feldman and Gareth Stedman Jones (London: Routledge, 1989), 264.

80 NW SA OTC. Winifred Kelly.

81 NW SA OTC. Margaret Kierman and Ivy.

82 *Catholic Herald,* 2 June 1934, 1.

83 Andrew Davies, *Leisure, Gender and Poverty,* 125.

84 Anthony P. Cohen, *Whalsay: Symbol, Segment and Boundary in a Shetland Island Community* (Manchester: Manchester University Press, 1987), 181.

85 L. Charles, Bishop of Salford, 'Lenten Pastoral Letter', *The Acta,* 1921, SDA.

86 NW SA OTC. Margaret Kierman.

87 Catholic Procession in Manchester, 28 May 1934, POFA 787.21.

88 NW SA OTC. Essie and Ronnie Strul (b.1926 and 1929).

89 NW SA OTC, Alma Todhill and Ivy Bolton.

90 Protestant Procession 1933, GMRCO Image Collection Ref. M38/39.

91 *Harvest,* 9 January 1932, 2.

92 *Harvest,* 7 June 1932, 172.

93 See Selina Todd, *Young Women, Work, and Family in England, 1918–1950* (Oxford: Oxford University Press, 2005), 19–20.

94 *Harvest,* 7 January 1932, 3.

95 Catholic Women's League 181/62 SDA.

96 MO A: WT 20/g

97 *Harvest,* 5 April 1938, 177.

98 Cohen, *Symbolic Construction,* 46–50.

99 T. G. Fraser, *The Irish Parading Tradition: Following the Drum* (Basingstoke: MacMillan, 2000).

100 Valiulis, 'The Politics of Gender in the Irish Free State, 1922–1937'.

101 Brown, *Death of Christian Britain,* 192.

102 Mike Cronin and Daryl Adair, *The Wearing of the Green: A History of St Patrick's Day* (London: Routledge, 2002).

Chapter 6

1 'Liverpool's Project for Great Cathedral', *NYT,* 21 September 1930, 12.

2 Sir David Manning, the British Ambassador to the United States, in a reception to honour the 75th anniversary of the British Embassy Residence, of which Edwin Lutyens was the architect. http://www.riba.org/go/RIBA/News/Press_5795.html

(accessed 30 May 2011). According to the Measuring Worth calculator, based on GDP, in today's money this would be over £500 million. www.measuringworth.com.

3 'Liverpool Metropolitan Cathedral', Rev. Joseph Howard, *The Cathedral Record: The Official Organ of the Archdiocese of Liverpool* (*LCR*) February 1939, 12.

4 http://www.liverpoolmetrocathedral.org.uk/history/history.html, 11 August 2011.

5 The estimated cost stood at £27,370,438 in 1954, Architect's Report, 13 September 1954, Liverpool Archdiocesan Archive (LAA) S2 VI C2. Gavin Stamp, *The Memorial to the Missing of the Somme* (London: Profile Books, 2007), 66.

6 Gibberd's cathedral, as it now stands, is 195 feet in diameter and 282 feet tall. Joseph Sharples, *Pevsner Architectural Guides: Liverpool* (London: Yale University Press, 2004), 86; Frederick Gibberd, *Metropolitan Cathedral of Christ the King* (London: Architectural Press, 1968), 46.

7 John Nelson Tarn, 'Liverpool's Two Cathedrals', in *The Church and the Arts: Papers Read at the 1990 Summer Meeting and the 1991 Winter Meeting of the Ecclesiastical History Society*, ed. Diana Wood (Oxford: Blackwell, 1994), 537–57; David Watkin, *English Architecture: A Concise History* (London: Thames & Hudson, 1979), 189–91; Sharples, *Pevsner Architectural Guides: Liverpool*, 84–6; Ernest Short, *The House of God: A History of Religious Architecture* (London: Philip Allan, 1955), 291–2; Christopher Hussey, *The Life of Sir Edwin Lutyens* (Suffolk: ACC Art Books, 1984), 527–41; Stamp, *The Memorial to the Missing of the Somme*; 66–9 and 134–6; Mary Lutyens, *Edwin Lutyens by His Daughter Mary Lutyens* (London: Murray, 1980); Clayre Percy and Jayne Ridley, *The Letters of Edwin Lutyens: To His Wife Lady Emily* (London: Harper Collins, 1985); Arts Council of Great Britain, *Lutyens: The Work of the English Architect Sir Edwin Lutyens (1869–1944)* (London: Arts Council of Great Britain, 1982).

8 Pat O'Mara, *The Autobiography of a Liverpool Irish Slummy* (London: Martin Hopkinson Ltd, 1934), 13.

9 On the impact of the famine on Irish migration, see Donald M. MacRaild, *Irish Migrants in Modern Britain, 1750–1922* (Basingstoke: MacMillan, 1999); Frank Neal, *Black '47: Britain and the Famine Irish* (Basingstoke: MacMillan, 1998).

10 Liverpool University Social Science Department: Statistics Division, *Migration to and from Merseyside: Home, Irish, Overseas* (Liverpool: The University of Liverpool, 1938), 17.

11 Very Reverend Canon Hughes, *A Concise Catholic History of Liverpool* (Liverpool: n.p., 1926), 41.

12 Ibid., 43; *Daily Dispatch Cathedral Supplement*, 1, c.1934 in LCL LSC Cuttings: *Cathedral Collection, 1929–1957*.

13 Hughes, *A Concise Catholic History of Liverpool*, 43.

14 John Belchem emphasizes the parish-based support network established by the Catholic Church in Liverpool where a report published in 1883, *Shocking Liverpool*, described the Catholic priest as 'the parson, the policeman, the doctor,

the nurse, the relieving officer, the nuisance inspector, and the school board inspector all rolled into one.' Quoted in John Belchem, *Merseypride: Essays in Liverpool Exceptionalism* (Liverpool: Liverpool University Press, 2000), 120. For an overview of the negative stereotypes about Scotland Road and the Liverpool Irish, see John Belchem, *Irish, Catholic and Scouse: The History of the Liverpool Irish, 1800–1939* (Liverpool: Liverpool University Press, 2007), 1–8.

15 O'Mara, *Autobiography of a Liverpool Irish Slummy*, 21.

16 Madeline McKenna, 'The Suburbanisation of the Working-Class Population of Liverpool between the Wars', *Social History* 16, no. 2 (1991): 181.

17 John Bohstedt, 'More than One Working Class: Protestant-Catholic Riots in Edwardian Liverpool', in *Popular Politics, Riot and Labour: Essays in Liverpool History, 1790–1940*, ed. John Belchem (Liverpool: Liverpool University Press, 1992), 216. James David O'Keefe, 'First World War Memorials and the Liverpool Cenotaph, 1917–1934', Unpublished MA Thesis, University of Manchester, 2004.

18 P. J. Waller, *Democracy and Sectarianism: A Political and Social History of Liverpool, 1868–1939* (Liverpool: Liverpool University Press, 1981), 325.

19 *MG*, 3 August 1931, 3.

20 *The Times*, 5 August 1936, 7.

21 Richard Joseph Downey (1881–1953), *Oxford Dictionary of National Biography* (accessed 4 June 2011).

22 Adrian Hastings, *A History of English Christianity 1920–1985* (London: Collins, 1985), 275.

23 Sir Edwin Landseer Lutyens (1869–1944), *Oxford Dictionary of National Biography*, http://www.oxforddnb.com/view/article/34638 (accessed 4 June 2011). See also Hussey, *The Life of Sir Edwin Lutyens*; Stamp, *The Memorial to the Missing of the Somme*; Lutyens, *Edwin Lutyens*; Arts Council of Great Britain, *Lutyens*.

24 Stamp, *The Memorial to the Missing of the Somme*, 66.

25 Ibid., 49.

26 As quoted, ibid., 66.

27 The Poor Law Guardians voted against the sale of the site to Downey and an act of law required the Guardians to sell to the Council who then sold it to Downey. Monsignor Cyril Taylor, 'The History of Liverpool's Catholic Cathedral', *Souvenir of Solemn Opening of the Metropolitan Cathedral Crypt* (Liverpool 1958), 5. LAA; *MG*, 5 June 1930.

28 *MG*, 15 June 1930.

29 LAA S2, VI, A1.

30 Archbishop Richard Downey of Liverpool (ed.), *A Cathedral in Our Time* (Liverpool, n.d.) inside pages, LAA, S1, V, D11.

31 *LPM*, 2 August 1929, LCL LSU Cuttings: *Cathedral Collection, 1929–1957*.

32 Stamp, *The Memorial to the Missing of the Somme*, 49.

33 Stamp, *The Memorial to the Missing of the Somme*, 142.

34 http://www.liverpoolcathedral.org.uk/cathedral/facts.asp (accessed April 2005).

35 Short, *The House of God*, 292; http://www.liverpoolmetrocathedral.org.uk/history/ history.htm (accessed 8 January 2007).

36 Short, *House of God*, 292.

37 *The Observer*, 4 June 1933, LCL LSU Cuttings: *Cathedral Collection, 1929–1957*.

38 Sheila Kaye-Smith, 'Building for the Future', *Solemn Blessing and Laying of the Foundation-Stone of the Liverpool Metropolitan Cathedral of Christ the King*, Monday 5 June 1933 (Liverpool: Liverpool Archdiocese, 1933), 28. LAA.

39 David Gilbert and Claire Hancock, 'New York and the Transatlantic Imagination: French and English Tourism and the Spectacle of the Modern Metropolis, 1893–1939', *Journal of Urban History* 33, no. 1 (2006): 95.

40 'Lutyens will Design Liverpool Cathedral: British Catholics, With Fund Near $1,000,000, Choose Him for Edifice in Modern Spirit', wireless to *NYT*, 31 July 1929.

41 Father Ronald Knox, 'A City Built to Scale', *Solemn Blessing and Laying of the Foundation Stone*, 30.

42 Ibid.

43 Patrick Allitt, *Catholic Converts: British and American Intellectuals Turn to Rome* (London: Cornell University Press, 1997), 3.

44 'National Catholic Congress: Celebration of Emancipation', *The Times*, 16 September 1929, 9.

45 Archbishop Robert Downey, 'Foreword', *Catholic Times Souvenir of Thingwall Park Centenary Celebrations*, 1929, 3, LAA S2, V5, D12.

46 Sullivan, 'The Scene at Thingwall park', 23.

47 Sheila Kaye-Smith, 'Building for the Future', 28.

48 Downey to I. A. Kirkpatrick, British Legation to the Holy See, 9 June 1933 LAA, S2, VI, B1.

49 Ibid.

50 'Lady Armstrong at Catholic Fete: Urges Members of the Circle to Play a Larger Part in Solving World Problems', 10 December 1933, *NYT*, 10. 'Cardinal Hayes praises Lady Margaret Armstrong for her charity work'; she had been president of Catholic Big Sisters for more than twenty-five years and chairman of Interdenominational Committee of Big Sisters for several years. *NYT*, 4 May 1930, 18; 'A Hard Age, This,' *NYT*, 23 March 1925, 20.

51 See, for example, *NYT*, 31 July 1929, 12; 21 September 1930, 12; 22 May 1932, 4; 6 June 1933, 25. In contrast, see the brief articles in *The Times*: 9 January 1933, 9 and 25 July 1934, 15.

52 As quoted in Rev. C. C. Martindale, *Liverpool Cathedral: The Foundation Stone Ceremony* (Liverpool: Liverpool Archdiocese, 1933), 2–3.

53 As quoted in the *LPM*, 6 June 1933, LCL LSC Cuttings: *Cathedral Collection 1929–1957*.

54 Archbishop Downey, *Address on the Cathedral Site after Singing the First Mass in the Crypt*, 31 October 1937, LAA, S1, V, D20.

55 Downey, *Address on the Cathedral Site*.

56 *A Cathedral in Our Time*, N. D., LAA, S1, V, D11.

57 Except from Archbishop Keating's pastoral letter, printed in *Liverpool Catholic Parishioner* (*LCP*), III, 11, November 1922, front page.

58 *LCP*, III, 12 December 1922.

59 Hastings, *A History of English Christianity*, 278.

60 Helen Forrester, *Tuppence to Cross the Mersey* (London: Harper Collins, 1993), 242.

61 Advent Pastoral Letter 1932, *Pastoral Letters 1932–1939*, LAA.

62 RM, Wrexham, *Evening Express*, 9 April 1930, LCL LSC Cuttings: *Cathedral Collection, 1929–1957*.

63 Helen Forrester, *Tuppence to Cross the Mersey*, 242–3.

64 Archbishop Richard Downey of Liverpool (ed.), *Rebuilding the Church in England* (London: n.p., 1933), 7.

65 Martindale, *Liverpool Cathedral*, 14.

66 Reported in *Evening Express*, 15 February 1937, LCL LSC Cuttings: *Cathedral Collection, 1929–1957*.

67 'Ways and Means', 1922–53, LAA S2 V A/6.

68 *Metropolitan Cathedral of Christ the King*, 54.

69 Archbishop Downey in Foreword, in *Blessing and Laying of the Foundation Stone*, 6.

70 LAA S2 V B10.

71 Charles H. Reilly, 'The Cathedral and the Town', in *Blessing and Laying of the Foundation Stone,* ed. Downey, 39. Reilly was a friend of Lutyens and they travelled around India together, 1927–8.

72 See Peter de Figueiredo, 'Symbols of Empire: The Buildings of the Liverpool Waterfront', *Architectural History* 46 (2003): 229–54.

73 Archbishop Richard Downey of Liverpool (ed.), *A Cathedral in Our Time* (Liverpool, n.d.), centre page spread.

74 Ralph Harrington, ' "The Mighty Hood": Navy, Empire, War at Sea and the British National Imagination, 1920–60', *Journal of Contemporary History* 38, no. 2 (2003): 181.

75 LAA S2 VI B1.

76 Martindale, *Liverpool Cathedral*, 3.

77 Commentator, *£3,000,000 Cathedral*, Universal Talking News, 1933. 35mm COMB B/W POS 628120.

78 'Legate Dedicates St. Louis Cathedral', *NYT*, 30 June 1926, 15.

79 Office of the Admiralty to Downey, 15 May 1933, LAA, S2, VI, B1.

80 The official radio broadcast (published in print form) lists the attendees and describes all the religious delegates but no military representative. Martindale, *Liverpool Cathedral*.

81 In March 1929, following the Roman-Vatican settlement of 1929, there was an Admiralty Fleet Order that decreed that that representatives of the Vatican 'should be regarded as representing the Pope in his capacity as head of the Roman Catholic Religion and not in his capacity as a temporal sovereign ... who are not entitled to salutes or military honours'. The Foreign Office responded by contradicting the Admiralty, asserting that Papal representatives 'should respectively receive the same honours as are accorded to Ambassadors and ministers'. A statement re-drafted the Admiralty's policy in May, which granted the Pope status as a chief of State. Admiralty Fleet Order National Archives (PRO) WO/32/3058.

82 The Chaplain-General called for the tradition of parades to continue because otherwise 'the Army will be divorced from religion ... it will become anti-religious of itself'. *Extracts from Minutes of the 63rd meeting of the Interdenominational Advisory Committee on Army Chaplaincy Services*, War Office 5 November 1930. PRO WO/32/4014.

83 For instance, no military representatives seem to have attended the consecration ceremony of Westminster Cathedral in 1910. *The Times*, 29 June 1910, 10.

84 LAA S2 VI B1.

85 See Allen Greenberg, 'Lutyens's Cenotaph', *The Journal of the Society of Architectural Historians* 48, no. 1 (1989): 5–23.

86 LAA S2 VI B1.

87 Raymond Jonas, *France and the Cult of the Sacred Heart: An Epic Tale for Modern Times* (London: University of California Press, 2000), 206.

88 'Cathedral Marks Feast of St John', *NYT*, 28 December 1922, 16; 'St. John to have a Jubilee', *NYT*, 16 December 1923, 7; ST. John's Service Fills Cathedral', *NYT*, 11 April 1927, 24; '3,500 Join Prayer for the Cathedral', *NYT*, 2 February 1925, 19.

89 *DD*, 5 June 1933, LCL LSC Cuttings: *Cathedral Collection, 1929–1957*.

90 *Solemn Blessing and Laying of the Foundation Stone of Liverpool Metropolitan Cathedral of Christ the King to be the Second Largest in the World, 1933*. 35mm COMB B/W POS Pathé 628121A.

91 Martindale, *Liverpool Cathedral*, 2.

92 *The Observer*, 4 June 1933, LCL LSC Cuttings: *Cathedral Collection, 1929–1957*.

93 Martindale, *Liverpool Cathedral*, 15.

94 *Liverpool Daily Post*, 14 September 1936, LCL LSC Cuttings: *Cathedral Collection, 1929–1957*; LAA S2 V B8.

95 Waller, *Democracy and Sectarianism*, 326.

96 *Protestant Times*, 12 January 1935, 3 and 4.

97 *Protestant Times*, 20 April 1935, Front Cover.

98 *DD*, 5 June 1933, LCL LSC Cuttings: *Cathedral Collection, 1929–1957*.

99 *DD*, 6 June 1933, LCL LSC Cuttings: *Cathedral Collection, 1929–1957*.

100   In 1931, for example, the *New York Times* reported Downey 'was made a target for stone-throwing while laying a foundation stone in the Edgehill district yesterday. He escaped injury. The incident came as a climax to strong feeling between religious factions in Liverpool.' *NYT*, 5 September 1931, 8. See also *NYT*, 15 July 1932, 10; *NYT*, 18 July 1932, 7

101   'Orangemen Mon British Church', *Chicago Daily Tribune*, 15 July 1932, 1; 'Liverpool Cathedral Stoned by Orangemen', *Daily Boston Globe*, 15 July 1932, 15; 'Orangemen Attack English Cathedral: Sing Hymns as They Shatter Stained-Glass Windows of Liverpool Catholic Edifice', *NYT*, 15 July 1932, 10.

102   'Ways and Means', Archive, 1922–53, LAA S2 V A/6.

103   Letter from Gerald J. Hardman and Company to Father Turner, 18 April 1940, LAA S2 B5.

104   Bishop of Salford to Downey, 4 July 1931, LAA S2 A35.

105   R. Ashbroke to Father Turner, 5 November 1936, LAA S2 B10.

106   Archbishop of Cardiff to Downey, 20 March 1931, LAA S2 A35.

107   Downey (ed.), *Rebuilding the Church in England*, 4.

108   Downey to Mackay – Mackay, advertisers.

109   'Liverpool Cathedral Second to St. Peter's: Preliminary Work on the Great Edifice is Proceeding Rapidly as Funds are Available', *NYT*, 22 May 1932, 4. See also 'Liverpool's Project for Great Cathedral: England Builds New Cathedral', *NYT*, 21 September 1930, 12; 'Lutyens Will Design Liverpool Cathedral: British Catholics, With Fund Near $1,000,000, Choose Him for Edifice in Modern Spirit', wireless to *NYT*, 31 July 1929.

110   *LPM*, 14 September 1936.

111   'Ways and Means', Archive, 1922–53, LAA S2 V A/6.

112   *Catholic Times*, 27 May 1922, 11.

113   *LCR*, January 1932, back page.

114   Correspondence from Imperial Agency to Downey, 29 September 1931, LAA S2 Box 5 A/34.

115   *LCR*, February 1933, inside page.

116   Report to Downey 3 July 1933, LAA S2 B13.

117   *LCR*, July 1933, back inside page.

118   *LCR*, April 1931, front inside page.

119   Report to Downey 3 July 1933, LAA S2 B13.

120   LAA S2 V B11.

121   *MG*, 17 December 1930, 18.

122   *Daily Mail*, 21 March 1935, LCL LSC Cuttings: *Cathedral Collection 1929–1957*. Again, this appears to mirror the fundraising activities for St John's in New York and many women raised vast sums of money for the cathedral.

123   LAA S2 V B11.

124   'Ways and Means', 1922–53, LAA S2 V A/6.

125 See, Maggie Andrews, *The Acceptable Face of Feminism: The Women's Institute as a Social Movement* (London: Lawrence and Wishart, 1996).

126 Allitt, *Catholic Converts.*

127 This statistic derived from the total number of recorded communions taken each year divided by the number of attendants at Mass on Easter Sunday. For example, in 1924 there were a total of 6,535,000 communions given out and divided by 258,000, the number of attendants at Mass on Easter Sunday. Taken from Canon Hughes, *A Concise Catholic History of Liverpool,* 43.

128 Peter Doyle, *Mitres and Missions in Lancashire: The Roman Catholic Diocese, 1850–2000* (Liverpool: The Bluecoat Press, 2005), 135.

129 Doyle, *Mitres and Missions in Lancashire,* 150.

130 http://www.liverpoolmetrocathedral.org.uk/history/history.html (accessed 11 August 2011).

131 Donors could take out life insurance on behalf of the cathedral, it cost as little as £1 12s. a year and paid the dividend on the donor's death. Cathedral Endowment Brochure, *Showing How You Can Help in a Big Way* (n.d.), LAA S2 VI A4.

132 According to his son, leading Catholic architect Francis Xavier Velarde (1897–1960) was asked by Downey (after a recommendation by Sir Charles Reilly) to complete Lutyens' design in 1948. Velarde apparently refused because he did not think it was appropriate considering the destruction Liverpool experienced in the Blitz, and also did not want to complete someone else's design. Giles Velarde, 'Strife of Reilly', *The Times,* 1 February 2007. http://www.timesonline.co.uk/tol/comment/debate/letters/article1308478.ece (accessed 6 June 2007).

133 Architect's Report, 13 September 1954, LAA S2 VI C2.

134 Ibid.

135 Watkin, *English Architecture,* 189.

136 John Summerson, 'Arches of Triumph: The Design for Liverpool Cathedral', in Arts Council of Great Britain, *Lutyens,* 52.

137 Liverpool Archdiocese, *A Cathedral for Our Time* (Liverpool: n.p., 1967), 8.

138 Title of an exhibition on Liverpool Archdiocese's attempt to build a Catholic cathedral during the interwar years held at the Walker Art Gallery, Liverpool, 27 January–22 April 2007. See http://www.liverpoolmuseums.org.uk/whatsonnet/displayexhibitions.aspx?mode=future&venue=2 as (accessed 27 December 2011).

Conclusion

1 The problem of housing persisted throughout the 1940s and 1950s, particularly in Manchester where possibilities for creating a new town emerged as soon as the war ended. 'Housing Problem for Manchester', *MG,* 25 June 1947, 8. Manchester Council bought Hattersley, to the east of the city, in the 1960s to create an overspill

estate to deal with the continued housing problem and Liverpool Corporation undertook an unpopular programme of clearance around Scotland Road in the early 1960s, moving many people out to Skelmersdale and Widnes.

2 'In Brief', *MG*, 5 August 1940, 6.

3 'Manchester's Whit Week', *MG*, 9 June 1941, 3.

4 'Lewis's', *MG*, 16 September 1939, 5.

5 Asa Briggs *Friends of the People: the Centenary History of Lewis's* (London B.T. Batsford Ltd, 1956), 199.

6 Michael D. Kandiah, 'Marquis, Frederick James, First Earl of Woolton (1883–1964)', *Oxford Dictionary of National Biography*.

7 James Greenhalgh, 'Building the Peace: Modernity, Space and the City in Britain, 1939-1957', Unpublished PhD Thesis, University of Manchester, 2013, 36–64.

8 'Manchester Raid Damage', *MG*, 20 January 1941, 6.

9 Stephen Essex and Mark Brayshay, 'Town Versus Country in the 1940s: Planning the Contested Space of a City Region in the Aftermath of the Second World War', *Town Planning Review* 76, no. 3 (2005): 44.

10 Phil Jones, 'Historical Continuity and Post-1945 Urban Redevelopment: The Example of Lee Bank, Birmingham, UK', *Planning Perspectives* 19, no. 4 (2004): 65.

11 Frank Mort, 'Fantasies of Metropolitan Life: Planning London in the 1940s', *Journal of British Studies* 43, no. 1 (2004): 129.

12 'Replanned Liverpool', *MG*, 11 December 1941, 3.

13 Martin Dodge and Richard Brook, 'Dreams of Helicopter Travel in the 1950s and Liverpool's Undeveloped Plans for a City Centre Heliport', *Transactions of the Royal Historic Society of Lancashire and Cheshire* 163 (2014): 111–25.

14 Rowland Nicholas, *City of Manchester Plan 1945* (London: Jarrold and Sons, 1945); Greenhalgh, 'Building the Peace', 92–3.

15 Greenhalgh, 'Building the Peace', 94.

16 Angus Calder, *The People's War: Britain 1939-1945* (London: Jonathan Cape, 1971).

17 Tristram Hunt, *Building Jerusalem: The Rise and Fall of the Victorian City* (London: Weidenfeld and Nicolson, 2004), 357.

18 Ken Young and Nirmala Rao, *Local Government since 1945* (Oxford: Wiley-Blackwell, 1997), 300.

19 Charlotte Wildman, '*A City Speaks*: The Projection of Civic Identity in Manchester', *Twentieth Century British History* 23, no. 1 (2012): 80–99.

20 Selina Todd, 'Phoenix Rising: Working-Class Life and Urban Reconstruction, c. 1945–1967', *Journal of British Studies* 54, no. 3 (2015): 680.

21 Alan Kidd, *Manchester* (Edinburgh: Edinburgh University Press, 2002), 215 and 224.

22 Jon Murden, ' "City of Change and Challenge": Liverpool since 1945', in *Liverpool 800: Culture, Character and History*, ed. John Belchem (Liverpool: Liverpool University Press, 2006), 394.

23 Frank Mort, 'Retailing, Commercial Culture and Masculinity in 1950s Britain: The Case of Montague Burton, the "Tailor of Taste"', *History Workshop Journal* 323, no. 3 (1994): 106–27; Janice Winship, 'New Disciplines for Women and the Rise of the Chain Store', in *All the World and Her Husband: Women in Twentieth-Century Consumer Culture*, eds. Maggie Andrews and Mary M. Talbot (London: Cassell, 2000), 23–45; Dawn Nell, Simon Phillips, Andrew Alexander and Gareth Shaw, 'Helping Yourself: Self-Service Grocery Retailing and Shoplifting in Britain, c. 1950–75', *Cultural and Social History* 8, no. 3 (2011): 371–91.

24 James Greenhalgh, 'Consuming Communities: The Neighbourhood Unit and the Role of Retail Spaces on British Housing Estates, 1944–1958', *Urban History* 43, no. 1 (2016): 158–74.

25 Mass Observation, *Change, No. 1 Bulletin of the Advertising Service Guild*, Clothes Rationing Survey, An Interim Report Prepared by Mass-Observation for The Advertising Guild (London, 1941).

26 Pat Kirkham, 'Beauty and Duty: Keeping Up the (Home) Front', in *War Culture: Social Change and Changing Experience in World War Two Britain*, eds. Pat Kirkham and Thoms David (London: Lawrence and Wishart, 1995), 13–28. At the same time, Sonya Rose stresses the problematic figure of the 'goodtime girl' during the war, associated with sexual deviance and with the power to bring down the British army. Sonya O. Rose, *Which People's War?: National Identity and Citizenship in Wartime Britain, 1939-45* (Oxford: Oxford University Press, 2003).

27 Carol Dyhouse, *Glamour: History, Women, Feminism* (London: Zed Books, 2011); Rachel Ritchie, ' "Beauty Isn't All a Matter of Looking Glamorous": Attitudes to Glamour and Beauty in 1950s Women's Magazines', *Women's History Review* 23, no. 5 (2014): 723–43; Catriona Beaumont, *Housewives and Citizens: Domesticity and the Women's Movement in England, 1928-1964* (Manchester: Manchester University Press, 2013). For an exception that stresses the continued appeal of movie star glamour, see Rachel Moseley, 'Respectability Sewn Up: Dressmaking and Film Star Style in the Fifties', *European Journal of Cultural Studies* 4, no. 4 (2001): 473–90.

28 Sarah C. Williams, *Religious Belief and Popular Culture in Southwark* (Oxford: Oxford University Press, 1999). See also Timothy Willem Jones and Lucinda Matthews-Jones (eds), *Material Religion in Modern Britain: The Spirit of Things* (Basingstoke: Palgrave, 2015).

29 Temporary Constitution of the Diocesan Board of Union Catholic Women Appointed by His Grace, the Archbishop of Liverpool, May 1940. LAA S1 VIII D1.

30 Callum Brown, *The Death of Christian Britain: Understanding Secularisation, 1800-2000* (London: Routledge, 2000).

31 Alana Harris, *Faith in the Family: A Lived Religious History of English Catholicism 1945–82* (Manchester: Manchester University Press, 2013).

32 https://catholicrelics.wordpress.com.

33 Marco Amati and Robert Freestone, 'All of London's a Stage: The 1943 County of London Plan Exhibition', *Urban History*, FirstView Article, August 2015, 3. http://dx.doi.org/10.1017/S0963926815000498.

34 Simon Gunn and James Vernon (eds), *The Peculiarities of Liberal Modernity in Imperial Britain* (Berkeley, CA: University of California Press, 2011); Frank Mort, *Capital Affairs: London and the Making of the Permissive Society* (London: Yale University Press, 2010). See also David Gilbert, David Matless and Brian Short (eds), *Geographies of British Modernity: Space and Society in the Twentieth Century* (Oxford: Wiley-Blackwell, 2003).

35 Ross McKibbin, *Classes and Cultures: England, 1918–1951* (Oxford: Oxford University Press, 1998), 276.

36 Joshua Landy and Michael Saler, 'Introduction: The Varieties of Modern Enchantment', in *The Re-Enchantment of the World: Secular Magic in a Rational Age*, eds. Joshua Landy and Michael Saler (Stanford, CA: Stanford University Press, 2009), 6–7.

37 Chris Waters, 'Introduction: Beyond 'Americanization': Rethinking Anglo-American Cultural Exchange between the Wars', *Cultural and Social History* 4, no. 4 (2007): 451–9.

38 *The Times*, 7 September 1931. As Andrew Davies shows, however, links with Chicago were not always positive as it was associated with gangsters, corruption and violence. Andrew Davies, 'The Scottish Chicago: From "Hooligans" to "Gangsters" in Interwar Glasgow', *Cultural and Social History* 4, no. 4 (2007): 511–27.

39 Frank Mort, *Capital Affairs*, 334.

40 Lesley Whitworth, 'Men, Women, Shops and "Little Shiny Homes": The Consuming of Coventry, 1930–1939', Unpublished PhD Thesis, University of Warwick, 1997.

41 Anthony Sutcliffe, *An Architectural History: London* (London: Yale University Press, 2006), 157.

42 Andy Foster, *Birmingham: Pevsner Architectural Guide* (London: Yale University Press, 2005), 59.

43 Colin G. Pooley and Jean Turnbull, 'Commuting, Transport and Urban Form: Manchester and Glasgow in the Mid-Twentieth Century', *Urban History* 27, no. 3 (2000): 360–83; Colin Divall and Winstan Bond (eds), *Suburbanizing the Masses: Public Transport and Urban Development in Historical Perspective* (Aldershot: Ashgate, 2003); J. W. R. Whitehand and C. M. H. Carr, *Twentieth Century Suburbs: A Morphological Approach* (London: Routledge, 2001).

44 Patrick Allitt, *Catholic Converts: British and American Intellectuals Turn to Rome* (London: Cornell University Press, 1997); Adam Schwartz, *The Third Spring: G. K. Chesterton, Graham Greene, Christopher Dawson, and David Jones*

(Washington, DC: Catholic University of America Press, 2005); Ian Turnbull Ker, *The Catholic Revival in English Literature, 1845-1961: Newman, Hopkins, Belloc, Chesterton, Greene, Waugh* (Indiana: University of Notre Dame Press, 2003); James R. Lothian, *The Making and Unmaking of the English Catholic Intellectual Community, 1910–1950* (Indiana: University of Notre Dame Press, 2009).

45 Robert Anthony Orsi, *The Madonna of the 115th Street: Faith and Community in Italian Harlem, 1880–1950* (London: Yale University Press, 1985); John T. McGreevy, *Parish Boundaries: The Catholic Encounter with Race in the Twentieth-Century Urban North* (London: University of Chicago Press, 1996).

46 For a recent example, see Andrew J. H. Jackson, 'Civic Identity, Municipal Governance and Provincial Newspapers: The Lincoln of Bernard Gilbert, Poet, Critic and "Booster", 1914', *Urban History* 42, no. 1 (2015): 113–29.

47 *Civic Week 1928*, 24.09.1928, 744.18 Pathé Online Film Archive.

48 Catriona Beaumont, *Housewives and Citizens: Domesticity and the Women's Movement in England, 1928-1964* (Manchester: Manchester University Press, 2013).

49 In Liverpool, there were a number of violent disturbances caused by protesters against unemployment during the early 1930s. For example, see 'Liverpool Riot Charges', *MG*, 23 November 1932, 2; 'Liverpool Riot Charges', *MG*, 13 January 1933, 3. There were protests against unemployment in Manchester too, but they appear less violent: 'Manchester Unemployment Demonstration', *MG*, 21 February 1935, 11; 'A Demonstration in Manchester', *MG*, 8 October 1931, 7.

50 Andrew Davies, *City of Gangs* (London: Hodder & Stoughton, 2013).

51 F. Goddard, 'What Is It Really Like to Live in Wythenshawe?' Secretary for Wythenshawe Community Council, *MEN*, 13 May 1947.

52 Sarah Lyall, 'How the Young Poor Measure Poverty in Britain: Drink, Drugs and Their Time in Jail', *NYT*, 10 March 2007.

53 McKibbin, *Classes and Cultures*, 527.

Bibliography

Primary sources

Archives

British Film Institute

Liverpool, 35mm Sil. B/W POS 6224595A.
Liverpool Civic Week 1926, 35mm St. B/W POS 603357A.
Procession and Crowning of the Rose Queen, 1928, 35mm St. B/W POS 606487A.
Whit Friday c.1928 35mm Sil. B/W POS 621290A.
Annual Whit Monday Procession c.1928 35mm Sil. B/W POS 622284A.
£3,000,000 Cathedral, Universal Talking News, 1933. 35mm COMB B/W POS 628120.
Solemn Blessing and Laying of the Foundation Stone of Liverpool Metropolitan Cathedral of Christ the King to be the Second Largest in the World, 1933. 35mm COMB B/W POS Pathé 628121A.
Opening of Manchester Civic Week 1926, 35mm B/W POS 621150A.
Liverpool Gateway of Empire, 16mm Sil. B/W POS 607837A.
A Cathedral in Our Time, VHS, 19 minutes, 1967.

John Lewis Archive

Bon Marché, Liverpool

Newspaper Cuttings Collection, post 1950.
1911–24 Total sales by department.
1926–35 Press Cuttings.
Photographic Collection.
1932–51 Special Events.
1936–44 Fashion Bargain Basement.

George Henry Lees, Liverpool

Newspaper Cuttings Collection and Adverts.
1914–34 Departmental Expenses.
The Inspirator, in-house magazine, August/September/December 1932.
1937–8 Publicity Leaflets.
John Lewis Press Cuttings.

Liverpool Archdiocesan Archives

Bishops' Papers: 1850–1921.
Downey Papers: 1928–53.
Catholic Action Archive.
Pastoral Letters, 1916–21, 1921–5.
Liverpolitana (Includes pastoral letters): 1928–31, 1932–4 and 1932–9.
Newspaper Cuttings File Four: Downey, 1917–28 Keating papers: to 1928.
Cathedral papers 1924–54.

Liverpool Local Studies Collection, Liverpool Central Library

City of Liverpool Finance Committee Minutes
Diary of Hilda Baines, 1928.
Ephemera relating to Civic Weeks
Liverpool Conservative Party Conference Minutes
Liverpool Housing Committee Minutes
Liverpool, The Mart of Nations, Promotional Map, 1924.
Liverpool promotional map, Civic Week, 18–25 September 1924.

Newspaper Cuttings

Cathedral Collection, 1929–1957.
Civic Week, 1926
Civic Week 1926, Volume 2.
Commerce and Industry.
Liverpool Civic Week, Wembley 1924.
Streets and Districts.
Transport, 1927–1959.
Visit of the Lord Mayor of Liverpool to the Mayor of New York City, May 1931.

Manchester Central Library Local Studies Collection

Finance Committee Minutes
Image Collection
Manchester Council Meetings Minutes
Manchester Council Records
Town Hall Committee Council Minutes
Town Planning Special Committee Minutes

Newspaper Cuttings

Manchester Corporation 'Parks Committee' 1939–44
Art Galleries Committee 1933–6 and 1937–45.

Box 102 *Buildings and Public Amenities.*
Box 207 *Trams, Tramways and Trolley-Buses.*
Box 421 *Architecture: Housing, Planning, Manchester Corporation.*
Civic Week, 1926, 6 Volumes.
Box 260 *Retail.*
Box 481–91 *Religion*
Civic Week, 1926, Volume 1.
Civic Week, 1926, Volume 2.
Civic Week 1926, Volume 3.
Civic Week, 1926, Volume 5.
Civic Week, 1926, Volume 6.

Mass Observation Archive

Mass Observation, *Change, No. 1 Bulletin of the Advertising Service Guild*, Clothes
    Rationing Survey, An Interim Report Prepared by Mass-Observation for
    The Advertising Guild (London, 1941).
Day Survey for 12 June 1937.
Directive Response:
    Personal Appearance April 1939
    Clothing May 1939
Diaries: Diarist No. 114, 1937.
File Report: Clothing and Personal Appearance, A17.
Topic Collections:
    18 Personal Appearance and Clothes.
    47 Religion.
Worktown Collection (Bolton).

The National Archives

Admiralty Fleet Order (PRO) WO/32/3058.
*Extracts from Minutes of the 63rd meeting of the Interdenominational Advisory
    Committee on Army Chaplaincy Services*, War Office 5 November 1930. PRO
    WO/32/4014.

North-West Sound Archive

Alec Greenlaugh, 'Mam, I can hear a band'.
Essie and Ronnie Strul.
Ivy Bolton b. circa 1925 and Edie Smythe b. c1920.
Margaret Kierman b.7.3.1925
Winifred Kelly b.1913.

British Pathé Online

234.21 Protestant Procession, Manchester 19.05.21.

234.41 Catholic procession, Manchester 30.05.21.

268.43 Whitsuntide Processions, Manchester 12.06.1922.

675.07 For the 131st Time, Whitsuntide 19.05.1932.

675.28 Faith of Our Fathers", Catholic Procession 23.05.1932.

713.15 Faith of Our Fathers 16.06.1930.

744.18 Civic Week 1928, 24.09.1928.

787.21 Catholic Procession in Manchester 28.05.1934.

787.28 Braving the Elements Protestant Procession 24.05.1934.

Salford Diocesan Archive

The Acta, 1919–21, 1925–9, 1930–4.

The Authorised Official Programme of the Catholic Whit-Friday Procession 1925.

The Authorised Official Programme of the Catholic Whit-Friday Procession 1931.

The Authorised Official Programme of the Catholic Whit-Friday Procession 1932.

Catholic Women's League Papers, Salford Branch, 1925–38.

Museums and Galleries Merseyside

Stewart Bale Photographic Archive

Published sources

Anon, 'Obituary: John Alexander Brodie', *Minutes of the Proceedings of the Institute of Civil Engineers* 240 (1935): 787–89.

Anon, *The Authorised Official Programme of the Catholic Whit-Friday Procession 1927* (Manchester: Salford Diocese, 1927).

Abercrombie, Patrick, 'Clearance and Planning: The Re-Modelling of Towns and Their External Growth', *The Town Planning Review* 16, no. 3 (1935): 195–208.

Barker, William (ed.), *Your City: Manchester, 1838-1938* (Manchester: Manchester Corporation, 1938).

Bowman, Frederick (ed.), *Liverpool Civic Week Programme and Cinema Souvenir, Profusely Illustrated* (Liverpool: Liverpool Organization, 1928).

British Medical Association, *The Book of Manchester and Salford* (Manchester: British Medical Association, 1929).

Brodie, John A., 'The Development of Liverpool and Its Circumferential Boulevard', *The Town Planning Review* 1, no. 2 (1910): 100–10.

Brodie, John A., 'Some Notes on the Development of Wide Roads for Cities', *The Town Planning Review* 5, no. 4 (1915): 294–9.

Burnham, Daniel, *Plan of Chicago* (New York: Da Capo Press, 1970).

Clay, Henry and K. Russell Brody (eds), *Manchester at Work: A Survey* (Manchester: Manchester Civic Week Committee, 1929).

Cotton, Vera E., *Liverpool Cathedral: The Official Handbook* (Liverpool, 1936).

Donaldson, A., *A New Catholic Cathedral Souvenir Handbook* (Liverpool, 1938).

Dougill, Wesley, 'Wythenshawe: A Modern Satellite Town', *The Town Planning Review* 16, no. 3 (1935): 209–15.

Downey, Richard, Archbishop of Liverpool (ed.), *Rebuilding the Church in England* (London: Burns, Oates and Washburne Limited, 1933).

Downey, Richard, Archbishop of Liverpool (ed.), *A Cathedral in Our Time* (Liverpool: Liverpool Archdiocese, c.1934).

Epstein, Jacob to Haskell, Arnold L., *The Sculptor Speaks* (London: William Heinemann, 1931).

Forrester, Helen, *Tuppence to Cross the Mersey* (London: Harper Collins, 1993).

Geddes, Patrick, *Cities in Evolution* (London, William and Norgate Ltd, 1949).

Gibberd, Frederick, *Metropolitan Cathedral of Christ the King* (London: The Architectural Press, 1968).

Greenwood, Walter, *Love on the Dole* (London: Vintage, 2004).

Jones, David Caradog (ed.), *The Social Survey of Merseyside* (3 vols., London: University Press of Liverpool, 1934).

Kelly's (Gore's), *Directory for Liverpool 1920* (London: Kelly's, 1919).

Kelly's (Gore's), *Directory for Liverpool 1932* (London: Kelly's, 1931).

Kelly's (Gore's), *Directory for Liverpool 1938* (London: Kelly's, 1937).

Kelly's (Gore's), *Directory for Manchester and Salford 1920* (London: Kelly's, 1919).

Kelly's (Gore's), *Directory for Manchester and Salford 1932* (London: Kelly's, 1931).

Kelly's (Gore's), *Directory for Manchester and Salford 1938* (London: Kelly's, 1937).

Liverpool Corporation, *Liverpool Civic Week Programme 1925* (Liverpool: Liverpool Corporation, 1925).

Liverpool University Social Science Department: Statistics Division, *Migration to and from Merseyside: Home, Irish, Overseas* (Liverpool: The University of Liverpool, 1938).

Liverpool Organization, *The Book of Liverpool: Civic Week, 1928* (Liverpool: Liverpool Organization, 1928).

Manchester and Salford District Committee of the Communist Party of Great Britain, *This is Our City: A Programme for a Modern Manchester* (Manchester: Communist Party of Great Britain, Manchester and Salford District Committee, 1937).

Manchester City Council, *Centenary Celebration of Manchester's Incorporation. Official Handbook to the Exhibition of Civic Services, City Hall*, Deansgate, May 2–7, 1938 (Manchester: Percy Brothers, 1938).

Manchester Civic Week Committee, *Manchester Civic Week Official Handbook* (Manchester: Civic Week Committee, 1926).

Manchester Corporation, *How Manchester Is Managed: A Record of Municipal Activities* (Manchester: Manchester Corporation, 1932).

Manchester Corporation, *How Manchester Is Managed: A Record of Municipal Activities* (Manchester: Manchester Corporation, 1933).

Manchester Corporation, *How Manchester Is Managed: A Record of Municipal Activities, with a Description of the City* (Manchester: Manchester Corporation, 1938).

Manchester Corporation, *How Manchester Is Managed: A Record of Municipal Activities* (Manchester: Manchester Corporation, 1939).

Manchester Corporation Transport Department, *General Statistical Information and Descriptions of Depots* (Manchester: Manchester Corporation, 1928).

Manchester Corporation Transport Department, *A Hundred Years of Road Passenger Transport in Manchester* (Manchester: Manchester Corporation, 1935).

Manchester City Council, *Centenary Celebration of Manchester's Incorporation, May 2–7 1938* (Manchester: Manchester Corporation, 1938).

Manchester Guardian, *Commercial Yearbook 1921* (Manchester: Manchester Guardian, 1921).

Manchester Guardian, *Commercial Yearbook 1925* (Manchester: Manchester Guardian, 1925).

Manchester Guardian, *Commercial Yearbook 1927* (Manchester: Manchester Guardian, 1927).

Manchester Guardian, *Commercial Yearbook 1928* (Manchester: Manchester Guardian, 1928).

Manchester Guardian, *Manchester Handy Book* (Manchester: Manchester Guardian, 1928).

Manchester University Settlement, *Ancoats: A Study of a Clearance Area. Report of a Survey Made in 1937–1938* (Manchester: Manchester University, 1945).

Ministry of Health, Annual Local Taxation Returns, 1925–35.

Nicholas, Rowland, *City of Manchester Plan 1945* (London: Jarrold and Sons, 1945).

O'Mara, Pat, *The Autobiography of a Liverpool Irish Slummy* (London: Martin Hopkinson Ltd, 1934).

Orwell, George, *The Road to Wigan Pier* (London: Penguin, 1989).

Pilcher, R. Stuart, *Road Passenger Transport: Survey and Development* (London: Sir Isaac Pitman and Sons Ltd., 1937).

Priestley, J. B., *English Journey: Being a Rambling but Truthful Account of what One Man Saw and Heard and Felt and Thought during a Journey through England during the Autumn of the Year 1933* (London: Penguin, 1977).

Reece, S., *Guide to Manchester and Salford* (Manchester: Sherratt & Hughes, 1939).

Reilly, Charles and Patrick Abercrombie, 'Town Planning Schemes in America', *The Town Planning Review* 1, no. 1 (1910): 54–65.

Reilly, Charles, *Some Liverpool Streets and Buildings in 1921* (Liverpool: The Liverpool Daily Post and Mercury, 1921).

Reilly, Charles, *Some Manchester Streets and Buildings* (Liverpool: The Liverpool Daily Post and Mercury, 1924).

Reilly, Charles, *Scaffolding in the Sky: A Semi-Architectural Autobiography* (London: Routledge, 1938).

Rowntree, B. Seebohm, *Poverty and Progress: A Second Social Survey of York* (London: Kongmans Green and Co., 1942).

Royal Institute of British Architects, *Town Planning Conference, London, 10–15 October, 1910: Transactions* (London: Royal Institute of British Architects: London, 1911).

Simon, E. D., *A City Council from Within* (London: Longmans, 1926).

Simon, Sheena, *A Century of City Government: Manchester, 1838–1938* (London: George Allen & Unwin, 1938).

Sommerfield, John, *May Day* (London: London Books, 1936).

Spender, Humphrey, *Worktown People: Photographs from Northern England, 1937–39* (Bristol: Falling Wall Press, 1982).

Spring, Howard, *Shabby Tiger* (Manchester: Memories, 1999).

Tylor, W. Russell, 'The Neighbourhood Unit Principle in Town Planning', *The Town Planning Review* 18, no. 3 (1939): 174–86.

White, Thomas, *Memorandum of the Chairman of the Mersey Tunnel Joint Committee on the Present Financial Position* (Liverpool: Liverpool Corporation, 1932).

Press

The Cathedral Record: The Official Organ of the Archdiocese of Liverpool
Catholic Herald
Catholic Times
Chicago Daily Tribune
Daily Boston Globe
Daily Courier
Daily Dispatch
Daily Mail
Evening Express
Harvest
Irwin's Weekly Chronicle
Liverpolitan
Liverpool Catholic Parishioner
Liverpool Post and Mercury
Manchester Dispatch
Manchester Evening News
Manchester Guardian
New York Times
Northern Voice
The Observer
The Tablet
The Times

Secondary sources

Books

Abelson, Elaine S., *When Ladies Go A-Thieving: Middle Class Shoplifters in the Victorian Department Store* (Oxford: Oxford University Press, 1989).

Aldcroft, Derek, *The Inter-War Economy: Britain, 1919–1939* (London: B.T. Batsford, 1970).

Allitt, Patrick, *Catholic Converts: British and American Intellectuals Turn to Rome* (London: Cornell University Press, 1997).

Andrews, Maggie and Mary M. Talbot (eds), *All the World and Her Husband: Women in Twentieth-Century Consumer Culture* (London: Cassell, 2000).

Anthony, Scott and James G. Mansell (eds), *The Projection of Britain: A History of the GPO Film Unit* (Basingstoke: Palgrave Macmillan, 2011).

Arts Council of Great Britain, *Lutyens: The Work of the English Architect Sir Edwin Lutyens (1869–1944)* (London: Arts Council of Great Britain, 1982).

Ayerst, David, *Guardian: Biography of a Newspaper* (London: Collins, 1991).

Baldwin, Peter C., *In the Watches of the Night: Life in the Nocturnal City, 1820-1930* (Chicago: University of Chicago Press, 2012).

Beaumont, Catriona, *Housewives and Citizens: Domesticity and the Women's Movement in England, 1928-1964* (Manchester: Manchester University Press, 2013).

Belchem, John (ed.), *Liverpool 800: Culture, Character and History* (Liverpool: Liverpool University Press, 2006).

Belchem, John, *Merseypride: Essays in Liverpool Exceptionalism* (Liverpool: Liverpool University Press, 2000).

Benjamin, Walter, *The Arcades Project*, translated by Howard Eiland and Kevin McLaughlin (London: Harvard University Press, 2002).

Benson, Susan Porter, *Counter Cultures: Saleswomen, Managers, and Customers in American Department Stores, 1890–1940* (Chicago: University of Illinois Press, 1988).

Bingham, Adrian, *Family Newspapers? Sex, Private Life, and the British Popular Press 1918-1978* (Oxford: Oxford University Press, 2009).

Bingham, Adrian, *Gender, Modernity, and the Popular Press in Inter-War Britain* (Oxford: Clarendon Press, 2004).

Bland, Lucy, *Modern Women on Trial: Sexual Transgression in the Age of the Flapper* (Manchester: Manchester University Press, 2013).

Bolton, Charles A., *Salford Diocese and its Catholic Past: A Survey* (Manchester, 1950).

Bowlby, Rachel, *Carried Away: The Invention of Modern Shopping* (New York: Columbia University Press, 2001).

Boyle, Raymond and Peter Lynch, *Out of the Ghetto? The Catholic Community in Modern Scotland* (Edinburgh: John Donald, 1998).

Breward, Christopher, Becky Conekin and Nancy Cox (eds), *The Englishness of English Dress* (Oxford: Berg, 2002).

Briggs, Asa, *Friends of the People: The Centenary History of Lewis's* (London: B.T. Batsford Ltd, 1956).

Brook, Richard and Martin Dodge, *Infra_MANC: Post-War Infrastructures of Manchester* (Manchester: Bauprint, 2012).

Brown, Callum, *The Death of Christian Britain: Understanding Secularisation, 1800-2000* (London: Routledge, 2000).

Bullock, Nick, *Building the Post-War World: Modern Architecture and Reconstruction in Britain* (London: Routledge, 2002).

Burman, Barbara (ed.), *The Culture of Sewing: Gender, Consumption and Home Dressmaking* (Oxford: Berg, 1999).

Buse, Peter, Ken Hirschkop, Scott McCracken and Bertrand Taithe, *Benjamin's Arcades: An UnGuided Tour* (Manchester: Manchester University Press, 2005).

Calder, Angus, *The People's War: Britain 1939-1945* (London: Jonathan Cape, 1971).

Carnevali, Francesca and Julie-Marie Strange (eds), *Twentieth-Century Britain: Economic, Cultural and Social Change*, revised & updated edn (Harlow: Pearson/Longman, 2007).

Catterall, Peter, Colin Seymour-Ure and Adrian Smith (eds), *Northcliffe's Legacy: Aspects of the British Popular Press, 1896-1996* (Basingstoke: MacMillan, 2000).

de Certeau, Michel, *The Practice of Everyday Life*, translated by Steven Rendall (Berkeley: University of California Press, 1984).

Clapson, Mark, *Anglo-American Crossroads: Urban Planning and Research in Britain, 1940-2010* (Bloomsbury: London, 2012).

Clapson, Mark, *Working-Class Suburb: Social Change on an English Council Estate, 1930-2010* (Manchester: Manchester University Press, 2012).

Clapson, Mark, *Suburban Century: Social Change and Urban Growth in England and the USA* (Oxford: Berg, 2003).

Clapson, Mark and Peter J. Larkham (eds), *The Blitz and Its Legacy: Wartime Destruction to Post-War Reconstruction* (Farnham: Ashgate, 2013).

Clendinning, Anne, *Demons of Domesticity: Women and the English Gas Industry, 1889-1939* (Aldershot: Ashgate, 2004).

Cohen, Anthony P., *The Symbolic Construction of Community* (Chichester: Ellis Horwood, 1985).

Cohen, Anthony P., *Whalsay: Symbol, Segment and Boundary in a Shetland Island Community* (Manchester: Manchester University Press, 1987).

Conekin, Becky E., *'The Autobiography of a Nation': The 1951 Festival of Britain* (Manchester: Manchester University Press, 2003).

Conekin, Becky E., Chris Waters and Frank Mort, *Moments of Modernity: Reconstructing Britain, 1945-1964* (London: Rivers Oram Press, 1999).

Conor, Liz, *The Spectacular Modern Woman: Feminine Visibility in the 1920s* (Bloomington: Indiana University Press, 2004).

Cook, Guy, *The Discourse of Advertising* (Routledge: London, 2001).

Cooke, Terry, *Scotland Road 'The Old Neighbourhood': The Yesteryears of Liverpool's famous Scotland Road* (Birkenhead: Countryvise, 1987).

Couch, Chris, *City of Change and Challenge: Urban Planning and Regeneration in Liverpool* (Aldershot: Ashgate, 2003).

Cox, Pamela and Annabel Hobley, *Shopgirls: The True Story of Life Behind the Counter* (London: Hutchinson, 2015).

Crossick, Geoffrey and Serge Jaumain (eds), *Cathedrals of Consumption: The European Department Store, 1850–1939* (Aldershot: Ashgate, 1999).

Darling, Elizabeth and Lesley Whitworth (eds), *Women and the Making of Built Space in England, 1870–1950* (Aldershot: Ashgate, 2007).

Daunton, Martin J. (ed.), *The Cambridge Urban History of Britain, Volume III 1840–1950* (Cambridge: Cambridge University Press, 2000).

Daunton, Martin J. and Bernhard Rieger, *Meanings of Modernity: Britain from the Late Victorian Era to World War II* (Oxford: Berg, 2001).

Davidoff, Leonore and Catherine Hall, *Family Fortunes: Men and Women of the English Middle Class, 1780–1850* (London: Hutchinson, 1987).

Davies, Andrew, *City of Gangs* (London: Hodder & Stoughton, 2013).

Davies, Andrew, *Leisure, Gender and Poverty: Working-Class Culture in Salford and Manchester, 1900-1939* (Buckinghamshire: Open University Press, 1992).

Davies, Andrew and Steven Fielding (eds), *Workers' Worlds: Cultures and Communities in Manchester and Salford, 1880–1939* (Manchester: Manchester University Press, 1992).

Davies, R. Bruce, *Peacefully Working to Conquer the World: Singer Sewing Machines in Foreign Markets, 1854–1920* (New York: Arno, 1976).

Davis, John, *A History of Britain, 1885–1939* (Basingstoke: MacMillan, 1999).

Divall, Colin and Winstan Bond (eds), *Suburbanizing the Masses: Public Transport and Urban Development in Historical Perspective* (Aldershot: Ashgate, 2003).

Doyle, Peter, *Mitres and Missions in Lancashire: The Roman Catholic Diocese, 1850–2000* (Liverpool: The Bluecoat Press, 2005).

Dyhouse, Carol, *Glamour: Women, History, Feminism* (London: Zed Books, 2011).

Esperdy, Gabrielle, *Modernizing Mainstreet: Architecture and Consumer Culture in the New Deal* (Chicago: Chicago University Press, 2008).

Fielding, Steven, *Class and Ethnicity: Irish Catholics in England, 1880–1939* (Buckingham: Open University Press, 1993).

Foster, Andy, *Birmingham. Pevsner Architectural Guide* (London: Yale University Press, 2005).

Fowler, David, *The First Teenagers: The Lifestyle of Young Wage-Earners in Interwar Britain* (London: Woburn Press, 1995).

Fraser, T. G., *The Irish Parading Tradition: Following the Drum* (Basingstoke: MacMillan, 2000).

Gamber, Wendy, *The Female Economy: The Millinery and Dressmaking Trades, 1860–1930* (Chicago: University of Illinois Press, 1997).

Gibberd, Frederick, *Metropolitan Cathedral of Christ the King* (London: Architectural Press, 1968).

Gilbert, David, David Matless and Brian Short (eds), *Geographies of British Modernity: Space and Society in the Twentieth Century* (Oxford: Wiley-Blackwell, 2003).

Giles, Judy, *Women, Identity and Private Life in Britain, 1900–50* (Basingstoke: MacMillan, 1995).

Glucksmann, Miriam, *Women Assemble: Women Workers and the New Industries in Inter-War Britain* (London: Routledge, 1990).

Gold, John R., *The Experience of Modernism: Modern Architects and the Future City, 1928-53* (London: Routledge, 2013).

Goodhart-Rendel, Harry Stuart, *English Architecture since the Regency* (London: Constable, 1953).

Gordon, George (ed.), *Regional Cities in the UK, 1890-1980* (London: Harper and Row, 1986).

de Grazia, Victoria, *Irresistible Empire. America's Advance through 20th-Century Europe* (Cambridge, MA: Harvard University Press, 2005).

de Grazia, Victoria, *How Fascism Ruled Women: Italy, 1922–1945* (London: University of California Press, 1992).

Green, S. J. D., *The Passing of Protestant England: Secularisation and Social Change, c.1920-1960* (Cambridge: Cambridge University Press, 2011).

Green, S. J. D., *Religion in the Age of Decline: Organisation and Experience in Industrial Yorkshire, 1870–1920* (Cambridge: Cambridge University Press, 1996).

Grimley, Matthew, *Citizenship, Community, and the Church of England: Liberal Anglican Theories of the State between the Wars* (Oxford: Clarendon Press, 2004).

Gunn, Simon, *The Public Culture of the Victorian Middle Class: Ritual and Authority and the English Industrial City, 1840–1914* (Manchester: Manchester University Press, 2000).

Gunn, Simon and James Vernon (eds), *The Peculiarities of Liberal Modernity in Imperial Britain* (Berkeley, CA: University of California Press, 2011).

Gunn, Simon and Robert J. Morris (eds), *Identities in Space: Contested Terrains in the Western City since 1850* (Aldershot: Ashgate, 2001).

Gurney, Peter, *Co-operative Culture and the Politics of Consumption in England, 1870-1930* (Manchester: Manchester University Press, 1996).

Hall, Peter, *Cities of Tomorrow: An Intellectual History of Urban Planning and Design in the Twentieth Century* (Oxford: Blackwell, 1996).

Harvey, David, *Paris, Capital of Modernity* (London: Routledge, 2004).

Haslam, Dave, *Manchester, England: The Story of a Pop Cult City* (London: Fourth Estate, 2000).

Hastings, Adrian, *A History of English Christianity 1920–1985* (London: Collins, 1985).

Herbert, Michael, *The Wearing of the Green: A Political History of the Irish in Manchester* (London: Irish Representation Group, 2001).

Higson, Andrew, *Waving the Flag: Constructing a National Cinema in Britain* (Oxford: Clarendon Press, 1995).

Hilton, Matthew, *Consumerism in the Twentieth Century: The Search for a Historical Movement* (Cambridge: Cambridge University Press, 2003).

Hilton, Matthew, *Smoking in British Popular Culture 1800–2000: Perfect Pleasures* (Manchester: Manchester University Press, 2000).

Hinton, James, *Nine Wartime Lives: Mass Observation and the Making of the Modern Self* (Oxford: Oxford University Press, 2010).

Houlbrook, Matt, *Queer London: Perils and Pleasures in the Sexual Metropolis, 1918–1957* (Bristol: Chicago University Press, 2005).

Hubble, Nick, *Mass-Observation and Everyday Life: Culture, History, Theory* (Hampshire: Palgrave MacMillan, 2006).

Hughes, Very Reverend Canon, *A Concise Catholic History of Liverpool* (Liverpool: n.p., 1926).

Hunt, Tristram, *Building Jerusalem: The Rise and Fall of the Victorian City* (London: Weidenfeld and Nicolson, 2004).

Hussey, Christopher, *The Life of Sir Edwin Lutyens* (Suffolk: ACC Art Books, 1984).

Hynes, Samuel, *A War Imagined: The First World War and English Culture* (London: The Bodley Head, 1990).

Jeffreys, James B., *Retail Trading in Britain, 1850–1950* (Cambridge: Cambridge University Press, 1954).

Johnson, Paul, *Saving and Spending: The Working-Class Economy in Britain, 1870–1939* (Oxford: Clarendon Press, 1985).

Jonas, Raymond, *France and the Cult of the Sacred Heart: An Epic Tale for Modern Times* (London: University of California Press, 2000).

Jones, Max, *The Last Great Quest: Captain Scott's Antarctic Sacrifice* (Oxford: Oxford University Press, 2003).

Jones, Timothy Willem and Lucinda Matthews-Jones (eds), *Material Religion in Modern Britain: The Spirit of Things* (Basingstoke: Palgrave, 2015).

Joyce, Patrick, *The Rule of Freedom: Liberalism and the Modern City* (London: Verso, 2003).

Ker, Ian Turnbull, *The Catholic Revival in English Literature, 1845-1961: Newman, Hopkins, Belloc, Chesterton, Greene, Waugh* (Indiana: University of Notre Dame Press, 2003).

Kent, Susan Kingsley, *Making Peace: The Reconstruction of Gender in Interwar Britain* (Sussex: Princeton University Press, 1993).

Kidd, Alan, *Manchester* (Edinburgh: Edinburgh University Press, 2002).

Kidd, Alan and David Nichols (eds), *Gender, Civic Culture and Consumerism: Middle - Class Identity in Britain, 1800–1940* (Manchester: Manchester University Press, 1999).

Kingsford, Peter, *The Hunger Marchers in Britain, 1920–1939* (London: Lawrence and Wishart, 1982).

Kuhn, Annette, *An Everyday Magic: Cinema and Cultural Memory* (London: I.B. Tauris, 2002).

Lambert, Sharon, *Irish Women in Lancashire 1922–1960: Their Story* (Lancaster: Centre for North-West Regional studies, University of Lancaster, 2001).

Lancaster, Bill, *The Department Store: A Social History* (London: Leicester University Press, 1995).

Landy, Joshua and Michael Saler (eds), *The Re-Enchantment of the World: Secular Magic in a Rational Age* (Stanford, CA: Stanford University Press, 2009).

Lawrence, Jon, *Electing Our Masters: The Hustings in British Politics from Hogarth to Blair* (Oxford: Oxford University Press, 2009).

Lawton, Richard and Catherine M. Cunningham (eds), *Merseyside: Social and Economic Studies* (London: Longman, 1970).

Lefebvre, Henri, *The Production of Space*, translated by Donald Nicholson-Smith (Oxford: Basil Blackwell, 1974).

Lennon, Mary, Marie McAdam and Joanne O'Brien, *Across the Water: Irish Women's Lives in Britain* (London: Virago Press, 1988).

Light, Alison, *Forever England: Femininity, Literature and Conservatism between the Wars* (London: Routledge, 1991).

Lothian, James R., *The Making and Unmaking of the English Catholic Intellectual Community, 1910–1950* (Indiana: University of Notre Dame Press, 2009).

Lutyens, Mary, *Edwin Lutyens by His Daughter Mary Lutyens* (London: Murray, 1980).

Maconie, Stuart, *The Pie At Night: In Search of the North at Play* (London: Ebury Press, 2015).

Maconie, Stuart, *Pies and Prejudice: In Search of the North* (London: Ebury Press, 2007).

MacPherson, D. A. J. and Mary J. Hickman (eds), *Women and Irish Diaspora Identities: Theories, Concepts and New Perspectives* (Manchester: Manchester University Press, 2014).

MacRaild, Donald M., *Irish Migrants in Modern Britain, 1750–1922* (Basingstoke: MacMillan, 1999).

Marchland, Roland, *Advertising the American Dream: Making Way for Modernity, 1920–1940* (London: University of California Press, 1986).

Marriner, Sheila, *The Economic and Social Development of Merseyside* (London: Croom Helm, 1982).

McGreevy, John T., *Parish Boundaries: The Catholic Encounter with Race in the Twentieth-Century Urban North* (London: University of Chicago Press, 1996).

McKibbin, Ross, *Classes and Cultures: England, 1918–1951* (Oxford: Oxford University Press, 1998).

McKibbin, Ross, *Parties and People: England 1914-1951* (Oxford: Oxford University Press. 2010).

McKibbin, Ross, *The Ideologies of Class: Social Relations in Britain, 1880-1950* (Oxford: Clarendon Press, 1990).

Morley, Paul, *The North (And Almost Everything In It)* (London: Bloomsbury, 2013).

Morris, Robert J. and Richard H. Trainor (eds), *Urban Governance: Britain and Beyond since 1750* (Aldershot: Ashgate, 2000).

Mort, Frank, *Capital Affairs: London and the Making of the Permissive Society* (London: Yale University Press, 2010).

Mulhern, Francis, *Culture/Metaculture* (London: Routledge, 2000).

National Museums of Liverpool, *The Cathedral That Never Was: Lutyens' Design for Liverpool* (Liverpool: Apollo, 2007).

Nead, Lynda, *Victorian Babylon: People, Streets and Images in Nineteenth-Century London* (London: Yale University Press, 2000).

Neal, Frank, *Black '47: Britain and the Famine Irish* (Basingstoke: MacMillan, 1998).

Orsi, Robert, *Thank You, Saint Jude: Women's Devotion to the Patron Saint of Hopeless Causes* (Yale: Yale University Press, 1996).

Orsi, Robert, *The Madonna of the 115th Street: Faith and Community in Italian Harlem, 1880–1950* (London: Yale University Press, 1985).

Otter, Christopher, *The Victorian Eye: A Political History of Light and Vision in Britain, 1800-1910* (Bristol: University of Chicago Press, 2008).

Parkinson-Bailey, John, *Manchester: An Architectural History* (Manchester: Manchester University Press, 2000).

Peck, Jamie and Kevin Ward (eds), *City of Revolution: Restructuring Manchester* (Manchester: Manchester University Press, 2002).

Peiss, Kathy, *Cheap Amusements: Working Women and Leisure in Turn-of-the-Century New York* (Philadelphia: Temple University Press, 1986).

Percy, Clayre and Jayne Ridley, *The Letters of Edwin Lutyens: To His Wife Lady Emily* (London: Harper Collins, 1985).

Rappaport, Erika D., *Shopping for Pleasure: Women in the Making of London's West End* (New Jersey: Princeton University Press, 2000).

Rea, Anthony, *Manchester's Little Italy: Memories of the Italian Colony of Ancoats* (Manchester: Neil Richardson, 1988).

Redford, Arthur, *The History of Local Government in Manchester, Volume 3. The Last Half Century* (London: Longmans, 1940).

Richards, Jeffrey, *The Age of the Dream Palace: Cinema and Society in Britain 1930–1939* (London: Routledge, 1984).

Richmond, Peter, *Marketing Modernisms: The Architecture and Influence of Charles Reilly* (Liverpool: Liverpool University Press, 2001).

Rieger, Bernhard, *Technology and the Culture of Modernity in Britain and Germany, 1890–1945* (Cambridge: Cambridge University Press, 2005).

Roberts, Elizabeth, *A Woman's Place: An Oral History of Working-Class Women, 1890–1940* (Oxford: Blackwell, 1984).

Robertson, Nicole, *The Co-operative Movement and Communities in Britain, 1914-1960: Minding Their Own Business* (Farnham: Ashgate, 2010).

Rooth, Tim, *British Protectionism and the International Economy: Overseas Commercial Policy in the 1930s* (Cambridge: Cambridge University Press, 1993).

Roper, Michael, *The Secret Battle: Emotional Survival in the Great War* (Manchester: University of Manchester Press, 2009).

Rose, Sonya O., *Which People's War?: National Identity and Citizenship in Wartime Britain, 1939-45* (Oxford: Oxford University Press, 2003).

Rotha, Paul, *Documentary Diary: An Informal History of the British Documentary Film, 1928-1939* (London: Martin Secker & Warburg Ltd, 1973).

Rushton, Pauline, *Mrs Tinne's Wardrobe: A Liverpool Lady's Clothes, 1900–1940* (Liverpool: The Bluecoat Press: 2006).

Salvidge, Stanley, *Salvidge of Liverpool: Behind the Political Scene, 1890–1928* (London: Hodder & Stoughton, 1934).

Schwartz, Adam, *The Third Spring: G.K. Chesterton, Graham Greene, Christopher Dawson, and David Jones* (Washington, DC: Catholic University of America Press, 2005).

Schwartz, Vanessa R., *Realities: Early Mass Culture in fin-de-siècle Paris* (London: University of California Press, 1998).

Sharples, Joseph, *Pevsner Architectural Guides: Liverpool* (London: Yale University Press, 2004).

Sharples, Joseph, Alan Powers and Michael Shippobottom, *Charles Reilly and the Liverpool School of Architecture, 1904-1933* (Liverpool: Liverpool University Press, 1996).

Sheldrake, John, *Municipal Socialism* (Aldershot: Avebury, 1989).

Short, Ernest, *The House of God: A History of Religious Architecture* (London: Philip Allan, 1955).

Smith, Carl, *The Plan of Chicago: Daniel Burnham and the Remaking of the American City* (Chicago: University of Chicago Press 2006).

Smith, Helen, *Masculinity, Class and Same-Sex Desire in Industrial England, 1895-1957* (London: Palgrave Macmillan, 2015).

Søland, Brigitte, *Becoming Modern: Young Women and the Reconstruction of Womanhood in the 1920s* (Oxford: Princeton University Press, 2000).

Stamp, Gavin, *The Memorial to the Missing of the Somme* (London: Profile Books, 2007).

Stevenson, John and Chris Cook, *The Slump: Society and Politics during the Depression* (London: Quartet, 1977).

Stevenson, John and Chris Cook, *The Slump: Britain in the Great Depression* (Harlow: Longman, 2010).

Strasser, Susan, Charles McGovern and Matthias Judt (eds), *Getting and Spending: European and American Consumer Societies in the Twentieth Century* (Cambridge: Cambridge University Press, 1998).

Summerfield, Penny, *Reconstructing Women's Wartime Lives: Discourse and Subjectivity in Oral Histories of the Second World War* (Manchester: Manchester University Press, 1998).

Sutcliffe, Anthony, *An Architectural History: London* (London: Yale University Press: 2006).

Sweet, Rosemary and Penelope Lane, *Women and Urban Life in Eighteenth-Century England: 'On the Town'* (Ashgate: Aldershot, 2003).

Swift, Roger and Sheridan Gilley (eds), *The Irish in Britain, 1815-1939* (London: Pinter, 1989).

Taylor, A. J. P., *English History: 1914–1945* (Oxford: Clarendon Press, 1965).

Thackeray, David, *Conservatism for the Democratic Age: Conservative Cultures and the Challenge of Mass Politics in Early Twentieth Century England* (Manchester: Manchester University Press, 2013).

Thane, Pat and Tanya Evans, *Sinners? Scroungers? Saints?: Unmarried Motherhood in Twentieth-Century England* (Oxford: Oxford University Press, 2014).

Tinkler, Penny, *Constructing Girlhood: Popular Magazines for Girls Growing up in England, 1920–1950* (London: Taylor and Francis, 1995).

Tinkler, Penny, *Using Photographs in Social and Historical Research* (London: Sage, 2013).

Todd, Selina, *The People: The Rise and Fall of the Working Class* (London: John Murray, 2015).

Todd, Selina, *Young Women, Work, and Family in England, 1918–1950* (Oxford: Oxford University Press, 2005).

Vernon, James, *Distant Strangers: How Britain Became Modern* (Berkley: California, 2014).

Wainwright, Martin, *True North: In Praise of England's Better Half* (London: Guardian Books, 2009).

Walkowitz, Judith, *Nights Out: Life in Cosmopolitan London* (London: Yale University Press, 2012).

Walkowitz, Judith, *City of Dreadful Delight: Narratives of Sexual Danger in Late-Victorian London* (London: Chicago University Press, 1992).

Walkowitz, Judith, *Prostitution and Victorian Society Women, Class, and the State* (Cambridge: Cambridge University Press, 1980).

Waller, P. J., *Democracy and Sectarianism: A Political and Social History of Liverpool, 1868–1939* (Liverpool: Liverpool University Press, 1981).

Ward, David and Oliver Zunz (eds), *The Landscape of Modernity: New York City, 1900–1940* (Baltimore: Johns Hopkins, 1997).

Waterhouse, Robert, *The Other Fleet Street: How Manchester Made Newspapers National* (Altrincham: First Edition Limited, 2004).

Watkin, David, *English Architecture: A Concise History* (London: Thames & Hudson, 1979).

Weinbaum, Alys Eve, Lynn M. Thomas, Priti Ramamurthy, Uta G. Poiger, Madeleine Yue Dong and Tani E. Barlow, *The Modern Girl Around the World: Consumption, Modernity, and Globalization* (London: Duke University Press, 2008).

Williams, Sarah C., *Religious Belief and Popular Culture in Southwark* (Oxford: Oxford University Press, 1999).

Wilson, Elizabeth, *Adorned in Dreams: Fashion and Modernity* (London: Virago, 1985).

Winter, Jay, *Sites of Memory, Sites of Mourning: The Great War in European Cultural History* (Cambridge: Cambridge University Press, 1995).

Woodhead, Lindy, *Shopping, Seduction and Mr Selfridge* (London: Profile Books, 2007).

Woolton, Earl of, *The Memoirs of the Rt. Hon. The Earl of Woolton* (London: Cassell, 1959).

Wrathmell, Susan, *Leeds Pevsner Architectural Guide* (London: Yale University Press, 2005).

Yearsley, Ian and Philip Graves, *The Manchester Tramways* (Glossop: Transport Publishing Company, 1988).

Young, Ken and Nirmala Rao, *Local Government since 1945* (Oxford: Wiley-Blackwell, 1997).

Chapters and journal articles

Alexander, Sally, 'Becoming a Woman in London in the 1920s and 1930s', in *Metropolis: London, Histories and Representations*, eds. David Feldman and Gareth Stedman Jones (London: Routledge, 1989), 245–71.

Alexander, Sally, 'Men's Fears and Women's Work: Responses to Unemployment in London between the Wars', *Gender & History* 12, no. 2 (2000): 401–25.

Amati, Marco and Robert Freestone, 'All of London's a Stage: The 1943 County of London Plan Exhibition', *Urban History*, FirstView Article (2015), 1–18. http://dx.doi.org/10.1017/S0963926815000498.

Auerbach, Jeffrey, 'The Great Exhibition and Historical Memory', *Journal of Victorian Culture* 6, no. 1 (2001): 89–112.

Ayers, Pat, 'The Hidden Economy of Dockland Families: Liverpool in the 1930s', in *Women's Work and the Family Economy in Historical Perspective*, eds. Pat Hudson and W. R. Lee (Manchester: Manchester University Press, 1990), 271–90.

Balderstone, Laura, Graeme Milne and Rachel Mulhearn, 'Memory and Place on the Liverpool Waterfront in the Mid-Twentieth Century', *Urban History* 41, no. 3 (2014): 478–96.

Barker, Hannah, 'Medical Advertising and Trust in Late Georgian England', *Urban History* 36, no. 3 (2009): 379–98.

Bean, Ron, 'Police Unrest, Unionization and the 1919 Strike in Liverpool', *Journal of Contemporary History* 15, no. 4 (1980): 633–53.

Beaven, Brad, 'Challenges to Civic Governance in Post-War England: The Peace Day Disturbances of 1919', *Urban History* 33, no. 3 (2006): 369–92.

Beaven, Brad and John Griffiths, 'Creating the Exemplary Citizen: The Changing Notion of Citizenship in Britain 1870–1939', *Contemporary British History* 22, no. 2 (2008): 203–25.

Beers, Laura, 'Education or Manipulation? Labour, Democracy and the Popular Press in Inter-War Britain', *Journal of British Studies* 48, no. 1 (2009): 129–52.

Bingham, Adrian, 'The British Popular Press and Venereal Disease during the Second World War', *The Historical Journal* 48, no. 4 (2005): 1055–76.

Bland, Lucy, 'White Women and Men of Colour: Miscegenation Fears in Britain after the Great War', *Gender and History* 17, no. 1 (2005): 29–61.

Britton, Sarah, 'Urban Futures/Rural Pasts: Representing Scotland in the 1938 Glasgow Empire Exhibition', *Cultural and Social History* 8, no. 2 (2011): 213–32.

Bohstedt, John, 'More than One Working Class: Protestant-Catholic Riots in Edwardian Liverpool', in *Popular Politics, Riot and Labour: Essays in Liverpool History, 1790–1940*, ed. John Belchem (Liverpool: Liverpool University Press, 1992).

Brewitt-Taylor, Sam, 'The Invention of a "Secular Society"? Christianity and the Sudden Appearance of Secularization Discourses in the British National Media, 1961–4', *20th Century British History* 24, no. 3 (2013): 327–50.

Bromley, Michael and Nick Hayes, 'Campaigner, Watchdog or Municipal Lackey: Reflections on the Inter-War Provincial Press, Local Identity and Civic Welfarism', *Media History* 8, no. 2 (2002): 197–212.

Brown, Callum G., 'Secularization, the Growth of Militancy and the Spiritual Revolution: Religious Change and Gender Power in Britain, 1901-2001', *Historical Research* 80, no. 209 (2007): 393–418.

Buckley, Cheryl, 'On the Margins: Theorizing the History and Significance of Making and Designing Clothes at Home', *Journal of Design History* 11, no. 2 (1998): 157–71.

Calder, Angus, 'Mass-Observation 1937–1949', in *Essays on the History of British Sociological Research*, ed. Martin Blumer (Cambridge: Cambridge University Press, 1985).

Caruana, Viv and Colin Simmons, 'The Promotion and Development of Manchester Airport, 1929–1974: The Local Authority Initiative', *The Local Historian* 30, no. 3 (2000): 165–77.

Caslin, Samantha, '"One Can Only Guess What Might Have Happened if the Worker Had Not Intervened in Time": The Liverpool Vigilance Association, Moral Vulnerability and Irish Girls in Early- to Mid-Twentieth-Century Liverpool', *Women's History Review* 25, no. 2 (2016): 254–73.

Clapson, Mark, 'The Rise and Fall of Monica Felton, British Town Planner and Peace Activist, 1930s to 1950s', *Planning Perspectives* 30, no. 2 (2015): 211–29.

Clapson, Mark, 'The Suburban Aspiration in England since 1919', *Contemporary British History* 14, no. 1 (2000): 151–74.

Cohen, Margaret, 'Walter Benjamin's Phantasmagoria', *New German Critique* 48 (1989): 87–107.

Constantine, Stephen. '"Bringing the Empire Alive": The Empire Marketing Board and Imperial Propaganda, 1926–33', in *Imperialism and Popular Culture*, ed. John M. MacKenzie (Manchester: Manchester University Press, 1986), 192–231.

Conway, Rebecca, 'Making the Mill Girl Modern?: Beauty, Industry, and the Popular Newspaper in 1930s' England', *Twentieth Century British History* 24, no. 4 (2013): 518–54.

Cosgrove, Denis, *Social Formation and the Symbolic Landscape* (Madison: University of Wisconsin Press, 1998).

Darling, Elizabeth, '"The Star in the Profession She Invented for Herself": A Brief Biography of Elizabeth Denby, Housing Consultant', *Planning Perspectives* 20, no. 3 (2005): 271–300.

Davies, Andrew, 'The Scottish Chicago: From "Hooligans" to "Gangsters" in Interwar Glasgow', *Cultural and Social History* 4, no. 4 (2007): 511–27.

Dodge, Martin and Richard Brook, 'Dreams of Helicopter Travel in the 1950s and Liverpool's Undeveloped Plans for a City Centre Heliport', *Transactions of the Royal Historic Society of Lancashire and Cheshire* 163 (2014): 111–25.

Doyle, Barry, 'The Structure of Elite Power in the Early Twentieth-Century City: Norwich, 1900-35', *Urban History* 24, no. 2 (1997): 179–99.

Emsley, Clive, 'Violent Crime in England in 1919: Post-War Anxieties and Press Narratives', *Continuity and Change* 23, no. 1 (2008): 173–95.

English, Jim, 'Empire Day in Britain, 1904–1958', *Historical Journal* 49, no. 1 (2006): 247–76.

Essex, Stephen and Mark Brayshay, 'Town Versus Country in the 1940s: Planning the Contested Space of a City Region in the Aftermath of the Second World War', *Town Planning Review* 76, no. 3 (2005): 239–64.

Evans, Caroline, 'Multiple, Movement, Model, Mode: The Mannequin Parade', in *Fashion and Modernity*, eds. Christopher Breward and Caroline Evans (Oxford: Berg, 2005), 125–45.

Fearon, Peter, 'A "Social Evil": Liverpool Moneylenders 1920s–1940s', *Urban History* 42, no. 3 (2015): 440–62.

Fielding, Steven, 'The Catholic Whit-Walk in Manchester and Salford, 1890–1939', *Manchester Regional History Review* 1 (1987): 3–10.

de Figueiredo, Peter, 'Symbols of Empire: The Buildings of the Liverpool Waterfront', *Architectural History* 46 (2003): 229–54.

Foucault, Michel, 'Of Other Spaces', *Diacritics* 16, no. 1 (1986): 22–7.

Gilbert, David. '"London in All Its Glory – or How to Enjoy London": Guidebook Representations of Imperial London', *Journal of Historical Geography* 25, no. 3 (1999): 279–97.

Gilbert, David, '*London of the Future*: The Metropolis Reimagined after the Great War', *Journal of British Studies* 43, no. 1 (2004): 91–119.

Gilbert, David and Claire Hancock, 'New York and the Transatlantic Imagination: French and English Tourism and the Spectacle of the Modern Metropolis, 1893–1939', *Journal of Urban History* 33, no. 1 (2006): 77–107.

Gleadle, Kathryn, 'Revisiting Family Fortunes: Reflections on the Twentieth Anniversary of the Publication of L. Davidoff and C. Hall (1987) *Family Fortunes: Men and Women of the English Middle Class, 1780–1850*', *Women's History Review* 16, no. 5 (2007): 773–82.

Greenberg, Allen, 'Lutyens's Cenotaph', *The Journal of the Society of Architectural Historians* 48, no. 1 (1989): 5–23.

Gunn, Simon, 'Class, Identity and the Urban: The Middle Class in England, 1800-1950', *Urban History* 31, no. 1 (2004): 29–47.

Gurney, Peter, '"Intersex" and "Dirty Girls": Mass-Observation and Working-Class Sexuality in England in the 1930s', *Journal of the History of Sexuality* 8, no. 3 (1997): 256–90.

Hamlett, Jane, '"Nicely Feminine Yet Learned": Student Rooms at Royal Holloway and the Oxford and Cambridge Colleges in Late Nineteenth-Century Britain', *Women's History Review* 15, no. 1 (2006): 137–61.

Harvey, David, 'From Space to Place and Back Again: Reflections on the Condition of Postmodernity', in *Mapping the Futures*, eds. Jon Bird, Barry Curtis, Tim Putnam, George Robertson and Lisa Tickner (London: Routledge, 1993).

Harrington, Ralph, ' "The Mighty *Hood*": Navy, Empire, War at Sea and the British National Imagination, 1920–60', *Journal of Contemporary History* 38, no. 2 (2003): 171–85.

Hasegawa, Junichi, 'The Rise and Fall of Radical Reconstruction in 1940s Britain', *Twentieth Century British History* 10, no. 2 (1999): 137–61.

Hatton, Tim, 'Unemployment and the Labour Market in Inter-War Britain', in *The Economic History of Britain since 1700. Volume 2: 1860-1939*, eds. Roderick Floud and Deirdre McCloskey (3 vols., Cambridge: Cambridge University Press, 1994), 359–85.

Hayes, Nick, 'Counting Civil Society: Deconstructing Elite Participation in the Provincial English City, 1900–1950', *Urban History* 40, no. 2 (2013): 287–314.

Hayes, Nick, ' "Calculating Class": Housing, Lifestyle and Status in the Provincial English City, 1900-1950', *Urban History* 36, no. 1 (2009): 113–40.

Hazley, Barry, 'Ambivalent Horizons: Competing Narratives of Self in Irish Women's Memories of Pre-Marriage Years in Post-War England', *Twentieth Century British History* 25, no. 2 (2014): 276–304.

Hewitt, Lucy E., 'Associational Culture and the Shaping of Urban Space: Civic Societies in Britain before 1960', *Urban History* 39, no. 4 (2012): 590–606.

Hilson, Mary, 'Women Voters and the Rhetoric of Patriotism in the British General Election of 1918', *Women's History Review* 10, no. 2 (2001): 325–47.

Houlbrook, Matt, ' "A Pin to See the Peepshow": Culture, Fiction and Selfhood in Edith Thompson's Letters, 1921-1922', *Past & Present* 207, no. 1 (2010): 215–49.

Houlbrook, Matt, ' "The Man with the Powder Puff" in Interwar London', *Historical Journal* 50, no. 1 (2007): 145–71.

Hulme, Tom, ' "A Nation Depends on Its Children": School Buildings and Citizenship in England and Wales, 1900–1939', *Journal of British Studies* 54, no. 2 (2015): 406–32.

Hulme, Tom, 'Putting the City Back into Citizenship: Civics Education and Local Government in Britain, 1918-1945', *Twentieth Century British History* 26, no. 1 (2015): 26–51.

Jackson, Andrew J. H., 'Civic Identity, Municipal Governance and Provincial Newspapers: The Lincoln of Bernard Gilbert, Poet, Critic and "Booster", 1914', *Urban History* 42, no. 1 (2015): 113–29.

Jarvis, David, 'British Conservatism and Class Politics in the 1920s', *The English Historical Review* 111 (1996): 59–84.

Jarvis, David, 'Mrs Maggs and Betty: The Conservative Appeal to Women Voters in the 1920s', *20th Century British History* 5, no. 2 (1994): 129–52.

Jerram, Leif, 'Space: A Useless Category for Historical Analysis?', *History and Theory* 52, no. 3 (2013): 400–19.

Johnes, Martin, 'Pigeon Racing and Working-Class Culture in Britain, c. 1870-1950', *Cultural and Social History* 4, no. 3 (2007): 361–83.

Jones, Phil, 'Historical Continuity and Post-1945 Urban Redevelopment: The Example of Lee Bank, Birmingham, UK', *Planning Perspectives* 19, no. 4 (2004): 365–89.

Judge, R., 'Merrie England and the Morris, 1881–1910', *Folklore* 104 (1993): 124–43.

Kirkham, Pat, 'Beauty and Duty: Keeping Up the (Home) Front', in *War Culture: Social Change and Changing Experience in World War Two Britain*, eds. Pat Kirkham and David Thoms (London: Lawrence and Wishart, 1995), 13–28.

Kong, Lily, 'Religious Landscapes', in *A Companion to Cultural Geography*, eds. J. Duncan, N. Johnson and R. Schein (Oxford: Blackwell Publishing, 2004), 365–81.

Kuhn, Annette, 'Cinema and Femininity in the 1930s', in *Nationalising Femininity: Culture, Sexuality and British Cinema in the Second World War*, eds. Christine Gledhill and Gillian Swanson (Manchester: Manchester University Press, 1996), 177–92.

Larkham, Peter J. and John Pendlebury, 'Reconstruction Planning and the Small Town in Early Post-War Britain', *Planning Perspectives* 23, no. 3 (2008): 291–321.

Larkham, Peter J. and Keith D. Lilley, 'Plans, Planners and City Images: Place Promotion and Civic Boosterism in British Reconstruction Planning', *Urban History* 30, no. 2 (2003): 184–205.

Lawrence, Jon, 'Class, "Affluence" and the Study of Everyday Life in Britain, c. 1930–64', *Cultural and Social History* 10, no. 2 (2013): 273–99.

Lawrence, Jon, 'The Transformation of British Public Politics after the First World War', *Past and Present* 190, no. 1 (2006): 186–216.

Lawrence, Jon, 'Forging a Peaceable Kingdom: War, Violence, and Fear of Brutalization in Post–First World War Britain', *Journal of Modern History* 75, no. 3 (2003): 557–89.

Leach, William R., 'Transformations in a Culture of Consumption: Women and Department Stores, 1890–1925', *The Journal of American History* 71, no. 2 (1984): 319–42.

Lees, Lynn Hollen, 'Urban Public Space and Imagined Communities in the 1980s and 1990s', *Journal of Urban History* 20, no. 4 (1994): 443–65.

Levine, Philippa, ' "Walking the Streets in a Way No Decent Woman Should": Women Police in World War I', *The Journal of Modern History* 66, no. 1 (1994): 34–78.

Markus, Gyorgy, 'Walter Benjamin or: The Commodity as Phantasmagoria', *New German Critique* 83, Special Issue on Walter Benjamin (2001): 3–42.

McCarthy, Helen, 'Service Clubs, Citizenship and Equality: Gender Relations and Middle-Class Associations in Britain between the Wars', *Historical Research* 81, no. 213 (2008): 531–52.

McKenna, Madeline, 'The Suburbanisation of the Working-Class Population of Liverpool between the Wars', *Social History* 16, no. 2 (1991): 173–90.

McKenna, Madeline, 'Municipal Suburbia in Liverpool, 1919-1939', *The Town Planning Review* 60, no. 3 (1989): 298–9.

Milne, Graeme J., 'Liverpool, Manchester and Market Power: The Ship Canal and the North West Business Landscape in the Late Nineteenth Century', *Transactions of the Historic Society of Lancashire & Cheshire* 157 (2008): 125–48.

Mitchell, Margaret, 'The Effects of Unemployment on the Social Condition of Women and Children in the 1930s', *History Workshop Journal* 19, no. 1 (1985): 105–27.

Morris, Jeremy, 'Secularization and Religious Experience: Arguments in the Historiography of Modern British Religion', *Historical Journal* 55, no. 1 (2012): 195–219.

Mort, Frank, 'Fantasies of Metropolitan Life: Planning London in the 1940s', *Journal of British Studies* 43, no. 1 (2004): 120–52.

Mort, Frank, 'Retailing, Commercial Culture and Masculinity in 1950s Britain: The Case of Montague Burton, the "Tailor of Taste"', *History Workshop Journal* 323, no. 3 (1994): 106–27.

Moseley, Rachel, 'Respectability Sewn Up: Dressmaking and Film Star Style in the Fifties', *European Journal of Cultural Studies* 4, no. 4 (2001): 473–90.

Nava, Mica, 'Modernity's Disavowal: Women, the City and the Department Store', in *Modern Times: Reflections on a Century of English Modernity*, eds. Mica Nava and Alan O'Shea (London: Routledge, 1996), 38–76.

Nell, Dawn, Simon Phillips, Andrew Alexander and Gareth Shaw, 'Helping Yourself: Self-Service Grocery Retailing and Shoplifting in Britain, c. 1950–75', *Cultural and Social History* 8, no. 3 (2011): 371–91.

Nicholas, Sian, 'The Construction of National Identity: Stanley Baldwin, "Englishness" and the Mass Media in Inter-War Britain', in *The Conservatives and British Society, 1880-1990*, eds. Ina Zweiniger-Bargielowska and Martin Francis (Cardiff: University of Wales Press, 1996), 127–46.

Noakes, Lucy, 'Demobilising the Military Woman: Constructions of Class and Gender in Britain after the First World War', *Gender and History* 19, no. 1 (2007): 143–62.

Otter, Christopher, 'Making Liberalism Durable: Vision and Civility in the Late Victorian City', *Social History* 27, no. 1 (2002): 1–15.

Peiss, Kathy, 'Making Up, Making Over: Cosmetics, Consumer Culture, and Women's Identity', in *The Sex of Things: Gender and Consumption in Historical Perspective*, eds. Victoria de Grazia with Ellen Furlough (London: University of California Press, 1996), 311–36.

Perkin, Joan, 'Sewing Machines: Liberation of Drudgery for Women?', *History Today* 52, no. 12 (2002): 35–41.

Pooley, Colin G. and Jean Turnbull, 'Commuting, Transport and Urban Form: Manchester and Glasgow in the Mid-Twentieth Century', *Urban History* 27, no. 3 (2000): 360–83.

Pooley, Colin G. and Sandra Irish, 'Housing and Health in Liverpool, 1870-1940', *Transactions of the Historic Society of Lancashire & Cheshire* 143 (1994): 193–219.

Prescott, Andrew, '"We Had Fine Banners": Street Processions in the Mitchell and Kenyon Films', in *The Lost World of Mitchell and Kenyon: Edwardian Britain on Film*, eds. Vanessa Toulmin, Patrick Russell and Simon Popple (London: BFI Publishing, 2004), 125–36.

Ritchie, Rachel, '"Beauty Isn't All a Matter of Looking Glamorous": Attitudes to Glamour and Beauty in 1950s Women's Magazines', *Women's History Review* 23, no. 5 (2014): 723–43.

Robertson, Nicole, 'Collective Strength and Mutual Aid: Financial Provisions for Members of Co-operative Societies in Britain', *Business History* 54, no. 6 (2012): 925–44.

Rowe, Michael, 'Sex, "Race" and Riot in Liverpool, 1919', *Immigrants and Minorities* 19, no. 2 (2000): 53–70.

Salmon, Frank and Peter De Figueiredo, 'The South Front of St George's Hall, Liverpool', *Architectural History* 43 (2000): 195–218.

Scott, Peter and James Walker, 'The British "Failure" that Never Was? The Anglo-American "Productivity Gap" in Large-Scale Interwar Retailing – Evidence from the Department Store Sector', *Economic History Review* 65, no. 1 (2012): 277–303.

Shapely, Peter, 'Civic Pride and Redevelopment in the Post-War British City', *Urban History* 39, no. 2 (2012): 310–28.

Smith, John, 'Urban Elites and Urban History', *Urban History* 27, no. 2 (2000): 269–74.

Sperber, Jonathan, 'Festivals of National Unity in the German Revolution of 1848–1849', *Past and Present* 136, no. 1 (1992): 114–38.

Stephen, Daniel Mark, ' "Brothers of the Empire?": India and the British Empire Exhibition of 1924-25', *Twentieth Century British History* 22, no. 2 (2011): 164–88.

Stephen, Daniel Mark, ' "The White Man's Grave": British West Africa and the British Empire Exhibition of 1924-25', *Journal of British Studies* 48, no. 1 (2009): 102–28.

Summerfield, Penny, 'Mass-Observation: Social Research or Social Movement?', *Journal of Contemporary History* 20, no. 3 (1985): 439–52.

Swenarton, Mark, 'Tudor Walters and Tudorbethan. Reassessing Britain's Inter-War suburbs', *Planning Perspectives* 17, no. 3 (2002): 267–86.

Tanner, Duncan, 'Electing the Governors/the Governance of the Elect', in *The British Isles, 1901–1951*, ed. Keith Robbins (Oxford: Oxford University Press, 2002), 43–71.

Tarn, John Nelson, 'Liverpool's Two Cathedrals', in *The Church and the Arts: Papers Read at the 1990 Summer Meeting and the 1991 Winter Meeting of the Ecclesiastical History Society*, ed. Diana Wood (Oxford: Blackwell, 1994), 537–57.

Tinkler, Penny, 'Cause for Concern: Young Women and Leisure, 1930–50', *Women's History Review* 12, no. 2 (2003): 233–62.

Tinkler, Penny, 'Picture Me as a Young Woman: Researching Girls Photo Collections from the 1950s and 1960s', *Photography and Culture* 3, no. 3 (2010): 261–82.

Tiratsoo, Nick, 'The Reconstruction of Blitzed British Cities, 1945–55: Myths and Reality', *Contemporary British History* 14, no. 1 (2000): 27–44.

Todd, Selina, 'Affluence, Class and Crown Street: Reinvestigating the Post-War Working Class', *Social History* 22, no. 4 (2008): 501–18.

Todd, Selina, 'Class, Experience and Britain's Twentieth Century', *Social History* 39, no. 4 (2014): 489–508.

Todd, Selina, 'Domestic Service and Class Relations in Britain 1900-1950', *Past and Present* 203 (2009): 181–204.

Todd, Selina, 'Phoenix Rising: Working-Class Life and Urban Reconstruction c. 1945–1967', *Journal of British Studies* 54, no. 3 (2015): 679–702.

Todd, Selina, 'Poverty and Aspiration: Young Women's Entry to Employment in Inter-War England', *20th Century British History* 15, no. 2 (2004): 119–42.

Todd, Selina, 'Young Women, Work, and Leisure in Interwar England', *Historical Journal* 48, no. 3 (2005): 789–809.

Valiulis, Maryann, 'The Politics of Gender in the Irish Free State, 1922–1937', *Women's History Review* 20, no. 4 (2011): 569–78.

Waters, Chris, 'Introduction: Beyond "Americanization": Rethinking Anglo-American Cultural Exchange between the Wars', Special Issue, *Cultural and Social History* 4, no. 4 (2007): 451–9.

Webster, Charles, 'Healthy or Hungry Thirties?', *History Workshop Journal* 13, no. 1 (1982): 110–29.

Wildman, Charlotte, 'Miss Moriarty, the Adventuress and the Crime Queen: The Rise of the Modern Female Criminal in Britain, 1918–1939', *Contemporary British History* 30, no. 1 (2016): 73–98.

Wildman, Charlotte, '*A City Speaks*: The Projection of Civic Identity in Manchester', *Twentieth Century British History* 23, no. 1 (2012): 80–99.

Wildman, Charlotte, 'Urban Transformation in Liverpool and Manchester, 1918–1939', *The Historical Journal* 55, no. 1 (2012): 119–43.

Winship, Janice, 'Culture of Restraint: The British Chain Store 1920-1939', in *Commercial Cultures: Economies, Practices, Spaces*, eds. Peter Jackson, Michelle Lowe, Daniel Miller and Frank Mort (Oxford: Berg, 2000), 15–34.

Whyte, William, 'The 1910 Royal Institute of British Architects' Conference: A Focus for International Town Planning?', *Urban History* 39, no. 1 (2012): 149–65.

Online resources

bbc.co.uk/legacies/immig_emig/england/manchester/index.shtml (Accessed 4 July 2012).

Charlottewildman.com

catholicrelics.wordpress.com

HM Treasury and The Rt Hon George Osborne MP 'Chancellor: "We need a Northern powerhouse"', 23 June 2014. https://www.gov.uk/government/speeches/chancellor-we-need-a-northern-powerhouse (accessed 9 July 2015).

liverpoolmetrocathedral.org.uk

manchestertransport.files.wordpress.com

measuringworth.com calculator

Oxford Dictionary of National Biography

Unpublished research

Broadley, Martin, 'The Episcope of Thomas Henshaw, Bishop of Salford, 1925–1938', Unpublished M.Phil Thesis, University of Manchester, 1998.

Greenhalgh, James, 'Building the Peace: Modernity, Space and the City in Britain, 1939-1957', Unpublished PhD Thesis, University of Manchester, 2013.

Hulme, Tom, 'Civic Culture and Citizenship: The Nature of Urban Governance in Interwar Manchester and Chicago', Unpublished PhD Thesis, University of Leicester, 2013.

Kandiah, Michael, 'Lord Woolton's Chairmanship of the Conservative Party, 1946-1951', Unpublished PhD Thesis, University of Exeter, 1992.

Milcoy, Katharine, 'Image and Reality: Working-Class Teenage and Girls' Leisure in Bermondsey during the Interwar Years', Unpublished PhD thesis, University of Sussex, 2001.

O'Keefe, James David, 'First World War Memorials and the Liverpool Cenotaph, 1917–1934', Unpublished MA Thesis, University of Manchester, 2004.

Whitworth, Lesley, 'Men, Women, Shops and "Little Shiny Homes": The Consuming of Coventry, 1930–1939', Unpublished PhD Thesis, University of Warwick, 1997.

Wright, Richard, 'Italian Fascism and the British – Italian Community, 1928–43: Experience and Memory', Unpublished PhD Thesis, University of Manchester, 2005.

Index

Abercrombie, Patrick   26, 191
Adelphi Hotel   1, 44
Affleck and Brown department store
 advertisements   97, 100–2, 206–7
 appeal to housewives   104
 in Civic Week   72
Ancoats
 ethnicity and religion   146–7, 152–3
 poverty   73, 91, 146
anthropology   114, 143, 145, 161
architecture
 American-style   1, 26, 41, 43–4, 47,
  95, 197
 Liverpool   34, 43–4, 56, 62, 87, 171,
  172–4, 179, 198
 Manchester   38–40, 42–3, 69, 149, 157
Armstrong, Harry Gloster   27, 45–7
Armstrong, Lady   27, 175

Baldwin, Stanley   10, 24
Beaven, Margaret   200
Benjamin, Walter   94
Blackpool   49, 115, 136, 150
Bolton   4, 15, 49, 55, 89, 92–4, 113–15,
 120–5, 130–9
Bon Marché department store
 advertisements   99, 101–2, 206
 promotional activities   62, 84, 92,
  104–7, 110
 shopping experience   119, 125, 136
boosterism   2, 18, 22–3, 30, 36, 43, 54,
 60, 73, 78
British Empire Exhibition
 Glasgow, 1938   50, 77
 Wembley, 1924   50, 52–4
Brodie, John Alexander   26, 34–6, 47
Burnham, Daniel   10, 25–6, 35

Catholicism
 modernity   17, 190, 195–6
 population   15, 29, 143, 146–7,
  169–70
 worship   144–5, 148–63, 182–4

Centenary of Catholic Emancipation,
  1929   151, 175
Charles, Bishop Louis   156
Chicago   10, 25–6, 45, 47, 84, 97
cinema   3, 40, 95, 106–7, 112–13, 116,
  161, 191
citizenship   11, 16, 25, 40, 47, 50–2, 68,
  73–8, 119, 157, 187, 198–200
City of Chicago Plan, 1909   10, 35
City of Manchester Plan, 1945   192
civic pride   11, 16, 22–3, 25, 36–7,
  48–9, 56, 58, 64–5, 68, 78, 185,
  198–200
Civic Week   16, 42, 49–74, 78–9, 94, 106,
  109, 117, 198–200
class   3–8, 16, 22, 24–5, 27, 47–8, 50–1,
  77–8, 83, 85, 92, 96, 98, 103,
  106, 108–10, 112–16, 122–3,
  130, 136, 138–40, 146–7, 176–7,
  193, 200–1
Communism   77, 176–8
Conservative Party   6, 24–5, 27, 35–6, 192
co-operative movement   130, 132,
  135–6, 163
cotton   2, 5, 13, 22–4, 31, 42, 61, 74,
  89–91, 100–1, 114
Cottonopolis   1, 24
County of London Plan 1943   14, 192
crime and policing   2, 28, 65, 93, 200

Downey, Archbishop Richard   167–8,
  170–89, 195

economic depression   3–4, 16, 21, 59,
  84–91, 93–8, 101, 109, 112, 135,
  176–7
electricity   28, 30, 40, 70, 75

fashion   16, 62, 72, 104–7, 112–14,
  116–19, 122–5, 128–40, 155–6,
  160–2, 194, 198, 201
Fields, Gracie   106–7
finance   28, 39, 60

First World War 5, 10, 14, 21–2, 24,
    28, 34, 98, 112, 146, 152, 155,
    169–70, 179, 198
Forrester, Helen, *Tuppence to Cross the*
    Mersey 4, 130, 178
fur 105–6, 119, 133, 137, 139

gas 28, 40, 75, 95
General Strike 21, 67, 149, 160
George Henry Lees department store
    advertisements and marketing 84,
        99, 101–2, 106–7
    shopping culture 103–4, 108, 110,
        118, 120–1, 136–7
glamour 88, 95, 103–7, 112–13, 116,
    119, 128, 134, 138, 161, 194
Greenwood, Walter, *Love on the*
    Dole 5, 116

Henshaw, Bishop Thomas 147, 149, 157,
    161, 163, 184–5
Hollywood 16, 103, 106, 119, 138, 140
home dressmaking 88–90, 113, 133–4,
    136, 160, 162
housing
    clearance 29–33, 146–7
    new estates 25, 28, 30–2 (*see also*
        Wythenshawe)
    problems 29, 147, 164, 201
Hulme 31, 33, 91, 146

illuminations 66, 70–1, 95
immigration 4, 7, 47, 143–6, 148, 156,
    162, 168–70, 174
IRA 11, 21, 155
Ireland and the Irish 4, 29, 146–8,
    151–2, 155–6, 162, 165, 168–9,
    170–2, 174–5, 183, 187
Italians 46, 143–4, 146–8, 150, 152,
    154–5, 165

Kendal's department store
    advertisements 97, 99–102
    architecture 42–3, 126–7
    retail culture 72, 109
King George V 36, 39

Labour Party 25, 27, 36, 170
Lewis's department store

advertisements 97, 99–102
innovations 59, 62, 84–6, 96–7,
    107–8, 190–1, 193
retail culture 63, 103–5, 110
Lime Street Station 34, 95
Liverpolitan 35, 83, 95–8, 118–19, 187
Liverpool Anglican Cathedral 172–4,
    189, 191
Liverpool Catholic Cathedral
    Edwin Lutyens' design 167–8, 172–5,
        188–9
    first attempts 170, 177, 186
    Frederick Gibberd's completed
        design 167, 189, 195
    pilgrimage and Masses 175, 180–3
Liverpool Echo 57, 97, 187
Liverpool Organization 59–65, 84, 97
local government 10–11, 22, 77,
    192, 196
local politics 15–16, 22–3, 24–7, 36, 48,
    50–1, 68, 85, 170
local press 17–18, 42–3, 97–8, 100–1,
    117–19
London 9, 13–15, 21, 34, 47, 49–50, 60,
    72, 175, 192, 196–7, 198
Lutyens, Edwin 42, 167–8, 170–81,
    185–9, 191, 195

Manchester Centenary Celebrations,
    1938 31–2, 37, 40, 49, 70–9
Manchester Central Library 38–9, 149
Manchester Evening News 97–101
Manchester Guardian 42, 64–9,
    97–101
Manchester Town Hall 38–40, 46, 67, 70,
    148, 192
Manchester Town Hall Extension 38–40,
    74, 201
mannequin parades 62–3, 65, 72, 107,
    109, 126, 129, 135
Marquis, Frederick 59–60, 62–3, 84–6,
    97, 108–10, 191
Mass Observation 4, 6, 17, 92–4,
    113–16, 120, 122–5, 127–8,
    130–40, 194
Mersey Tunnel 26, 34–6, 192
modernity 11, 13–14, 157, 161–2, 165,
    168, 187–90, 192–201
movie stars 16, 107, 116, 140

newsreel   154–5, 158, 162, 182
New York City   1, 26–7, 30, 38–9, 41–7, 58, 95, 113, 119, 143–4, 147, 150, 173–5, 182

O'Mara, Pat, *Autobiography of an Irish Slummy*   4, 168–9
Orwell, George, *The Road to Wigan Pier*   3–4, 105, 112, 116, 138

Philadelphia   38, 43
Pierhead, Liverpool   33–4, 62, 179
Police Strike   21, 28
Pope Benedict XV   155–6
Pope John Paul II   195
Pope Pius XI   178
post-1945 reconstruction   9, 14, 191–2
poverty   1–7, 22–4, 29, 90–1, 93, 146, 152, 159–61, 176–7, 200–1
processions   61–2, 144–65, 174, 182, 188, 190, 195
protest   73, 77, 171, 183–4, 200
public transport   9, 28, 33–4, 37–8, 61, 70, 76, 78, 86–7, 89, 198

race riots   21
Reilly, Charles
   journalism   1, 26, 38–9, 91, 95, 167, 179
   links with America   41–4, 175, 197
   University of Liverpool School of Architecture   43, 47, 168, 197
Rotha, Paul   22, 193
Rowse, Herbert   1, 43–4, 47

Salvidge, Archibald   27, 35–6, 47
Scotland Road   4, 29, 169, 173, 187
Second World War   9, 23, 59, 116, 134, 137, 156, 167, 188–9, 192, 194
sectarianism   148, 151, 165, 170, 183–4, 200
secularization   12, 143–4, 165, 195
Selfridge, Henry Gordon   84–5, 107–8, 110
Ship Canal   24, 27, 51, 75, 90
Ship Canal building   42, 67, 70

shipping   1, 4, 23, 49, 56–8, 64, 86
shopping   15–16, 62, 64, 66–7, 71–2, 77–9, 83–110, 112–27, 132, 138, 143–4, 149, 152, 162, 182, 190, 193–4, 198
shop windows   16, 40, 62, 91–4, 105, 110, 114, 117–18, 120, 124–7, 131, 133, 135, 138
showrooms   40, 94
Simon, Ernest   25, 27, 30, 47
Simon, Sheena   77
Spring, Howard, *Shabby Tiger*   5, 148
street hawkers   93, 150

taxation   21, 28, 204
Thompson, Edwin   29, 44–5
Tinne, Emily   119
Titt, George   45–6
town planning   10, 25–6, 31, 38
Town Planning Conference, 1910   9, 34
Trafford Park   24, 90

unemployment   1–7, 16, 21, 23–4, 29, 37, 86, 90–1, 114–15, 130, 133, 146, 160–1, 177, 183, 190, 193, 200–1
University of Liverpool School of Architecture   26, 43, 47, 168, 197
University of Liverpool Settlement   1, 59
University of Manchester Settlement   24, 146, 152

war memorials   170–2
Wembley Exhibition Hall   16, 49–50, 52–7, 198
women
   Catholicism   143–4, 150, 152, 155–8, 160–6, 187–8, 194–6, 198–200
   civic and political involvement   12–13, 40, 51, 62–3, 72, 76–7
   shopping   83, 88, 103–7, 113–40
Woodhouse, Percy   26, 47
Woolworth's   3, 29, 93, 120, 130, 139, 149
Wythenshawe   25, 30–1, 33, 67, 74, 109, 147, 164, 201